Rethinking Psychoanalysis and the Homosexualities

THE ANNUAL OF PSYCHOANALYSIS

VOLUME XXX

Rethinking Psychoanalysis and the Homosexualities

Edited by

Jerome A. Winer, James William Anderson,

Bertram J. Cohler, and R. Dennis Shelby

for the Chicago Institute for Psychoanalysis

and the Chicago Psychoanalytic Society

Routledge
Taylor & Francis Group
NEW YORK AND LONDON

Chapters in this volume are abstracted and indexed in
Psychoanalytic Abstracts.

First published 2002 by Analytic Press, Inc.

This edition published 2015 by Routledge
711 Third Avenue, New York, NY 10017, USA
2 Park Square, Milton Park, Abingdon, Oxon, OX14 4RN

First issued in paperback 2015

Routledge is an imprint of the Taylor & Francis Group, an informa business

ISSN: 0092-5055

ISBN 13: 978-1-138-00983-7 (pbk)

ISBN 13: 978-0-88163-366-5 (hbk)

Contents

III

CHANGING PSYCHOANALYTIC PERSPECTIVES ON HOMOSEXUALITY

IV

THE MEANING OF SEXUALIZATION IN CLINICAL PSYCHOANALYSIS

V

FEMALE HOMOSEXUALITY

VI

PSYCHOANALYSIS AND HOMOSEXUALITY IN CONTEMPORARY SOCIETY

Contributors

James William Anderson, Ph.D. (ed.) is Faculty, Institute for Psychoanalysis, Chicago, and Associate Professor of Clinical Psychology, Northwestern University Medical Schools.

Martin S. Bergmann, Ph.D. is Clinical Professor of Psychology, New York University Postdoctoral Program in Psychoanalysis and Psychotherapy and an Honorary member of the American Psychoanalytic Association.

Bertram J. Cohler, Ph.D. (ed.) is Professor, The Committee on Human Development and the Departments of Psychology and Psychiatry, at The University of Chicago; Faculty, Institute for Psychoanalysis, Chicago.

Jack Drescher, M.D. is Training and Supervising Analyst, William Alanson White Psychoanalytic Institute, New York; Editor-in-Chief, *Journal of Gay and Lesbian Psychotherapy*; and author of *Psychoanalytic Therapy and the Gay Man* (The Analytic Press, 1998).

Richard C. Friedman, M.D. is Clinical Professor of Psychiatry, Weill Medical College, Cornell University Medical School and a Lecturer in Psychiatry, College of Physicians and Surgeons, Columbia University, New York.

Robert Galatzer-Levy, M.D. is Faculty, Training and Supervising Analyst at the Institute for Psychoanalysis, Chicago.

Gary Grossman, Ph.D. is Assistant Clinical Professor, University of California, San Francisco and Member, San Francisco Psychoanalytic Institute.

Salee A. Jenkins, Ph.D. is Faculty, Institute for Psychoanalysis, Chicago, and adjunct faculty, Northwestern University Medical School.

Beverly P. Keefer, Ph.D. is Faculty, Psychoanalytic Center of Philadelphia, and in private practice, Philadelphia and Gladwyne, Pennsylvania.

Paul E. Lynch, M.D. is a Candidate, Boston Psychoanalytic Institute and a Clinical Instructor in Psychiatry, Harvard Medical School, Boston, Massachusetts.

Karen A. Martin, M.A., L.C.S.W. is Clinical Director of Youth and Family Counseling in Libertyville, Illinois, and a fifth-year candidate at the Chicago Institute for Psychoanalysis.

Martha C. Nussbaum, Ph.D. is an Ernst Freund Distinguished Service Professor of Law and Ethics, University of Chicago Law School.

Ethel S. Person, M.D. is Professor of Clinical Psychiatry, Department of Psychiatry, College of Physicians and Surgeons, Columbia University, New York; and Training and Supervising Analyst, Columbia University Center for Psychoanalytic Training and Research.

Sidney H. Phillips, M.D. is Training and Supervising Analyst, The Western New England Institute for Psychoanalysis, New Haven, Connecticut; and Associate Clinical Professor of Psychiatry, Yale School of Medicine.

Kelly J. Reene, Ph.D. is a Developmental Psychologist working in industry in Philadelphia, Pennsylvania.

Ralph Roughton, M.D. is Training and Supervising Analyst, Emory University Psychoanalytic Institute, Atlanta, Georgia; and Clinical Professor, Emory University, Department of Psychiatry and Behavioral Sciences.

Roy Schafer, Ph.D. is Training and Supervising Analyst, Columbia University Center for Psychoanalytic Training and Research, New York City, and in private practice.

R. Dennis Shelby, Ph.D. (ed.) is Faculty, Institute for Clinical Social Work, Chicago; Advanced Candidate, Chicago Institute for Psychoanalysis; and in private practice.

Marian Tolpin, M.D. is Faculty, Training and Supervising Analyst, Institute for Psychoanalysis, Chicago; and Clinical Professor of Psychiatry, Chicago Medical School.

Elisabeth Young-Bruehl, Ph.D. is Faculty, Columbia Center for Psychoanalytic Training and Research and in private practice, New York City.

Jerome A. Winer, M.D. (ed.) is Director, Institute for Psychoanalysis and Professor of Psychiatry, University of Illinois, Chicago.

Introduction

BERTRAM J. COHLER

The issue of same gender sexual identity has posed a challenge for our understanding of psychological development and psychological intervention. Understanding the dynamics of desire remains an enigma. As Chodorow (1992) observed, we still do not understand the foundations of heterosexuality let alone the factors leading to same gender sexual orientation. This problem has been rendered more complex because of social stigma which may interfere in the satisfaction of same gender desire. Nungesser (1983) observed that the possibility of men sharing a sexual relationship and intimacy arouses a particularly intense response among other men professing not to share these feelings.

Efforts to understand same gender desire and its consequences for morale and personal vitality across the course of childhood and adulthood have been rendered additionally complex as a result of the writing and teaching of a group of analysts in the postwar period who found it difficult to distinguish between their own values and beliefs and the process of clinical psychoanalysis as one of empathic understanding in which the analyst's own prejudices have no place. Recently analysts sharing this prejudice have joined with the Religious Right in the effort to portray same gender desire as both evidence of psychopathology and a moral evil. The psychoanalytic process is founded on a unique relationship in which the analyst monitors the analysand's material in order to maintain an atmosphere in which the analysand is able to sort out his or her own wishes and desires in the absence of anxiety on the part of the analyst which could disrupt this effort (Racker, 1968).

It is well known that Freud himself never adopted a moral stance regarding the expression of same gender desire or sexual orientation, sometimes portrayed as homosexuality. Responding to an American mother who had written Freud regarding the possibility that psychoanalysis could "cure" her son of his homosexuality, Freud (1935) demurred, and observed that homosexuality was neither a vice nor a virtue. Reviewing Freud's three different propositions regarding the dynamics of same gender desire, Lewes (1988) reported that Freud had responded to a query from Ernest Jones that sexual orientation had little relevance as a criterion for selection for psychoanalytic education. Freud's interest in sexual orientation, as in all aspects of sexuality, was primarily a consequence of his effort to find support for his epigenetic theory of personality development. Writing in the *Three Essays*, Freud (1905–1924) was quite careful to differentiate between same gender sexual orientation, or inversion, and what he termed the perversions in which there was a shift either in the aim of sexual satisfaction or a deflection from person to things or bodily parts and functions.

Freud's vision regarding the place of sexual orientation for personal development is well reflected in the position of the American Psychoanalytic Association that sexual orientation says little about suitability for becoming an analyst or for serving as a training and supervising analyst. This position of the Association, expressed in 1991, has been complemented by the 1999 position statement on psychoanalytic treatment, emphasizing that sexual orientation does not necessarily represent either psychopathology or personality deficit; that antihomosexual bias is a social prejudice that negatively affects mental health and further contributes to the analysand's enhanced sense of self-criticism and stigma; and that directed efforts to change sexual orientation only reinforces the analysand's experience of prejudice, which has led to enhanced personality distress (Meyer, 1995).

As important as it was for Freud to develop a theory of mental life, the significant contribution of psychoanalysis to contemporary society has been the clinical theory that focuses on the means for understanding wishes and actions over a lifetime (Klein, 1976). This experience-near mode of understanding (Kohut, 1959) represents the distinctive contribution of psychoanalysis to the human sciences and medicine. The psychoanalytic situation facilitates the analysand's ability to make meanings of experiences recounted over a lifetime, including those related to sexuality and sexual orientation, and leads to a narrative that fosters enhanced sense of personal integrity and vitality over that which occurs at the outset of the analytic process (Ricoeur, 1977; Schafer 1981). Understanding the sources of desire, of sexual orientation or identity, meanings made of sexual experiences, and fantasies regarding sexual desire are an important element of the work of clinical psychoanalysis. Indeed, such exploration is essential if the analysand is to realize an enhanced ability to enjoy sexual intimacy, as well as satisfying relationships. Nothing is ruled out as beyond understanding or consideration; analyst and analysand don't begin with any presumption regarding a sexual identity or orientation which is more or less "acceptable."

Although either or both analysand and analyst may believe that same gender sexual identity poses greater problems than a heteronormative orientation in the workplace, with family, or in the community, that belief itself must be understood. Psychoanalytic study and intervention founded on the perspective that the dynamics of sexual orientation must be a part of the psychoanalytic process, but without prejudice regarding the outcome of this exploration of wish and desire, has replaced a more traditional view emerging in the postwar period, that the goal of psychoanalytic inquiry must be the adoption of heterosexuality. As Chodorow (1992) has so well stated, all aspects of sexual desire represent "compromise formations," or means founded on personal development across the course of life for satisfying sexual desire, which have meanings and which must be understood. Psychoanalysis does not begin with prejudgment regarding any particular lifestyle as more or less acceptable. This issue poses a problem for so-called reparative or conversion psychoanalytic work which presumes that heterosexuality is the desired outcome following understanding of the analysand's story of factors leading to same gender sexual orientation. At the same time, as Drescher (1998) observed, the shared stigma regarding same gender sexual desire on the part of both analyst and analysand, regardless of their sexual orientation, may lead to some pressure in the direction of a heterosexual adjustment and pressure against accepting same gender identity as a desired outcome of psychoanalysis.

Recognition of the many complex factors leading to adoption of a particular sexual orientation was facilitated by clinical study such as that of Isay (1986, 1989) which suggested that one route for men identifying as gay was founded on early childhood experience of self and father. This focus on the analysand's experience of his father replaced a more traditional view based on a flawed and experience-distant method for the study of family relationships emphasizing presumed deficits in family ties accounting for same gender sexual identity (Bieber et al., 1962). Isay's discussion showed that it was possible to understand the dynamics of same gender sexual orientation but as a means for enhanced self-understanding and for realizing enhanced satisfaction in adult life by awareness of the factors leading to the choice of a particular sexual partner. The essays in this volume follow in the tradition of Isay's pioneering inquiry, using clinical psychoanalysis as a means for realizing a more satisfying and fulfilling life founded on enhanced self-understanding.

The volume opens with an essay by philosopher Martha Nussbaum showing the complex interplay between history and the understanding of desire, which points to the importance of understanding same gender sexual desire not as a universal construct across time and place but as embedded in a society of a particular time and place. The implications of Nussbaum's essay for clinical psychoanalytic inquiry is that we must focus on the meanings of particular sexual identity for the course of life within our own urban society at the present time. It is difficult to generalize to the expression of sexual desire in other times and places. This essay is followed by Roy Schafer's discussion of changing understandings of homosexuality within contemporary psychoanalysis; Martin Bergmann's reflections on this evolving view regarding understanding sexual orientation within psychoanalysis; and Gary Grossman's discussion of the impact of political and social change upon the very manner in which sexual orientation is understood within psychoanalysis. Drescher further adds to the implications of this view for clinical psychoanalytic intervention, whereas Richard Friedman raises some questions regarding the foundation of personal experience during childhood which leads a person to think of oneself as gay. The impact of this return to a focus on the meaning for the analysand of his own desire is highlighted in Ralph Roughton's reflections on the impact of this change for what he might have understood in different terms with a man in analysis prior to the present decade and renewed focus on psychoanalytic understanding of the experience of same gender desire. Discussion of Roughton's material by Cohler and by Tolpin further highlights this emphasis from within different psychoanalytic perspectives than the conflict model earlier presumed to be the only means of understanding wish and action.

A second major section of the book shows the contributions of clinical psychoanalytic study of same gender desire and sexual orientation for analyst and analysand alike. Phillips takes up the issue of the analyst's own sexual identity as an important factor shaping the analysand's experience of sexuality, whereas Shelby and Lynch each address the problem of stigma as a factor leading to the distortion of same gender desire. Roughton and Young-Bruehl elaborate on this issue of the effect of stigma and prejudice upon the analysand's experience of same gender sexual identity from somewhat different perspectives. A third section of the book explores the implications of a clinical psychoanalytic perspective for the study of gay and lesbian lives. Keefer considers the dynamics of the development of a lesbian identity, and Galatzer-Levy and Cohler review issues related to disclosure of this identity as gay or lesbian across the years of adolescence and adulthood. The chapters in this volume provide a timely overview of contemporary approaches to the study of sexual orientation within psychoanalysis and highlight issues important in psychoanalytic treatment with lesbians and gay men. The volume includes several case presentations (Martin, Shelby) originally presented at a conference sponsored by the Chicago Psychoanalytic Society and the Institute for Psychoanalysis in March 2000.

References

Bieber, I., Dain, H., Dince, P., Drellich, M., Grand, H., Gundlach, R., Kremer, M., Rifkin, A., Wilbur, C. & Bieber, T. (1962), *Homosexuality: A Psychodynamic Study of Male Homosexuals.* New York: Basic Books.

Chodorow, N. (1992), Heterosexuality as a compromise formation: Reflections on the psychoanalytic theory of sexual development. *Psychoanal. & Contemp. Thought,* 15:267–304.

Drescher, J. (1998), *Psychoanalytic Therapy and the Gay Man.* Hillsdale, NJ: The Analytic Press.

Freud, S. (1905), Three essays on the theory of sexuality. *Standard Edition*, 7:130–243. London: Hogarth Press, 1953.
——— (1935), A letter from Freud. *Amer. J. Psychiat.*, 107:786, published 1951.
Isay, R. (1986), The development of sexual identity in homosexual men. *The Psychoanalytic Study of the Child*, 41:467–489. New Haven, CT: Yale University Press.
——— (1989), *Being Homosexual: Gay Men and Their Development*. New York: Farrar, Straus & Giroux.
Klein, G. (1976), *Psychoanalytic Theory: An Exploration of Essentials*, ed. M. Gill. Madison, CT: International Universities Press.
Kohut, H. (1959), Introspection, empathy and psychoanalysis: An examination of the relationship between mode of observation and theory. In: *The Search for the Self: Selected Writings of Heinz Kohut, 1950–1978, Vol. 1*, ed. P. Ornstein. New York: International Universities Press, pp. 205–232.
Lewes, K. (1988), *The Psychoanalytic Theory of Male Homosexuality*, 2d ed. New York: Aronson, 1995.
Meyer, I. (1995), Minority stress and mental health in gay men. *J. Health & Social Behavior* 36:38–56.
Nungesser, L. (1983), *Homosexual Acts, Actors, and Identities*. New York: Praeger.
Racker, H. (1968), *Transference and Counter-transference*. New York: International Universities Press.
Ricoeur, P. (1977), The question of proof in Freud's psychoanalytic writings. *J. Amer. Psychoanal. Assn.*, 25:835–872.
Schafer, R. (1981), *Narrative Actions in Psychoanalysis*, Heinz Werner Lecture Series, Vol. 14. Worcester, MA: Clark University Press.

I

HOMOSEXUALITY IN TIME AND PLACE

Other Times, Other Places: Homosexuality in Ancient Greece

MARTHA C. NUSSBAUM

In E. M. Forster's novel *Maurice* (1971), two young men, strongly attracted to one another, begin their university study of Plato. Here is how the passage goes:

> They attended the Dean's translation class, and when one of the men was forging quietly ahead Mr. Cornwallis observed in a flat toneless voice: "Omit: a reference to the unspeakable vice of the Greeks." Durham observed afterwards that he ought to lose his fellowship for such hypocrisy.
> Maurice laughed.
> "I regard it as a point of pure scholarship. The Greeks, or most of them, were that way inclined, and to omit it is to omit the mainstay of Athenian society."
> "Is that so?" [says Maurice, who is very interested in this fact]
> "You've read the *Symposium?*" [says Durham]
> Maurice had not, and he did not add that he had explored Martial.
> "It's all in there—not meat for babes, of course, but you ought to read it. Read it this vac."
> No more was said at the time, but he was free of another subject, and one that he had never mentioned to any living soul. He hadn't known it could be mentioned, and when Durham did so in the middle of the sunlit court a breath of liberty touched him [p. 51].

In 1990, an American judge, a Reagan appointee to the U.S. Court of Appeals for the Southern Circuit, fulfills Clive Durham's reading assignment, reading the *Symposium* for the first time in order, as he says, "to plug one of the many embarrassing gaps in my education." In his book, *Sex and Reason* (1992), Judge Richard Posner describes the impact of that experience:

> I knew it was about love, but that was all I knew. I was surprised to discover that it was a defense and, as one can imagine, a highly interesting and articulate

> one, of homosexual love. It has never occurred to me that the greatest figure in the history of philosophy—or, for that matter, any other respectable figure in the history of thought—had attempted such a thing. It dawned on me that the discussion of the topic in the opinions in Bowers v. Hardwick was superficial [p. 1].

Discussing those opinions later in the same book, Posner argued that they betrayed both a lack of historical knowledge and a lack of what he calls empathy for the situation of gay men and lesbian women, the two being closely connected. "The less lawyers know about a subject," he writes, "the less judges will know, and the less judges know, the more likely they are to vote their prejudices" (p. 347). Thus he suggests that what he calls "the irrational fear and loathing" expressed in the Georgia law under which Michael Hardwick was prosecuted, and endorsed in the Supreme Court opinions upholding that law, might have been dispelled by a study of history, beginning, it would appear, with the study of Plato (p. 346).

In at least one subsequent judicial opinion of his own, Posner showed the effects of that classical education. In a blackmail case in 1993 (*U.S. v. Lallemand*, 989 F.2d 936), he spoke eloquently and with empathy of the special vulnerability of the closeted homosexual in contemporary American society, describing in some detail the nonnecessary character of the social prejudices that makes this class of persons so painfully susceptible to blackmailing schemes.

On October 15, 1993, I found myself on the witness stand in a courtroom in Denver, Colorado, telling State District Judge Jeffrey Bayless about Plato's *Symposium*. Because I had a very short time to testify as an expert witness, I focused above all on the speech of Aristophanes, which I had elsewhere argued to be one of the speeches in which Plato expresses his views that he wants his reader to consider especially seriously. I told the court the story of how human beings were once round and whole, but now were cut in half for our overambitiousness. We feel a sense of lost wholeness, and we run about searching for our lost other half (Plato, *Symposium*, §189C–193D).

There are, Aristophanes tells us, three types of search corresponding to three original species of human beings. There are males whose other half is male, females whose other half is female, and then there are people whose other half is of the opposite sex. The speech describes the deep feelings of intimacy and joy with which the lost other halves greet one another, and describes the activity of sexual intercourse as a joyful attempt to be restored to the lost unity of their original natures (192 B.C.).

Through that text—and some others in my testimony—I suggested that a study of history reveals a wide variety of judgments about same-sex acts and loving attachment and a valuable array of arguments on this topic, which might well cause us to ask what our own arguments in this area are like, and how well they stand up to the scrutiny of reason.

I believe that ancient Greek texts relating to same-sex relationships can be radical and valuable for us in just the way that Forster's (1971) character Durham and Posner say they are. That is, I think that they can make a contribution to contemporary legal and ethical thought in four ways. First, they force us to confront the fact that much that we take to be necessary and natural in our own practices is actually quite local and not at all universal. This, in turn, forces us to ask whether we have any good reasons for what we judge. Second, they permit us to question certain empirical claims that you commonly hear in this area today, such as the claim that, when same-sex acts and relationships are widely tolerated, the family and the social fabric will fall apart. Third, the Greek texts provide us with some valuable concrete arguments concerning important human goods that might be advanced in a sexual relationship of the same-sex sort. Finally, and I think most important, they promote what Posner found so sorely lacking in the opinions in *Bowers v. Hardwick*, that is, empathy for the hopes, fears, and human aims of people who are involved in such relationships.

It is very hard to study Greek views about sexuality, for the reason Forster gives—namely, silence. In this area, scholarly puritanism and evasiveness have exerted a very pernicious influence, distorting what Durham rightly holds to be a straightforward matter of scholarship (see Dover, 1989, p. vii). The omissions Clive and Maurice's tutor urged crept into all the scholarship. Whether they were prompted by shame or by the desire to make the revered Greeks look more like proper Victorians, they distorted not only the editing and translating of ancient texts, but also even the making of dictionaries and other technical tools of scholarship. If you looked up one of the words relating to a genital act, you would not know which one it was—they would just say "unnatural vice"—and you would find that under many different words. You wouldn't be able to tell which particular unnatural vice, so-called, was being discussed.

So, until very recently, there just were no reliable translations of Greek and Latin texts involving sexuality. This was true of sexuality in general, but particularly true of same-sex relationships. In the Loeb Classical Library, which has facing pages of translation, with English on one side and the original language on the other, the situation used to be that where the Greek concerned sexuality, on the right-hand side it would go into Latin rather than into English. If the left-hand side already had Latin, which was regarded as slightly more accessible to schoolchildren, then the right-hand side would go into Italian, as if any foreign language at all was a screen between the vulnerable young person and this terrible material.

There were also more radical omissions. There was one very canonical edition of the poems of Catullus, published by the Oxford University Press (Fordyce, 1961). If you knew the poems of Catullus, you would notice that about ten poems were just simply not there; then you would find in small print in the Introduction that "a few poems which for good reason are rarely read" had been omitted.

It was very interesting that the editor left in all the poems concerning urination, defecation, and also abuse of women; but any dealing with same-sex relationships was omitted. Apparently, we had a great deal of difficulty. But, by now, the situation is changed, and we do now have the evidence before us to review.

What is the evidence? What do we base our analyses judgments on? Of special importance is visual art. There are hundreds of vase paintings representing same-sex acts. These are paintings that are respectable: you can see from the use of the object that they are not intended to be pornographic. They were in central use in ritual and also in ordinary dinner table activities. As Kenneth Dover (1989) shows repeatedly throughout his pathbreaking work, *Greek Homosexuality*, which reprints dozens of such vase paintings, this is an extremely important source.

A second major source, also discussed extensively by Dover, is popular oratory. Public speeches made in courtrooms allude to sexual activities, and in these cases, because we have a courtroom system in which a decision is made by vote among jurors drawn from the whole citizen body by lot, you have some reason to think that people are going to say things that command wide acceptance. So that's a good way of getting at popular thought.

Another good way is comic drama. Again, you are going to put off the audience, they are not going to laugh, they will to be extremely shocked, if indeed what's represented is shocking to that audience. Now, interestingly, what's in this material is extremely shocking in many ways to a *modern* audience. Early in my career I was an actress, and I acted in a play of Aristophanes with the late Bert Lahr, who was playing the last stage role he ever played. Bert Lahr was a very conventional man, and he hated the jokes of Aristophanes. He ended up rewriting the entire script because he was afraid of losing his TV commercial contracts by saying these shocking things, some of which did concern, indeed, same-sex relationships. But to the Greeks, I think we can infer, the jokes were funny and not deeply shocking.

Finally, there is other literary evidence, and particularly the evidence of the philosophers. Now, this is tricky. Philosophers are not, in general, reliable sources for popular thought; they are a counterculture. But there are some exceptions. Plato's dialogues contain (because they are dialogues, set in the educated milieux of his time) speeches of at least some figures who are likely to represent widely held popular views. Among these, it is generally acknowledged, are the speech of Pausanias in the *Symposium* (to which I shall return later), and probably the speeches of Phaedrus and Aristophanes as well.

Finally, we have a very interesting book that comes from a few hundred years later (probably during the second century C.E.), a book of dream interpretation written by a Greek named Artemidorus of Daldis. He was a professional dream interpreter, with a diverse clientele. He says a lot about sexual norms and practices in the course of interpreting the dreams of his clients, and it has been convincingly argued that what he says represents continuous and widespread traditions of popular thought (Winkler, 1990, pp. 17–44).

So, what does the evidence show us? First, it shows a culture in which the sexual appetite per se is not looked on as particularly problematic or shameful. This is something that has been stressed both by Kenneth Dover, the great scholar of these matters, and by the philosopher Michel Foucault (1985)—namely, that there is a great distance between the Greek way of thinking about the sexual appetite and the Christian way, both in the general culture and in the philosophers. No appetite is wicked per se; the real problem is the proper control and management of appetite. However, it is important that all appetites need careful management—sex, like any other pleasure, may be used either well or badly.

Second, and this is something that Dover (1989) very much stressed, there is no general condemnation of same-sex acts as such, nor is there any view that the desire to perform a same-sex act is the sign of a wicked or depraved character. Dover (1941a) writes, "The Greeks regarded the sexual arousal of an older male by the sight of a beautiful younger male as natural and normal" (p. 1; see also Dover, 1989, pp. 60–68). He proceeds to demonstrate this in great detail. There are many texts, even by writers as conservative as Xenophon, the very moralistic and old-fashioned soldier-philosopher, where the arousal by a younger man is described as "among the necessities of nature" (Dover, 1989, pp. 60–68). Homosexual copulation was just not viewed as per se immoral or even taken to be criticized by the gods. Dover (1994a) summarizes: "The Greeks in general believed that many kinds of behavior, notably fraud, perjury, robbery, and the like, were offensive to the gods and incurred divine punishment in this world or the next. They certainly did not include homosexual copulation among those modes of behavior. Indeed, the gods themselves enjoyed it" (p. 2, see also Dover, 1989, pp. 196–203). Dover (1989) correctly contrasts that attitude to what he calls "the sentiment of a culture which has inherited a religious prohibition of homosexuality and, by reason of that inheritance, has shown until recently no salutary curiosity about the variety of sexual stimuli which can arouse the same person" (p. 203).

I think we can go even further than this. In Greek culture and practices, the gender of the partner assumes far less importance—not none, but far less—than it does in our own society, and it is usually taken as less salient than many other facts about a sexual act. Nor are people very often categorized socially in accordance with their orientation toward partners of a particular gender. It is assumed that abundant appetitive energy may find an outlet in intercourse with either gender, and the two possibilities are frequently treated as more or less interchangeable—youths and women being coupled together as likely pleasures for strongly appetitive men to pursue (see Halperin, 1990, pp. 15–40).

To give just one example of this: In Aristophanes's comedy, *Acharnians*, the delights of Peace (it's a play about making peace during the Persian war) are praised in a hymn to Phalles (the phallic god in whose honor a phallus is carried in the procession). The delights of Peace include sex with young men, adultery with married women, and the rape of a pretty Thracian slave girl. All are listed without any distinction as more or less interchangeable pleasures for the male hero (Aristophanes, *Acharnians*, lines 263–279; see analysis in Dover, 1989, p. 136).

As for actual practices, we find in Sparta evidence of a strong encouragement of male–male relationships in connection with the military culture (where people simply didn't live at home, they lived with other men) and also of female–female relations, as depicted in some erotic parts of Spartan choral poetry. For female–female relations elsewhere, the primary evidence is the poetry of Sappho. Now, like all poetic evidence, that material has to be used with a lot of caution when you reconstruct historical practices. The difficulty in the case of Sappho is much greater than usual, because only fragments survive, but I think we can still conclude that the text gives clear evidence of sexual acts, as well as romantic friendship in the world represented (see Winkler, 1990, pp. 162–187; Dover, 1989, pp. 183–184). And it's difficult to believe that this would be put forward to a highbrow audience as something that would be well received if it in no way corresponded to an accepted reality. Again, Aristophanes's speech in Plato mentions female–female relationships as something that Athenians will just know about and be familiar with (Plato, *Symposium*, §191E).

All those arguments have to remain a little bit speculative because the evidence otherwise for women's lives in general is so slight, but it's very interesting to see that at least the few references we have don't suggest that these relationships were particularly problematic.

Turning again to male–male relationships, and that is, of course, where most of our evidence is, here I think we find—and here again I am agreeing with Dover (1989)—no general condemnation of male–male relations and certainly not a general moral condemnation. Instead, it's clear first of all that visiting both male and female prostitutes was considered perfectly acceptable for a citizen male. Male prostitution is treated as a perfectly routine matter in texts of many kinds. Even in the midst of his moralizing denunciation of one of his enemies for selling himself as a prostitute—which, of course, was thought of as a very bad thing to do for a citizen—the orator Aeschines hastens to reassure his audience that he has no intention of discouraging the general practice of male prostitution. His aim, instead, is to guarantee that people who want casual sex with young men "turn to foreigners and resident aliens so as not to be deprived of what they prefer" (Aeschines, *Against Timarchos*, p. 195; see Halperin, 1990, p. 180 n. 3; Dover, 1989, pp. 20–22, 33–39, 42, 67, 107–109).

Where relationships between two male citizens are concerned, again we find no general condemnation, but there is a complex system of restrictions. We have to begin by noting that these relations, even when they involve people close to one another in age (and they frequently do), always involve an asymmetry of roles. There is the so-called *erastes*, or lover (the older partner), who actively pursues and courts the younger, drawn by the sight of youthful male beauty. The older one is supposed to be keenly interested in sexual intercourse, and this interest and the active, penetrative conduct that follows from it, is taken to be perfectly normal, natural, and manly. The younger partner—the so-called *eromenos* (or the beloved)—is likely to be pleased at being the object of admiration and interested in benefits, such as friendship, education, and political advancement that the relationship with a lover might bestow. So, in that sense, the relationship can involve real reciprocity of benefits and mutual affection.

The cultural norm dictates that there is something extremely problematic about being the recipient of sexual penetration. It smacks of womanliness, passivity, things that don't befit somebody who is about to become a citizen-leader. Therefore the cultural norm dictates that the younger partner is not supposed to have a keen sexual interest in being penetrated, nor to develop any habit of enjoying that kind of passivity—for that would be, in effect, to be turned into a woman and possibly for playing your later citizen role (see Dover, 1989, p. 103). This being the case, the relationship between the older and the younger male citizen is hedged round with a complex set of caveats.

First of all, no citizen may receive money for sex. Proof that you've done so disqualifies you for citizenship, because it is connected closely with the idea that you are available to the highest bidder, therefore with the potential for selling out your country. In a democracy where most major offices are filled by lot, one doesn't even want to have a citizen who is up for sale in that way—so that's why you could be disqualified from citizenship (Dover, 1989, pp. 107–109; Winkler, 1990, pp. 46, 57).

Second, there are grave strictures against any sexual violence and enticement, especially against the young. As Dover (1989) shows, the crime of hubris need not mean actual sexual assault, but it means some sort of coercive conduct—dishonest enticement, threats, blackmail, other forms of nonphysical coercion—and all of that needs to be ruled out (p. 36).

A third restriction, that is, habitual passivity, being habitually the one who gets penetrated, is much criticized. In fact, Aristotle, in a work called *Problemata* (which may be written partly by Aristotle himself and partly by others in his school), wonders why it is that there are some people who actually enjoy this, and he speculates that such a person might be physically malformed: ducts that in most people go to the penis go to the anus instead in this person. Aristotle finds this very puzzling. And then he adds, in a peculiar last sentence, "But for some people habit is a second nature" (IV, 26).

Finally, there is widespread criticism of people who seek casual bodily pleasure in their interactions with younger males, without caring for friendship, education, and other values (see Dover, 1989, p. 91).

So when one is dealing with a relationship between the older and the younger male citizen, a lot of care needs to be taken. The penetrative role is basically all right. With the young man who is going to be a citizen, much caution has to be taken not to corrupt him by excessive gifts and not to encourage habits of sexual passivity. For this reason, a cultural ideal that is prominently depicted in the visual art prefers what's called intercrural intercourse, that is, intercourse between the thighs of the younger partner, a kind of masturbation in which the younger person isn't really penetrated (see Dover, 1989, plates *passim*). It is generally thought that that is a cultural norm that probably doesn't correspond to reality, that there probably is quite a lot of anal intercourse really. However, the convention is that you don't acknowledge it, you don't say much about it, and certainly the younger person never gives evidence of enjoying it.

As for oral sex, the Greeks seemed to have had a very general aversion to oral sex, which they connect with uncleanness and with ideas of pollution. It's not a moral condemnation, but it does appear that there is just a very general condemnation, whether in same-sex or opposite-sex relationships.They say you don't want to kiss someone who has oral sex (see Winkler, 1990, p. 215).

Now we have to talk about age, because I found that in Colorado, right away, they look at these texts where the translation says "boy," and they say, "Oh, are they advocating sex with children?" Well, what are these so-called "man–boy" relationships? That is really a matter we can establish pretty clearly, again from the visual evidence (see Halperin, 1996). The younger partner is typically a person of full height; they almost always are as tall as the older one. On the other hand, they are not bearded. The height of beauty is supposed to be that thin window of opportunity between the time you reach basically your full height and manly athleticism, and the time that the beard starts to come in fully. Now, when was that in the ancient Greek world? It's a little hard to say, but there is reason to think that puberty came probably a little bit later than it does today. So one might say, the age of a high school senior or a college undergraduate, something like that.

There were also couples, it is clear, where the *eromenos* was even older than the standard norm, especially in relationships of long duration. Pausanias, the speaker in the *Symposium*, is a real historical character, and we know that he and the poet Agathon continued for at least 12 years a relationship that began when Agathon, the younger party, was 18 (Dover, 1989, p. 84). The Stoic philosophers held that a relationship should continue until the *eromenos*, the younger person, is at least 28, and they were mocked for this (Nussbaum, 1995). It was said, "Oh well, then they probably won't just have to shave their face, they'll probably have to shave their body as well." But, in any case, they did urge that, probably in connection with norms of friendship and education.

We should also consider the relationship between Plato and Dion of Syracuse, which is at least widely portrayed as a sexual relationship, and which evidently began when the parties were about 50 and 35, respectively (Nussbaum, 1986, pp. 228–233). We have as well the fact that Plato's characters, both Pausanias and Aristophanes, speak of their norm as that of a lifelong partnership. Pausanias insists that it shouldn't actually even begin until after the growth of the younger party's beard, just to make sure that it is based on character and mutual love, rather than on simply the desire for sex. Of course, by putting these ideas in the mouth of Pausanias, in a dramatic work where his loved one Agathon is present, Plato gives weight to these sentiments.

What about the issue of mutuality? It's true that the *eromenos* is typically depicted as deriving no sexual pleasure from this conduct. Some later writers do say that, on this basis, male-female sexual intercourse is better, because the woman derives pleasure, whereas the younger man does not, so that there is mutuality in sexual pleasure in the male-female relationship (Dover, 1989, p. 88). I think what's more significant is that it is perfectly clear that the sexual male-male relationship is depicted as producing many benefits for the younger man—love, friendship, education, political formation—and that frequently they feel intense affection for one another. So Phaedrus, in the *Symposium*, argues that if you had an army formed out of pairs of such lovers—and we know that there really was a real battalion in Thebes that was famous for doing this at around that time—they would outshine all other armies because of their mutual willingness to make sacrifices for each other (Plato, *Symposium*, §179B–180B). He says that there would be a combination of love and mutual emulation that would hold them together more tightly than any other group.

Now how about the philosophers? How are they related to this? Although, as I said, the philosophers are not exactly representative of popular culture, all the major Greek philosophers do, I think, develop a part of the Greek popular norm, namely, the idea that sexual relationships are better if they are focused on the soul rather than merely on bodily beauty, and that a stable, friendly love, rather than an unstable and promiscuous sexual love, should be sought. All believed that same-sex sexual desire, including a characteristic orientation of that desire, can be an extremely valuable element in human life, expressing goods of love and friendship and powerfully linked to other social and intellectual ends. Relationships that involve sexual desire of the same-sex kind can be major vehicles of human aspiration, and they are generally deemed to be more valuable as such vehicles than are marital relationships, whose ends are typically taken to be more physical and worldly, less profound. So, for example, in Plato's *Symposium*, Diotima says that it is only people who just think of the task of reproducing the next generation as merely that of physically making a child, who will want that kind of relationship. But if what you want to reproduce is of the spirit, what you think and what you care for, then you will prefer the same-sex relationship (Plato, *Symposium*, §208E–209A). Zeno's Republic, the ideal city of the Greek Stoics, was built around couples, most of them male couples, although it does look like they admitted some females to that category too (see Nussbaum, 1995; Schofield, 1991). The Stoics thought that the aspiration to civic virtue especially well pursued in the context of such a sexual relationship.

What do we make of all this? Looking at ancient Greek culture certainly should have for us the same result today that it did for Posner. That is, if we look at the Greeks not the way the Victorians did, hoping to find confirming images of ourselves, but as a strange people who organized things in some ways very differently, then we will be shaken into seeing that many ways of organizing things that we are accustomed to think normal or neutral are actually parochial. Thus Michel Foucault (1985) wrote, in the introduction to his second volume of *The History of Sexuality*, "The Greeks free our thought from what it silently thinks and so enable it to think differently" (p. 9). I think one thing that we see is that it is possible not to problematize the sexual appetite in a way that singles it out from the other appetites as a source of special anxiety and shame. We also see that it's possible not to categorize persons primarily in accordance with a binary division between the homosexual and the heterosexual. (You notice that even in Aristophanes, where there is a concept of innate original kinds, there are not two but three, because the idea that there is a binary division between same-sex and opposite-sex doesn't even occur to him.) It is also possible not to regard the nature of one's sexual partner as the most salient fact in the sexual coupling. It is possible to hold that same-sex relationships are not only not shameful per se, but also potentially of high spiritual and social value.

Now, obviously, none of this need make someone with different moral commitments change those judgments. It does, however, make that person ask on what evidence and argument those judgments are actually based. I think that is particularly important in our public culture today, where all too often we do not pause to look for reasons. Moreover, such a search for reasons is at the heart of some parts of the Christian tradition that have been especially active in criticizing same-sex relationships—in particular, the Catholic Natural Law tradition, which claims to derive its conclusions from reason unaided by revelation. For all these reasons, it is particularly important to ask, What are the reasons? Are they good reasons?

Second, when we look at the Greeks, and I think in general we do look at the Greeks as a culture we admire, not a total failure as a culture—after all, they are the source of some of our most cherished ideas and cherished cultural artifacts—we notice that the presence of same-sex relationships in Athens and in Sparta didn't have the result that is so frequently mentioned in scare stories about these matters, that is, the result of destroying the family and eroding the social fabric. Actually, one professor who testified in the Colorado trial, Harvey Mansfield (1994, pp. 117–118), argued that the recognition of same-sex relationships would cause the downfall of civilization. Well, in fact, we find widespread in Athens, as for instance in the speech of Phaedrus in the *Symposium*, the view that encouraging such relationships is a fine way of *strengthening* the social fabric, of making people who *will* fight for one another and will hold together the social fabric. In particular, in both Plato and the Stoics, the love of two people of the same sex is held to be closely connected to political liberty, because the idea is that these people will fight against tyrants. And they went back and thought about a famous pair of male lovers who were involved in the assassination of a tyrant, and they theorized that this pair, Harmodius and Aristogeiton, were able to do that because of their love for one another (Schofield, 1991).

In addition to the use of history to free thought and to test social hypotheses, I think this particular part of philosophy's history is significant because of the intrinsic interest of some of the moral arguments it develops on the issue. The texts argue, and argue repeatedly, that the passionate love of people of the same sex may serve many valuable social goals apart from procreation. In fact, Dover (1994b), having read the affidavits in the trial—he couldn't come to testify in person because of his age and illness—read one of the accounts that said that these relationships never achieve what the parties wish, they always end up degrading the parties and subverting the social fabric. This is what he wrote in an affidavit: "The Greeks were well aware that many sexual relationships did what the parties hoped and imagined, neither more nor less. If the participants imagined that they were achieving a thing which, for biological reasons, they could not achieve, then of course they would have been pursuing an illusion. But why should they have imagined that?"

Finally, I think that reading the Greeks has value in our moral and legal deliberations for the way in which they invite us to share the passionate longing of these same-sex lovers, to be moved by their hopes and anxieties and by their eventual joy. And this is how I myself got into this neck of the woods. I remember, as an undergraduate, searching for texts in which love of a man and a woman was depicted as a relationship of equality, mutuality, and sexual passion all together, and in which the two partners pursued, in the context of that sexual relationship, goals of intellectual aspiration and partnership with one another. It was an idea that drew me, but I didn't find it in any text dealing with men and women. There weren't any. Try to think about it. What novels are there? If there is one, then the woman dies very quickly. If you want that, then you can find that here is this depiction, both in parts of Plato's *Symposium* and especially in Plato's *Phaedrus,* of this beautiful relationship. You get into it and you imagine it as something quite wonderful, then you come back to your own society with a very different take on it. Why should people who pursue what seems so nice to pursue be treated in the terrible way that they are? In general, promoting a kind of empathy and understanding is a very, very important thing to do in this political and judicial culture.

Now, there are a few objections that one might make to this field of history, and I can only mention two, but I think it's important to do that.

One might first object that the ancient Greek world is just so different in its basic categories from our world that there is no point in looking back for anything pertinent to our own society when we look to the Greeks. We should just study it as it is, but what was salient then is very different from what is salient now. To that extent, the ancient world just lacks the modern concept of the homosexual, that is, a person with a lifelong disposition toward partners of the same gender (see Halperin, 1990). Now I think this is basically true. It says important things about the two cultures, and I agree with a lot of them. But this asymmetry between cultures is precisely what reading the Greeks is supposed, in my argument, to reveal to us. Namely, it is supposed to reveal to us the very fact that a society may tolerate, and even encourage, acts between members of the same sex without regarding this as the most salient feature about that act and without problematizing same-sex desire itself in a special way. The presence of the asymmetry doesn't defeat the comparative project; it's what makes it complicated and interesting.

I also want to say that any characterization of the Greeks that pushes this discontinuity to the limiting point of total noncomparability, denying that the Greeks had any concept of an erotic preference for members of one's own gender, cannot be quite right. It is refuted by the evidence of Plato, for both Pausanias and Aristophanes know and refer to people who have such stable preferences, indicating that they are referring to a widely accepted fact about human life. Such people, they say, may also marry and have children—to that extent their form of life is in fact different from that of many modern gay and lesbian people, although certainly not all. Their preference for same-sex acts is held to be a stable and a deep fact about their personalities.

The second, and I think the most serious, objection to the cross-cultural comparison is the claim that the Greeks high evaluation of same-sex activity is inseparable from Ancient Greek misogyny and the widespread Greek belief that one's deepest loves, aspirations, and political goals could not possibly be shared with a mere woman. You can see this in some of the evidence I have already mentioned. To that extent, shouldn't we rule out using the Greeks as any sign of what we might be, even in the very limited sense of that idea suggested by my argument here?

I think this is a serious issue, and we have to ponder these connections. But, in the end, I see no reason why we *should* draw this conclusion. First, the historical evidence actually suggests that encouragement of same-sex relationships varies to a large extent independently of women's role. In Sparta, women had much greater freedom, power, and property rights than they did at Athens. Yet Spartan culture gives especially prominent endorsement to same-sex relationships, both female and male. Second, the philosophers give us strong reasons for doubting that an interest in sex equality needs to be linked with a tendency to denigrate same-sex relations. Plato probably taught women in his school, and certainly argues very seriously for their equal education. He praises relationships that are rich in spiritual and intellectual value, and in his own culture, those are most likely to be between males because women are secluded and not educated. However, there is nothing in his argument itself to prevent an extension of the norm of love in connection with the extension of educational norm. Indeed, that's the extension that the Stoics themselves really make, defending very vigorously the equal education of women, and then suggesting that partnerships of all kinds, male-male, female-female, and male-female, are going to be present in the ideal city.

As for Aristotle, although women don't ever become completely equal, there is an idea of friendly love and reciprocity in both same-sex and opposite-sex relationships. As the scholar Anthony Price (1989) puts it very well in his recent book: "In both same- and opposite-sex relationships, Aristotle envisions the emergence of that reciprocal concern and respect which constitutes the best kind of friendship, linking individuals not only as satisfiers of one another's incidental needs but as partners in a life of personal self-realization" (p. 249).

Finally, we can all think for ourselves here, and we can see that the Greeks' defense of same-sex relationships as containing important human goods is in fact completely independent of their misogyny, both logically and empirically, no matter what the Greeks themselves thought on this point. For we can see, among other things, the great support that feminism has received from same-sex relationships, both female and male, and we can notice that the desire to enforce traditional gender roles and gender boundaries has been a major source of resistance to the goals of both feminists and lesbians and gay men in closely connected ways. Therefore it seems reasonable to suppose that the historically guided rethinking of the sexual orientation boundary may also free our minds to think differently about gender more broadly. That, of course, was the argument that was made in the Hawaii case, *Baehr v. Lewin*, that discrimination about gays and lesbians is itself a form of sex discrimination—not just sexual orientation discrimination—in that it reifies and reinforces the boundary between genders, which is the ultimate source of sex discrimination (*Baehr v. Lewin*, 852 P.2d 44 [Hawaii Supreme Court 1993]).

To conclude, the equation of the ancient with the modern, I think, shouldn't be done in a facile or naïve way, and it shouldn't be done in a romantic way, as if we could all just turn into Greeks. Indeed, I don't think we will reap the benefits of the comparison if we don't remain vigilant for differences and for problems, because it is from those that we want to learn. With the proper caution, the comparison may be very fruitful.

Finally, I think that the biggest benefit we get by engaging with the texts and arguments in this area is just that we are reasoning. We are employing curiosity and argument, whether historical or philosophical, and not the appeals to scare tactics or prejudice that usually you hear on these matters. And I do think that, if we face the issue with good arguments, appropriately illuminated by historical and cross-cultural understanding, over time we are going to prevail over prejudice and hatred, both in the courts and in the larger society of which they are a part.

References

Dover, Kenneth J. (1989), *Greek Homosexuality*. Revised ed. Cambridge, MA: Harvard University Press.

——— (1994a), Letter to Martha C. Nussbaum, February 11 (on file with the *Virginia Law Review* Association).

——— (1994b), Letter to Martha C. Nussbaum, March 15 (on file with the *Virginia Law Review* Association).

Fordyce, C. J. (1961), *Catullus: A Commentary*. Oxford: The Clarendon Press.

Forster, E. M. (1971), *Maurice: A Novel*. New York: W. W. Norton, 1987.

Foucault, M. (1985), *A History of Sexuality, Vol. II*, trans. R. Hurley. New York: Pantheon.

Halperin, D. M. (1990), *One Hundred Years of Homosexuality and Other Essays on Greek Love*. New York: Routledge.

——— (1996), Homosexuality. *The Oxford Classical Dictionary*, third ed. Oxford, NY: Oxford University Press, pp. 720–723.

Mansfield, H. (1994), Deposition of Harvey Mansfield (apropos of *Evans* v. *Romer*). On file with the *Virginia Law Review* Association.

Nussbaum, M. C. (1986), *The Fragility of Goodness: Luck and Ethics in Greek Tragedy and Philosophy*. Cambridge, UK: Cambridge University Press.

——— (1994), Platonic love and Colorado law: The relevance of ancient Greek norms to modern sexual controversies. *Virginia Law Review*, 80:1515–1651.

——— (1995), *Erôs* and the wise: The Stoic response to a cultural dilemma. *Oxford Studies in Ancient Philosophy*, 13:231–267.

Posner, R. (1992), *Sex and Reason*. Cambridge, MA: Harvard University Press.

Price, A. (1989), *Friendship and Love in Plato and Aristotle*. Oxford: The Clarendon Press.

Schofield, M. J. (1991), *The Stoic Idea of the City*. Cambridge: Cambridge University Press.

Winkler, J. J. (1990), *The Constraints of Desire: The Anthropology of Sex and Gender in Ancient Greece*. New York: Routledge.

On Male Nonnormative Sexuality and Perversion in Psychoanalytic Discourse

ROY SCHAFER

For some time, well-established propositions and forms of argument in the humanities and social sciences have been undergoing critical reappraisal. Strong arguments have been advanced against much of this received wisdom, claiming that it is replete with ideological precommitments, cultural narrowness, ahistorical perspectives, inconclusiveness, and self-contradiction. Meanwhile, pluralistic and antifoundational arguments have been gaining in persuasiveness and acceptance.

In many instances feminists have been showing how pervasive prejudice against women, based on the kind of thinking that is now in serious question, has insinuated itself into the canon in each of these fields of study. As part of this project, they have shown that the traditional and universalized psychoanalytic conceptions of normal and pathological development are biased in favor of men in that, tacitly and sometimes openly, they endorse conventional ideas of masculinity and femininity. Thus, in this major area of human desire, conflict, and forms of human relatedness, psychoanalysts have not consistently lived up to their ideals of sustained curiosity and openmindedness. Instead, they have presented moral value judgments as facts of nature, objective findings, or inevitable assumptions and conclusions, as though all their prejudiced assertions have been based on sound reality testing, rational inference, and biological sophistication.

Phallocentrism in psychoanalysis has already been discussed at length from within psychoanalysis. I have made a few contributions to this literature (Schafer, 1974, 1978, 1992b, 1993, 2001). A comparable upsurge has been taking place in the area of gay and lesbian studies (Abelove, Barale, and Halperin, 1993; Dominici and Lesser, 1995). Here, I try to add something to existing studies of the psychoanalytic conceptualization of male homosexuality; then, in an effort to strengthen my argument, I develop a correlated and much-needed critique of the concept of perversion. I focus first on the way sexual and gender prejudices often rest on confusions between norms and moral values, after which, with special reference to binary conceptualizations, I focus on the inimical influence of dichotomous or polarized thinking in the realm of sex and gender.

Norms and Moral Values

In his monograph *Psychoanalysis and Moral Values* (1960), Heinz Hartmann took up veiled moralizing. He pointed out that, in the course of child rearing, when parents and educators think they are simply conveying facts about things and practices and thus are being merely descriptive, they are likely to be conveying moral preferences or imperatives; at least, so they are understood by their children and young students. It can be said that it is very much that way in the case of gender development. For, when the boy is told, "Boys and men do this, not that," "Boys are this way, not that way"; "Boys aspire to this, not that"; "Boys look good this way, not that way"; and so on, he senses that he is being indoctrinated with moral prescriptions masquerading as factual statements about social norms. This we find to have been the case later on in our clinical analyses of adults, particularly in their struggles against certain thoughts, feelings, and desires in their transferences (see, for example, my essay, "Men Who Struggle Against Sentimentality" [Schafer, 1992a]). Similarly, "good for you," "bad for you," "the right way," "the wrong way," "nice," and "unpleasant," far from being merely descriptive, can imply moral preferences and imperatives and be so interpreted by children.

We enter here a major realm of object relations to which we were introduced psychoanalytically by Freud (1923) in "The Ego and the Id". There, he emphasized the child's identifying unconsciously with the parental unconscious superego. The boy's internalizing of moralistic traditions becomes the basis of his exerting the same influence when he is the parent of children, and so the process continues through the generations, whatever subsequent conscious modifications are introduced to suit the times. In clinical analysis, we find that, as children, our adult patients regularly drew moral lessons from what was ostensibly realistic instruction about the conventions of the social world. The "facts" about being a boy imply to the boy that he will be loved, admired, and safe from persecutory responses if he conforms to the norm without question or protest. At the opposite extreme, he will be scorned, punished, and otherwise emotionally abandoned if he does not, and that is the way it frequently works out.

Going further, however, the boy develops extravagant notions in conscious and unconscious fantasy about the rewards and punishments that await him in either case. These imagined and often permanent effects on his body, mind, or entire life can be simultaneously exciting and terrifying. The rationalistic parents who, later on, say, "But we never threatened or preached; we only informed, and we always explained," do not recognize the influence of unconscious communication, fantasy, and internalization processes. Thus, communicating what is normative perpetuates the moral import and impact of conformity and nonconformity in the realm of sexuality and gender.

The superego identifications of childhood include more than self-condemnation. They include as well support for the defensive tendency to project what is felt to be undesirable or unsafe and to become persecutory toward those into whom one projects one's own forbidden, unspeakable, or unnameable desires. To some extent, the way is prepared for this mode of defense by parents using projective identification in their child-rearing practices of what they cannot accept in themselves in their child-rearing practices; the child is assigned the burden of containing their unwanted, derogated, and feared selves.

Freud also prepared us to recognize and interpret these abuses, derogations, ostracisms, and discriminations. He showed how polarization affects many crucial developmental and social aspects of human life, including our views of the lives of others. We understand how this paranoid drama is played out between men and women when men use women as the garbage cans for their repudiated desires for such "female" or "feminine" experiences as passivity, yielding, penetration, and motherliness, and then go on to idealize what they have projected; thereby, they sharpen *the* difference between the sexes and derive further reassurance and sense of integration with regard to their own gender identity. On this basis, we also understand a good deal about why homosexual proclivities and practices are ridiculed and otherwise persecuted by the majority of conventionally heterosexual boys and men.

In psychoanalysis, these redistributions of sexual tendencies cannot be regarded simply as the result of an inborn, biological ground plan. Whatever nature may contribute in this regard—and we should remain skeptical of any arguments based on simple biological determinism—it is clear that nurture within cultural settings, as elaborated in unconscious fantasy, plays a tremendous role in the development of these projectively developed, dichotomous splittings within the self and these persecutory attitudes.

Binary Language and Values

Transmissions of superego dictates concerning maleness occur in ways other than the use of projective and introjective communication of normative facts to children. Indeed, the prime vehicle may be language. Language appears to be structured to serve sexual and gender biases. Typically, its coercive power is not felt as such; rather, language is felt to be a transparent medium that enables clear perception and rational, adaptive action in the world of social relations. No doubt it does enable organized thought and all the rest; however, it is also a medium so laden with moral messages that it regulates major aspects of our relations with ourselves, others, and events and things in the surrounding world. More than being enabling, language exerts moral control over what is enabled.

For instance, ideas of facticity and objectivity are directed and shaped by the words we use and how we use them. In learning language, we take it for granted that words refer to fixed realities. Binary divisions seem to describe the way things exist in nature. As a result, we often say "it" when all we can rightly say is that we are speaking from one possible perspective; we do not say, "as I see it" or some equivalently perspectival utterance. This reliance on "it" gives that "it" moral weight, as though we are being not only correct but "good" in being correct about "it." Like "it," binaries serve as organizers of the welter of information and impressions with which consciousness is flooded by our inner and outer worlds. We grow up blind to the way we receive constructions of nature. We add our own constructions as we go along, and we do not recognize the extent to which we realize only some of the possible versions of whatever "nature" might become for us. Anthropological research shows this to be so.

Binary terms pervade our thinking about identity formation and/in human relationships. Psychoanalytic discourse contains its full share of polarities that seem to reflect nature; upon reflection, however, we realize that they are merely established versions of nature and not the only ones possible. Masculine–feminine, heterosexual–homosexual, oedipal–preoedipal, genital–pregenital, paternal–maternal, active–passive: none of them are irreducible factual observations; all of them organizing concepts. We come to understand these terms as referring to natural and complete opposites; perhaps they may be juxtaposed or included in an aggregate, but certainly, we assume, their substructures are neither vague nor overlapping. Hence, "the opposite sex" and, in the usual absolute sense, "the difference between the sexes."

Contemporary critical theory has also brought out how these imposed polarizations implicitly set up hierarchies of value. Typically, they favor attributing a higher value to the first term of the two (masculine, active, etc.). Also, as already indicated, this structural feature of language leaves no room for overlap and gradations; it is as though the second term is the weak tagalong. The dichotomous wording is understood to refer to clear-cut, symmetrical units of nature.

To a large extent, Freud placed this polarizing, valorizing, and simplifying mode of thought at the center of his theorizing. In contrast, in his clinical thinking, Freud was not severely constrained by dichotomization. In most of his clinical works, he developed mixed and asymmetrical analyses. Often he subsumed these complex clinical accounts under the heading of overdetermination, and, as an advocate of scientific psychoanalysis and not realizing, as we can today, that narration is an aspect of all communication, he also regretted that they were novelistic. Our own clinical work follows Freud in these respects in that, as I understand it, we would all agree that we are constantly busy with mixed cases and questions of degree, and that much depends on the narrative skill with which we communicate our clinical work. In the same vein we mistrust presentations based on totally balanced, black-and-white contrasts.

In theory construction, however, the binary problem remains with us, for the constituents of the mixtures continue to be regarded as symmetrical opposites (for example, object love and narcissism). Also, hierarchic valorizations within the binaries have not been eliminated. Theory construction is the operation that most plainly exposes the way in which basic constituents of language have continued to control the formulation of numerous psychoanalytic principles just as they shaped Freud's foundational works. Perhaps the problem shows itself most plainly in the realm of sexuality. Discussions of homosexuality show this to be so.

As people develop in their cultural setting, always limited by the simplistic modes of primitive thinking and built-in valorizations of polarized language, they approach the ideas of "the paternal" and "the maternal" and "the masculine" and "the feminine" as symmetrical opposites and as somehow implying differences in value. In the same way, people in general tend to divide male and female bodies or genitals in this polarized way, as in the case of the erect penis and the female genitalia conceived as a hole to receive it: not just *a* hole; it is *the only* hole (the cloacal fantasy). Historical research has shown that, prior to modern times, anatomists considered this female "hole" the penis turned inside out (Laquer, 1989).

Much of my evolution as a clinician and theorist has consisted in trying to divest myself as much as I can of psychoanalytically endorsed ideas of "opposites." Opposites were in play during my personal development and my clinical training. Some are still in play in our discipline. For some time now, like many other analysts, I have been trying to focus my clinical attention on the ways in which my patients' thoughts are bound and blocked by dichotomous conceptions of the world and the self. Often enough, it turns out that when they seem to be using simple linguistic conventions, they are also giving signs that, unconsciously, they are controlled by powerful, black-and-white moral biases based on superego-enforced projections, introjections, and idealizations. Analytically, we understand these features to be associated with infantile anxiety, guilt, envy, and persecutory orientations.

At our analytic best, we focus on differences, not opposites. Difference, too, is a selectively organizing concept in that, arbitrarily, it can overlook much resemblance or identity; such is the case, for example, in thinking about men and women. Nevertheless, the idea of difference still leaves far more room than opposites for the analytic ideals of open-mindedness and curiosity. On balance, "difference" encourages us to individualize our analytic interpretations, and it pushes aside grand classifications and diagnoses. Thinking along these lines in connection with anthropological fieldwork, the noted methodologist Clifford Geertz recommended aiming for "thick description" of single scenes, events, and persons (1973).

As well as divesting myself as much as I can of binary classifications, I have developed a tentative, if not suspicious, attitude toward all universalizing propositions about men, women, fathers, mothers, sons, daughters, child-rearing practices, and psychosexual development. I think the key issues of psychoanalysis have been saddled with overambitious and unwarranted generalizations, and perhaps in response to the anxiety-inducing aspects of our work, we have been using these helpful but reductive classifications and diagnoses more than we should. Our doing so is inimical to the analytic attitude of empathic listening and graphic description. Too often, these generalizations are based on questionable dichotomizations and arbitrary symmetrical descriptions. Also, they promote ever new ways of interfering with individualized analytic thinking. As a result, the writings of many analysts seem repetitious, formulaic, and uninformative.

These remarks about individualization are not intended to argue that some pure phenomenology exists that is sacrificed in the process of generalizing. Phenomenology, too, is always shaped by existing conceptual and narrative commitments (Schafer, 1992). "Thick description," which serves individualization and the specification of differences, is necessarily guided by conceptual conventions. What is being argued here is that in the realm of sexuality and gender, binary thinking, with its moral implications, at least indirectly supports biased thinking. Of Freud, we may say that he wrote at cross purposes with himself, universalizing, generalizing, and dichotomizing, and, on the other hand, writing with impressive individualization about his patients and his work.

Male Nonnormative Sexuality

I turn now from this general scrutiny of psychoanalytic discourse and the place in it of unhelpful dichotomies and generalizations and intrusive values to focus on male nonnormative sexuality: the sexual desires for, fantasies about, and practices of men with men that are considered by many to be "altogether different" at best and "bad" or "evil" at worst. As I mentioned, it is particularly the nonconformist practices that threaten those who are polarized by binary thinking and who, on this basis, have become fierce advocates of whatever they believe is normative. Polarized men need to buttress their own identities by surrounding themselves in fact or fiction with "real men" and "real women," and to regard "others" as objectionable, dangerous, and even punishable.

Binary thinking naturalizes cultural and historical differences. These differences are made to seem no more than stable facts of nature. Once naturalized, any quality or process seems simply human and inevitable, and the idea that people are following norms and defending them vigorously need not be taken into account, for this is "the natural order of things." One of Freud's (1905) great contributions was his denaturalizing prevailing convictions about the sexual innocence of children and related convictions about the affects of disgust, shame, fear, and guilt. At the same time, however, and regrettably, he valorized the idea of a heterosexual, genital, reproductive culmination of development. He could not go all the way with the curiosity that led to his being able to denaturalize as much as he did in the realm of sexuality, which was plenty.

Although Freud's conscious orientation to sexual variation does not seem to be at all condemning or persecutory, he stopped being tirelessly analytic when confronted with men's nonnormative sexuality. Throughout his writings, he generalized that all nonnormative forms of sexuality are symptoms specifically of arrested development, that is to say, they are to be taken as signs of an individual's having been held up at one of the pregenital way stations to reproductive heterosexuality. Thus, nonnormative becomes a sign of disturbed development. Ostensibly nonjudgmental, this conclusion reaffirmed the morality of Freud's time, in what can be regarded as a pseudoscientific, hastily biologized way. For, unconsciously, there is no impermeable line between the idea that there is something different about you and something wrong with you; nor is there that line between psychologically wrong and morally wrong. That is one major reason why, to take a common clinical instance, most children and grown-ups tend to feel humiliated and vulnerable by admitting publicly that they need psychological treatment.

All the more so is this the case when it comes to gay proclivities. Today, many gay men have adopted a militant stance with regard to this moral pressure, but I think it ís safe to say that most people continue to regard every gay and "perverse" tendency as a stigma or sin against God or nature. Comparatively few remain aware of mixed cases and degrees of one tendency mixed with the other.

What Freud did in the realm of sexual orientation and practices was to mistake a norm as a fact of nature. How he came to reach this wrong conclusion in the realm of sexual orientation, object choice, and practices, and what was entailed by that conclusion, I first took up in my initial contribution to this topic, "Problems in Freud's Psychology of Women" (1974). There, I maintained (and I still maintain) that Freud's Darwinism led him to adopt an evolutionary ethic. In current terms, we might say instead that his conformist tendencies facilitated his using the Darwinism he valued as a scientist to support the evolutionary ethic. Viewing the individual as the carrier of the reproductive organs and substances designed to guarantee the survival of the species, he reasoned that it was essential that there be successful transmission of the germ plasm from generation to generation. It followed that psychosexual development should culminate in genital, heterosexual, reproductive sexuality. Anything else goes against the plan of nature. While he was taking this teleological set of assumptions for granted, Freud was also showing how many trials, tribulations, temptations, and deterrents the child encounters along the road to that "ideal" endpoint. He showed that there are many phases, modes, zones, pleasures, pains, and fantasies the boy must deal with along the way and that he can fixate on any one of them. Yet Freud continued to consider the procreative endpoint the only one that was complete and natural.

In this way Freud naturalized and implicitly moralized normative sexual inclinations and practices. He seemed not to see that he was leaping from biological norms to moral judgments when he assumed that development *ought to* culminate in reproductivity. He did not see the moralistic bias in reasoning that, because development *can* and usually does proceed to reproductivity, it *should* do so. But does this reasoning prove that only the reproductive heterosexual man is mature, normal, healthy, fully developed in his psychosexuality—a better-off person and by implication (which Freud consciously would have repudiated), a better sort of person—than others who have developed differently? Once Freud had idealized procreation in the conventional way, he had to see the other forms as immature, unfortunately arrested, perhaps irremediably so, although under ideal circumstances they might be amenable to the growth-enhancing method of psychoanalysis. Thus, just as in his phallocentric way he regarded the clitoris as a stunted organ, he regarded men who diverged from the procreative norm as stunted human beings.

Manifestly, Freud's stance was consistently empirical. He had what he took to be sound, supporting, empirical evidence for these conclusions. When he looked in depth at his sample of homosexually and otherwise so-called "perverse" patients and saw much unconscious sexual conflict and exaggerated defense involving fear, envy, rivalry, resentment, feelings of damagedness, narcissistic excess, and so on and so forth, he had, it seems, found all the evidence he needed to clinch his argument. But the conclusion of his argument was already in his mind; as can be seen in his much earlier correspondence with Fliess (Freud, 1954), the preconceptions and the value judgments were all there, poised to strike.

In fact, however, nothing conclusive follows from Freud's observations of the troubles of homosexual and otherwise "perverse" patients, for many heterosexual analytic patients show the same or similar conflicts, even the same intensity of conflict and defense, and the same or similar disturbing developmental circumstances. It was Freud himself who persisted in opening our eyes to this state of affairs. Furthermore, he recognized that psychoanalysis does not yield up the necessary and sufficient conditions to predict final outcomes of development; in his sounder methodological moments at various points in his writings, he pointed out that analytic explanation works much better retrospectively; that is to say, it provides a basis for postdiction, not prediction.

Freud seems to have used other observations to support his conclusions. For example, many heterosexually active, neurotic men seemed to derive therapeutic benefits from the analysis of unconscious conflicts over gender identity and sexual object choice. Again, it must be noted that, for several reasons, nothing conclusive follows from these observations. For present purposes, I shall emphasize only one of these reasons. Freud's Darwinian ideology committed him to try to bring his heterosexual patients to more integrated, comfortable, gratifying, heterosexual reproductive positions. For their part, almost all his patients appear to have been similarly committed. Once analysis helped them to recognize that unconscious "perverse" and "inverse" tendencies were crucial components of their pathogenic conflicts, they were eager to master them, if not get rid of them. Relieved of the weight of these difficulties by analysis, and helped toward a mixture of renunciation, sublimation, and continued repression, these men could hope to succeed in achieving genital heterosexual love, reproductivity, and pleasure instead of suffering. They and Freud were together in this. It was not the kind of togetherness that would have called attention to the considerable amount of transference-countertransference collusion in which they were engaged. Common cause has that blinding effect on clinical analytic work.

By and large, this common cause still seems to characterize many analytic treatments. Many, if not most, analysts and patients take heterosexual tendencies for granted. They agree that it is specifically conflict over these tendencies that should be examined, understood, and reduced. For example, one can see how much this is the case by observing the regularity with which analysts who are describing gains in their case reports emphasize the factors of getting married and having children or at least moving in that direction. In contrast, homosexual and "perverse" tendencies are considered central to psychological problems, and it is the temptation to act on them in fact or fantasy that is to be closely examined, understood, reduced, and emphasized in clinical reports. Strong cross-gender identifications must be modified, pregenital fixations loosened so far as possible, and the troublesome nonnormative tendencies finally subordinated to heterosexual genital primacy. Commonly, the patient will accept a degree of latent homosexuality and perverse leaning as natural and to be expressed through foreplay, aim-inhibited friendships, empathy, and creativity—presumably, just as their analysts do. Basically, however, renunciation is the implied goal.

In this situation, there is little or no recognition of the line of argument developed, for example, by Judith Butler (1990). She showed how one could use Freud's own explanation of the passing of the Oedipus complex, in his monograph "The Ego and the Id" (1923), to draw other conclusions. Specifically, she read Freud to be showing that identification with the lost oedipal object—the parent of the opposite sex—should favor a predominant identification with the opposite sex and thus promote normative homosexual resolutions of that complex. Although Freud noted this residual problem in his theory of psychosexual development, he did not deal with it effectively. He tended to fall back on *ad hoc* assumptions about constitutional differences and unspecified quantitative factors.

Perversion and Homosexuality

One aspect of Freud's (1905) idealization of normative heterosexuality is his characterizing the young child as "polymorphously perverse." Under this heading he included the homoerotic or "inverse." Polymorphous, yes, but why perverse? To confront the pejorative implications of the term perversion, one need only turn to the *Shorter Oxford English Dictionary* (1973): "Perversion: . . . turning aside from truth or right; perversion to an improper use; corruption, distortion." Furthermore, the history of the word perversion includes major legal and religious ideas of impropriety. Thus, there can be no question that "perversion" and "perverse" are loaded with moral connotations. Significantly, the *O.E.D.* uses a statement by Bacon as an illustrative quotation: "Women to govern men . . . slaves (to govern) free men . . . (are) total violations and perversions of the laws of nature and nations." The very choice of example naturalizes moral condemnation of those with feminist leanings along with nonnormative sexuality. We may recognize the same bias in daily speech when "straight" is used for normative heterosexuality: straight as opposed to what—crooked, twisted, off the mark?

We ought to ask why Freud used the word perverse in a conventional way. After all, he was repositioning his readers to adopt many new and radical points of view on sexuality. Why did he seem to stop thinking creatively here and simply go along with conventional linguistic distinctions? What blocked the further reach of his curiosity? I contend that, in his theorizing, Freud was looking backward from the teleologically prescribed endpoint of Darwinian sexual development. Even his use of the word pregenital indicates this looking backward, for that word implies that one is speaking of a normal future and thus of how the individual ought to get beyond inclinations of earlier times. It is implied that it is not enough to stay with such words as oral, anal, phallic-exhibitionistic, and dyadic. What is required is submission to the prescriptive use of the prefix *pre.*

The word preoedipal is closely allied with the word pregenital. Preoedipal, too, is a teleological, implicitly moralistic term. It naturalizes a conventional form of gender role development that, since Freud, has usually been understood in the sense of the "positive" (*sic*) oedipal. The positive oedipal is taken to be the crystallization, though not the culmination, of heterosexual development. Freud (1923) regarded the "negative" oedipal, which he identified and emphasized especially in "The Ego and the Id," as the site of homosexual love, as well as the capacity to identify with "the opposite sex." Nevertheless, the negative oedipal was relatively neglected in many of Freud's formal theoretical writings. In the same way, he usually neglected to go into detail about mothers in his patriarchically oriented case histories. And in his theories he usually situated this woman in positive oedipal contexts, where she remained the relatively unarticulated sex object of the positive oedipal boy and the unarticulated rival of the positive oedipal girl. It seems justified to conclude that the word preoedipal refers prescriptively to what is preheterosexual as well as pregenital.

Freud's restricted and restricting use of *pre* indicates that he stopped short of asking what he might have been expected to ask had he continued to exercise his enormous curiosity. Specifically with regard to castration anxiety, he did not ask, "What would there have to be about the boy's development prior to this moment of anxiety that would make him that vulnerable and impel him toward all the painful choices and consequences traced out by psychoanalysis?" To ask this question, Freud would have had to acknowledge the central and often disturbing role in development played by the early child-mother relationship. In his later years, and presumably under pressure from female colleagues, Freud did acknowledge the importance of that early relationship; however, he did so with some uncertainty and ambivalence, for in his very late paper on termination (1937) and in his "Outline" (1939) he regressed from this understanding when he said that castration anxiety and penis envy are the bedrocks. As such, they signify that the normal and proper outcome of psychosexual development is reproductive heterosexuality by way of a positive Oedipus.

Looking at the prefix *pre* in this light, as I believe we should, there seems to be no reason to include it in discussions of the gratifications, frustrations, attachments, and fears characteristic of the very first years of development. It is more consistently analytic to take up these features of early development on their own terms, so far as one can. Their subsequent transformations, if any, should not intrude into the very beginning of discussion. That is the way of unhampered curiosity; any other way, by implying that these features are not yet the real thing, marginalizes them. Certainly, contemporary, analytically oriented developmental research and contemporary clinical practice restore these early features to a major place in developmental theory without in any way minimizing the importance of their later transformations, the transformations on which Freud centered so rewardingly.

In this perspective, we can expect it to be just as helpful when looking forward to use the term postdyadic for the later development and, when looking backward, to speak of the preoedipal and pregenital. Only by looking in both temporal directions do we minimize the influence of value-laden teleological constraints. This bidirectionality throws into question the psychoanalytic use of "perverse" and "perversion."

It must be added that aesthetic value judgments and idealizations of the machine are often implied in the idea of reproductively oriented genital primacy. With regard to the aesthetic, Freud (1905) argued that normally oral, anal, and phallic exhibitionistic tendencies are subordinated to the heterosexual genital intercourse of adult sexual life. They are, he said, features suitable for foreplay. He implied then that, in that role, they may be pleasing without being indecorous. He also implied that it would go against the ideals of integration and maturity if, instead of repudiating or sublimating these tendencies, one were to linger too long over their direct gratification. Worse still, to be altogether gratified by them. He viewed their considerable sensuous and object-relational potential with great reserve. In an unobtrusive way, he added being decorously pleasing to the virtues of being stable, clear-cut, and continuing the species.

Idealization of the machine also flourished in the era of early Darwinian discourse. Both the powerful and efficient machine and the complex and intact organism were central to many metaphors and valorizations of his day. Often, they were, and they still are, metaphors for one another, as in the ideas "organic society" and the body as a "wonderful machine." The pressure is toward symmetrical conceptualization, unity, and efficiency: There should be no loose ends, everything in its expected place, and no Oscar Wildes to contend with. Blurred boundaries, unpredictability, conspicuous deviance in the realm of sex: none of them pleasing or productive.

Thus did materialistic-utilitarian values seem to join with aesthetic values as vehicles for moral proscription in the realm of sexuality and gender identity.

Conclusion

Freud may be viewed as having been working in conformity with the moral, aesthetic, and material dictates and linguistic turns of his culture. His powerful use of the language of his time and setting not only endorsed prevailing values, it loaded his discourse with them. The idea of perversion is one manifestation of this bias, and homosexuality as arrested development is another. Today, we realize more than ever that language is far more than a tool of thought or a transparent vehicle for the content of thought. We realize that words teach us what to think, how to think, how not to think, what to shun and persecute, and so how to get along in society.

References

Abelove, H., Barale, M. A. & Halperin, D. M., eds. (1993), *The Lesbian and Gay Studies Reader.* New York: Routledge.

Butler, J. (1990), *Gender Trouble: Feminism and the Subversion of Identity.* New York: Routledge.

Dominici, T. & Lesser, R., eds. (1995), *Disorienting Sexuality: Psychoanalytic Reappraisal of Sexual Identities.* New York: Routledge, pp. 187–202.

Freud, S. (1905), Three essays on the theory of sexuality. *Standard Edition,* 7:123–243. London: Hogarth Press.

——— (1923), The ego and the id. *Standard Edition,* 19:12–66. London: Hogarth Press.

——— (1937), Analysis terminable and interminable. *Standard Edition,* 23:216–253. London: Hogarth Press.

——— (1939), An outline of psychoanalysis. *Standard Edition,* 23:144–207. London: Hogarth Press.

——— (1954), *The Origins of Psychoanalysis: Letters to Wilhelm Fliess,* trans. E. Mosbacher & J. Strachey. New York: Basic Books.

Geertz, C. (1973), *The Interpretation of Cultures: Selected Essays*. New York: Basic Books.

Hartmann, H. (1960), *Psychoanalysis and Moral Values*. New York: International Universities Press.

Laquer, T. (1989), *Making Sex: Body and Gender from the Greeks to Freud*. Cambridge, MA: Harvard University Press.

Schafer, R. (1974), Problems in Freud's psychology of women. *J. Amer. Psychoanal. Assn.*, 22:459–485.

——— (1978), *Language and Insight: The Sigmund Freud Memorial Lectures 1975–1976 University College London*. New Haven, CT: Yale University Press.

——— (1992a), Men who struggle against sentimentality. In: *Retelling a Life: Narration and Dialogue in Psychoanalysis*. New York: Basic Books.

——— (1992b), *Retelling a Life: Narration and Dialogue in Psychoanalysis*. New York: Basic Books.

——— (1993), Gendered discourse and discourse on gender. *Psychiat. Humanities*, 4:1–21.

——— (2001), Conversations with Elisabeth von R. In: *Storms in Her Head: Freud and the Construction of Hysteria*, ed. M. Dimen & A. Harris. New York: Other Press, pp. 323–340.

The Shorter Oxford English Dictionary on Historical Principles, 2 volumes, rev. ed., ed. C. T. Onions (1973), Oxford, UK: The Clarendon Press.

The Relevance of History to the Psychoanalytic Controversy over Homosexuality

MARTIN S. BERGMANN

For a number of decades, the history of psychoanalysis has been a special interest of mine. In 1968, I coauthored a book entitled *The Revolution of Psychoanalytic Technique* and in 2000, a book entitled *The Hartmann Era*. To my knowledge, I am the only person teaching a course in the history of psychoanalysis within an academic frame of reference (New York University postdoctoral program in psychoanalysis and psychotherapy). I would like to participate in this discussion of homosexuality and psychoanalysis with a historical perspective in mind. One of the questions that has been of special interest to me is the question to what extent psychoanalysis develops from within by its own inner logic of development and to what extent it is responding to forces acting upon it from the outside world. Three such outside forces seemed to me of special significance: The pharmacological revolution and its impact, the feminist movement and its influence, and the effect of the gay liberation movement on the thinking of psychoanalysts about the nature of homosexuality.

The classical psychoanalytical position regarding homosexuality rests on the work of Karl Abraham (1924), who linked the stages of libidinal development with stages of object love. Human development, as Abraham saw it, went through six stages of development, beginning with the preambivalent oral phase and going through four ambivalent stages to end in a postambivalent capacity for genital love. In Abraham's table, the final genital phase was the sixth stage of libidinal development (p. 496). It corresponded to the highest stage that object love can reach and was labeled postambivalent. Almost *ex definicio* homosexuals were excluded from this highest stage of human development. The entire human development was conceptualized as aiming to reach this stage. Abraham's table was a great feat of organization and such feats of organization have a tendency to be cherished and held on to for a long time to come.

Abraham's table survived with only minor modification in Fenichel's (1945) classic. It is the main supporting structure of that book. Fenichel classified homosexuality under perversion because in perversion the desexualization of earlier stages of sexual development had not taken place. As Fenichel put it, a component of infantile sexuality remained and was cathexed and indispensable to bring about sexual orgasm. A last-ditch effort to save Abraham's table was attempted by Robert Fliess in 1948. But by that time, the table became so complex and cumbersome that it was no longer productive. Eventually, the table was modified by Anna Freud's (1965) developmental lines. However, even she retained the concept of genital supremacy with libidinal cathexes transferred to objects of the opposite gender outside of the family (p. 66). She also retained the traditional view that in perversions, component instincts of infantile sexuality outlast childhood and that genital primacy has either never been established or has not been maintained (p. 198). I found no evidence that classical analysis ever developed beyond this point. It may need stressing that Abraham's table was an idealized teleological structure and that homosexuals also may be capable of loving postambivalently, or the opposite thesis, that postambivalence is beyond human reach and was not considered within the classical frame of reference.

The first to question the usefulness of the concept of postambivalent genital love was Michael Balint (1947), who described genital love as follows:

> We know fairly well what an ambivalent love relation is—of postambivalent love we know hardly more than that it is, or at least ought to be, no longer ambivalent. This emphasis on the negative qualities . . . no greediness, no insatiability, no wish to devour the object, to deny it any independent existence. . . . There should be no wish to hurt, to humiliate, to boss, to dominate the object, etc., i.e. no sadistic features. . . . There should be no wish to defile the partner, to despise him (her) for his (her) sexual desires and pleasures; there should be no danger of being disgusted by the partner [p. 128].

Balint's criticism of the concept of postambivalent love created an uneasiness. It was as if suddenly the emperor had no clothes. Balint did not doubt that couples are in love and that many of them feel free from wishes to enslave each other, degrade each other, and all the other deplorable features that classical psychoanalysis contributed to the earlier stages of development. However, he was unable to supply a powerful theory comparable in its structure to that built by Abraham.

The next important contribution came in 1978 in a massive book of over 600 pages by Charles Socarides. The main achievement of that book was a clinical and theoretical separation between preoedipal and oedipal homosexualities. Socarides included in his theorizing the separation-individuation phases articulated by Margaret Mahler and her coworkers (Mahler et al., 1975). He saw the homosexual as one who never fully went through the separation-individuation phases and therefore remained subject to the fear of reengulfment by the mother and therefore by all other women (p. 73). To these categories, Socarides also added the degree of pathology of the internal object relations, eventually delineating five forms of homosexuality. The inclusion of developmental concepts and object relationship puts this book beyond the confines of classical psychoanalysis.

When I published my book *Anatomy of Loving* (Bergmann, 1987), I drew attention to another complication between life and Freudian theory. Freud's great discovery in 1905 was that all findings are in fact refinding. By that he meant that when a new love object is discovered, some characteristics of the old incestuous love object have to be refound in the new one. Contrary to what lovers experience, the excellence of the lover is never sufficient to evoke the emotion of love, as some refinding is necessary to kindle this emotion. What matters is that this refinding should not include the refinding of the oedipal taboo, and it is at this point that most neurotics come to grief. Refinding in love like refinding in transference can cross gender lines. Women often refind the mother in the husband, and men, the father in the woman. Refinding is as prominent among homosexuals as it is among heterosexuals. I therefore added to Freud's finding that if the earlier infantile objects were largely satisfactory and refinding without return to the oedipal guilt is achieved, love can be conflict free and happy. However, if these original objects were less than satisfactory when a person reaches adulthood, a conflict will take place between the wish to refind what one had and the need to find an object that is better than the original ones. The need to refind is therefore in a dynamic conflict with the equally powerful need for a corrective emotional experience. The same conflict between the two tendencies also takes place during transference, the two needs opposing each other. The conflict between refinding and corrective emotional experience is the lot of most lovers making postambivalence a rare phenomenon and not an expected stage in heterosexual love.

Freud was fond of quoting Mephistopheles' statement in Goethe's *Faust,* that gray is all theory and green the tree of life. Regrettably, the history of the relationship between psychoanalysis and homosexuality does not live up to this metaphor. It is not a happy story to retell. In 1973, the gay liberation movement was sufficiently powerful to make the American Psychiatric Association delete homosexuality from its diagnostic and statistical manual. Henceforth, homosexuality per se was no longer to be regarded as a form of mental illness. The American Psychoanalytic Association had always regarded itself as a component society of the American Psychiatric, so one would have expected that the American Psychoanalytic will follow the psychiatric resolution. But at this point, the difference between the two organizations becomes clear. The American Psychiatric is a professional association of physicians. Its approach to mental illness is free from ideological commitment. What works best and fastest is of primary consideration. By contrast, the American Psychoanalytic is based on the psychoanalytic method, and it is bound by the teachings of Sigmund Freud.

There was little emotional or theoretical interest at stake for American psychiatry to yield to the political pressure from the gay liberation movement and eliminate homosexuality as a mental illness. For American psychoanalysis, there was more at stake. It was only in 1991, that is, 18 years after the resolution of the American Psychiatric Association, that the American Psychoanalytic declared its opposition to discrimination in the acceptance of overt homosexuals into psychoanalytic training. It took another year and another resolution to declare that homosexuality should not be considered an obstacle to becoming a training and supervising psychoanalyst.

Contemporary psychoanalytic books such as that of Fogel and Myers (1991) suggest that a shift is discernible among psychoanalysts. Stoller (1991, 39) suggests that the whole concept of homosexuality be given up because in fact innumerable sexual behaviors are encountered in real life. In a similar vein Joyce McDougall (1991, p. 189) finds that the secret desire to transform homosexual patients into heterosexual ones once accepted as selfevident among psychoanalysts has been deplored. Homosexuality and other perversions remain mysterious, and what makes one person grow up straight and another gay has become inexplicable. In the same book, the sharp differentiation between neurosis and perversion is also blurred. Louise Kaplan (1991) states that perversion has always grown up alongside neurosis (p. 127). It seems that classical theory has not been replaced by another theory but rather that the classical theory has been given up.

The battle for recognition was carried on largely by Richard Isay (1996), who recorded this struggle in a moving book. The pain inflicted on homosexuals undergoing psychoanalytic treatment becomes evident when one reads his book. Although most psychoanalysts looked upon the wish of the homosexual to change her or his orientation as a sign of progress, a wish for healthy maturation, Isay thought otherwise.

> If a gay man wishes to change his sexual orientation, it is usually because early self-esteem injury and the internalization of social bias have resulted in an inability to consolidate and integrate his sexual orientation during adolescence and early adulthood, causing the instability of his homosexual identity [pp. 39–40].

What makes the problem even more difficult is the realization that this pain could have been averted had the training analyst kept in mind Ernst Ticho's (1972) differentiation between psychoanalytic goals and life goals (see also my essay on the subject, Bergmann, 2001). Strictly speaking, the sexual orientation of an analysand is a life goal and not a psychoanalytic goal, which should have restricted itself to understanding what happened and left the choice entirely in the hands of the patient. However, our sympathy should also go to Socarides, whose lectures were frequently threatened by demonstrations against him, sponsored by politically active homosexual groups.

For those of us who are not emotionally involved in this subject, the controversy offers a lesson in the interaction between outside forces, in this case, the gay liberation movement and the inner development of psychoanalysis. That such an interaction is not always smooth and often connected with human suffering seems inevitable. Greater wisdom could have averted much of the pain, but such wisdom is rarely available on the battlefields of history.

References

Abraham, K. (1924), A short study of the development of the libido, viewed in the light of mental disorders. In: *Selected Papers of Karl Abraham*, trans. D. Bryan & A. Strachey. London: Hogarth Press, 1948, pp. 418–501.

Balint, M. (1947), On genital love. In: *Primary Love and Psychoanalytic Technique*, 1953. New York: Liveright Publishing Corporation.

Bergmann, M. (1987), *The Anatomy of Loving*. New York: Columbia University Press.

——— (2001), Life goals and psychoanalytic goals from a historical perspective. *Psychoanal. Quart.*, 1:15–34.

Fenichel, O. (1945), *The Psychoanalytic Theory of Neurosis*. New York: W. W. Norton.

Fliess, R. (1948), An ontogenetic table. In: *The Psychoanalytic Reader: An Anthology of Essential Papers with Critical Introductions*, ed. R. Fliess. New York: International Universities Press.

Fogel, G. I. & Myers, W. A. (1991), *Perversions & Near-Perversions in Clinical Practice*. New Haven, CT: Yale University Press.

Freud, A. (1965), *Normality and Pathology in Childhood: Assessments of Development*. New York: International Universities Press.

Freud, S. (1905), Three essays on the theory of sexuality. *Standard edition*, 7:130–243. London: Hogarth Press, 1953.

Isay, R. (1996), *Becoming Gay: The Journey to Self-Acceptance*. New York: Pantheon Books.

Kaplan, L. J. (1991), Women masquerading as women. In: *Perversion & Near-Perversions in Clinical Practice*, ed. G. I. Vogel & A. M. Mayers. New Haven, CT: Yale University Press.

Mahler, M. S., Pine, F. & Bergmann, A. (1975), *The Psychological Birth of the Human Infant*. New York: Basic Books.

McDougall, J. (1991), Perversions and deviations. In: *Perversion & Near-Perversions in Clinical Practice*, ed. G. I. Vogel & A. M. Mayers. New Haven, CT: Yale University Press.

Socarides, C. W. (1978), *Homosexuality*. New York: Aronson.

Stoller, R. J. (1991), The term perversion. In: *Perversion & Near-Perversions in Clinical Practice*, ed. G. I. Vogel & A. M. Mayers. New Haven, CT: Yale University Press.

Ticho, E. A. (1972), Termination of psychoanalysis: Treatment goals, life goals. *Psychoanal. Quart.*, 41:315–333.

The Homosexualities

ETHEL SPECTOR PERSON

The editors' charge to me was to discuss what I was taught about homosexuality during my psychoanalytic education (very little) and how I now understand homosexuality. I did my psychoanalytic training at the Columbia University Institute for Training and Research concurrent with my psychiatric residency at Psychiatric Institute and graduated into a world where the burgeoning sex and gender social revolutions were to shape my thinking about homosexuality more than anything I learned during my training, with the single exception of Lionel Ovesey's work on pseudohomosexuality—more about that later.

Let me begin with what was happening in the world, before I turn more concretely to the evolution of my ideas about homosexuality. The way analysts now understand the homosexualities and masculinities and femininities was not born of brilliant insights we gleaned from interpreting our patients' dreams, fantasies, and sex acts as we sat behind our couches. Not long ago, Catherine R. Stimpson, dean of the Graduate School of Arts and Sciences at New York University, wrote an essay titled "Queers, Lesbians, Women, and Other Theoreticians" (presented at the Association on Psychoanalytic Medicine, February 6, 1996.) Her title says it all. The first analysts to reconsider homosexuality and gender did so on the basis of information and ideas that were initially garnered in the front lines of the sex and gender wars. The kickoff was the Stonewall Riot in Greenwich Village in 1969. A homosexual bar at the very epicenter of New York's gay subculture, Stonewall was usually protected against unannounced police raids because it was Mafia owned. The police, however, had the indiscretion to mount an unannounced raid the day after Judy Garland was buried, and a riot erupted (Heidenry, 1997, pp. 101–103). The twist within the twist is that the spontaneous riots against the police were led by drag queens in full regalia—so much for the automatic equation of masculine identifications with assertiveness, feminine identifications with passivity. There had been a gay movement for some 20 years; Stonewall put it on the map. What followed was an ongoing public debate between some who accepted or approved of homosexuality as a natural variant and others who condemned it as abnormal or amoral—some on religious grounds. (The ban on homosexuals in the Boy Scouts and the controversy it has generated is evidence of the ongoing intensity of this quarrel.) Although late to the front lines, it was of immense importance that the American Psychiatric Association took homosexuality off the sick list in 1973. Psychoanalysts were left, some rapidly, some more slowly or not at all, to come to terms with the political shifts emanating from the liberation movements which were subsequently theoretically elaborated in queer studies and in women's studies. The idea that homosexuality was not pathological was initially explored in the academy—only later within the psychoanalytic corpus. We were followers, not leaders. (Nor are our predominant, though not unitary, North American views shared by the majority of European and Latin American psychoanalysts even now.)

To repeat: The reevaluation of psychoanalytic views on homosexuality that took place in the 1970s and 1980s was first stoked by gay liberation and the revised views on gender were first sparked by the women's movement. Psychoanalytic thinkers did not lead the charge. That some analysts became open to revising long-held views about homosexuality was part of a seismic cultural shift. Retrospectively, it is clear that psychoanalytic theories on sex and gender reflected biases of a cultural hegemony and incorporated inconsistences that should have long been evident—and that were evident, to some degree, to Freud (1905) a hundred years ago. Initiative came from other quarters. For example, the poet and feminist Adrienne Rich (1980), in her classic essay "Compulsory Heterosexuality and Lesbian Existence," attacked our culture's assumptions about the "normative" status of heterosexuality by recognizing that "heterosexuality, like homosexuality, represented a narrowing of sexual possibilities."

The major influences on my ideas about homosexuality came from two sources concurrently. One derived from my close relationship with Lionel Ovesey, a psychoanalyst at the Columbia University Center for Psychoanalytic Training and Research. When I graduated from psychoanalytic training, he asked me to participate with him in some cross-gender studies and he became my mentor. He launched me into sex research. Having proposed that we write a book on sex and gender, he looked at the outline, saw that neither of us had any experience with transvestites or transsexuals, and sent me off to find some and start interviewing them. He was rigorous in insisting on having sufficient data to draw conclusions and highly critical of those analysts who he thought "sucked it out of their thumb."

The second influence came from a long-standing connection to the homosexual community through the aegis of two extremely close gay friends, one a hairdresser, the other an academic. Through the hairdresser, who befriended me at a crisis moment in my life, I became privy to a world in which homosexuals lived a rich social life, were not seeking therapy, could be high spirited, and were able to provide some of the most engaging companionship to be had anywhere—not to mention caregiving, a quality poignantly portrayed in *The Birthday Party*, one of the first plays about gay society (maybe the first) to make it to the big boards. My hairdresser friend looked after me, let me attend what I think were some of the first gay weddings around, but sent me home before the party got to be an orgy. (Orgies peaked in the heterosexual world later.) The academic traveled in a different world, no promiscuity whatsoever but a taste for sequential relationships, the most significant of which was with a woman he loved and married. As one might imagine, they were ultimately sexually incompatible, divorced, and remained best of friends.

In 1974, I was a founding member of a "Women in Society" seminar at Columbia University, which included both heterosexual and lesbian women. In the mid-1970s, I participated in a seminar on homosexuality at Columbia sponsored primarily by members of the Department of English interspersed with some analysts from the Columbia Center for Psychoanalytic Training and Research, a seminar that was severely limited by what was an antihomosexual bias among some of its most prominent participants. When I was invited by the sociologist Richard Sennett to join a seminar on homosexuality at the Institute for Humanities at New York University in 1979, I first told him I was unwilling to participate if the seminar was to be exclusively heterosexual. He assured me it wasn't. In fact, it was comprised of a group of remarkably gifted male homosexuals, several of whom subsequently became quite famous, leavened with a few heterosexual or bisexual men and the writer Frances FitzGerald and me. This was a valuable experience in terms of my coming to appreciate the difference in knowing about something as an insider as distinct from the position of an observer, even a friendly one.

Because of these various relationships and activities, I was well situated to observe what was happening in the culture and to play that off against some of the views that were then prevalent within the psychoanalytic community. But most of what I have written has been about masculinity and femininity (masculinities and femininities as they now are designated [Chodorow, 1994]) and cross-gender disorders, not about homosexuality. The women's movement was an important influence in my thinking, and women's issues became as familiar to me as the back of my hand. I had access to a sufficient number of transsexuals and transvestites (courtesy of the "father" of transsexualism, the late physician and sexologist Harry Benjamin), and I had started traveling the transvestite party and drag queen ball circuits to delineate some of the differences and similarities between different kinds of cross-dressers, some straight, some gay, others virtually asexual, so that I felt I had an adequate grasp of those worlds. Part of the reason that I have written very little about male homosexuality compared with what I have written about other aspects of sex and gender is that I came to see fairly early that homosexuality was not a single entity (any more than heterosexuality is), and I knew too many vital, vibrant, gay men to consider homosexuality *de facto* a neurosis. The idea that homosexuality was far from unitary was already implicit in Ovesey's work very early and in mine as well (Ovesey, 1969; Ovesey and Person, 1973; and Person, 1975). In 1978, Bell and Weinberg proposed a "typology of homosexualities." There is now a consensus that there are not just homosexuals and heterosexuals but a variety of homosexualities and of heterosexualities, too (a distinction parallel to the insistence on masculinities and femininities).

Ovesey was a man of his time, and, he, like others of his generation, regarded homosexuality as emanating from neurotic conflict. He did not view it as perverse however. He conceptualized homosexuality as the avoidance of the female genital; he thought the avoidance stemmed from a fear of the female per se (the vagina dentata fantasy) or alternatively from fear of the rival father. He undertook to treat a number of homosexuals, the aim of the intervention being to enable them to function heterosexually. However, we must put this into perspective. This was at *their* request. It was not only psychoanalysts who believed homosexuality was neurotic if not perverse. A considerable number of homosexuals shared this judgment, many of whom consulted psychoanalysts with the specific goal of changing their orientation. Although it is now forgotten, a number of men were able to make that conversion. We now know that some of those men who were "cured" ultimately felt thwarted and came out after gay liberation was well underway. Nonetheless some happily remained in their marriages. This might suggest that some few instances of homosexuality *are* the result of neurotic inhibition. (If we really believe in a range of homosexualities, maybe there is room to consider that homosexuality may occasionally have neurotic roots just as heterosexuality can.)

One of my very first patients was such a homosexual, someone from a distinguished family, whose fantasies were homosexual but who desperately wanted to be heterosexual. I saw him in a lengthy treatment, and his commitment to being heterosexual never wavered. He was someone who had had very little homosexual experience but many homosexual fantasies and longings and no heterosexual experience. To some degree he was an atypical homosexual, ultraconservative, uninterested in any of the things that so many gays are. He had been brutalized by his father, and in part his homosexuality appeared to be the function of an impairment of assertion not only in the sexual arena, but also in the professional world as well. That is, he feared retaliation should he be successful in love or in work. Nonetheless, he was determined to make a conversion in his sexual orientation, and so he did. I know a great deal about the long-term outcome of his therapy because he stayed in touch with me intermittently over the years—to chat, to let me know when the children were born, what the other milestones were. Although he still had homosexual fantasies, he was never tempted to act on them. He had a very successful marriage with a woman he adored, never regretted it, and reinitiated more sustained contact with me when his wife died at a relatively young age. He was overcome by grief as he had continued to be passionately in love with her throughout their marriage. After an interval of time, he connected with another woman, though it was clear that the love of his life was his late wife. (Even under this stress, and overcome by his loss, he did not at any time seek homosexual consolation.) He never regretted his heterosexual life, was an exemplary husband and father. In addition, he achieved considerable success in his work but nothing near the astonishing success of his father.

Ovesey had long cut himself loose from classical psychoanalytic theory, particularly from libido theory, in the way that he thought about homosexuality (and other issues, too). Self-described as a proponent of adaptational theory, he is best understood in today's terms as an intuitive object relations theorist or a self psychologist long before those theories existed as such. He made a major contribution in delineating what he called pseudohomosexuality, an important concept that runs contrary to today's emphasis on bisexuality and the reputed prevalence and fluidity of sexual object choice and gender. Nonetheless, pseudohomosexuality remains the best explanation for a number of clinical findings.

For many patients, a ready solution to the problem of frustrated dependency comes through symbolizing sustenance in sexual terms, mobilizing either the breast or the penis as dependency objects. Dependency problems can get disguised as sexual desire, in which a woman and her breast or a man and his penis become symbols of dependent security and power. These adaptations were theorized in great detail by Ovesey (1969). He observed that there were two fantasies in which the penis could be co-opted to the function of a breast. In the first, the father's penis appears to be a feeding organ, similarly to the mother's breast, and the semen is equated with milk. Then a patient may produce a dream image of sucking the penis. The second involves the incorporation of the father's penis by mouth or vagina or anus in the female, or by mouth or anus in the male. In this way, the donor's "masculine" strength becomes available to the dependent subject.

Fantasies that make use of the penis for dependent gratification may also occur in a heterosexual man in the form of a homosexual wish. Such fantasies are fostered by a man's belief that he requires vicarious strength from his father as a function of his own weakness or helplessness. That is what Ovesey called pseudohomosexuality to distinguish it from true homosexuality.

Ovesey developed the idea of pseudohomosexuality in relationship to his work with men who had homosexual fantasies and worried that they might be homosexual, but possessed little or no homosexual desire. They might, however, be strongly inhibited in their sexual congress with women. He postulated that the homosexual fantasy (and sometimes enactment) served the purpose of providing imagined masculine strength through the incorporation of male semen. Some of the group performed well heterosexually and experienced pleasure in their encounters, but were troubled by their "homosexual" fantasies. Some of the patients had come to fear they were latent homosexuals.

Although some contemporary theorists may feel that the diagnosis of pseudohomosexuality is a rather ingenious way to disavow homosexuality or bisexuality, I remain convinced that the concept of pseudohomosexuality has relevance to current clinical work with some individuals. One patient whom I saw over many years was always involved with women (including several wives), but suffered from mild to moderate inhibitions vis-à-vis any woman he was officially paired off with. His sexual life revolved almost obsessively around a woman other than the official woman in his life. He was tortured by these split relationships—by his sexual submission to the "other" woman and by his resentment of the "primary" woman. But in moments of great stress, typically centering on business issues and challenges from competitors, he would resurrect in fantasy a memory he had from early adulthood when he had had a single homosexual experience, in which he performed fellatio and swallowed the semen. The memory of this incident became his default fantasy for countering high anxiety. He did not self-identify as homosexual, and came to interpret the occasionally recurring fantasy as a balm to whatever anxiety he was feeling in the moment. In the "homosexual" fantasy, the patient was more of a suckling than a sexual creature. The fantasy was invoked as a security patch and was not accompanied by sexual arousal though it had clearly been enacted at least once in his earlier life. However the distinguishing factor for me is that he invariably experiences sexual desire as desire for the opposite sex, and so I interpreted the fantasy as a pseudohomosexual fantasy. I have observed a variation of this kind of sporadic fantasy in several different men over the years. I make the point to emphasize that we should not be too hasty in assuming that every "sexual" fantasy necessarily represents a repressed strand of sexual identity.

By this time it's self-evident that I have not discussed homosexuality in women. There are a number of women whose development toward homosexuality is a mirror image of that of a great many male homosexuals in that the girl eschews feminine interests from early on and by adolescence has formed some attraction to girls. However, there are other groups which have been less coherently depicted. One of these groups consists of women who by their own account have heretofore entertained no same sex interests (except in an occasional dream or two if one plumbs hard enough to find it) and who come to a sudden conversion only after the dissolution or breakup of a heterosexual relationship or the disillusion with one. In the past decade or so, I have seen a number of such women in consultation, a few in treatment. For some, their conversion does not occur until midlife or later. Yet when they seek consultation or treatment, they are not asking for an exploration of this turnaround, but rather help with adjusting to a new life situation. The change in orientation is already a *fait accompli*. There are several different ways to understand this pattern. Although it extends beyond the purview of this essay, it suggests to me that there may be a significant difference in the ability of the two sexes to suppress or disavow sexual desire.

Retrospectively, the requirements of sexologists and psychoanalysts that an etiological explanation be provided for homosexuality but not for heterosexuality makes no sense. Just as Freud's insistence that masculinity is innate while femininity is acquired as a response to the girl discovering her penis-lessness now appears illogical, so, too, does the idea that homosexuality requires explanation but not heterosexuality. We now know that homosexuals may or may not be perverse, and heterosexuals, too. Just as we have a more complex notion of biological sex and of gender, so, too, do we require a much more complex theory of sexuality than the one we now have.

Constructionism (constructivism) attempts to provide that more complex theory. One important charm of constructivist theory is simply that it is a nonessentialist theory of sex, holding that sex is not simply the expression of a biological force but that the form it takes is socially constructed. This is important enough to take constructivism seriously. Jeffrey Weeks (1986), a major constructionist and historian of sex, writes that "the critique of essentialism . . . has been very useful in casting light on hidden but controlling assumptions, and in opening up the sexual field to new questions, about history, power, meanings, diversity, choice, and so on" (p. 113). In this I concur.

The study of the history of homosexuality, among other things, opens up the intersection of psyche and culture. Freud (1905) made a particularly valuable contribution to historical relativity when he pointed out that "the most striking distinction between the erotic life of antiquity and our own no doubt lies in the fact that the ancients laid the stress upon the instinct itself, whereas we emphasize its object" (in a footnote added in 1910, p. 149). Sacrifices to Aphrodite aside, what this means, as a practical matter, is that for the ancients what you did, whether you were active or passive and not with whom you did it (whether man or woman), defined acceptability. As a result, same-sex sex among men had a very different meaning in antiquity than it does today.

Even though homosexual behavior has undoubtedly always been with us, the self-concept of *being* homosexual is relatively new. That homosexuals now self-identify as homosexual has central significance not only to psychoanalysts but also to historians and sociologists. The phrase "coming out" refers to the public acknowledgment of one's homosexuality, but there is an analogous internal "coming out," and it is just as important. An individual comes to construct (perhaps develop is a better word) an identity as homosexual out of his or her sexual tendency in the context of culture. Although this process of interaction between cultural identity and sexual desire now seems almost inevitable, nonetheless a cognitive category of sexual identity must preexist in order for a homosexual-behaving person to self-identify as a homosexual person. Historians point out that homosexual self-identification probably did not occur as such before the nineteenth century. Weeks (1979) suggests that by the mid-nineteenth century a distinctive male homosexual subculture had emerged, much like the contemporary one—one that attained a distinctive style and manner of speech. Interestingly, this identity niche preexisted by a couple of decades the formal declaration of such a category by medico-legal authorities in the second half of the nineteenth century. Boswell (1980) pointed to a gay subculture with its own literature and argot as early as the eleventh and twelfth centuries. Participation in such a subculture shapes the individual's homosexual identity.

Why the category "homosexual" emerged, first as a subculture and then as a classification, and then as a revised subcultural identity, raises many questions. What the psychological ramifications are of identification within the subculture, what functions it serves for society at large, and the meaning of the profound homophobia such self-labeling invokes in others have become the basis for major inquiries in both sociology and history. These analyses make significant contributions to understanding the way homosexuals' identities evolve, particularly through mutual interaction within the subculture. To some degree, development as it is understood within psychoanalysis can be expanded to embrace the concept of constructionism insofar as the precepts of the culture get incorporated into a developmental pathway.

Even so, sociological and historical analyses that rely solely on a constructionist or a scripting frame of reference are unable to account for the origins and divergence of homosexual and heterosexual trajectories. Therefore, it still remains for neuropsychiatrists, psychoanalysts, and developmental psychologists to ponder, though not to pontificate on, the origins of sexual object choice. It would seem odd to me to assume *a priori* that there may not be more than one route by which one becomes either homosexual or heterosexual. Put another way, it seems fair to say that we do not fully understand how each of us is launched on a pathway toward same or opposite sex object choice, or as I should more correctly say on the path toward one or another kind of heterosexuality or one or another kind of homosexuality (and sometimes bisexuality). In this context, we should not lightly discard the possibility of some innate tendency, in addition to theories of constructivism.

An important question remains the degree to which essentialism plays a role in some forms of homosexuality (and in heterosexuality, too). It seems to some observers that there is a group of feminine boys, in whom "feminine" characteristics appear very early in their lives. The psychologist and researcher Coates, among others, has demonstrated there are a variety of predisposing familial constellations in boyhood effeminacy, but it may be equally true that there are biological predispositions as well, perhaps including those which Coates has identified with regard to boyhood sensory sensitivities, and other factors too. Of the group of effeminate boys, a certain percentage will grow up to be gay (Coates and Wolfe, 1995). (Incidentally, Coates is adamant that it is totally unethical to offer to treat a child with the proffered premise that this may prevent later homosexuality.) Other evidence exists that essentialism plays some role in object choice and gender role behavior: some studies appear to demonstrate that androgens stoke aggression in boys while also causing "malelike" behaviors (more aggressive play, diminished doll-play, low maternal rehearsal, etc.) in girls with the adrenogenital syndrome (AGS) and perhaps a greater tendency to homosexual object choice in girls with AGS (Money, Schwartz, and Davis, 1984).

Loughery (1998) describes a subgroup of homosexuals who report feeling ostracized by virtue of their contemporaries' rejection of them as boys, *before* they had any conscious awareness of being homosexual. But they do begin life by experiencing themselves as different, that is, sexuality by itself does not constitute the whole of a gay identity. In his book on homosexuality, Loughery argues:

> One does not have to subscribe to the notion of gay men "as a people" to feel ill at ease with the denial of all meaningful inner differences. . . . The contention of a difference-denying straight-gay sameness overlooks the truth that such was not the case for many men when they were six or twelve or sixteen. If before puberty they did not know what to make of the masculine code their fathers anxiously pressed upon them, if they knew in their teens that they longed for the touch of another boy and fantasized about a forbidden companionship and love of the sort that their male peers found with girls, then they also knew that they had to keep a secret whose enormity other children in adolescence could not imagine. They felt *touched* by a profound difference. And it is unfathomable that so grave . . . a dilemma would not have meaning, if only as a source of a certain kind of potential later in life. A better part of a gay man's adolescence and adulthood may be spent in purging himself of the dangerous mannerisms that felt right in childhood and in erasing or mitigating the marks of alienation, deception, and assaults. . . . But the marks are there, not merely to be cultivated as a grievance or contemplated as a painful scar . . . but to be the basis for a life more attuned to other ways of seeing the world, more critical of unquestioning conformity, more open to doubt and change than might otherwise have been the case [pp. 447–448].

Here we are given an exceptional description of the inner experience of some *prehomosexual* boys. But their experience also highlights how we see in the developmental experience of many *preheterosexual* boys the impulse to exclude those who do not fit into their preexisting mind set of what "boyness" is. Whatever we as adults believe, children come to their own conclusions about what is appropriately feminine and what is appropriately masculine.

Of course, not all boys who will become homosexual have felt ostracized, another piece of evidence that homosexuality is not a single entity. When boys do feel ostracized, as Loughery suggests, those early life traumas may have an upside. He importantly observes that "outsiders" may have unusually cogent insights into the culture's biases and fault lines, a clarity of vision such as comes from minority status. The negative consequences of not being part of the in-group are perhaps better known than the ways in which outsider status can be a surprising gift as well as an affliction.

What I learned from gay liberation and the women's movement (and before them from the civil rights movement) is that we can be blinded by adherence to a preexisting ideology, particularly as it touts the superiority or "mental health" of one group relative to another. Such cultural hegemony is by definition linked with issues of power. The way preexisting ideologies impose power constraints on our lives, including our sexual lives, was first vociferously pointed out in the liberation movements mounted by minorities. These insights entered the academy, not only through revised psychoanalytic formulations but just as importantly through postmodernist studies, among them the contributions of Foucault (1979). The biases with which most of us grow up reflect ideologies we have internalized and which are part of what I have elsewhere called the cultural unconscious. The cultural unconscious encompasses among other things ideas about who has power and who is powerless (Person, 1995, 1999, in press). Within our field, much of our theoretical reformatting had come from women, homosexuals, and other minorities, and from a few "searchers" who were drawn to postmodern interpretations by virtue of a major theoretical bent. Those of us most willing to reformat our thinking are often those who may in some preconscious way have felt the impact of cultural powerlessness in our own psychological lives. Those who command power by virtue of their sex, race, religion, or class affiliation seldom give it away by virtue of their own free will. The resistance to unjust power generally is first mounted by those who have in one or another way felt the sting of disenfranchisement.

References

Bell, A. & Weinberg, M. (1978), *Homosexualities: A Study of Diversity Among Men and Women*. New York: Simon & Schuster.

Boswell, J. (1980), *Christianity, Social Tolerance and Homosexuality*. Chicago: Chicago University Press.

Chodorow, N. (1994), *Femininities, Masculinities, Sexualities: Freud and Beyond*. Lexington: University of Kentucky Press.

Coates, S. & Wolfe, S. (1995), Gender identity disorder in boys: The interface of constitution and early experience. *Psychoanal. Inq.*, 15:6–38.

Foucault, M. (1979), *The History of Sexuality Vol. 1: An Introduction*. London: Penguin.

Freud, S. (1905), Three essays on sexuality. *Standard Edition*, 7:130–243. London: Hogarth Press, 1953.

Heidenry, J. (1997), *What Wild Ecstasy: The Rise and Fall of the Sexual Revolution*. New York: Simon & Schuster.

Loughery, J., (1998), *The Other Side of Silence: Men's Lives and Gay Identities: A Twentieth-Century History.* New York: Henry Holt.
Money, J., Schwartz, F. & Davis, V. G. (1984), Adult erotosexual status and fetal hormonal masculinization and de-masculinization: 46, XX congenital virulizing adrenal hyperplasia and 46, XY androgen-insensitivity syndrome compared. *Psychoneuroendocrinology,* 9:405–415.
Ovesey, L. (1969), *Homosexuality and Pseudohomosexuality.* New York: Science House.
——— & Person, E. (1973), Gender identity and sexual psychopathology in men: A psychodynamic analysis of homosexuality, transsexualism and transvestism. *J. Amer. Acad. Psychoanal.,* 1:53–72.
Person, E. (1975), The treatment of male homosexuality. *J. Amer. Psychoanal. Assn.,* 25:183–199.
——— (1995), *By Force of Fantasy: How We Make Our Lives.* New York: Basic Books.
——— (1999), *The Sexual Century.* New Haven, CT: Yale University Press.
——— (in press), *Feeling Strong: The Achievement of Authentic Power.* New York: Morrow.
Rich, A. (1980), Compulsory heterosexuality and lesbian existence. *Signs,* special issue, ed. C. Stimpson & E. Person 5:631–660. Reprinted in Stimpson & Person (1980).
Stimpson, C. & Person, E., eds. (1980), *Women: Sex and Sexuality.* Chicago: University of Chicago Press.
——— (1996), Queers, lesbians, women, and other theoreticians. Paper presented at meeting of Association for Psychoanalytic Medicine, New York City, February 6.
Weeks, J. (1979), Movements of affirmation: Sexual meaning and homosexual identity. *Radical Hist. Rev.,* 20:164–179.
——— (1986), *Sexuality.* New York: Routledge.

II

THE QUESTION OF ORIGINS

Causes and Becauses: On Etiological Theories of Homosexuality

JACK DRESCHER

> *The story of origins is thus a strategic tactic within a narrative that, by telling a single, authoritative account about an irrecoverable past, makes the constitution of the law appear as a historical inevitability.*
>
> —Judith Butler, *Gender Trouble*

Although some claim to know what causes either homosexuality or heterosexuality, the origins of human sexual attraction remain an unsolved mystery. In the absence of certain knowledge, theories of etiology seek to provide both explanations and an ontological rationale for the way things are. From another perspective, however, etiological theories can be listened to as narratives that communicate the values of the theorizer.

Consider the following: "In the beginning God created man." This etiological story then goes on to relate the subsequent creation of woman. Patriarchal religions have traditionally argued that being first made man the better of the two. Some feminists, however, read the same biblical story as making a case for the later model improving upon the first (de Beauvoir, 1952). Who decides which position is better and which is worse? How does a person's place in the developmental line of an origin story relate to his or her place in a social hierarchy? How does an etiological narrative serve an individual's need for self-definition or a culture's need to define itself? And how do individuals or cultures decide which values are preferred in making these decisions? In the following sampling of homosexuality's etiological theories, this paper explains not only the narratives of immaturity, pathology, and normal variants, but also the morality tales that underlie them as well.

Narratives of Immaturity

Narratives of immaturity regard homosexuality as a normal step toward the development of adult heterosexuality. These theories define same-sexuality as a passing phase, that is, homosexuality is something that one outgrows. In fact, many heterosexual men believe they have advanced beyond their own childhood homosexual activity, but that adult gay men have not. For example, one patient, despite a lifetime attraction to men, married and raised children into adulthood. He then told his wife about his homosexual attractions, and they subsequently divorced. After writing to tell his father about these changes in his life, he received a letter admonishing him for "childish behavior." The patient's father said that he, too, had had homosexual experiences as a teen-ager. "Nevertheless," the patient's father went on, he had "put aside his selfish pursuit of pleasure and taken on the responsibilities of marriage and a family." Of course, so had the patient, although his father was unable to comprehend the announcement of his son's coming out as anything other than a childish act.

The most renowned tale of immaturity in psychoanalysis is found in "Three Essays on the Theory of Sexuality" (Freud, 1905).[1] In Freud's developmental model, instincts had to traverse two immature psychosexual stages, the oral and anal phases, before they were capable of attaining more mature expressions of sexuality. This meant that adults who achieved sexual excitement by other means—fellatio or receptive anal sex, for example—were said to suffer from either fixations or regressions of libido. It was hypothesized that these latter activities were expressions of immature sexuality, as contrasted with mature forms of genital, (hetero)sexual expression.[2]

Freud's instinct theory, which grew out of his clinical work with hysterics (Breuer and Freud, 1893–1895; Freud, 1896a, b), is central to his narrative of immaturity. In so-called normal people, perverse instincts were repressed and pushed out of consciousness. They could, however, emerge in dreams in disguised forms and were either forgotten (repressed) or consciously regarded as meaningless (Freud, 1900). In hysterics, the repressive mechanism did not function normally and unacceptable instincts were transformed, through displacement and conversion, into physical symptoms. Perverts, unlike hysterics, acted upon instincts that were not in conflict with a repressive mechanism. This led to Freud's (1905) claim that "neuroses are the negative of perversions" (p. 165) and his

---

[1] Harry Stack Sullivan (1953) also saw childhood homosexuality as a normal phase toward the development of adult heterosexuality.

[2] Freud (1908) considered nongenital, meaning nonpenile–vaginal, sexual acts to be immature, regardless of the sexual orientation of the individual. However, since same-sex activities preclude penile–vaginal intercourse, in this nosology, homosexual acts can only be regarded as immature forms of sexual expression.

assertion that homosexuality was not a psychoneurotic illness (1935), which he defined as symptoms arising from intrapsychic conflict (1926). Although homosexuality was not technically an illness, Freud's theory of immaturity did not quite constitute a clean bill of health. For it is worth noting that in everyday conversation, calling someone immature may not be as offensive as calling them sick, but neither appellation is particularly respectful.

Freud (1910) saw homosexuality primarily as a developmental arrest, a fixation, or a sign of psychological immaturity. He claimed that Leonardo da Vinci's homosexuality resulted from an identification with his mother in which he took someone who resembled himself as a younger man for a love object. In blaming Leonardo's homosexuality on his close relationship with his mother, Freud's etiological theory evoked the stereotype of the mama's boy.

Do mothers cause homosexuality? Many psychoanalysts seem to believe so. These beliefs are, however, based upon cultural stereotypes of homosexuality, the "mama's boy" being a case in point. In fact, the idea that too much closeness to mothers "causes" boyhood gender nonconformity is rather common in the general population. Although a belief in the supposed demasculinizing effects of mothers is cross-cultural, the solutions to the problem may vary from culture to culture. For example, a tribe in Papua New Guinea, also concerned about boys being too close to their mothers, ironically offers a homosexuality-as-immaturity solution to the problem of developing a future heterosexual identity:

> Seven-to-ten-year-old Sambia boys are taken from their mothers when first initiated into the male cult, and thereafter experience the most powerful and seductive homosexual fellatio activities. For some ten to fifteen years, they engage in these practices on a daily basis, first as fellator, and then as fellated. Elders teach that semen is absolutely vital: it should be consumed daily since the creation of biological maleness and the maintenance of masculinity depend on it. Hence, from middle childhood until puberty, boys should perform fellatio on other youths. Near puberty the same initiates become dominant youths. Ritual helps remake their social and erotic identity, the bachelors becoming the fellated partners for a new crop of ritual novices. And at the same time, youths and boys must alike must absolutely avoid women, on pain of punishment. This dual pattern—prescribed homosexual activities and avoidance of women—persists until marriage [Herdt, 1994, pp. 2–3].

Narratives of Pathology

Just as theories of immaturity naturalize the same-sex experiences of early life, theories of pathology define adult homosexuality as a disease or abnormal condition that deviates from a biologically predetermined, heterosexual development. These etiological narratives are based upon several assumptions: First, adult heterosexuality is the normal, nondiseased state. Second, deviations from conventional gender role expectations are symptoms of the homosexual disease.[3] Finally, an external, pathogenic agent traumatizes and turns an individual from the straight path leading to normal heterosexuality. The external event can occur pre- or postnatally and, among others, includes intrauterine hormonal exposure (Dörner, 1986), too much mothering (Bieber et al., 1962), insufficient fathering (Moberly, 1983), or even excess masturbation:

> Nothing is prone to contaminate—under certain circumstances, even to exhaust—the source of all noble and ideal sentiments, which arise of themselves from a normally developing sexual instinct, as the practice of masturbation in early years. It despoils the unfolding bud of perfume and beauty, and leaves behind only the coarse, animal desire for sexual satisfaction. If an individual, thus depraved, reaches the age of maturity, there is wanting in him that aesthetic, ideal, pure and free impulse which draws the opposite sexes together [Krafft-Ebing, 1886, p. 248].

Although Freud rejected Krafft-Ebing's pathologizing in favor of a theory of immaturity, neoFreudian analysts repathologized homosexuality. Sandor Rado (1969) played a major part in shaping these later theories. He made the neo-Darwinian claim that human psychology is linked to reproductive survival and labeled nonprocreative sexual activity as maladaptive.[4] Instead, "homogeneous pairing" as he termed it, was entirely based on a deviation from the "male–female" design as two men seeking sexual intimacy with each other were hopelessly engaged in a misguided attempt to mimic heterosexual encounters:

> What evidence enables me to assume that every homosexual act or homogeneous relationship is a statement of the male-female design? If male desires male, why does he seek out a male who pretends to be a female? Why does a male affect femininity if he wants to express a male's desire for a male? Why does a female turn to a masculine acting female if she is expressing the desire of a female for a female? How else can the crucial fact be explained that in male pairs one male impersonates a female and in female pairs one female impersonates a male? Sometimes evidence for the male–female pattern is deeply repressed, *but I think it can be found with a thorough search.* They are pretending to be a male-female pair. The male-female sexual pattern is dictated by anatomy [pp. 211–212; emphasis added].

Rado's "homosexual" was narrowly constructed of butch and femme stereotypes that made no distinctions between gender roles, gender identity, and sexual attraction. He believed that biology, rather than custom, ultimately determined the mimicry of heterosexual gender roles in same-sex couples. That is to say,

---

[3] These beliefs are embodied in the *DSM-IV's* diagnosis of gender identity disorder of childhood (APA, 1994).

[4] These beliefs also led Rado (1940) to reject Freud's theory of innate bisexuality.

even the environmental factors that caused homosexuality could not overcome the biological drives to create some semblance of male–female pairs. Rado (1969) saw parental behavior as the pathogenic agent:

> Why is the so-called homosexual forced to escape from the male-female pair into a homogenous pair? . . . the familiar campaign of deterrence that parents wage to prohibit the sexual activity of the child . . . causes the male to see in the mutilated female organ a reminder of inescapable punishment. When . . . fear and resentment of the opposite organ becomes insurmountable, the individual may escape into homosexuality. The male patterns are reassured by the presence in both of them of the male organ. Homosexuality is a deficient adaptation evolved by the organism in response to its own emergency overreaction and dyscontrol [pp. 212–213].

Rado had an enormous impact upon later psychoanalytic narratives of pathology. For example, Bieber et al.'s (1962) comparison study of homosexual and heterosexual men in psychoanalysis began with Rado's assumption "that heterosexuality is the biologic norm and that unless interfered with all individuals are heterosexual" (p. 319) and labeled "homosexuality . . . a pathologic biosocial, psychosexual adaptation consequent to pervasive fears surrounding the expression of heterosexual impulses" (p. 220). The Bieber group claimed that a marital relationship in which the father's authority was undermined by the mother was a contributory factor in causing male homosexuality. They found "the best interparental relationships," meaning those least likely to produce homosexuality, in those families where "father dominates but does not minimize mother" (p. 158). Whatever its shortcomings, this theory did lend the weight of medical authority to a cultural belief that a father should be the head of his household. However, as a story about a boy who is closer to his mother than he is to his father, it also evoked the image of the mama's boy again.

Blaming mothers for homosexuality is routine in western culture. One patient, after describing a fight with his mother, said she was always on the defensive with him because "I'm gay." The therapist wondered why his being gay would make her feel defensive. The patient replied that his mother had always dominated his father and that was why he was gay: "She feels guilty because she made me gay." When the therapist told the patient that the actual causes of homosexuality were unknown, he responded with surprise. A few months later, he admitted always blaming his mother for his being gay and, subsequently, blamed her for his being HIV positive. Further exploration revealed that blaming his mother for being gay represented his own unwillingness to accept his homosexuality. When told that it was not a fact that his mother was responsible (see Bell, Weinberg, and Hammersmith, 1981), he had to directly address his own unaccepting feelings. As he did so, he began to feel less angry with his mother, and as a result, their relationship improved significantly.

Narratives of Normal Variants

There are narratives that consider homosexuality as a phenomenon that occurs naturally and therefore is not a sign of illness or pathology. Theories of normal variants claim that gay men are born different, but that their differences are natural. Left-handedness is often used as an analogy in these stories. Is left-handedness a disease or a normal variant? Today, the presence of left-handedness in a minority of people is not defined as an illness, although being left-handed may have disadvantages. In the past being left-handed did lead to social opprobrium;[5] and historically, analogous to gay men, left-handed children were often treated as if they were abnormal and cured of their antisocial habit by forcing them to write right-handed.

It is primarily outside the analytic literature that one finds the earliest normal variant theories. The most influential of these theorists is Alfred Kinsey (Kinsey, Pomeroy, and Martin, 1948) whose approach is based on Darwin's observation on the evolutionary importance of variations within a species. It regards sexual behaviors as one of many possible variations within the human species, like hair or skin color. Kinsey's now-famous 7-point scale categorizes variations along a spectrum of sexual possibilities. At one end is the Kinsey 0, the man who was exclusively heterosexual and had never had an orgasm as a result of physical contact with another man or been aroused by someone of his own sex. At the other end was the Kinsey 6, the individual whose physical contacts and psychological responses were exclusively homosexual. The ratings of 1 to 5 represented different degrees of bisexuality with the Kinsey 3 being equally homosexual and heterosexual in both behavior and/or psychological attraction.

Kinsey and his collegues reported that 37 percent of the male population he surveyed had some homosexual experience leading to orgasm between adolescence and old age. He challenged the stereotypes of homosexuality in the psychiatric and psychoanalytic literature of his time: "The homosexual male is supposed to be less interested in athletics, more often interested in music and the arts, more often engaged in such occupations as bookkeeping, dress design, window display, hairdressing, acting, radio work, nursing, religious service, and social work. The converse to all these is supposed to represent the typical heterosexual male" (p. 637).[6]

In the 1980s, analytic writers outside the psychoanalytic mainstream began incorporating normal variant themes into psychoanalytic theory and practice. Richard Isay (1989, 1991, 1996) has the historic distinction of being the first psychoanalyst to write in this area as an openly gay man. Isay, (1989) attributes homosexuality's causes to unelaborated constitutional factors and describes the dilemma of a normative homosexual adaptation in a heterosexual world:

---

[5] The word *sinister* is derived from a Latin root connoting the left side.

[6] See Kenneth Lewes's (1995) work for an account of the psychoanalytic attack on the Kinsey studies that disagreed with prevailing analytic theory of its time

> I have come to believe that at ages three, four, five and six some homosexual children assume opposite gender characteristics in order to attract and sustain the attention of the father. These are usually such attributes as sensitivity, gentleness, and a lack of interest in aggressive sports. Some homosexual children may also seem noticeably feminine in manner, dress and behavior. I believe that they develop these characteristics for the same reason that heterosexual boys may adopt certain of their father's attributes, in order to attract, first the mother's interest and later, someone like the mother [p. 19].

Isay's approach is to reinterpret earlier psychoanalytic findings. He rejects the contention of Bieber et al. (1962) and Socarides (1968) that distant fathers contribute to the development of homosexuality in their sons. According to Isay, homosexuality is not caused by withdrawn fathers. Instead, fathers who sense their sons' innate same-sex attractions will anxiously withdraw from their own future gay child. In actuality, his alternative theory deftly illustrates that the psychoanalytic unconscious often serves as a projective screen open to multiple interpretations by analvsts holding differing views of human development.

Although gay patients may present with a belief that homosexuality is a normal variant, those stories are usually a later, cognitive acquisition. A patient with these beliefs often holds them in a tenuous relationship with more affectively charged narratives of pathology and immaturity acquired earlier in life. Such was the case of another patient who sought a consultation after being treated by a psychoanalyst for more than twenty years. Many of those years were spent trying to "cure" the patient of his homosexuality. The patient had been married when he began treatment, but was now divorced and identified himself at the time of the consultation as a gay man. He explained why the previous therapy had ended. During a session in which the patient spoke of the possibility that his homosexuality might be genetic in origin, he said the analyst called him "stupid." He left the office in an agitated state, and the analyst subsequently called him at home to express concern about what had happened. The patient explained that he was upset because "you called me stupid." The analyst proceeded to clarify his statement and told the patient, "I didn't say you were stupid, I said the idea was stupid." The patient responded, "Well, it's the same thing, isn't it?"

When asked what he found so distressing about his interaction with the previous therapist, the patient had several associations. At one level, he felt the analyst had been rude and had called him stupid. But there was something more troubling to him. It had taken the patient a long time to reevaluate the theory of pathology that had, in part, motivated his earlier wish to change his sexual identity. He was now more comfortable with the idea that his homosexuality might be considered normal. Like many people today, he believed that if homosexuality has a genetic or biological origin, and that "gay people are born that way," then being gay should be considered normal. And if homosexuality was biologically normal, then it was not necessarily a bad thing. However the patient's newly acquired belief in a normal variant theory also coexisted with his much older theory of pathology. Whatever the analyst's motive for denigrating the biological, normal variant theory, the patient experienced it as an attack on his belief that being gay was good.

Morality Tales

As the patient's experience illustrates, embedded within etiological theories are moral concerns about the meaning of homosexuality. From this perspective, etiological theories can be read as stories about the impact of homosexuality on the social order, on an individual's worth within that order, or the relationship between homosexuality and the intent of a higher force. These tales offer instruction about what is valuable and what is devalued. Among the key words in the morality tales that underlie etiological theories are "social benefit" and "social harm," "good and evil," "health and illness," "adaptive and maladaptive," "holy and sinful," or "mature and childish."

One lesson to be learned from narratives of immaturity was that one could grow up to fulfill one's adult potential and become something better. In Freud's (1924) work, the resolution of the Oedipus complex was the *sine qua non* of adult development. It was only by achieving this step that one identified with the parents, gave up infantile sexual wishes, and came to accept reality. This was Freud's explanation of how one attained the psychological status of an adult. Adulthood, however, required the mature exercise of one's sexual responsibilities:

> Since normal intercourse has been so relentlessly persecuted by morality—and also, on account of the possibilities of infection, by hygiene—what are known as the perverse forms of intercourse between the two sexes, in which other parts of the body take over the role of the genitals, have undoubtedly increased in social importance. These activities cannot, however, be regarded as being as harmless as analogous extensions [of the sexual aim] in love relationships. They are ethically objectionable, for they degrade the relationships of love between two human beings from a serious matter to a convenient game, attended by no risk and no spiritual participation [Freud, 1908, p. 200].

Freud's pronouncements on homosexuality could be similarly judgmental. Joseph Wortis (1954), during an analysis with Freud, asked why people shouldn't express both aspects of "bisexuality." Freud responds as if his analysand were an unruly child:

> Normal people have a certain homosexual component and a very strong heterosexual component. The homosexual component should be sublimated as it now is in society; it is one of the most valuable human assets, and should be put to social uses. One cannot give one's impulses free rein. Your attitude reminds me of a child who just discovered everybody defecates and who then

> demands that everybody ought to defecate in public; that cannot be [pp. 99–100].

Like theories of immaturity, narratives of pathology also contain underlying values, seen in their tendency to speak of illness as a synonym for immorality. In other words, the illnesses described in these theories are metaphoric. For example, medicine's deficiency model of illness attributes physical symptoms to the absence of an external substrate required for normal growth and development. Physical examples are vitamin deficiencies, like scurvy or rickets. Moberly (1983), a fundamentalist Christian therapist who defines homosexuality as an illness, takes literary liberties with the deficiency model and proposes that as a child, a gay man lacked "a good relationship" with his father: "the homosexual . . . has suffered from some deficit in the relationship with the parent of the same sex. . . . Any incident that happens to place a particular strain on the relationship between the child and the parent of the same sex is potentially causative" (pp. 2–3). Moberly cannot objectively define an ideal parental–child relationship, for, unlike a vitamin, the nature of this particular nutrient is entirely subjective:

> The common factor in every case [of homosexuality] is disruption in the attachment to the parent of the same sex, however it may have been caused. Whatever the particular incident may be, it is something that has been experienced as hurtful by the child, whether or not intended as hurtful by the parent . . . it must be emphasized that this relational defect may not be evident, or not more than partially evident to appearances. At the conscious level an adjustment may be made that leaves few or even no signs of disturbance. The family relationships of a homosexual may in a number of instances seem to be good, indeed, in such cases they are good at a certain level. This is not an objection to the present hypothesis, since what we are speaking of is intrapsychic damage at a deep level, much of which may not be overt or conscious. Similarly, it may not always be readily evident what led to the deficit in the first place. The cause may not be readily recognized, or recognized for what it is [p. 4].

Moberly's *post hoc* reasoning offers few useful guidelines on how to supply adequate psychological nourishment to prevent homosexuality.

In contrast to those who pathologize homosexuality, normal variant theorists have a view of the social order that sees potential value in individual variation:

> Until the extent of any type of human behavior is adequately known, it is difficult to assess its significance, either to the individuals who are involved or to society as a whole; and until the extent of the homosexual is known, it is practically impossible to understand its biologic or social origins. It is one thing if we are dealing with a type of activity that is unusual, without precedent among other animals, and restricted to peculiar types of individuals within the human population. It is another thing if the phenomenon proves to be a

fundamental part, not only of human sexuality, but of mammalian patterns as a whole [Kinsey et al., 1948, pp. 610–611].

This approach is typified in sociobiology (Wilson, 1975), which can be read as an evolutionary morality tale that hypothesizes the social benefits provided by gay people. Wilson begins with the assumption that homosexuality's ongoing presence in populations, despite cultural stigma and a "homosexual's" lack of self-reproduction, suggests a biological origin of adaptive value. As it is built upon stereotypes of homosexuality, the fact that gay people can and do reproduce is irrelevant to this theory's narrative thread. It is a story that rests upon two underlying biological analogies: sickle-cell anemia and the altruistic behavior of social insects.

Sickle-cell anemia is a condition present in individuals who have two autosomal recessive genes (SS) for a type of hemoglobin that causes red blood cells to have an abnormal or sickle shape that leads to many damaging medical complications. The sickle-cell trait persistence in populations, despite its illness-causing potential, may be due to the prevalence of malaria, an infectious disease endemic to areas whose populations show the sickle-cell trait. Heterozygous individuals (designated HS) are more resistant to malaria than the homozygous dominant (designated HH) who has normal hemoglobin and no sickle-cell trait at all. However, in malarial zones, the so-called healthy individual (HH) is at greater risk than the sicker heterozygote (HS). Illustrating nature's aversion to the clear-cut distinctions so prized by human beings, the same gene (S) that causes debilitating illness in one setting (SS) can afford an adaptive measure of protection and greater health in another (HS). Analogously, genetic homosexuality should lead to extinction as gay men are "less likely" to reproduce. But if the hypothetical gay gene offered some adaptive value in the manner of the sickle-cell trait, that could explain its continued presence in populations.

This leads to Wilson's other analogy, drawn from studies of social insect species. Among bees and wasps, most members of the colony do not reproduce themselves, but may derive a genetic benefit in helping their queen reproduce. The feeding of the fertile queen and the care of her young by nonreproducing workers is defined as *altruistic* behavior. Because workers share some of the genetic traits of their queen, they have a reasonable likelihood of continuing their own genetic line by providing scarce resources to the queen and her offspring. This phenomenon, referred to as *kin selection,* could be called a genetically selfish solution masquerading as altruistic behavior.

The next step in Wilson's line of reasoning is the theory of homosexual altruism. He hypothesizes that a gene causing homosexuality, while interfering with the individual's own reproductive capacity, may guarantee him a measure of genetic success even if he is incapable of reproducing himself. The "homosexual" increases the likelihood of passing on his own DNA by taking care of the children of his reproducing siblings. Having an increased number of caretakers per child would be likely to increase the child's reproductive success and favor transmission of the homosexual gene. Unsurprisingly, Wilson's altruistic "homosexual," like his counterparts in theories of immaturity and pathology, is constructed from stereotypic gender roles. In this case, being a gay man is defined as being a helper rather than a hunter. That is to say he fits the stereotypes of a man who is not as athletic as other men or as one who is interested in domestic or other feminine pursuits.

Conclusions

For any particular patient, an etiological theory is likely to have a personal meaning and an affective charge. A gay man asking "What is the cause of my homosexuality?" may simply be asking "Why do I feel different from everybody else?" A heterosexual analyst asking, "Why is my patient gay?" may be asking, "Why is this person different from me?" Therefore, focusing on homosexuality's etiology is not the most meaningful way to conduct a psychotherapy, any more than it would be meaningful to conduct a therapy that spent inordinate amounts of time searching for the origins of a patient's heterosexuality. The time-consuming search for etiologies is quite widespread in the psychoanalytic treatments of gay men and is often done at the patient's own request. However, recognizing the often irrational underpinnings of the search for origins may allow the focus of treatment to shift from finding the causes of homosexuality to helping patients understand what their same-sex feelings mean. This is a psychoanalytic approach that instead of asking 'What is wrong with the patient?" asks "Who is the patient?"

References

American Psychiatric Association (1994), *Diagnostic and Statistical Manual of Mental Disorders, 4th ed.* Washington, DC: American Psychiatric Press.

Bell, A., Weinberg, M. & Hammersmith, S. (1981), *Sexual Preference: Its Development in Men and Women.* Bloomington: Indiana University Press.

Bieber, I., Dain, H., Dince, P., Drellich, M., Grand, H., Gundlach, R., Kremer, M., Rifkin, A., Wilbur, C. & Bieber T. (1962), *Homosexuality: A Psychoanalytic Study.* New York: Basic Books.

Breuer, J. & Freud, S. (1893–1895), Studies on hysteria. *Standard Edition,* 2. London: Hogarth Press, 1955.

de Beauvoir, S. (1952), *The Second Sex.* New York: Vintage Books, 1978.

Dörner, G. (1986), Hormone-dependent brain development and preventive medicine. *Monogr. Neural Sci.,* 12:17–27.

Freud, S. (1896a), Heredity and the aetiology of the neuroses. *Standard Edition*, 3:142–156. London: Hogarth Press, 1962.

——— (1896b), The aetiology of hysteria. *Standard Edition*, 3:189–221. London: Hogarth Press, 1962.
——— (1900), The interpretation of dreams. *Standard Edition*, 4 & 5. London: Hogarth Press, 1953.
——— (1905), Three essays on the theory of sexuality. *Standard Edition*, 7:123–246. London: Hogarth Press, 1953.
——— (1908), "Civilized" sexual morality and modern mental illness. *Standard Edition*, 9:177–204. London: Hogarth Press, 1959.
——— (1910), Leonardo da Vinci and a memory of his childhood. *Standard Edition*, 11:59–138. London: Hogarth Press, 1957
——— (1924), The dissolution of the Oedipus complex. *Standard Edition*, 19:73–79. London: Hogarth Press, 1961.
——— (1926), Inhibitions, symptoms and anxiety. *Standard Edition*, 20: 75–175. London: Hogarth Press, 1959.
——— (1935), Anonymous (letter to an American mother). In: *The Letters of Sigmund Freud*, ed. E. Freud. New York: Basic Books, 1960, pp. 423–424.
Herdt, G. (1994), *Guardians of the Flutes: Idioms of Masculinity*. Chicago: University of Chicago Press.
Isay, R. (1989), *Being Homosexual: Gay Men and Their Development*. New York: Farrar, Straus and Giroux.
——— (1991), The homosexual analyst: Clinical considerations. *The Psychoanalytic Study of the Child*, 46:199–216. New Haven, CT: Yale University Press.
——— (1996), *Becoming Gay: The Journey to Self-Acceptance*. New York: Pantheon.
Kinsey, A., Pomeroy, W. & Martin, C. (1948), *Sexual Behavior in the Human Male*. Philadelphia, PA: Saunders.
Krafft-Ebing, R. (1886), *Psychopathia Sexualis*, trans. H. Wedeck. New York: Putnam, 1965.
Lewes, K. (1995), *Psychoanalysis and Male Homosexuality*. Northvale, NJ: Aronson.
Moberly, E. (1983), *Homosexuality: A New Christian Ethic*. Cambridge, UK: James Clarke.
Rado, S. (1940), A critical examination of the concept of bisexuality. *Psychosomatic Med.* 2:459-467. New York: Basic Books.
——— (1969), *Adaptational Psychodynamics: Motivation and Control*. New York: Science House.
Socarides, C. (1968), *The Overt Homosexual*. New York: Grune & Stratton.
Sullivan, H. S. (1953), *The Interpersonal Theory of Psychiatry*. New York: Norton.
Wilson, E. (1975), *Sociobiology: The New Synthesis*. Cambridge, MA: Belknap Press.
Wortis, J. (1954), *Fragments of an Analysis with Freud*. New York: Charter Books.

Homosexuality

RICHARD C. FRIEDMAN

Recent revision of previously accepted psychoanalytic theories and practices about homosexuality have been profound. My book, *Male Homosexuality: A Contemporary Psychoanalytic Perspective* (Friedman, 1988) influenced this paradigm shift. Subsequently, Jennifer I. Downey and I have continued our work on psychoanalysis and sexual orientation (Friedman and Downey, 1993, 1995; Downey and Friedman, 1998). The circumstances that led to my 1988 book, however, not only place our own contributions, but also much about this phase of psychoanalytic thought, in historical perspective.

In the 1970s it had become apparent to me that generally accepted psychoanalytic ideas about male homosexuality were invalid. I was influenced in my thinking at the time by my work with the *DSM-III* (American Psychiatric Association, 1980) Committee, my psychoanalytically informed research on homosexuality, and my experiences as a candidate at The Columbia Psychoanalytic Institute.

The DSM-III

Soon after Robert Spitzer led a successful effort to delete homosexuality as a diagnosis from the *DSM,* I became a member of an advisory committee to the *DSM* Task Force on Human Sexuality. At that time the psychoanalytic community was involved in a struggle with the *DSM* Committee about the appropriate theoretical substructure of the entire psychiatric nomenclature. The previous two editions of the *DSM* had been based on psychoanalytic theory. The third edition of the *DSM,* however, was influenced by Kraepelin much more than Freud, and utilized a descriptive, atheoretical stance toward psychopathology. Rather than framing illness in terms of unconscious, maladaptive, irrational motivations, it was conceptualized in terms of suffering and disability.

The publication of *DSM-III* (1980) marked the beginning of a gradual decline of the influence of psychoanalysis on clinical psychiatry. This turned out to have dramatic influence on social-political attitudes about homosexuality in the United States. Prior to *DSM-III,* public policy about gay/lesbian people (then called "homosexual") was based on the psychiatric/psychoanalytic judgment that they were either sociopathic, or sexual deviants. The former idea was based on the assumption that adequate superego functioning results from paternal identification, which is (inevitably and necessarily) impaired in gay males (Lewes, 1988). The notion that homosexual desire is evidence of what today would be termed a paraphilia was based on the psychoanalytic belief that resolution of oedipal and preoedipal conflicts would inevitably lead to heterosexuality. The pathological model of homosexuality had adverse consequences for gay/lesbian people with regard to immigration policy, child custody, federal employment, and in many other areas as well (Gonsiorek and Weinrich, 1991). A continually reverberating negative cycle of negative assumptions about gay/lesbian people occurred in many sectors of American society which was contributed to by (now obsolete) psychoanalytic ideas.

In addition to being critical of the new framework for interpreting psychiatric illness in the DSM, many psychoanalysts were specifically opposed to the depathologization of homosexuality which they believed to have occurred as a result of political pressures by the gay rights movement. Spitzer's view, however, and that of the DSM Committee and the American Psychiatric Association, was different. Gay and lesbian people simply had not been shown to be more likely to experience distress and disability than heterosexual people (except as a consequence of antihomosexual prejudice).

Teaching about Homosexuality at Psychoanalytic Institutes

The publications of Socarides were probably the most influential at the Institutes of The American Psychoanalytic Association (Socarides, 1963, 1968). Socarides viewed predominant or exclusive homosexuality as a pathological response to unresolved preoedipal conflicts.

I was a psychoanalytic candidate at The Columbia Psychoanalytic Institute in the 1970s where the most influential psychoanalytic educator in the area of sexual orientation was Ovesey. Ovesey had observed that homosexual dream imagery was frequently used by heterosexual men to express feelings about competitive defeat, or yearnings for dependent gratification, and termed this phenomenon "pseudohomosexuality" (Ovesey, 1954, 1955a, b, 1969). Ovesey's theoretical ideas about pseudohomosexuality were anchored in an adaptational psychoanalytic perspective, originally formulated by his teacher and the first director of The Columbia Psychoanalytic Center, Sandor Rado (Rado, 1940). Ovesey was more circumspect about homosexuality itself. Unlike most analysts at that time, he did not consider homosexuality to be a perversion, but rather a sexual neurosis whose etiology was not known.

Psychoanalytically Informed Research on Homosexuality

As a result of my work on the DSM committee, I read a study by Evelyn Hooker demonstrating that Rorschach protocols of homosexual men were indistinguishable from those of heterosexual control subjects (Hooker, 1957, 1965). Interestingly, Hooker's work had never been discussed either during my psychiatric or psychoanalytic training. Her study was so thoughtfully designed and meticulously executed that it stimulated me to question generally accepted psychoanalytic ideas about sexual orientation. I found myself becoming wary of the evidence that psychoanalysts used as a basis for their conclusion that homosexuality was inherently pathological. Review of the psychoanalytic publications on the topic raised many questions. The literature was unsystematic: different types of patients were discussed in a global way, basic assumptions tended to be uncritically accepted, and systematic research hardly existed. Despite these limitations, psychoanalysts who were influential not only in psychoanalysis, but also in psychiatry as well, publicly expressed the view that homosexual orientation itself was inherently pathological. This generalization applied to all homosexual people, not just patients.

Prior to the years of my psychoanalytic training, the psychoanalytic community had carried out only one research project on male homosexuality. This was a well-known study of The Committee of Medical Psychoanalysts under the direction of Bieber (Bieber et al., 1962). This investigation was not designed to test assumptions about the psychopathology or normalcy of homosexuality. The authors noted that all psychoanalytic theories of homosexuality assumed it to be pathological—an assumption that they retained. Rather, the purpose of their study was to compare development and family histories in homosexual male psychoanalytic/psychotherapy patients with heterosexuals. In this study, the homosexual and heterosexual patients did indeed have different family profiles. The authors concluded that a specific type of familial configuration caused homosexuality: close binding mothers, and hostile and/or detached fathers. This assumption has not been validated, although gay men more often than heterosexual men do tend to describe difficulties with their fathers during development (Friedman, 1988). Isay has speculated that this may be primarily due to anxiety experienced by the fathers in reaction to their sons' homosexuality (Isay, 1989).

Uneasy about the state of the psychoanalytic literature on homosexuality and unwilling to accept the conclusions of most senior analysts at that time about the development and psychological functioning of homosexual people, I had not yet formed an opinion about alternative ways that psychoanalysts might think about human sexual orientation. I decided to carry out psychoanalytically informed research on male homosexuality, partly in the hope that new data might help me resolve some of my uncertainties about the state of the field. This research was also motivated by practical considerations.

I had accepted an academic post at The Institute for Human Reproduction at Columbia-Presbyterian Medical Center, which required that I carry out a research project in some area of human sexuality. Serendipitously, a study had just appeared in the prestigious *New England Journal of Medicine* indicating that serum testosterone was higher in a sample of heterosexual than homosexual men (Kolodny et al., 1971). This research attracted much attention because the media was anxious to be able to report that homosexuality is "biological" (e.g., has a simple biological "cause"). I attempted to replicate Kolodny's finding and was one of a number of investigators who found that there is, in fact, no difference in blood levels of testosterone, or other hormones, between hetero- and homosexual men (Friedman et al., 1976; Friedman and Frantz, 1977). Downey subsequently found that the same was true in women of divergent sexual orientation. Unlike other biological researchers, however, I decided to interview my subjects about their development and psychological functioning in addition to measuring their sex steroid hormones. The latter part of my research was designed to acquire additional psychodynamic data about men similar to those who had been studied by Hooker (1957, 1965). Would the psychodynamics and psychopathology of homosexual men in my study be similar to her subjects, or to those described by psychoanalysts who had carried out psychoanalytic treatment of homosexual patients?

Unfortunately, there was no educational structure by which research was considered part of psychoanalytic education. Research such as mine, though not considered antipsychoanalytic, was rather viewed as being extrapsychoanalytic—not relevant to psychoanalytic theory or practice. In order to carry out this project, therefore, it was necessary to take a leave of absence from psychoanalytic training. In my research, I compared both blood levels of sex steroid hormones and psychodynamics in socially well-adjusted highly functional men of homo- and heterosexual orientation. Failing to find evidence that the homosexual group was more "pathological" than the heterosexual group, I concluded that the generally accepted psychoanalytic paradigms of homosexuality were incorrect. As a result of this research and my close reading of the analytic and nonanalytic literature on homosexuality, I realized that other important psychoanalytic assumptions about sexual and personality development that I learned in the Institute classrooms were also not valid. My conclusions about this were at odds with those of senior analysts, including most training analysts at that time. Virtually the entire faculty of The Columbia Psychoanalytic Institute, for example, including my own analyst, accepted Rado's view that heterosexuality was a biologically based norm, and homosexuality the result of developmental derailment (Rado, 1940). The vast majority of psychoanalytic institute faculty throughout the United States accepted the models about homosexuality advanced by Charles Socarides as being valid (1963, 1968). The single exception to this general trend was Judd Marmor (1965, 1980), who was the first major psychoanalyst/psychiatrist to reject the pathological model of homosexuality. Marmor's view was not generally accepted, however, and at that time I had never met him. The intellectual tradition at The Columbia Psychoanalytic Institute was rich, but as was generally true throughout psychoanalysis, scholarly work was carried out in groups led by training analysts. At Columbia a chronological line of thought existed with regard to homosexuality that had begun with Rado and Kardiner, and included Karush, Ovesey, Gaylin, and Ethel Person, a mentee of Ovesey's (Person, 1999). Both Bieber and Socarides were graduates of Columbia, and their work was in keeping with the perspectives established and accepted there. In contrast, my work on psychoanalysis and homosexuality was carried out in isolation from this tradition. Karush and Gaylin had been analytic supervisors of mine, and I learned a great deal from each man. The patients I treated during analytic training were heterosexual, however, and the topic of homosexuality was mentioned only in passing during my supervision. The process of skeptical scholarly detachment from local authority figures, although tolerated, was not encouraged or supported in psychoanalysis at that time.

Paradigm Revisions

Three books published in the 1980s proposed far-reaching revisions in psychoanalytic ideas about male homosexuality.

In a critical analysis of psychoanalytic articles, Lewes (1988) convincingly demonstrated that bias had influenced psychoanalytic ideas about male homosexuality. Discussing publications throughout the history of psychoanalysis, he showed that the type of bias was influenced by the particular phase of psychoanalytic history in which an article was published. The biases had cascading effects that ultimately shaped the way that homosexuality was perceived by psychoanalysts at the time his book was written.

At the turn of the century, Ellis (1905) had observed that homosexual and heterosexual people were similar save for their sexual orientation. This point had been overlooked in psychoanalytic discourse until the publications of Isay. Isay (1989) proposed that homosexuality was innate and that the developmental pathways of gay men were influenced not by psychopathology, but rather, defensive and prejudicial treatment by the heterosexual majority, including their own fathers. The first openly gay psychoanalyst in The American Psychoanalytic Association, Isay used his own psychobiography as further evidence in support of his ideas. He particularly emphasized that attempts by psychoanalysts to change the sexual orientation of their patients were not only likely to fail, but to be harmful. Isay's ideas met with considerable resistance from the psychoanalytic establishment. Perhaps the single concept that stimulated the most extreme defensive reactions was that because gay/lesbian people seemed to be able to work and love at a similar level as heterosexual people, heterosexuality should not be used as a developmental norm by psychoanalytic psychology.

By the 1980s, new psychoanalytic ideas about women and gender identity development had become widely accepted. These were strongly influenced by the extrapsychoanalytic research of Masters and Johnson (1966), and Money and Ehrhardt (1972). Stoller's publications (e.g., 1968) were particularly important in explaining how relevant these new areas of research were for psychoanalysis. Similar cross-discipline communication had not yet occurred in the area of sexual orientation, however. In *Male Homosexuality: A Contemporary Psychoanalytic Perspective*, I discussed ways in which descriptive research on human sexual behavior, such as, for example, had been carried out by Kinsey et al. (1948, 1953), and genetic and neuroendocrine research were relevant for psychoanalytic theory and practice. Critical review of the psychoanalytic literature on narcissism, masochism, and paranoia did not provide support for the pathological model of homosexuality. I suggested that most psychoanalytic discussions of sexual orientation included four basic components: conscious sexual fantasy, sexual activity, sense of identity as gay or heterosexual, and social role (advertisement of one's sexual identity to others). Rejecting the notion of constitutional bisexuality and unconscious homosexuality as lacking empirical support, I noted that Freud had died long before the emergence of modern gender psychology. Identifications and partial identifications with significant others of both genders are universal. Consciously experienced erotic desire for opposite-sexed persons, although common, is not. A relatively small group of people (although a large number) never experience such desire during their entire lives. Some people have experienced homo- and heteroerotic desire at various points and phases of the life cycle. Of these, some label themselves "gay" and some feel that they belong to the heterosexual majority (Friedman and Downey, 1999). Data about sexual orientation change during psychoanalysis were sparse. I suggested that when sexual orientation seemed to change, it was probably among bisexual men. What usually changed in such men was not the sexual imagery itself, but rather the significance attributed to the imagery for the person's sense of identity and social role.

I also observed that homosexual imagery in gay men is autonomous, and is not a reaction to unconscious anxiety about heterosexuality as some psychoanalytic theoreticians had proposed (Friedman, 1988).

Subsequent Psychoanalytic Developments

During the 1990s the pathological model of homosexuality was formally abandoned by American psychoanalysis. This altered perspective had come about as a result of the influence of extraanalytic, psychoanalytically informed contributions from mental health professionals (Cabaj and Stein, 1996), the ongoing social/political/educational efforts of The Homosexual Issues Committee of The American Psychoanalytic Association, and psychoanalytic publications as well (Isay, 1989, 1991, 1996, 1998; Magee and Miller, 1997; Drescher, 1998; Cohler and Galatzer-Levy, 2000).

During the past decade Downey and I continued our scholarly work on sexual orientation.

Among the points we discussed were:

(1) The need for psychoanalysts to use a standardized way of describing erotic fantasy and activity in publications. The literature about homosexuality and bisexuality still contains many examples of authors calling a behavior by the same name, "homosexuality," but actually discussing quite different phenomena.
(2) The necessity to conceptualize sexual orientation as a function of the gender of the person. Female sexual orientation must be understood as part of the psychology of women; male sexual orientation as part of the psychology of men. The development of men and women is different in many respects from earliest childhood. These differences include different interpersonal and cognitive styles, different sexual and romantic fantasies, and different ways of experiencing all aspects of sexuality (Friedman and Downey, 2000). Boys tend to experience the onset of consciously experienced erotic fantasy in response to a visual stimulus—not in the context of an intimate relationship. Once experienced, erotic fantasy seems to act as a limit. That which is outside the delimited frame of consciously experienced erotic fantasy profile is responded to as nonerotic. For example, men who have been gay from childhood do not tend to respond erotically to imagery of nude women. Men who have been exclusively heterosexual in fantasy from childhood do not tend to respond erotically to imagery of nude men. Unlike men, girls and women tend to experience the onset of consciously experienced erotic fantasy in the context of a meaningful relationship. Once formed, their erotic fantasy patterns tend to be more plastic than those of males. Women, for example, sometimes experience entirely new homoerotic fantasy arousal patterns following intimate relationships with other women in middle age, or even later. This occurs very rarely among men (Downey and Friedman, 1998). Psychoanalytic experience and extrapsychoanalytic research indicates that the psychosexual functioning of lesbians is similar to those of heterosexual women, much more than gay men. The psychosexual functioning of gay men is much more similar to that of heterosexual men, much more than lesbians.
(3) The importance of recognizing the influence of bias in the psychoanalytic literature about human sexuality. One of the most important biases has been

a tendency toward emphasizing the sexuality of males more than females. For example, the psychoanalytic literature on male homosexuality has been far more abundant than that about female homosexuality. Another crucial bias has been toward heterosexism—a tendency to privilege heterosexual developmental and social organization and to view heterosexual development as a norm. Many other sociocultural and historical biases have been present as well (Lilling and Friedman, 1995; Cabaj and Stein, 1996; Friedman and Lilling, 1996). It is quite important for the psychoanalytic community not to assume that the problem of bias about sexual orientation has been solved despite progress in awareness that has occurred recently. Bias, and the influence of ideology on thinking about sexual orientation, are ongoing problems in psychoanalysis, and continuous critical scrutiny is necessary to counteract deleterious effects. In the United States, the topic of homosexuality is part of a political struggle between Conservatives and Liberals that includes religious dimensions. Antihomosexual prejudice remains a major social problem, although improvements have obviously occurred in recent years. It is not easy for psychoanalysis as a discipline and profession to maintain an appropriate boundary in such a turbulent social climate. Despite external pressures, the attitudes, values, and judgments of psychoanalytic practitioners must somehow continue to rest on scientific/clinical perspectives, and not be determined by immediate political pressures (no matter how well-intentioned the response to such influences might seem at the moment).

(4) The need for psychoanalysis to critically scrutinize its assumptions in the light of ongoing psychoanalytic and extrapsychoanalytic research and to abandon ideas and theories that have not stood the test of time. We have suggested, for example, that one of Freud's most cherished and tenaciously held convictions was probably invalid: the universality of the incestuous wish. We have discussed the rationale for this despite the experience of psychoanalysts that triangular oedipal psychodynamics are crucial in psychological functioning and development. We have discussed the way in which psychoanalytic experience with gay men and lesbians provides data that help resolve this apparent contradiction (Friedman and Downey, 1995). Freud's conclusions about the "biological bedrock" underlying motivation also require revision. We have discussed the rationale for abandoning the notion of penis envy as a developmental norm, for example (Downey and Friedman, 1998).

(5) In addition to revision of theoretical models, we have discussed clinical issues as well. Homophobia is probably the single most important clinical topic that has recently emerged as crucial in understanding gay/lesbian patients. In the early 1970s, an educator and psychologist who lectured on the topic of homosexuality and regularly encountered virulent antihomosexual

> attitudes in audiences, coined the term "homophobia" to connote such behavior. About a decade later, a psychotherapist observed that gay/lesbian people often suffered because they had been reared in environments of antihomosexual bias. Internalizations of antihomosexual attitudes and values led to diverse types of psychological difficulties. He termed these negative internalizations "internalized homophobia" (Malyon, 1982). Homophobia and internalized homophobia did not originate as psychoanalytic concepts, since the behaviors they connote are, as a general rule, not phobic in the sense that psychoanalysts use the term. Nonetheless they have become part of clinical parlance, and in keeping with traditions of common usage, we have incorporated them into our psychoanalytic vocabulary.

Patients who are or have been in situations where they have been exposed to antihomosexual prejudice may suffer from symptoms of traumatic stress. This is common particularly in children, adolescents, and young adults. Successful treatment of anxiety resulting from homophobic abuse generally requires some type of environmental change in addition to psychotherapy. If patients are young enough to still be living with or closely involved with homophobic family members, family therapy may also be indicated.

Negative valuation of the self for being homosexual may lead to dramatic and severe symptoms, including suicidal behavior, substance abuse, and various types of sexual symptoms. Many patients who suffer guilt and shame about being homosexual respond positively to gay affirmative supportive psychotherapy. Others, however, particularly those who have multiaxial psychiatric disorders, require exploratory psychotherapy or psychoanalysis, and frequently, concurrent psychopharmacology. A particularly important unconscious mental mechanism in internalized homophobia is identification with the aggressor. Patients may identify with bullies and abusers from different childhood phases and subsequently attack themselves as they were attacked during childhood and adolescence. Often such childhood abuse comes from male peers and authority figures and is triggered by a boy's cross-gender stereotypic role behavior. Girls and women tend to be more tolerant of gender nonconformity than boys and men (Friedman and Downey, 1994, 1995, 1999; Downey and Friedman, 1996).

Conclusion

Much remains to be learned about the culture of psychoanalysis from the study of the history of psychoanalytic ideas about sexual orientation. How did a field that prided itself on insightful and helpful understanding of behavior become so seriously in error about such a crucial aspect of psychological functioning as sexual orientation? Although psychoanalysis appears to have righted itself with regard to the psychological development and functioning of gay/lesbian people, ongoing monitoring is necessary in order to guard against the emergence of similar misunderstanding of other types of behavior. Revision of psychoanalytic ideas about homosexuality resulted—at least in part—from an increasingly enthusiastic attitude of organized psychoanalysis about research. Hopefully this trend will continue and contribute to the ongoing critical scrutiny of hypotheses that is necessary for the continued vitality of psychoanalytic psychology.

References

American Psychiatric Association (1980), *Diagnostic and Statistical Manual of Mental Disorders, 3rd ed.* Washington, DC: American Psychiatric Press.

Bieber, I., Dain, H. J., Drellich, M., Grand, H., Gundlach, R., Kremer, M., Rifkin, A., Wilbur, C. & Bieber, I. (1962), *Homosexuality: A Psychoanalytic Study of Male Homosexuals.* New York: Basic Books.

Cabaj, R. P. & Stein, T. S., eds. (1996), *Homosexuality and Mental Health: A Comprehensive Textbook.* Washington, DC: American Psychiatric Press.

Cohler, B. J. & Galatzer-Levy, R. M. (2000), *The Course of Gay and Lesbian Lives.* Chicago: University of Chicago Press.

Downey, J. I. & Friedman, R. C. (1995), Internalized homophobia in lesbian relationships *J. Amer. Psychoanal Assn.,* 46:471–506.

——— & ——— (1996), The negative therapeutic reaction and self-hatred in gay and lesbian patients. In: *Homosexuality and Mental Health: A Comprehensive Textbook,* ed. R. Cabaj & T. Stein. Washington, DC: American Psychiatric Press, pp. 471–484.

——— & ——— (1998), Female homosexuality: Classical psychoanalytic theory reconsidered. *J. Amer. Psychoanal. Assn.,* 46:471–506.

Drescher, J. (1998), *Psychoanalytic Therapy and the Gay Man.* Hillsdale, NJ: The Analytic Press.

Ellis, H. (1905), *Studies in the Psychology of Sex, Vol. 1.* New York: Random House.

Friedman, R. C.(1988), *Male Homosexuality: A Contemporary Psychoanalytic Perspective.* New Haven, CT: Yale University Press.

——— & Downey, J. I. (1993), Psychoanalysis, psychobiology and homosexuality. *J. Amer. Psychoanal. Assn.,* 41:1159–1198.

——— & ——— (1994), Special Article: Homosexuality. *New Engl. J. Med.,* 331: 923–930.

——— & ——— (1995), Biology and the Oedipus complex. *Psychoanal. Quart.* 64: 234–264.

——— & ——— (1999), Sexual fantasy and behavior: Selected clinical issues. In: *Masculinity and Sexuality: Selected Topics in the Psychology of Men.,* ed. R. C. Friedman & J. I. Downey. Review Series. Washington, DC: American Psychiatric Press.

——— & ——— (2000), Psychoanalysis and sexual fantasies. *Arch. Sexual Behavior,* 29:567–586.

——— Dyrenfurth, I., Linkie, D., Tendler, R. & Fleiss, J. L. (1976), Hormones and sexual orientation in males. *Amer. J. Psychiat.,* 134:571–572.

——— & Frantz, A. Z. G. (1977), Plasma prolactin levels in male homosexuals. *Hormones & Behavior,* 9:19–22.

——— & Lilling, A. A. (1996), An empirical study of the beliefs of psychoanalysts about scientific and clinical dimensions of male homosexuality. *J. Homosexuality* 32:79–89.

Gonsiorek, J. C. & Weinrich, J. D. (1991), *Homosexuality: Research Implications for Public Policy.* Newbury Park, CA: Sage.

Hooker, E. (1957), The adjustment of the male overt homosexual. *J. Proj. Tech.,* 21: 18–31.

——— (1965), Male homosexuals and their worlds. In: *Sexual Inversion: The Multiple Roots of Homosexuality,* ed. J. Marmor. New York: Basic Books.

Isay, R. (1989), *Being Homosexual: Gay Men and Their Development.* New York: Farrar, Straus, Giroux.

——— (1991), The homosexual analyst: Clinical considerations. *The Psychoanalytic Study of the Child,* 46:199–216. New Haven, CT: Yale University Press.

——— (1996), *Becoming Gay: The Journey to Self-Acceptance.* New York: Pantheon Books.

——— (1998), Heterosexually married homosexual men: Clinical and developmental issues. *Amer. J. Orthopsychiat.,* 68:424–432.

Kinsey, A. C., Pomeroy, W. B. & Martin, C. E. (1948), *Sexual Behavior in the Human Male.* Philadelphia: Saunders.

——— ——— ——— & Gebhard, P. H. (1953), *Sexual Behavior in the Human Female.* Philadelphia: Saunders.

Kolodny, R. C., Masters, W. H., Hendryx, J. H. & Toro, G. (1971), Plasma testosterone and semen analysis in male homosexuals. *New Engl. J. Med.,* 285:1170–1174.

Lewes, K. (1988), *The Psychoanalytic Theory of Male Homosexuality.* New York: Simon & Schuster.

Lilling, A. & Friedman, R. C. (1995), Bias towards gay patients by psychoanalytic clinicians: An empirical investigation. *Arch. Sexual Behavior,* 24:563–570.

Magee, M. & Miller, D. (1997), *Lesbian Lives: Psychoanalytic Narratives, Old and New.* Hillsdale, NJ: The Analytic Press.

Malyon, A. K. (1982), Psychotherapeutic implications of internalized homophobia in gay men. *J. Homosexuality,* 7:59–69.

Marmor, J., ed. (1965), *Sexual Inversion: The Multiple Roots of Homosexuality.* New York: Basic Books.

——— (1980), *Homosexual Behavior.* New York: Basic Books.

Masters, W. H. & Johnson, V. E. (1966), *Human Sexual Response.* Boston, MA: Little, Brown.

Money, J. & Ehrhardt, A. A. (1972), *Man and Woman, Boy and Girl: The Differentiation and Dimorphism of Gender Identity from Conception to Maturity.* Baltimore, MD: Johns Hopkins University Press.

Ovesey, L. (1954), The homosexual conflict: An adaptational analysis. *Psychiatry,* 17: 343–250.

——— (1955a), The pseudohomosexual anxiety. *Psychiat.,* 18:17–25.

——— (1955b), Pseudohomosexuality, the paranoid mechanism and paranoia: An adaptational revision of a classical Freudian theory. *Psychiatry,* 19:341–351.

——— (1969), *Homosexuality and Pseudohomosexuality.* New York: Science House.

Person, E. S. (1999), *The Sexual Century.* New Haven, CT: Yale University Press.

Rado, S. (1940), A critical examination of the concept of bisexuality. *Psychosomatic Med.*, 2:459–467.
Socarides, C. (1963), The historical development of theoretical and clinical concepts of overt female homosexuality. *J. Amer. Psychoanal. Assn.*, 11:386–414.
——— (1968), A provisional theory of etiology in male homosexuality: A case of preoedipal origin. *Internat. J. Psychoanal.*, 49:27–37.
Stoller, R. (1968), *Sex and Gender.* New York: Science House.

III

CHANGING PSYCHOANALYTIC PERSPECTIVES ON HOMOSEXUALITY

The Two Analyses of a Gay Man: The Interplay of Social Change and Psychoanalytic Understanding

RALPH ROUGHTON

The interplay of social change and psychoanalytic understanding is demonstrated by how we have dealt with homosexuality, more than by any other issue—more, even, than female psychology. For example, Freud was a leading voice against the repressive forces of his day, in particular against laws that criminalized homosexual behavior (1930). In a newspaper interview in 1903, he stated categorically, "Homosexual persons are not sick." By the 1980s, however, the American Psychoanalytic Association had become the most conservative and tradition-bound of the mental health organizations, our theories and our attitudes reflecting the thinking of decades past. Social change had left us far behind.

Consider, for example, the early homophile organizations, the Stonewall uprising that catalyzed the modern gay rights movement, the growing acceptance of gay men and lesbians in mainstream culture in the 1980s, the formation of a cohesive gay community to fight the AIDS crisis, and the rise in academia of gay and lesbian studies. Nothing in our professional literature nor any discussions at our national meetings would indicate an awareness of this social upheaval as a progressive current.

In the bitter 1973 fight over removing homosexuality from the American Psychiatric Association's list of diagnosable disorders, the American Psychoanalytic Association took no official position. Nevertheless, a petition signed by many of our members, and a letter from our president urging the APA leadership to postpone any decision, left little doubt that "the psychoanalysts" opposed this change (Bayer, 1987).

Was it rigid adherence to our theories of neutrality and psychic reality, designed to prevent our clinical work from being too easily swayed by external reality, that kept us uninvolved and ignorant of social change? Were we too self-important to think we might learn something from the larger world of ideas and social movements, as well as from colleagues in other clinical disciplines? Or was there an underlying antihomosexual bias that blinded us to new understandings of the lives of gay men and lesbians?

We like to think that our advances arise, not from political or social pressure, but from better explanations and solutions to clinical problems. In other words, change comes slowly from inside. In the case of homosexuality, however, I believe it is the other way around. It has not been scientific discoveries but breathtaking social changes in popular culture, in courtroom decisions, in public policies, and even in religious organizations, that have goaded us into rethinking homosexuality and have inevitably evicted psychoanalysis from its heterosexist closet.

I do not mean to imply that unscientific or inappropriate changes were forced upon us by politics and society. Rather, psychoanalysis had so isolated itself from other scientific and clinical disciplines, and had so girded itself in the mantle of pure analytic process as the source of all knowledge and wisdom, that it took some rather dramatic changes to wake us up. It became apparent that we had lost the place of leadership in the world of ideas that psychoanalysis once enjoyed.

In 1993, when the national organizations of all other mental health professions (psychiatrists, psychologists, social workers, and others) formed a coalition to support President Clinton's initiative to allow gay men and lesbians to serve openly in the military forces, this group did not even ask the American Psychoanalytic Association if we would like to join them. They apparently either assumed that we would decline or, more likely, simply did not think of us at all. We had become irrelevant.

Not only were our ideas considered bankrupt, our clinical services were widely considered harmful to gay men and lesbians. Even analysts who were otherwise friendly and supportive of gay colleagues advised them not to seek treatment with psychoanalysts. In the audience of a gay-themed play on Broadway in the early 1990s, just the mention in the dialogue of someone going to a psychoanalyst evoked loud hoots and jeers from the audience.

Of course, not all psychoanalysts were so blind and misguided. A few joined the debate with newer thinking, and many quietly went about their clinical work, respecting their gay patients' autonomy. But, as a profession, we allowed the most biased thinkers among us to speak for us. And our patients, our profession, and our members—both straight and gay—suffered.

Some have claimed that the "gay activist movement" in the American Psychoanalytic Association forced its agenda upon us (Socarides, 1995). How ludicrous! In the 1991 watershed year, when the nondiscrimination policy was finally adopted, we had exactly one self-identified gay member. Although Isay was a forceful voice who deserves much credit for initiating changes, he hardly constituted an invincible movement that could overpower our governing bodies.

Rather, our members began to see the absurdity of cherishing a theory that could not explain these new observations in the world around us. New, nonstereotypical images of gay men and lesbians were everywhere—on TV, in movies, in a few of our colleagues, in some of our friends, and in many of our children. When openly gay candidates were accepted in a few institutes in 1993, some faculty members admitted that it was their first experience of actually knowing a homosexual person other than as a patient. Now they found themselves teaching impressive, sometimes outstanding candidates who openly identified themselves as gay, lesbian, or bisexual. A few colleagues were emboldened to openly declare their own gay identities.

A gaping disparity grew between our old stereotypes and these new images. So when new leaders arose in our organization, our members were ready to institute changes in our policies and attitudes. We were neither hijacked by the ACLU nor shamed into political correctness. Rather, we rethought the issues with greater wisdom, surmounted our heterosexist bias and ignorance, and began to look and listen differently. If unbiased observations of lesbians and gay men did not fit our theories, perhaps it was the theories that needed changing. And, at the least, discriminatory policies and practices based on those theories could be corrected without waiting for new theories to be developed.

At the Conference on Women and Power at Emory University in Atlanta, Georgia, Ethel Person (2000) made the important observation that social change is never initiated by powerful insiders. Change in our psychoanalytic understanding of gender and sexual orientation began in the women's movement and in gay liberation movements out there in the culture, not from within our field.

Now that we have embraced social justice for gay men and lesbians and have made our organizations more gay friendly, we have the long, slow task of reformulating our concepts of development. We are just beginning to think in terms of a normative developmental course, rather than a pathological one, for boys and girls who will grow up to be gay (Corbett, 1996; Goldsmith, 2001; Phillips, 2001).

Clinical Changes

New theories of development will evolve slowly. Fortunately, our clinical work needs no new theory—only the unbiased application of psychoanalytic principles. But that will require conscientious work on the part of individual analysts to overcome their bias, heterosexism, countertransference, and lack of knowledge about the lives of lesbians and gay men.

Much of the problem with treatment for homosexual individuals in the past was that it was simply bad analysis. We overlooked the departures from neutrality, the use of directive-educative methods, and the manipulation of compliant transferences for the misguided goal of changing sexual orientation (Mitchell, 1981).

Psychoanalytic principles were abandoned in the zeal to cure homosexuality. What a different perspective we have when we do not automatically assume that a gay or lesbian orientation represents pathology but in fact may be the natural sexual expression for this person.

For example, a typical subtle communication from a presumably unbiased analyst occurs when his male patient, who is struggling to clarify his sexual desires, is aware that his analyst seems interested when he talks about his date with a woman but remains coolly silent when he mentions his recent date with a man. The analyst may be unaware of his different responsiveness, but it will not escape the gay or bisexual man who has spent his life attuned to subtle disapproval of his "abnormal" desires.

I do not mean that homosexual object choice is never defensive, never represents the sexualization of other needs, never has compulsive or perverse uses. What I do recommend is that we begin our analytic explorations from the perspective that sexual orientation and psychopathology are independent dimensions (Cohler and Galatzer-Levy, 1996) and that we conclude otherwise only when there is supporting evidence. This will help to overcome the small voice of bias within the analyst that says, "It's not normal for a man to date a man; it probably represents his fear of women." In fact, it may simply represent his sexual desire that was fixed in him at a very early age and is as natural for him—and as unlikely to change—as an opposite-gender object choice is for others (Freud, 1920; Roughton, 1999, 2000b). His apparent anxiety when dating women may simply be the discomfort that would be reasonable for a man to feel when he is expected to act on a desire that he does not feel, along with shame for not feeling it. The subtle disapproval communicated by his analyst will reinforce that anxiety and shame.

Clinical Case

Now I present some clinical material from 1975, which represented a turning point in my understanding of homosexuality, and then look at the same material from today's perspective as another turning point. Hence, "The Two Analyses of a Gay Man," borrowing from Kohut's 1979 title, "The Two Analyses of Mr. Z." In fact, my patient had only one analysis, the implied second one being a reconceptualization of old material from a new perspective—as we now know was also true of Kohut's second "analysis" (Strozier, 2001).

It was 1975, just three years after I had graduated from the psychoanalytic institute, when Ben[1] sought treatment with me. Our meager classroom discussions of homosexuality had focused on the concept of homosexuality as phobic

[1] This case was summarized in my 2001 essay, "Four Men in Treatment: An Evolving Perspective on Homosexuality and Bisexuality, 1965 to 2000."

avoidance of the opposite sex and the possibility for change through analysis (Rado, 1949; Ovesey, 1969) At first, this had generated hope, because it now defined homosexuality as a neurosis that could be cured rather than as an unchangeable perversion. But this new approach had not worked for me personally. My five-year analysis that ended in 1970 proved to be a pseudocure, based on the exploitation of a compliant transference, which evaporated shortly after termination.

Being married with two young daughters, I was determined to make another attempt to rid myself of homosexual feelings. So I began a second analysis with a different analyst in 1973, two years before I began seeing Ben. I was also reading the early self-psychology work of Kohut, (1971), Goldberg (1975), and Lachmann (1975), in which they described the self-restorative function of sexual behavior. Although their focus was primarily on heterosexual patients, I began to understand that homosexual acts might also represent attempts to maintain or restore a cohesive sense of self. This not only made sense to me intellectually, but it was also an analytic perspective on homosexuality that conveyed a feeling of respect and empathy for the patient—a quality present in Freud's writings but lost in much of the later psychoanalytic literature. It also resonated with my own second analysis, which was now less focused on getting rid of my homosexual desires than on understanding their place in my life and in my self-identification as bisexual.

I give this brief personal background in order to set the context for my work with Ben—there were rich, parallel analytic processes, leading to the possibility for enhanced understanding but also for countertransference distortions and enactment complications.

Ben was 27. He had an MBA and a promising career as a financial analyst, and he was married to a professional woman five years his senior. During the second year of analysis, a baby daughter was born, and his joyful involvement in being a father was striking.

Ben sought help for depression and a sense of emptiness. Difficulty with male authority figures was a central concern, in that he was both highly competitive and intensely sensitive to either praise or criticism. Lately he had been finding some relief for his anxious longings through anonymous sexual encounters with men, which left him feeling a deep sense of shame. He was a bright and aggressive achiever, who blazed a trail of success through high school and his first year of college. But then something happened that reversed all this. He was severely depressed, began spending his weekends escaping into a fantasy world induced by hallucinogens, and dropped out of all other social activity. Six months later, in danger of ruining his academic record, he managed to pull himself together and, without any professional help, returned to proving himself through achievement.

As we sought to understand what triggered this depression, it became clear that he had responded to feeling rejected by a series of close male friends *toward* whom he had felt a special bond of intimacy and love. Although for Ben this closeness was somewhat erotized, none of these was an overt sexual relationship. Nevertheless, his intense need apparently frightened each of them away, which compounded the shame he already felt because of his dimly perceived sexual attractions to these friends. His solution was to numb the feelings and escape. And, to avoid ever being this vulnerable to hurt and shame again, he closed up emotionally and secretly ruminated about his masculinity and his sexual orientation.

Ben had some heterosexual experiences with two different women before he met the woman he married. He found it very pleasurable, particularly enjoyed prolonged foreplay and intimacy, and usually felt relaxed and tranquil afterward. Sex with his wife was less satisfactory, because she was inhibited and less interested than he was. Before he married, Ben's sexual experiences with other males had been limited to a few instances of mutual masturbation. He was attracted to good-looking men with well-developed bodies, but he thought his longing was more for intimacy than for sex.

In 1975 my understanding of Ben's pathology was in terms of narcissistic deficits and vulnerability to shame, and I thought of his homosexual preoccupations as an attempt to repair his incomplete sense of self through mirroring experiences with other men. Ben seemed a good example of my new understanding that sexual activity may be one way of restoring a fragile sense of self. This would seem especially apt in same-sex behavior in that the fragile, vulnerable self finds a reassuring mirror image. In fact, the analytic work with Ben was carried out largely around the vicissitudes of a narcissistic transference, periods of homosexual "acting out" (as I thought of it then), along with very real progress in growth and self-understanding.

After initially feeling exposed and vulnerable, he became more comfortable and quickly regressed to a surprising degree, giving the first indication of circumscribed areas of narcissistic pathology in what had initially appeared to be a relatively well-integrated personality. Regressive moments were characterized by mild episodes of depersonalization related to his fear of merger or engulfment when he felt too close to me or when boundaries were in some way threatened. In the fourth month, he developed an idealizing transference, which progressed over several months to an expanding sense of himself and some grandiosity. This was confined to analytic material and showed up outside only as derivatives that enhanced his life (weight lifting, reading books on the use of power, etc.).

In many ways, Ben was an ideal analysand. Workable regressions during the sessions were paired with a remarkable self-observing capacity. He quickly grasped and integrated insights, with the interpretations often coming from him rather than me. Ben had evolved three ways of restoring a sense of wholeness: The first was in his competitive struggles and remarkable achievements. This left him fearful of the inevitable conflicts with authority figures and vulnerable to retaliation from competitors, as well as a constant pressure to avoid the pain of failure. Ben's second avenue of compensation was in relationships with other men, which he initially sought in intimate friendships. Finding the rejection by these friends too painful to risk again, he turned to anonymous sexual encounters. As analysis progressed, a third avenue came into being in the transference relationship, where his longing for intimacy began to find some solid reality but was periodically displaced by anger or sexual acting out, whenever he needed to create a safe distance to reassure himself of his autonomy.

Rather than giving a systematic case presentation, I have chosen to follow certain threads: Ben's feeling inadequate and needing to prove himself, his desire for love and intimacy, and the meaning that having sex with men had for him. Was it acting out, as I thought at the time, even though I accepted its useful function in filling his narcissistic needs? Or was it, as I now think, the natural expression of his sexuality? Or both?

In the second month of treatment, Ben's apprehension about resuming analysis after a week's vacation led him to talk of his many early fears: he remembered being afraid to go to school, to ride the bus, to go to the lunchroom, to play baseball. What was he afraid might happen, I asked. Being beat up by bigger boys, getting in a fight, he replied. He felt he couldn't hit back. His father had been disappointed and critical because he was not good at baseball. He would pray for God to help him be a good baseball player. Then he expressed anger at his father for expecting so much and not being supportive. This early, I chose not to interpret the transference aspects, but today I might do so.

In the next session, he reported having felt angry with me after the last session. He felt uptight about telling me his weakness, and he knows nothing about me and my weakness. I commented that he feels this as competition and feels at a disadvantage with me. He then talked about how important physical appearance is to him—both his own and those with whom he has a relationship. He worries about how he looks to me; then he said he finds my appearance "acceptable." He feels sheepish to be so concerned about this. I thought, but didn't say it, that he shifted from feeling disadvantaged in competition with me to the one area where he felt superior—that of appearance.

The next day he spoke of experiences in the past when he had to prove his manhood and was afraid. As an exchange student in Peru, he lived with a family whose sons were learning the art of bullfighting. He was afraid but forced himself to get in the ring with a bull. His next associations were to a few months ago when he went into an adult bookstore, which turned out to be a gay establishment with private video booths where men could engage in sexual acts. He left, but then came back and allowed himself to be picked up by a man and went home with him. They engaged in mutual masturbation and then had a nice talk afterward. He felt kindly toward the man but had no desire to do it again. He thought that he had rationalized away the guilt but found that it was still there. He especially didn't want to tell me.

The next day, he was anxious, afraid of my disapproval. I pointed out that he didn't feel guilty until he thought about what I might think. He said he really felt bad about the experience but that it did have one positive aspect—a friendly intimacy. He felt better after talking about it, and he felt my tacit acceptance.

I skip now to a session a year later, fourteen months into treatment. For two sessions he had talked of feeling lonely. He wanted me somehow to fill the empty void in him, but he knows that's not my role. He spoke of wanting to be "in love" with someone. As he was leaving, he told me that he would be away the week after next, which reminded me that I needed to tell him that I would be away the Thursday and Friday prior to that. This was poor timing on my part.

Not surprisingly that night, feeling lonely, he went to the book store but left without making contact with anyone. When he got to his car, he found that he had locked his keys in the car and had to break a window. This attracted attention and embarrassed him there in the parking lot. He still felt secretive and ashamed about going to a gay bookstore. Then he talked more about wanting to be loved, to have someone who loves him and wants to make him happy. In the next session, my notes are only a brief summary, but I wrote a comment to myself: "he really opened up in the area of the narcissistic deficit, which he tries to fill with the homosexual acting out."

The next day, he felt better and was more able to talk about his sexual fantasies. Getting a blow job has a "selfish component," he says. He gets satisfied and the partner only gets gratified through admiring and pleasing him. At this point he had only received oral sex.

A few weeks later, he felt afraid of the deepening emotional relationship with me—a fear of being vulnerable, of being hurt, but also just a fear of having to talk about feelings. He told of seeing a beautiful man coming out of the gay bookstore, and he felt "a strong emotional charge," a mixture of desire and fear. He identified this as looking for his idealized self, but also for someone who shares this secret side of himself, that is, an attraction to men. He associated to having seen me on a recent Saturday at a mall wearing jeans. That was like having a view of my private life, again like sharing a secret. He likened this to seeing a mirror of himself and feeling whole. With the man at the gay bookstore, it's sharing this secret attraction. With me, it's feeling understood, that I'm in tune with him; and it has the same effect. Following this session, he struggled with resistance, intellectualizing and talking about outside events, and he forgot to come to one session. He was able to talk about his fear of the closeness: it's like he runs away at the slightest hint of it, he says, like being in the woods at night, hearing a sound and being afraid.

A week later, he continued to explore this "secret life" and what it means to him—an exciting sense of freedom from being trapped in a straight, dull world. It's also acting out some undefined need. And it's best of all when it is a shared secret with a close friend, giving him companionship with total acceptance. In college it was the drug scene; recently it's been the gay bookstore experiences.

The next day, he was having some mild dissociative feelings—a vague, dreamy feeling with someone, maybe his mother, saying to him, "You're bad, really awful, so bad you're not worth being around." This was not a memory but a felt reconstruction. He talked about not feeling lovable after having exposed his inner life. "Always there is the feeling of the 'bad me' that has to hide and cover it with a 'good me' through achievement." This was just before my summer vacation, which he insisted was no big deal. He resisted my suggestion that his feeling unlovable might be linked to my going away. But then he wryly warned me to watch out for sharks if I went anywhere near the beach. The session ended with his saying he was having warm feelings that he wanted to keep private.

Two weeks later, on my return, he had "almost" decided to quit analysis. He is in a lot of pain in his outside life and fears that analysis will blow everything up, change his whole life, that he will give up everything. At first I thought that he was only paying me back for going away. But "blowing up, changing his whole life, and giving up everything" suggested something else. I asked what had happened while I was away that he was uncomfortable telling me.

He had been in San Francisco on a business trip, had gone to a gay bathhouse, and had a sexual encounter. He really liked this man; there was a lot of affection and shared feelings; and with much reluctance he let me know that he had tried giving oral sex—and that he had liked it. After telling me about this, he decided maybe he didn't have to quit analysis after all. His fears of my disapproval were eased, but what about his fear of changing his whole life and giving up everything? Astonishingly, in retrospect, we did not explore the meaning of those phrases. What I did write as a note to myself, however, was: "But explore the acting out aspect of this." That is, I focused on the transference meaning of his "acting out," rather than his fear of the possible life-altering consequences of allowing himself to acknowledge and act on his homosexual desires.

What I thought we should explore was the transference meaning of this happening while I was away. But that implied that I thought his need to compensate for, or retaliate against, my absence was the determining factor; whereas now I would at least be open to the possibility that he was finally allowing himself to follow his natural sexual wishes, even if he could only do so when I was away. That is, doing something new while I was away may be acting out; but it also may represent greater freedom to try out new, adaptive behavior at a time when having to tell me about it is temporarily in abeyance. This differs from older interpretations, where we always assumed only the pathological meaning for behaviors that were outside heterosexual norms and failed to explore how they might represent the norms of same-sex life.

In the next session, he said he had felt so much better, that it only takes a few words of acceptance to turn his whole mind-set around. Then, following my note to myself, we explored the San Francisco experience in the context of my absence. In the course of this, I referred to him as "a hungry guy," explaining that I meant that his need for love and approval was like an appetite and that he was always hungry. This struck a very responsive note with many associations: as a child he was always hungry, and his mother chided him for eating too much. He tries to quell his hunger and not demand what he wants, because he has no right, or because it will overwhelm others. He also associated this with feeding his baby daughter her bottle and feeling love and intimacy with her, something he didn't feel from his parents.

When I reread these notes after twenty-five years, I cringed. Calling him a hungry guy sounded so much like his mother chiding him for wanting too much. But I think I conveyed by my tone an understanding of what it feels like to be hungry and unable to ask for what you want. And his response was one of opening up.

Several months later, at the end of the second year of analysis, he said that the two hardest things for him to talk about were his sexual feelings for men and his positive feelings for me. It's easier for him to tell me that he hates me than that he loves me. The next day, he felt annoyed, vaguely angry with me. He's aware of rapidly alternating desire for closeness, then annoyance. That night he went to the bookstore again and had a very passionate, satisfying experience. He said it was a transient physical and emotional intimacy and implied that oral sex had been mutual. He said he felt very good afterward, and I had the impression that he stopped just short of saying that he felt fulfilled. The next morning he was very turned on and wanted sex with his wife. They did have intercourse, but her rigidity pretty much ruined it for him.

That was on the weekend, and now on Monday he is castigating himself, referring to sex with the man as "acting out," feeling guilty, and again afraid to talk about it with me. He spoke rather gloomily of feeling trapped in his life. In hindsight, sex with men seemed more exciting and fulfilling than with his wife.

Later, he confirmed the mirror aspect of the sexual object choice—he prefers someone his age, his size, nice looking, intelligent, warm, accepting. "I guess if I looked in the mirror, that would be it." But that wasn't it either. He emphasized that it wasn't just a mirror. He wants contact with another person; it's very important to him to be loved by a man. He is aware that, in spite of his fears and doubts, he is beginning to break out of the old restrictions, at least in sessions with me and when he has sex with a man. But he has to trust me to know what is happening, because this territory is new and frightening to him.

Another time, he said, "My self-concept comes almost entirely from the reflections from other people. That's why people are so important. If they aren't there, I don't exist. I feel like a bubble in the ocean—everything on the outside and nothing on the inside. [Pause] Somehow this is connected with the sex thing." I said, "Yes, when you find a mirror image that seems like part of yourself and merge with it through sex, then you feel whole. No wonder it feels so good."

What I intended to convey was that his sexual activity with men, as well as his liking it, were understandable. But he focused on my unintended implication that having sex with men was pathological and therefore something he should work to rid himself of. He responded angrily: "It's my secret thing; leave me alone with it. If you understand it, it will go away or else you'll expect me to give it up."

Over the next few sessions, we continued to work with this interpretation and his response. I clarified the difference between identifying the need and having to give up the behavior; and with further working through over time, he came to realize, "that you really want me to be free . . . to develop in my own way; and you make no claims on me." Later he said, "I have this contented, centered feeling, like I'm becoming myself."

With this progress in building a more cohesive sense of himself, Ben was able to reclaim some of the power he had delegated to me. His fears of merger and rejection diminished, and he began to feel a sense of wholeness that came from within himself. At this point, feelings of competition resurfaced but now were tinged by the angry desire to defeat other men, rather than needing to win primarily to bolster his self-concept. This introduced what seemed another motive in having sex with men—revenge and the wish to dominate. Linking this to his anger at his father and authority figures, including me in the transference, he then saw how some of his acting out had expressed his anger at me.

With further analysis of both the competitive and the mirroring needs in the transference, Ben experienced a shift in his feelings about physical relationships with men. He still felt attracted, but it was now more for closeness and less a sexual urge. I interpreted this as his beginning to undo the sexualization with which he had invested other needs (Coen, 1981). My retrospective view is that this interpretation again assumed that his homosexual feelings were not valid as sexual feelings and that they had only a defensive or reparative function and meaning.

As we approached the end of Ben's third year of analysis, he had come to feel more and more a sense of wholeness. His vulnerability to slights had diminished significantly, allowing him to feel more contented with his life in general. He was gaining a national reputation in a highly competitive profession and was being rapidly promoted within his company. Despite some disappointments in his marriage, his daughter was such a vital part of his life that he did not consider divorce as an option.

His mother developed a fatal brain tumor, and her impending death spurred him to work through the conflicts that had prevented his being close to her. As part of the same process, he explored more deeply the rivalry with his father, which allowed him to have a more mature friendship with him.

This phase of Ben's analysis was consistent with what Kohut (1977) described in the analysis of some narcissistic patients. After prolonged analytic work on the deficits in self-structure has led to improvement in self-cohesion, there often follows a period in which oedipal issues emerge and are rather quickly worked through, more like a normal developmental phase than a pathological template. Oedipal conflicts with his father came into the analytic material, were easily interpreted and worked through. It is important to note that during this oedipal phase there was no increase in his homosexual yearnings nor any noticeable decrease following it.

There was a parallel shift to oedipal configurations in the transference as well, and again interpretation and resolution of conflicts went forward easily. Ben's relationship with me both deepened and took on a more mature character so that, when he informed me that his insurance benefits were soon to run out and he would like to cut back in frequency of sessions, I suggested that instead we consider his readiness for a planned termination. He readily agreed to this suggestion, which ushered in a six-month termination period. During this phase of the analytic work, Ben experienced some mild regressions, and he reverted occasionally to "acting out" sexually; but overall it was a very productive termination process that consolidated his insights and led to further resolution of the transference. At the end, he remarked on how profoundly his life had changed, and I felt very satisfied that this had been a good analysis and an appropriate termination.

However, in looking back over this material, I noted a particular session during the termination period. It was Ben's thirtieth birthday. He spoke about his goals in life. When he thinks about making a major career change, for example, he still feels an emptiness. And he conceives of this emptiness being filled only by loving someone—and being loved—really touching someone in a way that isn't fully met by his wife and daughter, whom he does love. I wrote a note to myself: "This is still the hunger that he tried to satisfy in sex with men; but what is an alternate solution? He hasn't quite found it yet." How prophetic.

Six months after termination, Ben called to tell me that his wife was suing for divorce. Either being careless, or perhaps unconsciously intending to be caught, he had left the phone number of a man he was having an affair with where his wife could find it. His concern was not so much that his marriage was ending but that his wife thought he must have lost his mind, and he wanted to discuss how to talk with her and help her understand. We met for one session, and I learned that he had fallen in love with a man, that the relationship fulfilled both sexual excitement and loving intimacy, and that he was now convinced that this was the direction he wanted his life to go.

About a year later we met by chance in a public place, and he proudly and happily introduced me to his lover. Fifteen years later (1993), I read in a newspaper article that he had died of AIDS. Named as survivors were his daughter and his companion. His professional credits mentioned that he was a senior vice president of a nationally recognized financial institution and that he had been identified as one of the outstanding men in his field by a leading business magazine.

Knowing little of Ben's life following termination, we are left with more questions than answers. I wondered about unresolved transference and self-destructive acting out, both in his choice of life course and in his acquiring HIV. He had tended to withdraw or act out whenever there was some empathic failure on my part, especially when he felt rejected by me. And, of course, it was my suggestion that we consider terminating, when he had only wanted to decrease the frequency for financial reasons.

However, those thoughts are based on the assumption that Ben's choice about his sexuality was pathological and that getting AIDS resulted from taking life-threatening risks. If analysis in the 1970s had freed Ben to seek the sexual life he wanted with carefree abandon, this would have occurred prior to our knowledge of how HIV is transmitted and therefore would not have been knowingly self-destructive.

It seems clear, as I thought in 1975, that Ben's acting on his homosexual feelings during the analysis did serve a self-repairing function and did at times represent acting out—just as heterosexual activity may serve the same purposes. But I now also think that the homosexual part of his bisexuality was the stronger and that divorce and a committed relationship with a man represented growth and freedom rather than pathology. Perhaps intimacy and fulfillment eluded him in marriage, because his desire could not be fulfilled with a woman. Or perhaps it was not a matter of differential strengths of sexual desires but that he met an individual, who happened to be a man, with whom he could have the intimacy he lacked with his wife (Roughton, 2000a). I emphasize the "perhaps," because this is speculation and illustration. We have no way of proving any formulation.

Would I do anything differently today? In 1975 I thought that Ben was bisexual and that the homosexual need was activated primarily to fill his emptiness and to restore his less than cohesive sense of self. I thought that need had diminished with analysis and that he would then be able to sublimate the homosexual part of his bisexuality and maintain a marriage that he wanted to continue. Now, 25 years later, I would more fully explore his homosexual yearnings beyond the use of them as narcissistic repair. And I would be more aware of the need to avoid even subtle implications that his homosexual feelings represented only pathological or restorative use of sexuality.

Another way of putting this is that my older understanding would focus on the homosexual behavior and how that was activated and used in the service of narcissistic compensation or acting out. In my newer way of thinking, the focus would be on the self needs, realizing that sexual behavior may be used in the service of narcissistic compensation or acting out. If one is a gay male, that sexual behavior would be with another male just as, if one is a straight male, that sexual behavior would be with a female. But one is neither gay because he is narcissistic, nor narcissistic because he is gay. He is narcissistic and gay, and the two have no more necessary causative or pathological link than would be presumed in someone who is narcissistic and straight.

The attitude I communicated to Ben in 1975, I believe, was an acceptance of his homosexual yearnings as a symptom, but not as a natural part of his sexuality. I look back to several missed opportunities to explore this: the greater intimacy and fulfillment in sex with men than he experienced with his wife; the San Francisco experience that he feared would lead him to give up everything; his realization that sex with men was not just a mirror but a desire for shared love with a man; the way he had always tried to quell his hunger and not ask for what he wanted; feeling that he was trapped in his life; and my prophetic note about his not having found an alternate satisfaction for the hunger he tried to fill with sex with men. Perhaps the reason was that the hunger for men was just that—his natural affection, love, and sexual desire (Roughton, 2000b).

In our current emphasis on intersubjectivity and the analyst's emotional participation in the analytic process, this retrospective reanalysis calls for a closer look at my role in Ben's analysis and in his life decisions. It is difficult to reconstruct my actual day-to-day feelings from 25 years ago, but events in Ben's life and my own at that time point to a parallel process.

Why, for example, did I overlook those opportunities to explore Ben's homosexual desire as natural, rather than defensive or compensatory? At the time, I was in my own analysis and struggling with whether I was going to accept my homosexual feelings as real and what I was going to do about it. I was consciously invested in finding a solution that allowed me to continue my own marriage. This was also Ben's conscious intent at the time of termination.

I was certainly not aware of trying to influence Ben's decision about marriage, but did he take my avoidance of a fuller exploration of his homosexual desire as a message? How he would have interpreted that message could be anything, from feeling that I was uncomfortable in talking more about his desire, to feeling my disapproval of his considering leaving his marriage.

What I can say is that, as far as I was consciously aware, my intent was helping Ben find what felt authentic for him, rather than having an agenda for him. On the other hand, Renik (1993) points out that what we analysts are less able to acknowledge about our own subjectivity is what we are more likely to enact with own patients.

Ben's marriage lasted only a short time after his analysis terminated. He then chose to live his life as a gay man. Although my similar choice to divorce and live my life as a gay man was made only many years later, there is no doubt that, during Ben's analysis, that course of action felt like a forbidden desire that

I could not bring myself to choose. Did I somehow communicate that conflicted wish to Ben by what I chose to explore and to ignore? Some would suggest that Ben picked up my unspoken wish, constructed from subtle clues in my selective focus on his material, and that he acted out my forbidden wish for me.

What do I think was the extent of my influence on Ben's choices—first, to stay married, and then later to accept his homosexual desire? I do think that an analyst cocreates the analytic process, that what material he chooses to comment on constitutes a "back-channel" of communication beyond what he says in words, and that he exerts a strong influence on the interaction in the analytic session.

We must be careful, however, about assuming that a plausible explanation of a behavioral choice means it was causative. Although the analyst's subjectivity may partly determine what gets explored and what is avoided in the analytic process, it is unlikely to be the determining factor in the patient's major life choices, except possibly in those patients whose psychopathology makes them especially malleable and vulnerable to influence. Ben wanted approval and validation, and he may have sensed that I would approve a decision he also wanted. But he was also robustly independent enough to make his own decisions based on what he wanted.

At most, I believe that my own parallel conflicts may have influenced how the material unfolded, may have limited the participation he needed from me to explore his desire, and may have interfered with his being able to work through his decision while he was still in analysis.

Could the outcome have been different with my current understanding and perspective? My conjecture is that Ben's choice of a male partner would have been the same, but that he might have been able to work through to this choice during his analysis, and therefore with greater understanding and better integration of his sexual desire. As it was, both the psychoanalytic theory of the time, and my own investment in not being homosexual myself, steered us away from helping Ben explore this as an acceptable option for himself. We can see how easily such subtle steering by the analyst can happen within what appears to be an unbiased, nondirective analytic process.

Summary

I want to return to one of my original points. We do not need a new technique for working with lesbians and gay men in analysis. We simply need to rid ourselves of our old (mis)understandings of the origins and development of homosexual and bisexual orientation and object choice; we need to rid ourselves of the heterosexist assumptions about what is normative in human life; and we need to be aware of antihomosexual bias in its masked and subtle forms, of countertransference, and of how little most of us know about the lives of gay men and lesbians. Only then can we approach our gay and lesbian patients with the unbiased openness and respect that can make analysis the same for them as for our straight patients.

References

Bayer, R. (1987), *Homosexuality and American Psychiatry: The Politics of Diagnosis.* Princeton, NJ: Princeton University Press.

Coen, S. (1981), Sexualization as a prominent mode of defense. *J. Amer. Psychoanal. Assn.,* 29:892–920.

Cohler, B. & Galatzer-Levy, R. (1996), Self psychology and homosexuality: Sexual orientation and maintenance of personal integrity. In: *Textbook of Homosexuality and Mental Health,* ed. R. Cabaj & T. Stein. Washington, DC: American Psychiatric Press, pp. 207–223.

Corbett, K. (1996), Homosexual boyhood: Notes on girlyboys. *Gender & Psychoanal.,* 1:429–461.

Freud, S. (1903), Letter. *Die Zeit* (Vienna), October 27.

——— (1920), The psychogenesis of a case of homosexuality in a woman. *Standard Edition,* 18:145–172. London: Hogarth Press, 1955.

——— (1930), Open Letter. *Wiener Arbeitzeitung,* May 16.

Goldberg, A. (1975), A fresh look at perverse behavior. *Internat. J. Psychoanal.,* 56:335–342.

Goldsmith, S. (2001), Oedipus or Orestes? Homosexual men, their mothers, and the women in their lives. *J. Amer. Psychoanal. Assn.,* 49:1269–1287.

Kohut, H. (1971), *The Analysis of the Self.* New York: International Universities Press.

——— (1977), *The Restoration of the Self.* New York: International Universities Press.

——— (1979), The two analyses of Mr. Z. *Internat. J. Psychoanal.,* 60:3–27.

Lachmann, F. (1975), Homosexuality: Some diagnostic perspectives and dynamic considerations. *Amer. J. Psychother.,* 29:254–260.

Mitchell, S. (1981), The psychoanalytic treatment of homosexuality: Some technical considerations. *Internat. Rev. Psycho-Anal.,* 8:63–80.

Ovesey, L. (1969), *Homosexuality and Pseudohomosexuality.* New York: Science House.

Person, E. (2000), On dominance, hierarchy, and gender. Presented at conference on "Women and Power," Emory University, Atlanta, GA, February 25.

Phillips, S. (2001), The overstimulation of everyday life: I. New aspects of homosexuality. *J. Amer. Psychoanal. Assn.,* 49:1235–1267.

Rado, S. (1949), An adaptational view of sexual behavior. In: *Psychosexual Development in Health and Disease,* ed. P. Hoch & J. Zubin. New York: Grune & Stratton, pp. 159–189.

Renik, O. (1993), Analytic interaction: Conceptualizing technique in light of the analyst's irreducible subjectivity. *Psychoanal. Quart.,* 62:553–571.

Roughton, R. (1999), Repair, analyze, or affirm? Reflections on treatment for gay men. Presented at American Psychoanalytic Association meeting, New York, December 17.

——— (2000a), Bisexuality. Presentation at Panel on Contemporary Views on Bisexuality in Clinical Practice. American Psychoanalytic Association meeting, Chicago, May 13.

——— (2000b), Sometimes a desire is just a desire. *Gender & Psychoanal.*, 5:259–273.

——— (2001), Four men in treatment: An evolving perspective on homosexuality and bisexuality, 1965 to 2000. *J. Amer. Psychoanal. Assn.*, 49:1187–1217.

Socarides, C. (1995), *Homosexuality, A Freedom Too Far.* Phoenix, AR: Adam Margrave.

Strozier, C. (2001), *Heinz Kohut: The Making of a Psychoanalyst.* New York: Farrar, Straus & Giroux.

Two Analyses, Two Times: Discussion of Ralph Roughton's Chapter

BERTRAM J. COHLER

Roughton has presented us with both paradox and challenge. The paradox is how to explain changes in the clinical theory of psychoanalysis, while the challenge posed for clinical psychoanalysis requires reconsideration of received wisdom regarding the analysis of persons with alternative sexual lifestyles such as gay women and men (Herdt, 1997; Hostetler and Herdt, 1998). Much of what we presume to be the received view regarding homosexuality as evidence of either oedipal or deficit psychopathology in personality development is founded on a theory of development as adaptation which was initially posed by Rado (1945–1955, 1949) at the Columbia Psychoanalytic Center in the postwar period (Isay and Friedman, 1986). As Lewes (1988) has shown, Freud never maintained this view of homosexuality as the psychopathology which has so often been attributed to him. Although there is yet little information regarding the adjustment of gay men and women followed from early adulthood into oldest age, virtually all cross-sectional study of gay and lesbian lives in adulthood, more than a thousand such reports to date, has shown absolutely no relationship between personal distress and sexual orientation except as the consequence of a lifetime of experience of stigma and antigay prejudice on the part of the larger society (Meyer, 1995).

Roughton challenges us to reconsider not only our presuppositions regarding this relationship between psychopathology and sexual lifeways, but also to reconsider presuppositions regarding both our understanding of the course of gay and lesbian lives, as well as the dynamics of change in psychoanalytic work with gay men and women. His sensitive, honest, case presentation raises particular questions regarding the nature of the transference, focusing on the analysand's search for mirroring and twinship (Tolpin, this volume).

Roughton also challenges us to reconsider our views regarding the meaning of wish and action among those men and women identifying with alternative sexual lifestyles. As Mannheim (1928) had observed, and as supported by Toulmin's (1990) discussion of the sociology of knowledge, formal education such as that imparted in psychoanalytic education fosters a generationally founded understanding of a discipline, including particular ways of understanding sexuality, normality, and adjustment. It may be painful to reconsider long-held tenets regarding psychoanalytic theory and practice which arise as a result of larger scale historical and social change together with subsequent formulations of the clinical theory within psychoanalysis (Mitchell, 1981; Schafer, 1993, 1995). Schafer (1995, this volume) emphasizes that different does not equal pathological. Rather than asking about the impact of psychoanalysis on the study and treatment of persons with a gay identity, we should address the question of the contributions of the study of bisexual, lesbian, and gay lives to our understanding of the psychoanalytic situation and in fostering increased appreciation of psychoanalytic perspectives on the study of lived experience across the course of life.

Social Change and Psychoanalytic Understanding of Gay Lives

From the outset, understanding the interplay between the intrapsychic and the social has posed problems for psychoanalysis (Chodorow, 1999). The therapeutic relationship reflects this interplay of personal life experiences within particular social and historical contexts. As historian of psychoanalysis Lawrence Friedman (1988) has shown, our understanding of the curative dynamic of psychoanalysis necessarily reflects these larger social and historical changes. Social and historical change affects both the external reality that analysands confront and the manner in which we and our analysands make meanings of these aspects of lived experience. For example, changes in the sequence and timing of transitions into adulthood across the postwar period led young people into ever more delayed entrance into the world of work. The emergence of a period termed "Youth" (Keniston, 1960, 1970) posed particular issues for the psychoanalysis of young adults. In a recent volume reporting on the followup of child analyses into adulthood (Cohen and Cohler, 2000), Calvin Colorusso and Arthur Rosenbaum both report on their analytic work with their former child analysands, then youth entering into the adult world of the late 1980s and 1990s, at a time of particular difficulty in finding a job, and at a time when there had been significant changes in the presumed course of early adult lives. These events define a cohort for a generation of people.

Understood from this perspective, the psychoanalytic process reflects the interplay of generationally defined understandings of self and others. The analysand's expression of wish and intent is founded in a presently told life story including both social context and particular life circumstances woven into an account or narrative of presently understood lived experience. The analyst's own empathic response to this account, including a particular interpretive stance, is also based on generationally defined understandings of lived experience (Toulmin, 1990) founded on particular life changes, and framed within the sociohistorical context of a particular time. It is as a consequence of larger historical events taking place at any particular time, that study of wish and meaning becomes so particularly complex. Nowhere is this more evident than in the study of sexual orientation. Not only in the manner in which sexual orientation is understood within the larger society, but also in the understandings which successive cohorts have of their own sexuality, the origins of being straight, gay or bisexual (Boxer and Cohler, 1989; Chodorow, 1992; Chauncey, 1994; Katz, 1995).

Mitchell (1978) has suggested that adult homosexuality should be understood in terms of its present meanings for the analysand, apart from speculation regarding presumed origins in early childhood. Schafer (1995) has expressed a similar view, urging in addition that we recognize the complexities involved in the transformation of early childhood experience for adult lives. This complexity has been represented in more recent presentations such as Wolfson's (1987) panel report in which Joyce McDougall's essay reflected a dramatic shift from her earlier concern with female homosexuality as psychopathology to concern with the meanings for her lesbian analysands of their sexual wishes and their experience of their own sexuality with their partner. For McDougall, this presentation represented a dramatic shift from her earlier concern with lesbian lives as expression of primitive psychopathology.

Accompanying the social changes of the "sixties," a new form of the study of social life emerged in America and Europe. As the historian John D'Emilio (1983) has observed:

> Human sexuality is amazingly malleable and can organize itself in many sorts of ways. How that desire is understood and hence experienced is what counts. Only in some societies and eras do desires coalesce into a social role, or identity, that gets labeled homosexual, or gay, or lesbian, and that corresponds to how individuals organize their emotional, intimate, and erotic lives. And for reasons that still can only remain speculative, the modern West appears to be one such place and time [p. 254].

The dramatic and rapid nature of social change led to a reconsideration of the interplay of generation *and* social change. That which was most interesting in the study of lives was no longer the extent to which people stayed the same over time but the extent to which they changed (Neugarten, 1969). This shift had a profound impact on psychoanalysis as a developmental psychology (Emde, 1981, 1983; Cohler and Freeman, 1993; Cohler and DeBoer, 1996). From this perspective, what is significant about lives is less the extent to which early childhood factors directly shape adult expression of wish and desire than the means people use to maintain a sense of personal continuity or coherence over time. From this perspective, sexual orientation itself is but one of several factors in various ways salient to understanding lives over time.

The significance of social changes in the period roughly from 1965–1975 has not been fully appreciated within psychoanalysis. These changes profoundly impacted the expression of desire and intimate relations (Tipton, 1982; Gitlin, 1987; Echols, 1989; Duberman, 1993) and are well demonstrated in Roughton's discussion of changes in the very ways in which he understood his analysand's efforts at finding his own gay identity at the outset of this period of rapid social change until the present time. Roughton's present discomfort, reflecting back on his limitations in appreciating the significance of his analysand's struggle to realize his gay identity, must be understood in terms of the time at which the analysis took place and the dramatic change in our understanding of the dynamics of the transference-countertransference configuration in the analysis of gay men and women in the meantime. Indeed, Roughton has himself been a pioneer in raising these issues, and we are all in his debt for providing new understandings of the dynamics of the analytic relationship as a consequence of work with gay and lesbian analysands.

Making Meaning of the Lesbian and Gay Experience

Considering issues of clinical theory posed by Roughton's presentation, which are relevant in the analysis of gay men and women, it is important to begin with a caveat: the reality that some men and women realize enhanced sense of intimacy and vitality from same gender socioerotic relationships does not mean that wish and feeling associated with such relationships should necessarily be excluded from consideration within psychoanalysis. Although my own analyst once observed that it is impossible to analyze love, and it is possible to explore the meanings that we make of all aspects of our experience, including those associated with these same gender socioerotic relationships. Why we choose the partners we choose, our experience of ourselves and our partners during even the most stimulating and intimate moments, and associated fantasies and their foundation in our presently told story of the course of our lives all must become aspects of study within the psychoanalytic situation.

Learning How to "Go Gay"

The problem posed by this perspective so familiar to us as psychoanalysts is that—as our colleague Drescher (1998) has observed in his recent book, *Psychoanalytic Therapy and the Gay Man*, and as highlighted by Roughton in his presentation—prejudice regarding gay lives learned over a lifetime by gay and straight analysts and analysands alike may lead the analyst to discourage the analysand from realizing a gay sexual identity, or to see aspects of the struggle to come to terms with a gay identity as evidence of a breakdown product or deficit state rather than as an aspect of learning what it means to be gay. Roughton narrates Ben's struggles to learn about his own gay identity as he visits bookstores and bathhouses in the effort to learn how to be gay. Although, particularly in former times, these visits might have been seen as a acting-out or as a means of protection against the experience of an enfeebled self, Roughton now understands his patient's visits to erotic venues as a means of learning about how it is to "go gay" (Plummer, 1981; Savin-Williams, 1990, 1997).

Consider the observation made by an analysand, a man in his early thirties, who observed that in high school, all his straight friends learned how to date girls, what to do on a date, and what sex with girls was all about. However, there was no one to tell him how to meet and date men, what happened on a date, and how to have sex with other guys. He had to learn that on his own, feeling ashamed of going to the back rooms of "adult" bookstores in order to make that discovery. Across prior generations of gay men there was little socialization into being gay such as there was into being straight. In their book *Children of Horizons*, Herdt and Boxer (1996) describe a gay youth group where such supportive socialization is available; it is particularly striking in this account both how important it was for group members to have the affirming support of their peers in learning what it means to be lesbian or gay, and also the ease of these gay and lesbian teens in their relationships with each other and the community. Their lifestyle, relationships, and adjustment were little different from their straight counterparts apart from the gender of their partner. Savin-Williams (1997) reports similar experiences among gay youth attending college in upstate New York.

Clearly, there have been social changes; my younger patients are more concerned regarding problems in managing intimacy and blocks to feeling close to their partners than regarding their sexual identity. These men and women seek analysis, just as their straight counterparts, in order to realize more intimate and caring relationships, help in realizing career goals, and help in dealing with issues within their family. In the words of activist gay commentator Andrew Sullivan (1995), these students are "virtually normal," with all the ambivalence which this term implies. Growing up at a time when there were few consociates able to mirror Ben's own struggles, he was left to find the way to be gay on his own, a particularly lonely struggle.

Gender-Role Stereotyping and Gay Childhood

Ben's struggle to realize his identity as a gay man is one commonly encountered in clinical work with gay men. Roughton notes Ben's long-standing distress regarding his feelings of failure to comply with the expectation that he be a "typical" boy, showing the usual interests in athletics. There is presently much controversy regarding the dynamics of development among gay youth. Corbett (1997) has observed that:

> Homosexual boyhood as a conceptual category does not exist. The existence of homosexual boys has until now either been silenced or stigmatized. Bullies identify sissies. Psychiatrists identify sissy-boy syndromes. There has been virtually no effort to speak of the boyhood experience of homosexuals other than to characterize their youth as a disordered and/or nonconforming realm from which it is hoped they will break free. The fate of these boys is contemplated with the kind of hushed charity that obscures antipathy [p. 108].

Corbett maintains that the boy with nontraditional gender interests such as competitive sports and enjoyment of so-called rough-and-tumble play, neither masculine nor feminine in gender identification, poses a dilemma for a society that insists upon categorizing gender roles as either feminine or masculine. He (1997a) suggests that the paradox and mystery of homosexuality is that it questions this binary categorization of gender roles and cautions against a rush to judgment regarding the meaning of nontraditional gender interests such as boyhood interests in theater or music: "I wish simply to propose that early cross-gendered experience is interimplicated with later developing homosexuality in complex ways that remain unaccounted for within current developmental theories" (1997a, pp. 111–112).

Boys with nonstereotyped gender interests do not define themselves as girls, although they may enjoy some activities such as cooking which were thought to be stereotypically feminine in earlier cohorts. However, these boys also do not define themselves as boys in the manner most often portrayed by the larger society. Indeed, they maintain strong identifications with attributes and interests of both mothers and fathers and, in this way, challenge accepted psychological theories regarding the development of gender identification. Corbett (1998) suggests that Richard Friedman's (1997) endorsement of "rough-and-tumble" play as evidence of the course of expected boyhood development put misplaced emphasis upon the value of aggression as a prototypic masculine attribute. This critique is founded on Friedman's own explicit acknowledgment of a biological basis as the explanation for the presumed more typical "rough-and-tumble" play of early childhood (R. Friedman, 1988, 1997, p. 490) as the precursor to a hetereosexual sexual identity. Friedman accuses Corbett of lack of familiarity with this biological literature, and Corbett (1997b) challenges Friedman's essentialist model of psychobiological development.

Corbett's remarks highlight the problems created in the use of essentialist, often presumed biologically founded, explanations for development in which, in a manner presumed consistent with the tenets of social evolution, masculine aggressivity is presumed essential in order to realize reproduction of the species. Recent writing on the struggles of boys growing up in contemporary America, required to carry on this image of masculinity, have highlighted the high personal cost for the boys' well-being involved in such efforts to impose a stereotyped view of masculinity (Kindlon and Thompson, 1999). Added to this problem was the anxiety expressed by Ben's father that Ben might have other than the expected developmental course together with Ben's profound sense of shame at not living up to his father's expectations for him, and disappointment that his father was unable to affirm and support him in his effort to find his own way through the boyhood years.

A promising younger classical musician came to treatment seeking help in his relationship with his family. He recalled how, in second grade, his teacher had expressed concern to his parents that he did not show the usual boyhood interests in athletics, preferring instead the violin. Terrified that their son might be gay, his parents had rushed to put him in little league, soccer, and other competitive athletic pursuits. Later, my patient even became captain of his college football team and president of his fraternity while feeling all the time ever more estranged from himself. Moving to Chicago after college to pursue his study of music, through his study and work, the patient met other gay men and ultimately began a relationship with another man which has been highly rewarding for each of them.

Some Clinical Implications of Psychoanalytic Work with Gay Men and Women

In his continuing effort nationwide to educate psychoanalysts about issues posed in the analysis of gay men and women, Roughton stresses the importance of appreciating the differences in meaning regarding the very issue of sexuality itself in work with lesbian and gay analysands. Too often, it is presumed that only a gay or lesbian analyst will be able to work with a gay or lesbian analysand. Clearly, this is not the case. Indeed, as Drescher (1998) has noted, there may be a particular problem posed for the gay analyst by the gay patient who avoids talking about a particularly dicey problem by saying that as a person the analyst surely knows what the analysand is experiencing.

Sexual Identity Match and the Analysis of Gay Women and Men

Two related issues are posed by this discussion: the issue of match of analyst and analysand, such as discussed by Kantrowitz (1995, 1996) in her recent work reports on the findings from her program of research into successful outcome in psychoanalysis, and also the related issue of disclosure of the analyst's own sexual identity. The question of the role of similarity of analyst and analysand in terms of shared gay sexual orientation also raises the larger question of analyst–analysand "match" (Kantrowitz, 1995, 1996). Following Cooper (1987) and

Viederman (1991), Kantrowitz suggests that compatibility in terms of character structure may be more significant in fostering a sense of collaboration facilitating analytic progress than such apparent sources of similarity as gender, ethnicity, or sexual orientation.

Although the analysand may believe that an analyst who is also gay may be the most likely to "understand" what it means to be gay or lesbian, and most able to provide a source of mirroring, this may be less a source of compatibility fostering a working alliance and a positive facilitating transference than other less obvious aspects of the analyst. A straight analyst, able and willing to learn about gay lifeways from gay and lesbian analysands, might more readily foster such an alliance than an ideological gay analyst with specific views regarding the impact of sexual orientation upon personality and lifestyle. Kantrowitz's (1995, 1996) discussion highlights particularly subtle aspects of the analyst's personality likely to be important in determining a good "match" between analyst and analysand.

The analysand's expectation of perfect automatic understanding by virtue of shared sexual orientation, reflecting a mirroring transference, may obscure the content of particular wishes enacted anew in the analytic relationship. For example, a talented younger actor developed characters in his work by merging with the character, attempting to think as his character would feel in similar circumstances. He had sought referral to a gay analyst. This technique of merger with the character was enacted anew in the transference. He assumed his analyst shared his experiences and could be one with him as he described both his search for intimacy and his almost compulsive cruising. When his analyst asked him to describe in greater detail his experience while cruising, the analysand regarded this query as an inability to be one with him through what the analyst assumed were similar experiences of cruising.

Presumption of a shared set of experiences and implicit understandings by either or both analyst and analysand can easily permit the analysand to avoid personally painful topics by appealing to the analyst's shared understanding of "what it means to be gay." Sometimes knowledge of the analyst's sexual lifeway does not foster a sense of safety in the therapeutic situation. A young adult seen in intensive psychoanalytic psychotherapy at a mental health center serving the gay and lesbian community feared that his therapist might seduce him; assuming that his therapist must be gay, he was afraid that a lifelong pattern would be enacted once again—an older man, beginning with a distant relative, would befriend him only to try to sexually exploit him. Another gay man explicitly stated that he did not want a gay therapist; disparaging himself, his self-hatred extended to a possible therapist. He was sure that a gay therapist would be another object of disparagement and, in addition, like himself, would hate himself and be self-disparaging, whereas a straight therapist would be able to feel good about himself.

The issue of analyst–analysand match on sexual identity has special significance for gay male and lesbian clients. Along with the feeling of being alone, the reality of difference and alienation even in the family of origin constitutes the distinctive pain of early gay experience, unparalleled in the family experiences of members of other oppressed groups. The perpetuation of that pain in therapy with a nongay therapist is one of the commonly reported reasons for gay male and lesbian client's dissatisfaction or failure in traditional psychotherapy (Rochlin, 1982, p. 23). The gay therapist is assumed to be more readily able to follow the gay client's references to gay settings and issues that would be outside the experience of straight therapists. Finally, the gay therapist is assumed to be familiar with the gay world and able to guide the client in avoiding the pitfalls of being gay and using the resources of the community. Rochlin (1982) and Isay (1989, 1991, 1993, 1996b) claim that as a result of the antigay prejudice in our society, gay women and men are likely to feel safer and more accepted working with a gay rather than a straight analyst.

However, issues of safety and shared understanding of the problems and possibilities of being gay may be more complex than Rochlin and Isay acknowledge. The experience of being gay has changed in dramatic and surprising ways across cohorts of gay women and men. The middle-aged gay analyst who relies on his or her own experience is almost as likely to misunderstand the gay young adult's experience as a straight analyst, but may be at even greater risk of not acknowledging this misunderstanding, especially if easy understanding between analyst and patient is seen as highly desirable. Furthermore, as Malyon (1982) maintains, antigay prejudice is so ubiquitous in our society that the gay analyst is as likely as straight counterparts to maintain some residual sense of antigay prejudice. Further, as Blechner (1995) and Drescher (1995) note, gay men and women who completed their psychoanalytic education before the opening of the institutes to openly lesbian and gay candidates are likely to have particularly complex and unsatisfactory experiences of integrating homosexuality into their larger lives and their personal analyses.

The Issue of the Analyst's Self-Disclosure and the Gay Analysand

Unlike ethnicity and gender, sexual orientation is neither obvious nor customarily acknowledged within the psychoanalytic situation. Thus the process of gay prospective analysands explicitly seeking referral to gay analysts presumes public acknowledgment of an aspect of the analyst's life ordinarily not made public. As a result of antigay prejudice, and the very checkered past in psychoanalytic understanding of different expressions of desire, many gay men and women seek the presumed safety of analysts sharing a similar sexual orientation. The issue of self-disclosure in the analysis of gay and lesbian analysands is one fraught with issues. Isay (1991, 1993, 1996b) makes the most explicit recommendation advocating the analyst's self-disclosure of sexual orientation. He argues that many gay men, having experienced the emotional withdrawal of their own fathers in response to awareness of the young boy's erotic attraction, need an affirmative and caring man who can provide a good role model and who can see that sexuality and intimacy can be found together. Further, the reality of antigay prejudice within the community requires that the psychoanalytic situation provide a sense of safety free of such prejudice, presumably uniquely possible when gay analysands know that their analyst shares their sexual lifeway. Finally, Isay believes that the analyst's acknowledgment of shared sexual orientation provides for the analysand affirmation that details of his desire and lifestyle are implicitly understood.

Although generally sympathetic with the work of Isay (1989, 1996a, 1996b), Drescher (1998) is more cautious in recommending self-disclosure for precisely the reasons that Isay (1996b) urges it. Drescher observes that because the gay analysand is aware of a shared lifeway with his analyst, the gay analysand may seek to avoid talking about such issues as the meaning of being gay which otherwise would come into the analytic process. Raphling and Chused (1988) have raised the issue of gender similarity in the analytic relationship. They note that either the same or different gender between analyst and analysand poses distinctive issues for the course of the analysis. Shared gender may be a source either of increased safety and comfort in the analysand's presumption of a shared set of life experiences, or as Drescher (1998) suggests, of resistance to analysis, failing to consider the meanings of such status characteristics as gender, marital status, sexual orientation, or even ethnicity and race for the analysand's lived experience (Holmes, 1992).

Isay's concern that the analysand find a positive role model in a gay man well adapted to his sexual lifeway ignores the reality of a lifetime of exposure to antigay prejudice (Herek, 1991, 1996) experienced by analyst and analysand alike and which itself must become a part of the therapeutic situation. Isay believes that through adopting a gay affirmative position, it is possible to provide something akin to a "corrective emotional experience" through fostering an idealizing transference. A part of the work with gay and lesbian analysands consists precisely in working through these often personally painful experiences; it is neither desirable or even possible to avoid the therapeutic work directed at making peace with these often traumatic life experiences. Isay (1996b) tries to emphasize that gay men can have satisfactory lives and fulfilling intimate relationships. Reflecting the life experiences of his cohort of middle-age gay men, it is understandable that he should express such affirmative statements. However, for many younger adults this is not an issue; these gay and bisexual men and women implicitly understand that there is little necessary connection between sexual lifeway and well-being.

Self-disclosure on the analyst's part raises important issues for study of the analytic situation. The analysand comes to the first meeting with the analyst having already made particular meanings of this information regarding the analyst's own sexual identity; clearly, the meanings that the analysand makes of this information regarding the analyst's sexual identity must be reviewed anew across the course of the analysis. The question is whether and in what circumstances the analyst's self-disclosure is in the best interest of the analysand and in facilitating the analytic alliance. The decision to disclose some aspect of the analyst's own life to the analysand rests on the assumption that as a result of the analyst's own personal analysis and continuing self-inquiry (Gardner, 1983), the decision to disclose some aspect of the analyst's own life has been well considered apart from issues of so-called countertransference responses or complementary identifications (Racker, 1968).

Renik (1993, 1995) has discussed this issue of the analyst's self-disclosure in particular detail and notes the paradox in contemporary psychoanalytic practice in which the analyst is presumed to be withholding personal revelations even as the model for practice has become one of recognition of the personal relationship of analyst and analysand. Renik disputes presumptions about self-analysis as a guide to self-disclosing, noting that such self-inquiry usually follows rather than precedes the self-disclosure. He suggests that our model is still one of objective neutrality, presumably always a factor, whereas our practice is in reality intersubjective (Stolorow, Atwood and Brandchaft, 1994; Hoffman, 1998). The reality, as Renik (1993) sagely observes, is that experienced analysts are likely to foster a real, personal relationship within the analytic setting. Further, Renik observes that: "every effective clinician learns that appropriate gratifications for analyst and analysand are an essential feature of the successful analytic process. In practice we struggle to determine which gratifications are effective and appropriate and which are counterproductive and exploitative" (1993, p. 565).

This issue of self-disclosure becomes particularly complex in the case of the gay analyst and either gay or straight analysands. Although the analyst's partnership status is always an issue within the transference, the stigma and prejudice still attached to same-gender sexual orientation suggest that gay analysts will be confronted with particular issues. There is no way of avoiding this issue given the reality that the analytic community is small and that analysands often know far more about their analyst than is generally recognized. Further, analysands look for even the most subtle clues regarding their analyst's marital status. It is most common in contemporary bourgeois society for all married women and most married men to wear wedding rings. The analysand most often silently digests this information regarding marital status from the first diagnostic interview before beginning analysis. The lack of a wedding ring poses unique transference fantasies, including the analyst's sexual availability. Some lesbian and gay analysts have commitment rings, often worn on the right hand, which conveys yet additional information. The analyst listens for evidence regarding the manner in which the analysand understands this presence or absence of a ring, as well as other clues, including the analyst's dress and demeanor, office furniture, books and pictures, and even the analytic couch itself.

The inclusion of all aspects of what is experienced within this unique collaboration of analyst and analysand does not vitiate the importance of fostering shared understanding of the meaning of all aspects of this collaboration. What it does mean is that the analysand begins analysis with knowledge of who the analyst is, and that this knowledge grows. Acknowledgment of this knowledge and its significance for the analysis contributes to therapeutic change. These considerations apply to the analyst's sexual orientation. For example, in Phillips' (1996) account of an analysis of a straight man by a gay analyst, it is clear in retrospect that the patient knew Phillips was gay. The choice is usually how, rather than whether, the analysand will learn of the analyst's sexual orientation. Our discussion presumes that, at least at a conscious level, gay analysts can be comfortable and open about their sexual orientation and recognize the impact of this sexual lifeway upon colleagues, analysands, and the larger community, even while recognizing the many and complex issues, including the continuing internalized homophobia discussed throughout this work. The issue of disclosure can itself be a fruitful topic for analytic work.

A bright, intuitive young professional who valued interpersonal honesty, sought a referral from a psychiatrist friend for a gay therapist. At the first meeting with his therapist, he repeated his interest in working with a gay therapist and wished to confirm that reality. His therapist, known in the community for his work in mental health and sexuality, assented that he was indeed gay but noted that it was important for them to explore what this meant to the client. The client's lifelong struggle with his own self-hatred was repetitively enacted through tearoom encounters followed by self-denigration and shame. He feared being "out" though he worked at a newspaper with an accepting atmosphere where people were "out." After a year of work devoted to the client's problems realizing a wished-for sustained intimate relationship, his therapist canceled an appointment scheduled during the following month. The client asked where the therapist was going, to which the therapist honestly said he was going to a professional meeting without providing additional information. The client then asked if the therapist was going with anyone, which led to another somewhat impulsively posed question—whether the therapist had a partner.

Following the perspective provided by Cooper (1987), with tact and consideration for the client's sensitivity about feeling rebuffed as he felt had been the circumstance within his family when he was a child, the therapist noted that either a yes or no answer might pose a burden for the client. After a few minutes' pause, the client grinned and said that his therapist was right in not disclosing this information: A yes answer would lead the client to feel envious and angry, and a no answer would mean that his therapist was as unable as he to find a relationship. In so doing he began to explore the meanings of both these ideas for himself. From the point of view of furthering analysis, disclosure of sexual orientation and related matters may be viewed as like other disclosures by the analyst, not a matter to be prejudged or resolved by reference to authoritative prescriptions but an issue to be evaluated in each instance based on what is likely to move the analytic work forward.

Conclusion

Discussion of the psychoanalytic situation in the analysis of men and women identifying as gay poses important issues more generally for psychoanalysis. Roughton has presented a paradox and provided a challenge to reconsider such important aspects of the psychoanalytic process as the role of the analyst in facilitating the analysand's search for enhanced personal integration. The questions which Roughton has asked resonate with reconsideration of the dynamics of change in psychoanalysis posed by positions as disparate as those of self psychology and the constructivist-intersubjective perspective elaborated by the late Gill (1994) and by Hoffman (1998).

Clinical study of gay and lesbian lives has much to offer to psychoanalysis. For example, a focus on issues of internalized homophobia (Malyon, 1982), inevitably shared by analyst and analysand alike, leads to new understanding of the dynamics of the relationship of analyst and analysand and enhanced understanding of what Racker (1968) has characterized as the analyst's complementary and concordant identifications, and the role of the analyst's own attitudes as a factor possibly interfering in the maintenance of that empathic understanding so central to realization of clinical change in psychoanalysis (Kohut, 1984).

Analytic work with lesbians and gay men also inevitably raises questions regarding self-disclosure. As a result of antigay prejudice, and the very checkered past in psychoanalytic understanding of different expressions of desire, many gay men and women seek the presumed safety of analysts sharing a similar sexual orientation. This search, which raises important issues for the analysis of the transference, often leads to a situation at some point in the analysis in which the analyst discloses his or her own sexual orientation. Sometimes, as in the case of Isay, analysands come for analysis because of the analyst's sexual orientation which is well known in the community. Issues of self-disclosure on the analyst's part raise important issues for study of the analytic situation itself and lead to important additional understanding of what Gill (1994) has referred to as a "two-person" psychology.

Clinical psychoanalysis remains in a quandary regarding intervention within the lives of gay men and women. In part, this quandary is a reflection of cohort differences in psychoanalytic education. It is understandable that a more senior group of analysts, educated in the postwar period, and influenced by a generation of clinician-teachers themselves wedded to a scientistic conception of psychoanalysis, should have difficulty with more recent perspectives, such as that of Schafer (1995, this volume) regarding same-gender sexual orientation as nonnormative but not evidence of psychopathology. For example, Friedman and Lilling (1996) have reported that even though most analysts no longer believe that homosexuality is necessarily evidence of psychopathology, many analysts are reluctant to cast aside received wisdom from their own psychoanalytic education and continue to believe that homosexuality must serve as a means of protecting oneself against heterosexual wishes.

Mitchell's (1996) musings regarding the meaning of homosexuality for psychoanalysis also reflect this quandary. Mitchell notes that once sexuality and reproduction are viewed as separate, it is no longer possible to regard homosexuality as evidence of psychopathology. As Mitchell honestly acknowledges, the origins of homosexuality may never be known, and we must rely on our own self-reflection in dealing with the dilemmas presented for the analyst in exploring with the analysand the meanings of particular life choices and outcomes. Consistent with Mitchell's reflections concerning the dilemmas posed for psychoanalysis in work with gay and lesbian analysands, we are indebted to Roughton for posing today the paradox and challenge provided for psychoanalysis as an ever-evolving and changing clinical theory in his discussion of psychoanalysis and homosexuality.

References

Blechner, M. (1995), The shaping of psychoanalytic theory and practice by cultural and personal biases about sexuality. In: *Disorienting Sexuality: Psychoanalytic Reappraisals of Sexual Identities*, ed. T. Domenici & R. C. Lesser. New York: Routledge, pp. 265–288.

Boxer, A. & Cohler, B. (1989), The life course of gay and lesbian youth: An immodest proposal for the study of lives. In: *Gay and Lesbian Youth*, ed. G. Herdt. New York: Harrington Park Press, pp. 315–355.

Chauncey, G. (1994), *Gay New York: Gender, Urban Culture and the Making of the Gay Male World, 1890–1940*. New York: Basic Books.

Chodorow, N. (1992), Heterosexuality as a compromise formation: Reflections on the psychoanalytic theory of sexual development. *Psychoanal. & Contemp. Thought*, 15:267–304.

——— (1999), *The Power of Feelings: Personal Meaning in Psychoanalysis, Gender, and Culture*. New Haven, CT: Yale University Press.

Cohen, J. & Cohler, B. (2000), *The Psychoanalytic Study of Lives over Time: Clinical and Research Perspectives on Children Who Return to Treatment in Adulthood*. New York: Academic Press.

Cohler, B. & deBoer, D. (1996), Psychoanalysis and the study of adult lives. In: *Psychoanalytic Perspectives on Developmental Psychology*, ed. J. M. Masling & R. E. Bornstein. Washington, DC: American Psychological Association, pp. 151–220.

——— & Freeman, M. (1993), Psychoanalysis and the developmental narrative. In: *The Course of Life: Early Adulthood. Vol. 5*, ed. S. Greenspan & G. Pollock. Madison, CT: International Universities Press, pp. 99–177.

Cooper, A. (1987), The transference neurosis: A concept ready for retirement. *Psychoanal. Inq.*, 7:569–585.
Corbett, K. (1997a), Homosexual boyhood: Notes on girlyboys. In: *Sissies and Tomboys: Gender Nonconformity and Homosexual Childhood*, ed. M. Rottnek. New York: New York University Press, pp. 107–139.
——— (1997b) Speaking queer: A response to Richard C. Freedman. *Gender & Psychoanal.*, 2:495–514.
——— (1998), Gross-gendered identifications and homosexual boyhood: Toward a more complex theory of gender. *Amer. J. Orthopsychiat.*, 68:352–60.
D'Emilio, J. (1983), *Sexual Politics, Sexual Communities: The Making of a Homosexual Minority in the United States, 1940–1970*, 2nd ed. Chicago: University of Chicago Press, 1998.
Drescher, J. (1995), Anti-homosexual bias in training. In: *Disorienting Sexuality: Psychoanalytic Reappraisals of Sexual Identities*, ed. T. Domenici & R. C. Lesser. New York: Routledge, pp. 227–242.
——— (1998), *Psychoanalytic Therapy and the Gay Man*. Hillsdale, NJ: The Analytic Press.
Duberman, M. (1993), *Stonewall*. New York: St. Martin's Press.
Echols, A. (1989), *Daring to Be Bad: Radical Feminism in America, 1967–1975*. Minneapolis: University of Minnesota Press.
Emde, R. (1981), Changing the models of infancy and the nature of early development: Remodeling the foundation. *J. Amer. Psychoanal. Assn.*, 29:179–219.
——— (1983), From adolescence to midlife: Remodeling the structure of adult development. *J. Amer. Psychoanal. Assn.*, 33(supplement):59–61.
Friedman, L. (1988), *The Anatomy of Psychotherapy*. Hillsdale, NJ: The Analytic Press.
Friedman, R. C. (1988), *Male Homosexuality: A Contemporary Psychoanalytic Perspective*. New Haven, CT: Yale University Press.
——— (1997), Response to Ken Corbett's "Homosexual boyhood." *Gender & Psychoanal.*, 2:487–494.
——— & Lilling, A. (1996), An empirical study of the beliefs of psychoanalysts about scientific and clinical dimensions of male homosexuality. *J. Homosexuality*, 32:79–89.
Gardner, R. (1983), *Self-Inquiry*. Hillsdale, NJ: The Analytic Press.
Gill, M. (1994), *Psychoanalysis in Transition: A Personal View*. Hillsdale, NJ: The Analytic Press.
Gitlin, T. (1987), *The Sixties: Years of Hope, Days of Rage*. New York: Bantam Books.
Herdt, G. (1997), *Same Sex, Different Cultures*. Boulder, CO: Westview Press.
——— & Boxer, A. (1996), *Children of Horizons*, 2nd ed. Boston: Beacon Press.
Herek, G. (1991), Myths about sexual orientation: A lawyer's guide to social science research. *Law and Sexuality: A Review of Lesbian and Gay Legal Issues*, 1: 133–172.
——— (1996), Heterosexism and homophobia. In: *Textbook of Homosexuality and Mental Health*, ed. R. Cabaj & T. S. Stein. Washington, DC: American Psychiatric Press, pp. 101–113.
Hoffman, I. (1998), *Ritual and Spontaneity in the Psychoanalytic Process*. Hillsdale, NJ: The Analytic Press.

Holmes, D. E. (1992), Race and transference in psychoanalysis and psychotherapy. *Internat. J. Psychoanal.*, 73:1–11.

Hostetler, A. & Herdt, G. (1998), Culture, sexual lifeways, and developmental subjectivities: Rethinking sexual taxonomies. *Social Research*, 65:249–290.

Isay, R. (1989), *Being Homosexual: Gay Men and Their Development*. New York: Farrar, Straus & Giroux.

——— (1991), The homosexual analyst: Clinical considerations. *The Psychoanalytic Study of the Child*, 46:199–216. New Haven, CT: Yale University Press.

——— (1993), On the analytic therapy of homosexual men. In: *Affirmative Dynamic Psychotherapy with Gay Men*, ed. C. Cornett. Northvale, NJ: Aronson, pp. 23–44.

——— (1996a), *Becoming Gay: The Journey to Self-acceptance*. New York: Pantheon.

——— (1996b), Psychoanalytic therapy with gay men: Developmental considerations. In: *Textbook of Homosexuality and Mental Health*, ed. R. Cabaj & T. S. Stein. Washington, DC: American Psychiatric Association Press, pp. 451–469.

——— & Friedman, R. C. (1986), Toward a further understanding of homosexual men. *J. Amer. Psychoanal. Assn.*, 34:193–208.

Kantrowitz, J. (1995), The beneficial aspects of the patient–analyst match. *Internat. J. Psychoanal.*, 76:299–314.

——— (1996), *The Patient's Impact on the Analyst*. Hillsdale, NJ: The Analytic Press.

Katz, J. (1995), *The Invention of Heterosexuality*. New York: Dutton/Plume Books.

Keniston, K. (1960), *The Uncommitted: Alienated Youth in American Society*. New York: Harcourt, Brace & World.

——— (1970), *Youth and Dissent*. New York: Harcourt Brace Jovanovich.

Kindlon, D. & Thompson, M. (1999), *Raising Cain: Protecting the Emotional Life of Boys*. New York: Ballantine Books.

Kohut, H. (1984), *How Does Analysis Cure?* ed. A. Goldberg & P. Stepansky. Chicago: University of Chicago Press.

Lewes, K. (1988), *The Psychoanalytic Theory of Male Homosexuality*, 2nd ed. New York: Aronson.

Malyon, A. (1982), Psychotherapeutic implications of internalized homophobia. *J. Homosexuality*, 7:59–70.

Mannheim, K. (1928), The problem of generations. In: *From Karl Mannheim*, 2nd ed., ed. K. H. Wolff. New Brunswick, NJ: Transactions Books, 1993, pp. 351–398.

Meyer, I. (1995), Minority stress and mental health in gay men. *J. Health & Social Behavior*, 36:38–56.

Mitchell, S. A. (1978), Psychodynamics, homosexuality, and the question of pathology. *Psychiatry*, 41:254-263.

——— (1981), The psychoanalytic treatment of homosexuality: Some technical considerations. *Internat. Rev. Psycho-Anal.*, 8:63–80.

——— (1996), Gender and sexual orientation in the age of postmodernism: The plight of the perplexed clinician. *Gender & Psychoanal.*, 1:45–73.

Neugarten, B. (1969), Continuities and discontinuities of psychological issues into adult life. *Human Development*, 12:121–130.

Phillips, S. (1996), A new analytic dyad: Homosexual analyst and heterosexual patient. Paper presented at fall meeting, American Psychoanalytic Association, New York, December.

Plummer, K. (1981), Going gay: Identities, life cycles and life styles in the male gay world. In: *The Theory and Practice of Homosexuality*, ed. J. Hart & D. Richardson. London: Routledge & Kegan Paul, pp. 93–110.
Racker, H. (1968), *Transference and Counter-Transference*. New York: International Universities Press.
Rado, S. (1945–1955), *Adaptational Psychodynamics*, ed. J. Jameson & H. Klein. New York: Aronson, 1995.
——— (1949), An adaptational view of sexual behavior. In: *Psychosexual Development in Health and Disease*, ed. P. H. Hoch & J. Zubin. New York: Grune & Stratton, pp. 159–189.
Raphling, D. & Chused, J. F. (1988), Transference across gender lines. *J. Amer. Psychoanal. Assn.*, 36:77–104.
Renik, O. (1993), Analytic interaction: Conceptualizing technique in light of the analyst's irreducible subjectivity. *Psychoanal. Quart.*, 62:553–571.
——— (1995), The idea of the anonymous analyst and the problem of self-disclosure. *Psychoanal. Quart.*, 64:466–495.
Rochlin, M. (1982), Sexual orientation of the therapist and therapeutic effectiveness with gay clients. *J. Homosexuality*, 7:21–29.
Savin-Williams, R. (1990), *Gay and Lesbian Youth: Expression of Identity*. Washington, DC: Hemisphere Publications.
——— (1997), *. . . And Then I Became Gay: Young Men's Stories*. New York: Routledge.
Schafer, R. (1993), In the wake of Heinz Hartmann. In: *Tradition and Change in Psychoanalysis*. Madison, CT: International Universities Press, pp. 3–21
——— (1995 /1997), The evolution of my views on non-normative sexual practices. In: *Tradition and Change in Psychoanalysis*. Madison, CT: International Universities Press, pp. 237–252.
Stolorow, R., Atwood, G. & Brandchaft, B., eds. (1994), *The Intersubjective Perspective*. New York: Aronson.
Sullivan, A. (1995), *Virtually Normal: An Argument about Homosexuality*. New York: Knopf.
———. (1998), *Love Undetectable: Notes on Friendship, Sex, and Survival*. New York: Knopf.
Tipton, S. (1982), *Getting Saved from the Sixties: Moral Meaning in Conversion and Social Change*. Berkeley: University of California Press.
Toulmin, S. (1990), *Cosmopolis: The Hidden Agenda of Modernity*. New York: The Free Press.
Viederman, M. (1991), The real person of the analyst and his role in the process of psychoanalytic cure. *J. Amer. Psychoanal. Assn.*, 39:451–90.
Wolfson, A. (1987), Towards the further understanding of homosexual women. *J. Amer. Psychoanal. Assn.*, 35:165–812.

Discussion of Ralph Roughton's Chapter

MARIAN TOLPIN

I am going to do Ben's third analysis, with the benefit of hindsight. The analysis is unusual, not only because of its brevity. I try to do it as though I were Ralph Roughton, a male analyst, and elicited the same kind of transference he did, that is, an upsurge of Ben's intense unconscious needs and fears, expectations and hopes, disappointment, anger, and shame experienced primarily with the analyst as childhood father.[1] I shall try to understand Ben's larval transference as it emerges in several hours in the second month of treatment and briefly mention the "beautiful man" and "hungry guy" transference in the second year of the analysis. I also give some examples of my idea of *trial interpretations*.[2] First some introductory:

I share Roughton's belief that we can move psychoanalysis toward what he means by a "good theory," that is, a theory that does not continue to pathologize homosexuality. My agenda is even more ambitious than his: I want to enlarge our theoretical and interpretive framework to overcome the psychoanalytic blind spots that lead to pathologizing in general and prevent us from seeing the

---

[1] There is little evidence of a maternal transference until Roughton's interpretation of Ben's hunger. Then Ben remembers his mother chiding him for eating too much, and his associations suggest that he internalized what amounted to her rejection and disapproval of his psychological hunger; then he chided himself for his needs and. tried to quell them.

[2] Trial interpretations are tentative in order to invite the patient to join in and go ahead on his own, or to object if they are not on the right track. In others words, tentative interpretations invite patients to join in the analytic work of understanding themselves, The interpretations I make are intended to put a "spotlight of consciousness" (Kohut lectures on Freudian metapsychology in Rubovits-Seitz, 1999) and felt emotion on all aspects of the transference: the reviving healthy developmental urges; the unconscious defensive measures used to preserve the self-organization the patient has managed to build up; and the self-pathology in its revived developmental context. The importance of interpretations and reconstructions and how they are made includes illumination of psychic depths; and, in and of themselves, they also begin to reverberate with the patient's psychic depths because they act as the carriers or conduits, if you will, for the analyst's positive and negative selfobject functions.

transferences of health I describe as *forward edge transferences.* These consist of patients' still-remaining normal developmental needs, strivings, expectations, and hopes (in revitalized forms) to find their own kind of selfhood from the analysis and the analyst. I think Roughton's frank self-disclosure is in the service of his agenda and mine to try to live up to the analytic "group-self" ideal (Freud, 1923) to do psychoanalysis that, "does not set out to make pathological reactions impossible, but to give the patients's ego [self] *freedom* to decide one way or another" (p. 50, footnote). In other words, we share the goal to give the patient freedom of choice.

The ideal that Freud formulated for analysis means that the analyst does not get to decide what is good for the patient. Thus, what Roughton calls "good" analysis should mean that cure for patients, in general, for gay and lesbian patients, in particular, means that they acquire the *inner freedom* to choose the sexual orientation and life they want. I am in agreement with him that because of pathomorphic theory the working-through process that might have given Ben (and Roughton himself) freedom of choice—to be gay (openly) or not to be gay (remain closeted)—was short-circuited. Ben's "second analysis" took place when Roughton understood Kohut's newly introduced concept of sexualization of structural deficits as though it were intended to *explain* homosexuality and, thereby, to change the patient's orientation. (He was not alone in misunderstanding the concept.) However, Kohut's theory of sexualization is neither intended to explain homosexuality as a choice, nor to do away with it, anymore than it is intended to explain or do away with the choice of heterosexuality. Sexualization, like "aggressivization," is a measure of defense. The utilization of sex and/or aggression is seen so frequently in a whole spectrum of disorders because both serve to temporarily alleviate the depression, depletion, anxiety, and so forth, which are the symptomatic and characterological consequences of weakness of self-organization. Specifically, sexualization, because of the intensity and excitement associated, first with infantile sexuality, and later with adult sexuality, is used by boys, girls, men, and women (straight, gay, bisexual, or whatever) in compulsive (over and over again) efforts to shore up or invigorate a fragmented or depleted self.

For now, at least, I think the theory of self-development in a facilitating self-selfobject matrix comes closest to a good theoretical guide for a "good analysis" of any and all patients. To use the theory to its fullest, however, we have to learn to see what I illustrate in connection with Ben's analysis: namely, that selfobject transferences consist of a "forward edge" of remaining health, as well as a "trailing edge" that repeats what Freud (1914) described as the "artificial illness" that, so to speak, replaces the childhood illness by taking over all its features (p. 154). This is way of saying that we are now able to analyze healthy and pathological dimensions of a "total transference" (Racker, 1968, pp 151–152, used this term, writing in a Kleinian framework). Sexuality, gay and straight, may be part of the healthy "forward edge" of self-development, or part of the "trailing edge" or pathology of self-development. (Shelby, this volume, in "About Cruising and Being Cruised," calls attention to what can be considered "trailing edge" self-fragmentation and the use of transient same-sex encounters to hold the self together, and distinguishes this emergency sexuality from being gay.) And now for the third analysis. Before turning to the therapeutic process I want to briefly outline what I mean by forward and trailing edge transferences.

A Brief Discussion of the Concept of Forward and Trailing Edge Transferences

Psychoanalysis has regarded transference exclusively as an "artificial illness," a "new edition" of core childhood psychopathology that is revived and compulsively repeated with the analyst as the original childhood imagoes. Freud (1914) put it this way, "Transference makes it possible to treat [the] illness not as an event of the past, but as a present-day force . . . the illness [can be] brought, piece by piece, within the field and range of the operation of the treatment" (p. 151). This view of transference is a source of theory-induced clinical blind spots. In the psychoanalytic situation, these act silently, for the most part, to prevent the analyst from discovering and analyzing a resurgent "new edition" of the patient's remaining core of health. By definition, "forward edge" transferences are reanimated new editions of health in which the analyst is unconsciously experienced as a reinstated mirroring, idealizing, and alter ego selfobject. At first, this form of transference consists of fragile unconscious "tendrils" (albeit in thwarted, stunted, crushed, or distorted forms) of still-intact strivings for growth-enhancing self-selfobject experiences.

Blind spots due to theory place unintended iatrogenic limits on therapeutic action. When we fail to see that there are strivings ("tendrils") for recognition, strengthening, and alikeness experiences and fail to facilitate their emergence (primarily by recognizing and interpreting them as such), we contribute to crushing them again and crowding them out. Freud (1912) regarded an aspect of the transference as positive and unobjectionable—that made the patient cooperative and amenable to suggestion, and therefore it didn't have to be analyzed, but utilized to promote the work. In either case, the remaining healthy development is not engaged and fully reactivated in depth, and as a consequence, still viable motivations, expectations, and strivings are not accessible to an essential transformative, working-through process. It is the bit-by-bit process of interpretation and reconstruction and working through of transferences of health that is the condition for gradual expansion, stabilization, and transformation of healthy aspects of the child self and for the integration of these aspects into a changed psychic reality that shifts the intrapsychic balance, "just enough," from repetitions of the past (trailing edge of development) to constructive forward moves.

To repeat my main point: at one and the same time, theory-induced blind spots restrict our clinical vision of the patient's (and our own) psychic reality because they lead us to expect transference repetitions of nuclear childhood pathology and its later derivatives. They also obscure the subtle hints of bona fide transferences that derive their force and momentum from still-viable tendrils of healthy childhood motivations, strivings, expectations, and hopes of getting what is needed from the analyst. It is crucial to stress that tendrils of remaining health are not apparent on the surface—my clinical examples show that we have to be primed to look for them in order to see them and to tease them out from the trailing edge pathology in which they are invariably entwined. For instance, tendrils of forward edge strivings have to be disentangled from manifestly pathological mergers, idealizations, grandiosity, "narcissistic entitlement" (Murray, 1964), rage, envy, and depreciation; from "intermediate" defenses and compromise formations that protect the self the patient has managed to build up and, at the same time, inhibit, restrict, and further compromise normal development. In effect, when the joint analytic work required to see, interpret, and foster the healthy tendencies is done by patient and analyst, the persisting "urge to complete development" and regain "developmental momentum" (noted by Bibring, 1937; A. Freud, 1965) is given an enormous boost. In other words, these otherwise vague "curative factors" are now grounded in the clinical theory of analyzable forward edge transferences. Analysis of these configurations, as well as trailing edge transferences (of childhood illness), restarts and reinvigorates an expectable developmental process in an expectable selfobject environment.

Resurgence of Health: Seeing and Interpreting Forward and Trailing Edge Transferences

Ben returns from a one-week vacation. He missed his sessions, but that wore off and he had a good time. Now that he is back he feels anxious, a vague apprehensive feeling that reminds him of his early childhood fears—he was afraid to go to school, ride the bus, go to the lunchroom, play baseball. The analyst asks Ben a good question, "Do you know what you were afraid of?" (The "empathic inquiry" into his fears is "good' because it catalyzes a stream of free associations that begin to illuminate the inner childhood world and give hints about thwarted needs of the nuclear self at the core of his disorder.) Ben is open in his answer: he was afraid of being beaten up by bigger boys, afraid to fight because he felt he couldn't hit back. The spontaneous revival of his childhood fears on Ben's return to "analytic school," catalyzed by the analyst's inquiry, makes him think of his father's criticisms and disappointment in him because he wasn't any good at baseball. He used to pray for God to give him strength to be a good baseball player. He's angry because his father expected so much and wasn't supportive.

Although he sensed a transference (which he did not make explicit), Roughton did not make an interpretation. I think this is the time to respond to both sides of the transference—that is, to what can be considered the forward edge of the transference, his hope for the strengthening, supportive experience he needed with an idealizable father, and to the "trailing edge" of the transference, his longstanding fears, his disappointment and feeling of weakness, and his feelings that he is a disappointment. The interpretation might go something like this: "You prayed to God for strength so you wouldn't be afraid, so you'd be good at what your father approved of, so he'd be proud of you and you'd be proud of yourself. You wished you had his warm glow of approval instead of his harsh criticism; then you'd feel that warm glow inside of yourself instead of your own harsh self-criticisms and disappointment in yourself."

The above interpretation encompasses both forward and trailing edge of the patient's development—his hopes and needs, his disappointments, anxiety, and chronic sense of inadequacy. What of the transference anger at the father who expects so much of him and is unable to be encouraging and reassuring? Is it true that self psychologists avoid anger and are only "nice"? There will be ample time for that. There are already intimations of Ben's anger and rivalry, shame and withdrawal; or even the threatened loss of feeling real (depersonalized) when he feels unsupported and criticized, feels he is no good, and is self-critical (for example, when the analyst/God lets him down). In fact, the analyst does not have to wait long. (Roughton took the patient's loss of feeling real/depersonalized as a manifestation of retreat from feared closeness to the analyst, whereas I see it as the loss of feeling real because needs and hopes for closeness to an uplifting god are dashed again.)

In fact, Ben says he is angry at the analyst and "resistant" to the analysis in the next hour. He doesn't want to tell the analyst about his weakness because he doesn't know anything about the analyst and *his* weakness. Roughton interprets, "You feel resistant and angry because you feel this to be a competition in which you are disadvantaged compared to me." The interpretation leads to a shift from the hoped-for idealization to defensive sexualization (hyperinvestment in his own and the analyst's body and physical being). God did not answer his prayers for strength—maybe he didn't even hear them. Ben says physical appearances are very important to him—his own and those of others with whom he has relationships. He's concerned about how *he* looks to the analyst—the analyst's appearance is (only) "acceptable" to him. He feels "sheepish" that he is concerned about appearances. Roughton did not interpret the patient's shift, from looking to him as God, to their respective bodies. He noted, however, the shift and considered it to be defensive one-upmanship (instead, I would see the shift as suggestive of the genetics of the self-disorder—loss of the idealized father and sexualization may be the hallmark of the patient's self disorder). Ben "shifted from feeling disadvantaged in competition with me to the one area where he felt superior—that of appearance." (Did he feel the sting of Ben's depreciation of him?)

The self-psychology framework prompts me to inquire into the developmental context for the defense of turning the tables on the analyst, and to think of the use of this self-protective reaction as a signal for a trial interpretation and reconstruction: "I think you must have felt exposed yesterday—perhaps because I didn't say anything you feel ashamed telling me about your fears and feelings of weakness, that I have the upper hand [like your father, perhaps]; and then, understandably, you want to reassure yourself by asserting, at least, that you are better looking than I am." In other words, I address Ben's vulnerability and his "competitive" defense against shame (and anger over feeling shame) and his expectation that, the analyst, like his father, looked down at him, when the father/analyst remained silent after he exposed himself by showing his fears, his weakness, not being any good, and his prayers for support to feel he was good and whole.

There is another possible meaning and another interpretation. When idealizing needs for the father's strength were inadvertently rebuffed by the analyst's silence, Ben turns to another (compensatory) pathway to self-expansion, vigor, and pride in himself—the kinship/twinship alternative he tried out in college. That is, he turns away from the father/analyst who again thwarts a valid developmental need for support, and he turns toward the alter ego-twin/analyst in a new edition of a variation on boys' muscle-flexing contests: "We two are alike; maybe you have something missing like I do; but I can go toe-to-toe with you and beat you when it comes to looks." The patient's "sheepishness" may well reflect embarrassment about his impulse to do tit-for-tat and put the analyst down; but it may also reflect his shyness and fears about a concealed *unconscious wish to play* with a twin/ or father/analyst in a friendly rivalry in which, finally, he can come out ahead (note his depression and drug use when his twinship needs with college buddies were rejected).

In the following hour the "continuous and undisturbed thread" (Freud, 1909, p. 143) of a compensatory try at a twinship with Roughton continues: Ben remembers forcing himself to keep up with the boys in adolescence when he was afraid but felt he had to prove his manhood. Like the time the boys in Peru were learning bullfighting and he forced himself into the ring (he was not free to decide one way or another what he was or what he wanted). The analyst does not chime in (as I would): this is another bit of therapeutic process that affords an opportunity for understanding another tendril of expectation and hope to feel stronger through treatment, so that he can, so to speak, be one of the boys and learn to step up to the plate or take the bull by the horns; he wants support and acceptance (by analyst/twin) so he doesn't continue, as in his adolescence and boyhood, to be so afraid and self-critical.

What next? Without the equivalent of reciprocity and fatherly support (provided by an interpretation), Ben's need for a twinship with the analyst takes a sexual form: he is reminded of mutual masturbation with the man who picked him up at the gay bookstore a few months earlier. He tried to rationalize away the guilt, didn't want to tell the analyst. Roughton does not recall making any comment. This is another chance for an interpretation that resonates with his primary need—to echo what he said about proving his manhood. I would add that he is still in search of his manhood, perhaps now with men like himself; and now with me (I hope that the transference interpretation will deepen his search for himself with me).

Tendrils of his idealizing or twinship needs unrecognized, Ben returns the next hour feeling guilty, anxious, and depressed; he is afraid of Roughton's reaction to his revelations about his sexual encounter. Roughton tells Ben he didn't feel guilty until he thought what others, including Roughton would think and notes, "He felt better after talking about it and he felt my tacit acceptance." Notwithstanding the importance of tacit acceptance, the analyst's acceptance is not enough—it does not illuminate the thwarted transference needs and hopes (to overcome his fears and establish his manhood) and therefore cannot sink into the depths of the stunted man-self. In effect, acceptance acted as reassurance that unintentionally left Ben alone again with his fears and shame about his weakness, his longings to feel manly, and his anguished self-criticism about his furtive efforts to find what he is looking for on his own.

Let's fast forward to the second year of the analysis and a brief mention of the transference meanings of the "beautiful man," the "hungry guy," and the foreclosing of Ben's working though to a real choice. It is no wonder that Roughton himself was still too constrained (by forces "inside" him and "outside" in a homophobic analytic world) to be able to analyze what might have been the flowering of a health-promoting "gay transference," and the making of a gay man. (Ben's transference is an admixture of all the selfobject transferences rolled into one, probably including sexual desires toward the analyst—but none of them particularly sexualized, at least so far.) Instead of analyzing the transference, Roughton inadvertently deflected it; and he now thinks (rightly) that his interpretations of sexualized "acting out" to fill in structural deficits were misguided. He thinks that Ben's sexual encounters can be better explained as experiments in following his natural sexual wishes, although Roughton notes that Ben seeks out men for sex only when the analyst goes away. (I think he senses a contradiction here—if Ben is experimenting with natural inclinations why is that limited to the analyst's absence?)

I think there are better theoretical explanations that make for better analysis now—the transference has to be addressed instead of being side-stepped. (Understanding, interpretation, and reconstruction are the royal road to curative action and inner change, as much as dreams are a royal road assisting us to recognize transference.) For example, I would interpret that, for Ben, the analyst in jeans whom he saw at the mall, and wondered about, is unconsciously (consciously?) one side of a coin; the "beautiful man" coming out of the gay bookstore—the man in whose reflection Ben could see himself and feel whole—is the other side of the same coin. That is to say, the "gay transference"—Ben's idealizing-twinship experiences of the analyst—was not acknowledged openly and explained and reconstructed as the experiences he needed as a young boy, an adolescent, and young man to restore himself and the feeling of wholeness.

It is clear that the unanalyzed selfobject experiences with Roughton had a profound effect on Ben's beginning sense of cohesion. At the time of the analyst's two-week vacation, before Ben went to the baths in San Francisco, the interpretation might have been that he wanted the analyst to openly acknowledge the kinship bond that makes him feel whole; that the frustration of the coming interruption makes him want to put these positive feelings about himself in tandem with the analyst on hold. In other words, the transference experience of intimacy and closeness with the analyst was beginning to make him feel whole. He forgot, intellectualized, dissociated, went to the baths, and feared an explosion in his life more because his *secret (unconscious) twinship transference* was not shared in the light of analyzing it.

Finally, what made Roughton cringe? I think the only thing wrong with his interpretation to Ben that he is a "hungry guy" is that it was " incomplete." The work of interpretation starts with such a spontaneous comment and simply needs to go further—to explain the idealizing and twinship experiences he is hungry for in order to establish his masculine self. In Kohut's *metaphorical language for selfobject functions that provide sustenance, Ben is hungry for "psychological food."* In a "good" analysis "food" is available to the patient via self-selfobject experiences that are analyzed. These experiences can be bit-by-bit digested, metabolized, transformed, and integrated into a firmed self organization as sustenance-providing, approving, self-supportive capacities (Kohut, 1984). In personal communications, Kohut frequently analogized the process of transmuting internalization—building cell structures—as follows: "We drink cow's milk but it is transformed into our own protein and cell structure" (Kohut, 1977).[3]

Conclusion

When Roughton analyzed Ben, he was still in the midst of coming to terms with his choice to be gay or not to be gay. Kohut's theory was new, and he, like the rest of us, was uncertain in his first efforts to apply it, particularly the concept of sexualization of structural deficits. He experienced first hand the complex interplay between his own psychology, his marriage, his analytic training, and his personal goals and ambitions for himself, as well as the myriad social biases of his time and place. I think the combination of all these led, paradoxically enough, to tacit acceptance of Ben's sexual desires and to inadvertent discour-

[3]See, for example, Kohut's (1977) discussion of the "empathic-responsive milieu [of selfobjects] . . . that contains an optimal amount of oxygen" (p. 85). The same can be said for food. See also Kohut (1984), where he refers to selfobject functions as "nutriments" (p. 70).

agement of his unconscious forward edge transference bids for strengthening through idealization and basic alikeness. The deflection of the idealizing and twinship transferences inadvertently encouraged Ben to displace his thwarted needs for affirming experience—from the psychoanalytic situation and the psychoanalyst to the secret source of affirmation derived from the twins he met in the bookstores and baths. In short, I do not think Ben's "natural inclination" or primary motivation was to find himself in the baths when the "beautiful man" did not recognize his health-fostering transference needs. I think his natural inclination and hunger was to find himself with, and in, the idealized analyst or the twin–analyst and the analysis. It required another time and another place to fully engage the variations on twinship and idealizing transferences of men such as Ben. That time and place is now, provided that we overcome the blind spots that limited our vision of psychic reality to pathology and prevented us from analyzing and strengthening still-healthy needs that set growth of the firmness and wholeness of the self in motion. Analysis that leads to inner change gives the patient enough freedom from past constraints to decide his or her particular sexual orientation and preferences, one way or the other.

References

Bibring, E. (1937), Theory of the therapeutic results of psychoanalysis. *Internat. J. Psycho-Anal.*, 18:170–189.

Freud, A. (1965), *Normality and Pathology in Childhood*. New York: International Universities Press.

Freud, S. (1909), Analysis of a phobia in a five-year-old boy. *Standard Edition*, 10: 5–149. London: Hogarth Press, 1955.

——— (1912), The dynamics of transference. *Standard Edition*, 12:99–108. London: Hogarth Press, 1958.

——— (1914), Remembering, repeating, and working-through. *Standard Edition*, 12:147–156. London: Hogarth Press, 1958.

——— (1923), The ego and the id. *Standard Edition*, 14:13–66. London: Hogarth Press, 1961.

Kohut, H. (1977), *The Restoration of the Self*. New York: International Universities Press.

——— (1984), *How Does Analysis Cure?* ed. A. Goldberg & P. Stepansky. Chicago: University of Chicago Press.

Murray, J. M. (1964), Narcissism and the ego ideal. *J. Amer. Psychoanal. Assn.*, 12: 477–511.

Racker, H. (1968), *Transference and Countertransference*. London: Hogarth Press.

Rubovits-Seitz, P. F. D. (1999), *Kohut's Freudian Vision*. Hillsdale, NJ: The Analytic Press.

IV

THE MEANING OF SEXUALIZATION IN CLINICAL PSYCHOANALYSIS

The Overstimulation of Everyday Life: II. Male Homosexuality, Countertransference, and Psychoanalytic Treatment

SIDNEY H. PHILLIPS

In Part I,[1] I asserted that everyday life within Western, heterosexual culture is overstimulating for the homosexual boy. Certain common child-rearing practices and regular school activities—all based on implicit heterosexual norms—surround the homosexually inclined boy in an atmosphere of sexual overstimulation that affects his development, symptom formation, and adult sexual adaptation. I only discovered this when I began to look more carefully at the adolescent longing of some homosexual boys for heterosexual boys so frequently reported in the analyses and psychotherapies of gay men. I explored the common finding in psychoanalytic work with my adult gay male patients that they described one or more experiences during midadolescence of falling in love with and pining away for heterosexual adolescent boys.

I acknowledged in Part I somewhat of a paradox in referring to sexual overstimulation as being "everyday." The central case presentation in Part I of a gay man who grew up from early childhood into adolescence sharing a family bed with his younger brother is hardly a universal or "everyday" experience. One might even call it the sexual overstimulation of overcrowded family life. Yet on the other hand, the analytic literature is so accustomed to associating sexual overstimulation with the extreme cases of brutal molestation that Shengold (1967) described in his classic paper on rat people that the case in Part I, which did not involve any molestation, seemed quotidian by comparison. There was another way in which the sexual overstimulation of everyday life seemed an apt description of my subject matter. Many gay and lesbian patients report having

[1]See Phillips (2001).

contended on a daily basis in their youth with such overstimulation. Even if not everyday, these experiences are not uncommon and are reminiscent of Freud's (1905, pp. 173–206) original observations on infantile sexuality.

In Part I, I reported on the treatment of a group of adult men in their twenties or early thirties who presented as openly gay and yet also reported various neurotic or character-related symptoms, including difficulties in establishing and sustaining relationships with men. All described histories of being sexually attracted to other boys and/or men from age four years and older. During treatment, each man over time told me in rich detail about their first loves of midadolescence. The stories were remarkably similar. They fell "head over heels" in love with a heterosexual boy. These sexually unconsummated love affairs went on for many months. The homosexual boy had to overcome some reluctance on the heterosexual boy's part to permit greater and greater physical intimacy, especially sleeping in the same bed together. The heterosexual boy's reservations were invariably overcome by the homosexual boy's ingenious rationalizations and energetic persistence.

What was striking in all these stories was how both participants attended to and would not cross what seemed like a carefully constructed boundary against *manifest* erotic behavior or dialogue. As long as all proceeded under the "innocent," permissive guise of mutual, close friendship, the relationships continued. These strange love affairs between homosexual and heterosexual adolescent boys predictably all ended the same way: The heterosexual boy eventually turned his attentions to a heterosexual girl. In Part I, I questioned how to understand these love affairs so similarly depicted by all of these patients. In particular, I inquired as to how we could understand both the homosexual adolescent's choice of a heterosexual love object and the unrequited love. I presented an explanation offering a new synthesis of developmental theory.

Blos (1967) described adolescence as "the second individuation process" insofar as the adolescent struggles to separate psychologically from his parents, this time using peers as substitutes and displacements for the internal, parental objects (p. 163). Blos also viewed adolescence as a reprise of the oedipal drama in which new resolutions are attempted and integrated. But although offering us a useful developmental framework, Blos wrote manifestly and primarily about heterosexual adolescents.

Isay (1989) offered a major theoretical advance for reconsidering the development of gay men when he proposed a developmental pathway specific to homosexual men that entailed an early homosexual orientation. He reported that gay men experienced homoerotic fantasies from at least age four or five years, a finding that is replicated in this study. He noted that this period of development is "analogous to the oedipal stage in heterosexual boys, except that the primary object of homosexual boys is their fathers" (p. 29). Goldsmith (2001), in a crucial expansion of Isay's developmental framework for the homosexual boy, argued that during this oedipal phase not only is the "father the boy's primary love object, but his mother becomes the chief rival for father's affection" (p. 1273).

Isay (1989) showed persuasively how resolution of diverse symptomatology during the analyses of gay men depended on their becoming conscious of and accepting emotionally their homoerotic, incestuous fantasies and desires for their fathers (p. 46). It is important to recall that Isay's theoretical revision included a new understanding of the stereotypical "absent" or "withdrawn" father of homosexual sons so prominently depicted in earlier mainstream psychoanalytic theory. Absenting or withdrawn fathers do not create homosexual sons, he asserted. Rather, the homosexually inclined boy exhibiting oedipal attraction to his (conflicted) father precipitates his withdrawal. Goldsmith (2001) argued convincingly based on clinical data "for a successful resolution of this stage of development, the homosexual boy must learn to master both his anger and aggression toward his mother and his fear of reprisal from her" (p. 1273).

Here then was the necessary developmental framework to understand these unrequited love affairs. The homosexual adolescent boy reworks a version of his oedipal passions: He falls in love with a heterosexual adolescent boy as a displacement of his childhood love affair with his (heterosexual) father. Accordingly, it was of such vital importance to the homosexual adolescent boys in these affairs that the heterosexual boys *returned their passionate love in depth* even though it never encompassed a manifestly erotic dimension. An essential feature of these friendships for the homosexual boy was that they were deeply felt *on both sides*: The *love* was mutual even if erotic attraction was not. These friendships were clearly an effort by the homosexual boy, in this adolescent version of this oedipal drama, to heal and repair the effects of the paternal withdrawal and/or repulsion during the original oedipal passions so poignantly described by Isay.

Even though ultimately not an erotic triumph, since in the denouement the heterosexual boy always gets his girl, the homosexual boy—perhaps for the first and formative time in his life—basks in the warmth of another male's love. Now we can understand how and why the erotic boundary is so carefully constructed and maintained in these affairs: It is an obvious repetition of the incest taboo but surely also an effort to avoid the erotic triggers to the original paternal retreat. It is not merely a repetition of the wish for the "full" oedipal triumph, though surely it is this, too. But it is also an expression of the homosexual boy's deepest wish that someday, somehow, someone can love him wholly and completely without having to step lightly around the erotic perimeter.

In Part I, I then presented the case of Mr. E, a 32-year-old man, who was well established and successful in his career but was unhappy in his love life. Despite having been aware of sexual excitement and arousal for other boys and men since the age of five years and even though he described himself as openly gay when he began treatment, he had been unable to have a relationship with another gay man. His love life was as I have described earlier: He fell in love with heterosexual men and pined away for them. This pattern had begun in childhood when Mr. E's two-year-younger brother became old enough to leave his crib and was placed into a double bed with the patient. They continued this sleeping arrangement until the patient left home for college.

I then described a detailed account of the analysis with Mr. E who had been referred to me as an openly gay analyst. First, I review the salient points of this analytic work; then I extend my thoughts on everyday overstimulation to countertransference and psychoanalytic treatment. During the analysis, any time Mr. E became aware of erotic feelings within the transference, he would fall silent and report that he had "hit a wall" or his thoughts had "gone blank." My invitations to see what came to mind about the "wall" and the "blank" were met with a trancelike prelude to actually falling asleep on the couch. Several efforts to analyze this as *resistance*—attempting to note what the patient had been talking about just prior to falling asleep—went nowhere. It was only when I recognized and interpreted the *expressive* aspects of this enactment that the analysis deepened. Mr. E was repeating with me both the sexual arousal he had once felt in bed with his brother, as well as his dissociative efforts not to think about what he was experiencing. The autohypnotic, trancelike prelude to falling asleep on the couch represented a signal here-and-now in the analytic session itself of conscious but disavowed feelings and sensations of sexual arousal toward the analyst. This pattern was analyzed and worked through many times in dreams, associations, and enactments.

The work proved pivotal in the analysis, and it led to an opening up of many new pathways for exploration in his treatment. One obvious one followed quickly on the heels of this one. Because he knew that I was gay, what if he became aroused in the session, and instead of shaming him, I became aroused, too? Would I seduce or exploit him? Would *I* be able to contain the excitement? Without having to feel so ashamed of *his* excitement, what would stop him from seducing me? And so on. This work opened up to analytic scrutiny the oedipal longing, rivalry, and disappointment that lay behind the overstimulated relationship with his brother, freed him to engage more deeply and passionately in his relationship with his partner, and made possible a planned and successful termination of the analysis.

By the overstimulation of everyday life, then, I referred to the frequent experiences, for example, of homosexually inclined children and adolescents who are placed again and again in the company of same gender parents, siblings, and peers in various degrees of undress or nakedness and the internal, subjective states generated by those experiences. It is a wholly different experience for a homosexually inclined boy to take a shower with his father or to sleep in the same bed with his brother than it is for a heterosexually inclined boy to do so. The homosexually inclined child or adolescent may be repeatedly overstimulated by gender pairings that paradoxically were meant to protect against just such a risk.

In Part I, I emphasized the relation between everyday overstimulation and shame. I noted that the same experiences that lead to the overstimulation of everyday life would also tend to evoke shame: exposure of the sexually aroused state. For homosexually inclined children, this everyday overstimulation creates a double vulnerability to shame: They not only fear exposure of their sexual arousal, but they also dread exposure of the *homoerotic* source of their arousal. I presented a clinical vignette that demonstrated the "usual horror" for the homosexual adolescent boy who lives in daily fear of exposure of his sexually aroused state in same-gender athletic locker rooms. I noted that the example of the homosexual boy contending with the psychology of the locker room illustrates Yorke's (1990) point that the "awareness of an observer is a reflection of the link between shame, pride, and exhibitionism/voyeurism and the defenses against them that underlie *the need to hide*" (p. 381).

I also elaborated on the inner, subjective states of homosexual boys subjected to everyday overstimulation. Their internal landscape is best described as a tantalized inner world of longing. Relentless cycles of attraction, hope, excitement, and arousal *alternating with states of disappointment, loss despair,* and *grief* give their inner world a unique form and content. *Webster's* (1976) definition of longing is "an eager desire especially for something remote or unattainable (synonyms: craving, pining away)." So how is it that the outcome of *some* unmet desire is frustration while *other* unmet desires result in longing? When desire meets an obstacle (a "no," for example), there are two possible outcomes. If the "no" is accepted, the result is frustration followed by grief. Grief is a process that integrates the frustration (or loss) with the desire (i.e., the idea that "I cannot have this now" is emotionally accepted and integrated). If the grief process is "successful" at integrating the initial desire with the loss, the result will be some adaptation to the loss—for example, the person might wait, hoping that the desire could be gratified later, or the person might seek a displacement or substitute gratification.

But what if the "no" is not accepted? The "no" or unavailability of that which is desired may be repudiated or may be denied and magically undone in fantasy. There is a quality of longing or yearning—distinct from mere frustration—that holds "I still want it; I must have it; I will have it." The repudiation of the "no" by magical undoing and denial would thereby create an expectation of, a renewed hope for, gratification. In this scenario, rather than being extinguished or quieted, desire would be heightened and intensified.

Is longing, then, a closed emotional loop of failed grief and unintegrated loss? It is the oscillation between the "yes" in fantasy and the "no" in reality that gives longing its peculiar quality of "delicious pain." Thus a new psychoanalytic definition of longing emerges: an affective state that stems from a repudiation, disavowal, and magical undoing of the loss of the unavailable object and the lack of integration of the pain, disappointment, and sadness accompanying that loss, resulting in a repetitive but derailed and incomplete process of grief. The defenses of magical undoing and disavowal operate against the integration of the pain of the loss. Note how these defenses are within the same dissociative continuum (denial, disavowal, dissociation, vertical splits in the ego) that I pointed to in Mr. E's treatment when he was attempting to stave off the reenactment of his tantalized, inner world within the transference.

I turn now to a discussion of the countertransference to the overstimulation of everyday life. Broadly speaking, analysts may react to patients' reexperiencing this type of everyday overstimulation in the transference in two different directions. The analyst may unwittingly collude with patients in their dissociative defenses against the overstimulation in sessions by developing countertransferential reactions along the dissociative continuum. In reaction to a patient's conscious and determined efforts not to address his arousal here and now within the hour, the analyst may feel distracted, bored, and/or sleepy in response to such circumstantial detail evinced by a patient. When only partially recognized, this type of reaction in the analyst is likely to give rise to interpretive efforts of the patient's resistance: looking for the moment that his associations defensively derailed and bringing this to the patient's attention, just as I initially tried with Mr. E. In my experience, this type of intervention is almost never productive because the defenses at work in the patient are not fully unconscious—for example, obsessional displacement and isolation—but rather are a conscious disavowal of currently active, affective experience. The analyst misses and fails to address a transference-countertransference enactment: the expressive rather than resistant side of the interchange.

The other broad category of countertransference reaction the analyst may experience is a version of the sexual overstimulation itself. The analyst may find himself feeling mildly sexually aroused in the session while having explicitly erotic fantasies about the patient or a displacement figure. Even without breaking any boundaries with the patient, analysts may react to having such explicitly erotic fantasies about patients with shame and guilt as though such reactions represent (internal) exposure of moral and professional failures—dangers to be warded off at all cost. These reactions—both the mild arousal associated with explicit sexual fantasies as well as the shame and/or guilt in response to such fantasies—can prove to be extremely illuminating about the patient's early, warded off experiences of everyday overstimulation when recognized and brought into self-analytic scrutiny by the analyst.

With Mr. E, for example, my initial reaction to his more explicit expressions of erotic desire toward me was to feel slightly aroused and then promptly to feel mild shame. Because sexual attraction or mild arousal to patients on previous occasions had served as important clues to the transference-countertransference matrix, I was perplexed by my shame response. It slowly dawned on me that *my* shame in reaction to feeling aroused might well be resonant with a similar response in Mr. E. My countertransference proved to be a crucial determinant to the pivotal interpretation I made to Mr. E about *his* arousal and shame within our sessions.

Let me illustrate the nature and potential usefulness of this type of countertransference in somewhat greater clinical detail. Mr. F was 20 years old when he first consulted me. In his initial presentation, he claimed only to be seeking treatment at the urging of his mother who was worried about him. After returning home from his first year of college, there had been many family arguments, and he had felt alienated from his parents and siblings. His disclaimer about seeking treatment for himself quickly yielded to his telling me in great detail about his conflicts about "being gay" and having "come out" to his family during the previous school year. Despite having "come out" to his family—all of whom had eventually reacted in relatively loving and supportive ways—he found himself unable to tolerate his own romantic and sexual yearnings for gay peers, several of whom had expressed explicit affectionate and sexual interest in him. Gradually he described his inhibitions and conflicts about initiating and sustaining sexually intimate relationships with other men. He felt ashamed of his sexual desire for other men and had chosen instead to surround himself with heterosexual male friends from high school and college for whom he secretly pined away. He recognized this pattern himself and thought it was related to his being afraid of his family discovering that he was gay. He hoped that he could "cure it" by "coming out" to his family. Their warm reaction had pleased him but failed to relieve his inhibitions and conflicts.

By the time he consulted me, he was in the early phases of a smoldering depression as manifested by stark expressions of cynical nihilism and thinly veiled hopelessness. He quickly settled into twice-weekly sessions and began to tell me about himself. Though he was aware of his attraction to and arousal by other boys and men since early childhood, he had been more troubled by this attraction since puberty. That other boys were starting to show an interest in girls made him feel threatened "that my friends would figure me out." The furtive pleasure he took in masturbatory fantasies about male sports figures was staunchly in conflict with his Catholic upbringing and religious training. When episodic forays into asceticism and prayer failed to resolve his conflict, he became interested briefly in "black magic" and checked out some library books on the occult and devil worship. That offered no relief either, and for a time he secretly read about Hitler and the persecution of the Jews. He became preoccupied with Nazi torture and execution and found it confusing that he identified at different times with both perpetrator and victim.

As we explored this material, he recalled an incident from his early adolescence. He had taken his brother's dog with him on a hike into the woods. The patient began to pitch rocks up in the air and catch them. One rock ricocheted off an overhanging tree limb and accidentally struck the dog in the head. When the dog seemed dazed, he picked it up and ran home. Omitting any mention of the blow to the head, he told his mother that the dog had become ill on their hike. The mother raced the dog to the vet where it seized and died. The patient had never before told anyone of this incident and wept openly and profusely in the session. His tears were affectively condensed expressions of pent-up, searing guilt. Between sobs and gasps, he managed to ask out loud a question with which he had been silently agonizing for years: Had he killed his brother's dog to get back at his brother? But for what, he wondered? He did not know.

After linking more directly his poignant grief and guilt over the dog's death to his brother, he told me more about that relationship. He had "idolized" his two-year older brother as a young boy. They had shared a bedroom growing up, and Mr. F had been curious about and aroused by his brother's athletic body. He recalled trying to catch glimpses of his brother in the shower. Once he had spent most of the day constructing a makeshift periscope from thick cardboard and mirrors from his mother's old compacts in order to watch his brother in the shower without being observed. He recalled when they were both in school how painful it had been that his brother had "spurned" him for male peers. The patient had felt rejected and hurt.

"But how could I be turned on by my own brother? It's almost incest, for God's sake, but worse," he exclaimed. The reference to God, I soon discovered, had been no trivial expletive. He began to quote verses from the Book of Leviticus and from St. Paul's Epistle to the Romans which condemned homosexuality as an abomination that deserved the death penalty. Homoerotic incestuous desire, in *his* mind, was a "deadlier" sin than the heterosexual version.

I interpreted that he was expecting this attitude of condemnation from me, and this seemed to help him feel comfortable enough to proceed to talk about his first homosexual experiences. He had met a young man at college. As they became acquainted in a class, they regularly sat next to one another in a large lecture hall. One day in class, Mr. F's leg had brushed up against his friend's leg. His friend left his leg pressed up against Mr. F's throughout the lecture. The patient was instantly aroused though he tried to hide it by continuing to look at the lecturer. He felt paralyzed with mounting excitement and hopeful expectation. At the end of class, they exchanged knowing looks and adjourned to Mr. F's room for an afternoon of passionate lovemaking.

At one point in what had been a freely flowing description of Mr. F's first sexual and romantic encounter with another man, he fell silent. I commented on this abrupt shift and inquired as to what had changed. Averting his eyes which were teeming with tears, he told me in halting, shame-ridden terms about having discovered his predilection to be penetrated anally by his sexual partner. He literally squirmed in his chair and winced in silent expectation of my reaction.

When I suggested that he seemed once again to be anticipating the condemning words of Leviticus or St. Paul to come spewing forth from me, he gradually relaxed and told me how confused he was about anal sex. He found it the most intensely pleasurable erotic experience he had ever had. On the other hand, he felt intensely ashamed that he liked it so much. He felt such desire was "unmanly" and would surely be ridiculed by his male heterosexual friends.

This was typical of how this time-limited, psychotherapeutic work proceeded: open, graphic descriptions of a never-before-spoken aspect of his sexual life followed by an awkward silence in which he worried his "confession" would result in the harshest condemnation or humiliation from me. Interpretation of this pattern relieved his sense of dread; the work would deepen until this pattern was repeated again. I present this perhaps commonplace psychotherapeutic work with a man struggling with conflicts about his sexual orientation not to suggest it was unusual or groundbreaking in any way, but rather as background to what was quietly transpiring in the countertransference which seemed a remarkable and dramatic example of the impact of an everyday overstimulating transference on the therapist/analyst.

This treatment began in the summer months when the patient worked at an outdoor, manual labor job. He always arranged to shower and to put on fresh clothes prior to his sessions. He usually wore a sleeveless T-shirt neatly tucked into his knee-length short pants and sandals. He had handsome features with a muscular physique. Upon arriving for sessions, his hair was often still wet and glistening from the recent shower. I had from the beginning found his boyish good looks attractive and his affable, slightly reserved demeanor appealing.

As he told me more of his story, I noticed a building sexual attraction to him. In response to his appearance, demeanor, and the content of our sessions, I found myself having a particular recurrent fantasy. I imagined a variation of a scene from a film entitled *The Unbearable Lightness of Being*. In this scene at a hospital, the irresistibly handsome protagonist, a neurosurgeon, said to an O.R. nurse, "Take off your clothes." He said this to her almost off-handedly as she passed through the room in which the surgeon was sitting. She looked at him somewhat surprised and asked him what he had said, as though she had not heard him. He looked directly at her and repeated himself declaratively, "Take off your clothes." The nurse paused briefly and then unbuttoned her white surgical tunic, opening it fully to the surgeon. The audience views this scene from behind the nurse through a window in another room. We see the neurosurgeon's gazing at what we presume to be the nurse's naked body. Unbeknown to either the surgeon or the nurse, two male surgeons have witnessed the entire scene through the window. They shook their heads at one another both in dismay and yet also somewhat in awe of the neurosurgeon's boldness and success with women.

Repeatedly in sessions, I imagined myself in the neurosurgeon's role, saying unabashedly to my patient, "Take off your clothes." In my fantasy, the patient complied, which then led, I imagined, to explicit sexual relations. I always interrupted the fantasy with the thought, "You ought to be ashamed of yourself," and continued to castigate myself while actually feeling mildly ashamed. I did not feel tempted to act on this fantasy, yet I remained puzzled and curious at its persistence.

As the treatment unfolded in the pattern I have described, I had suggested early on to the patient that the cause of his inhibitions that left him unable to enjoy romantic, sexual relationships with available men must reside outside of his emotional awareness as his own efforts "to figure it out" intellectually and to "cure" himself by "coming out" to his family had not succeeded. One day he began a session by telling me that he had happened on something that he thought was important to the origin of his inhibition. He reported that his aunt, his father's sister, dabbled in the art of Rolfing—a form of deep, sometimes painful massage intended to relieve emotional tension by relaxing muscles and recovering warded off distressing or unsettling memories connected to specific areas of the body. The patient had discussed with his aunt his sexual inhibition, and she had suggested a trial Rolfing massage to see what might come to mind.

While his aunt massaged his upper back, shoulders, and arms, the patient had a startling memory dating from age five years. He recalled sitting in his bedroom with his best friend, another five-year-old boy:

> I had always been attracted to my friend. We often played "make-believe," and I used to make up stories that required his having to take off his shirt. Then I would look at him and find a way in the story that led to our wrestling so I could touch him and press my body up against his. Sometimes my friend was reluctant to do this. One time we were sitting on the floor of my bedroom facing one another. I was feeling so frustrated and aroused that I couldn't see and touch his body that I just blurted out, "Take off your clothes!" The door to my bedroom was open, and my father happened to be walking by just at that moment and overheard me. He yelled at me, "You ought to be ashamed of yourself."[2]

---

[2] Because of how this event was "recovered," as well as the emphatic importance the patient attributed to it, the question naturally arises as to whether this is a screen memory—depicting real or imagined primal scene material—rather than a remembered "actual" event from the patient's childhood. The time-limited nature of this treatment and the fact that we were meeting twice weekly—making unlikely the possibility of its deeper and more extensive associational unraveling—probably contributes to its qualities as a screen memory. Though, of course, not answering the question with this patient, psychoanalytic work with several other gay men suggests just how commonplace similar memories are from the childhoods of such patients. *These* reports, which lack the artifactual complications of *this* one, seem to hold up under the veridical scrutiny of entire analyses. This is unlike the usual analytic fate of screen memories, which often do not acquire an enduring conviction of having actually occurred in external, material reality.

I was stunned by the seemingly uncanny convergence of Mr. F's memory and my persistent fantasy. How do we account for its specificity? I suggest this fantasy is an example of the "reverie" about which Ogden (1994) wrote:

> . . . a major dimension of the analyst's psychological life in the consulting room with the patient takes the form of reverie concerning the ordinary, everyday details of his own life (that are often of great narcissistic importance to him). . . . these reveries are not simply reflections of inattentiveness, narcissistic self-involvement, unresolved emotional conflict, and the like; rather, this psychological activity represents symbolic and proto-symbolic (sensation-based) forms given to the unarticulated (and often not yet felt) experience of the analysand as they are taking form in the intersubjectivity of the analytic pair [p. 12].

To apply Ogden's conceptualization to my own, could the analyst's reverie also be an intersubjective reflection of the patient's disavowed state of everyday overstimulation? As I thought about the overlapping relations between the form and content of the patient's verbal discourse, his appearance in the sessions, and my fantasy—as well as the parallels to my own life, present and past—the uncanny quality of the convergence waned.

It is, of course, virtually impossible for a gay analyst to sit with a patient who is struggling with "coming out"—generational differences notwithstanding—and not be reminded of his own experience. This was personal terrain that I knew well. My "choosing" a scene of *heterosexual* seduction as the countertransferential vehicle of resonance recapitulated the conflictual shapes of *my* past while equally representing the patient's wishes and fears. Likewise, that I consciously identified with the male protagonist rather than the woman character, with the seducer rather than seduced, replicated old and familiar struggles of my own—all areas of conflict for the patient as well.

In trying to understand these countertransference reactions, Gabbard (1994) wrote that a key part of the "reflective process is determining which role, if any, one is playing in the patient's internal cast of characters. Sexual arousal in the analyst is frequently connected to one of these characters that has been thrust upon the analyst by the coercion of the patient's behavior in the analytic setting" (p. 1091). Given the conjunction of the patient's conflictual life and my own, it is perhaps arguable the degree to which his "internal cast" was "thrust" upon my stage or my "internal characters" were "drawn" to his. Thus, the likelihood of an intersubjective "coproduction" has a more compelling feel to it in this instance.

In retrospect, the sessions were "drenched" in voyeurism. The patient's history with his childhood friend was a scene of voyeuristic excitement and seduction which was then *observed* by the father. The patient's relationship with his brother involved repeated episodes of voyeurism that culminated in constructing the periscope to *view* him secretly in the shower. A film—from which my fantasy derived—is, of course, *watched* by an audience. The very nature of a film is that its characters are, in effect, "unaware" of being *viewed* by the audience. The particular scene in the film, from which my fantasy was constructed, depicted the two surgeons *watching* the nurse disrobe in front of the protagonist who in turn *gazed* at the nurse's body. In the psychotherapy sessions themselves, the patient was voyeuristically stimulating me by his revealing attire, as well as by verbally referring to and demonstrating the wet vestiges of his recent shower.

Gabbard (1996) points to a growing consensus and more general awareness in contemporary psychoanalysis about the nature of countertransference: "[It] is generally a joint creation involving contributions from both patient and analyst. The exact form of the countertransference is inextricably linked to a 'fit' between what the patient is attributing to the analyst and the internal and self and object representations within the analyst that may or may not provide a 'hook' for what the patient is projecting" (p. 260). Roughton (1993) cautions that such resonance between analyst and analysand can become the source of unrecognized resistance in the analysis:

> Analysts recognize and work effectively every day with situations created by their analysands to gain gratification by winning in a power play or through some favor granted. This *intrapsycyhic role relationship* consists of a role in which the analysand casts himself, a complementary role for the analyst, and an attempt to impose a transference interaction which will actualize and gratify an underlying wish in a disguised way. The analyst listens, not just with free-floating attention, but also with "free-floating responsiveness" (Sandler, 1976a, pp. 64–65). And it is just because of the subtlety of the appeal, or the triviality of the act involved, or the specific fit with a blind spot or countertransference vulnerability of the analyst that such interactions stay outside the awareness of both parties. What is most important to recognize is that such actualizations may become silent resistances and go unanalyzed, to the detriment of the analysis [p. 460].

Although I did not disclose to the patient my elaborate countertransference fantasy, it was actively in my awareness and the object of ongoing self-analytic investigation—both for what it revealed about this particular psychotherapy as well as what I learned about myself.[3] Neither did I disclose my homosexuality to Mr. F, though he may well have intuitively discerned this fact during our conversations. Irrespective of whether Mr. F "knew" it, my being a gay man who easily remembered my own struggles with "coming out" would seem to be

---

[3] Smith (1997) notes that "the analyst's conflicts, resistances, and self-analysis intersect with the patient's conflicts, resistances, and psychoanalysis, and that in dealing with one, we cannot avoid the other, but also and more importantly that the focus on the one inevitably functions both to facilitate and to oppose the work on the other" (p. 29).

the type of "fit" between analyst and patient to which Gabbard (1996) refers. Further, familiar memories of my own childhood voyeurism—interestingly, also involving showers—provided the object relational "hook" for what Mr. F was projecting onto me regarding his erotic attraction to his brother.

Another powerful overlap involved the pattern of the patient's discourse—his frequently reporting scenes with arousing, erotic content followed by expressions of the most profound shame or expected humiliation—which so clearly derived from the childhood memory of the patient's being "caught" and humiliated by the father. This in turn was repeated in my own reaction of shame when I, in effect, "caught myself" in my fantasy of seduction. Other overlaps between the content of the patient's discourse and the film included: (1) they both entailed the poignant depiction of the death of a beloved family dog; and (2) they both involved references to fascism (nazism by the patient; communism in the film).

The most profound convergence, however, concerned the central theme of the film: the way the "lightness of being" as represented by sexual promiscuity defends against the unbearable psychic pain of unmourned and unmournable losses in life. In a similar way, the overstimulation of everyday life generates a closed emotional loop of adolescent longing that is reflected in derailed grief and disavowed loss. Gabbard (1994) writes that

> Myriad factors contribute to sexual excitement in the analyst. These include hostility and contempt toward the patient, the perception of a deficit state in the patient with a corresponding fantasy that the analyst can fill the void left by others, and denial of the reality of transference and countertransference connected with a wish to be the patient's exclusive love object. *The defensive aspects of sexualization should also be investigated, particularly in regard to the avoidance of grief and loss in both analyst and patient* [pp. 1102–1103; emphasis added].

The psychotherapy with Mr. F offered him the first opportunity to acknowledge his unmourned, unconsummated, adolescent love affair with his brother. The "lightness" of sexualization defending against "unbearable" loss is the central theme of the film from which I unwittingly chose to construct my countertransference fantasy. Mr. F's losses—as well as my own—converged in this fantasy.

Now it is seems clear that Mr. F's treatment was under the sway of a quintessential overstimulating transference. Mr. F was taunting me sexually on many different levels, creating within me and between us a tantalizing state of erotic longing interrupted by experiences of the most deeply felt shame and humiliation. He unwittingly conveyed how powerfully he was in the developmentally arresting/arrested grip of unbearably intense but disavowed psychic pain where neither regressive retreat nor progressive release seemed possible. Mr. F oscillated within an anal-sadistic mode of organization between enraged fratricidal fantasy only tenuously displaced onto the brother's dog and a punitive reaction against such murderous wishes, the searing guilt of "an-eye-for-an-eye" sphincter morality as manifested in his preoccupation with torture and execution. Within an oedipal level of organization, he vacillated between repeating and reworking his incestuous love affair with his brother—displaced onto his classmate—and reacting with vehement shame and self-loathing against his newly discovered passionate desire to be penetrated anally by a loving partner. Feeling caught in a savagely vicious circle of desire, shame, rage, and despair that was largely disavowed, he took refuge in his nihilistic attitudes and dabbling with devil worship. If a loving God (Old Testament or New) would not answer his prayers, then he would defiantly worship at a satanic altar, seeking relief from his sense of powerlessness from "black magic(al)" undoing and the power of the occult.

This essay has focused on the impact of the sexual overstimulation of everyday life on development, symptom formation, adult sexual adaptation, and psychoanalytic treatment with some homosexual men. I have described the everyday nature of this overstimulation during the childhood and adolescence of some gay men both as a way of emphasizing its common and cumulative effects in the lives of these individuals; as well as to alert clinicians that this phenomenon has gone unrecognized and remained hidden by and imbedded within "normative" assumptions of heterosexual culture. The overstimulation gains some of its pathogenic power by being both everyday and unseen, a relentless force in the lives of these individuals that goes unnoticed, unspoken, unarticulated. Finally, I have presented the typical countertransference reactions to this type of overstimulation with a detailed case illustration. The essay demonstrates with a dramatic clinical vignette the complexity of recognizing and making effective use of commonly occurring countertransference reactions to the varieties of overstimulating transferences. In particular, the analyst's defensive guilt and/or shame in reaction to explicitly erotic fantasies about the patient can prove clinically illuminating if brought under self-analytic scrutiny.

References

Blos, P. (1967), The second individuation process of adolescence. *The Psychoanalytic Study of the Child*, 22:162–186. New York: International Universities Press.

Freud, S. (1905), Three essays on the theory of sexuality. *Standard Edition*, 7:130–243. London: Hogarth Press, 1953.

Gabbard, G. O. (1994), Sexual excitement and countertransference love in the analyst. *J. Amer. Psychoanal. Assn.*, 42:1083–1186.

——— (1996), The analyst's contribution to the erotic transference. *Contemp. Psychoanal.*, 32:249–273.

Goldsmith, S. J. (2001), Oedipus or Orestes? Homosexual men, their mothers, and other women revisited. *J. Amer. Psychoanal. Assn.*, 49:1269–1287.

Isay, R. A. (1989), *Being Homosexual: Gay Men and Their Development.* New York: Farrar, Straus & Giroux.
Ogden, T. (1994), The analytic third: Working with intersubjective clinical facts. *Internat. J. Psychoanal.*, 75:3–19.
Phillips, S. H. (2001), The overstimulation of everyday life: I. New aspects of male homosexuality. *J. Amer. Psychoanal. Assn.*, 49:1235–1267.
Roughton, R. E. (1993), Useful aspects of acting out: Repetition, enactment, and actualization. *J. Amer. Psychoanal. Assn.*, 41:443–472.
Shengold, L. (1967), The effects of overstimulation: Rat people. *Internat. J. Psychoanal.*, 48:403–415.
Smith, H. F. (1997), Resistance, enactment, and interpretation: A self-analytic study. *Psychoanal. Inq.*, 17:13–30.
Webster's Third New International Dictionary (1976), Springfield, MA: G. & C. Merriam.
Yorke, C. (1990), The development and functioning of the sense of shame. *The Psychoanalytic Study of the Child*, 45:377–409. New Haven, CT: Yale University Press.

Sexualization and the Disavowal of Tender Longings

R. DENNIS SHELBY

This case illustrates a number of issues discussed in this volume and the clinical literature in general; straight or gay therapist; the traumatic loss of a partner to AIDS and its intrapsychic consequences; the manner in which various personalities experience and defend against what has come to be called internalized homophobia; working with an erotized transference; the role of sexualization in the maintenance of the self; and letting the transferences be our guide when faced with a very complicated patient. This case was originally for discussion by a panel, hence the clinical process is emphasized over my formulations though they come through in the way the material is handled and interpreted. The write up is a summary of the unfolding of the first 10 months of treatment, hopefully conveying how the patient and I got to the point of beginning to engage highly traumatized and disavowed aspects of his personality and the related challenges he poses in working more directly with transference material.

The clinical process with this patient centered around recognizing that the initial erotized transference was defensive in nature but also reflected the manner in which he managed considerable depletion, depression, and disavowed longings. Accepting, and working with the defensive transference, allowed the development of a more stable mirror transference and a quiet idealizing transference. Strong twinship elements are present as well. The mirror transference became the vehicle for accessing disavowed longings and the deeper, depleted, and vulnerable aspects of the patient's personality.

ID Data

The patient is a 40-year-old man. A devoted bodybuilder, his appearance is quite striking given his considerable muscle mass on an average frame. He tends to present himself like a farmer or a laborer, often swaggering and lumbering when he walks. He can present in a defiant, provocative, acutely polite, or acutely sad and tearful manner. In sharp contrast to his muscular body, clothes that are chosen to show off his muscles, and teeth that are capped and so white they appear like dentures, his hair is often disheveled and totally incongruent with his general presentation. He flies cargo jets and transferred to Chicago six years ago from one of the coasts.

Presenting Problems

The patient's presenting complaints included being in the midst of relations with two men and unable to choose between them. Capt. B had been with partner A for four years when he began seeing partner C. He was terrified one or both of them would end the relationship. It soon became clear that he was experiencing considerable anxiety and depression and was afraid of falling apart and/or being overcome with sadness, deep depression, and of giving in to long standing suicidal ideation. Capt. B was referred by the therapist who was working with him and partner A in couples treatment. The therapist reported that the patient had left treatment with a straight therapist and wanted to reenter treatment with a gay therapist.

History

Capt. B is the youngest of a sibship of three boys and was born and raised in a small rural southern town. He described his childhood as lonely, confusing, and bleak. The family history is remarkable for its contrasts and unevenness in functioning. The families were generally well off with considerable landholdings. About half of each side of his extended family were professionals, or successful farmers, while the other members had considerable alcohol problems and were marginally functional.

He described his mother as a drunk, a "major drunk," and father as a "fat, blowhard failure." As the history emerged in the treatment, it appeared that mother's alcoholism took hold when the patient was around 10, and was triggered by the death of her father. There were many hospitalizations throughout his adolescence in efforts to get her alcoholism under control. In his midteens, father left the family for an extended period and invited the patient to go with him, but the patient declined because he was afraid that his mother would die without any one looking after her. He described many nights of setting his alarm so that he could wake up and check on her, instances of her passed out on the floor, and numerous multiweek binges. During one of the many episodes of father dragging his mother off to the psychiatric hospital, father yelled at the patient, "this is all your fault!" There were numerous bitter fights between the parents that would often begin at the dinner table and continue through the evening. When speaking of his parents, there is a pronounced, bitter, contemptuous tone. Despite considerable money, the house and yard were in disarray. Capt. B related his attempts to clean up the yard and plant a garden, but his mother did not notice, and his father was critical. Around age nine he began having sexual relations with an adolescent cousin. Capt. B was devastated when, after several years, the cousin lost interest in him and focused on girls. Father's business failed around this time, and he declared bankruptcy. Capt. B felt abandoned by the extended family as well. No one seemed to notice that his parents were in a steep decline, and he longed for one of the many relatives to take him into their home.

The patient's brothers were out of the home when mother descended into alcoholism, and he is quite dismayed by their lack of appreciation for what he went through. Both parents are deceased for several years. Capt. B remains quite involved with his oldest brother's family, though he is finding the relationships increasingly distressing. His brother was a graduate of a prestigious military academy; though he intended to become a pilot he washed out of training early on. He, too, has declared several bankruptcies. Capt. B put one nephew through college, and is the administrator of a trust funded through sale of the family land. The purpose of the trust is to educate the grandchildren.

Early on he viewed education as a way out of the town and his family system. Capt. B was a straight A student, though he reported that he had to study very hard because he felt he was not that smart. He was admitted to a prestigious university with an aviation department. With great dismay he reported that his father never seemed to recognize his achievements. Father was a pilot during the war; his brother washed out of training and did not succeed. He had succeeded, but again he felt no one noticed. For several years he flew passenger jets, and moved about the country.

Capt. B met his first partner in his late twenties and reported that it was the first time he felt loved. He described the partner's voice as "like warm chocolate syrup flowing over me." Two years into the relationship, the partner was diagnosed with AIDS, developed cryptospiridium, and was dead six months later. During the course of the illness, which involved uncontrollable diarrhea, the partner lost half of his body weight. Capt. B had been quite fond of his partner's parents and came to view them as his real mother and father. Following the death, they withdrew, and Capt. B went into several years of depression. Following the death of his partner, Capt. B switched to flying cargo. He reported becoming preoccupied with his responsibility for so many lives, and could no longer bear the burden.

He transferred to Chicago to move up into larger aircraft and met partner A soon after. They bought a home, and Capt. B took the lead on restoring it as buying and rehabbing homes was a hobby and side business. Several years into the relationship, partner A went into what sounds like a significant depression and withdrew into an anxious state. Capt. B then found partner C via the Internet and saw him for several months before the affair became obvious. When the treatment began, Capt. B was living in a borrowed apartment, was seeing both men, and unlike originally reported, was still in treatment with his individual therapist. Capt. B reported that *he* could not bear to talk about sexual matters with his therapist, that it would be like talking to his father about "being a fag." He refused my request to speak with his therapist, and declared me his new therapist. It also felt that he was declaring my office his new home.

Course of Treatment

The patient called and left a pager number only. I thought it was a bit odd, but we were eventually able to connect. An acutely polite man called, and we set up a time to meet. When I went to get him in the waiting room, I was struck by his size and demeanor. He was again polite, if not somewhat timid, then lumbered, almost swaggered back to my office.

In response to my asking how I could be of help, he replied, "I am a queer, I suck cock and love to fuck butt, I was fucked by my cousins from nine on, and I *loved* it." He then went into fine detail of his sexual exploits with his two men, adding that he was also infatuated with a hustler as well. After a while he paused and said, "Damn. It feels good to finally be able to say these things." I was struck by the venomous tone in the way he said queer, not the "I am queer," as the younger generation is prone to say, but a way that conveyed intense self-loathing. But also, of all the ways to introduce himself, this was the way he chose.

Captain B began to hint at how hard it was to keep both men pleased, that he often used Viagra to perform, and that he was often exhausted. He added that neither of them knew he was still having sexual relations with the other. He was torn between the two of them, was afraid one or both of them would end it, and felt guilty because he was lying to each one about the other. He had assured both that he was not sleeping with the other. I began to feel that I was watching a porno movie as he filled me in on his current situation.

I asked about his saying that it felt good to talk about these things. He said that he could never talk to his other therapist about sexual stuff. That it would be too embarrassing and humiliating. It would be like talking to his father about being a fag and he *would not, could not* bear the idea. He was thankful to the therapist in that he could now think about being alone—prior to his treatment, being alone was intolerable. He was clear that he had no problems with Dr. L, that it was *he* who did not want to talk about sexual matters.

Capt. B's affect shifted markedly as he filled me in on his history. He told me about his mother's descent into alcoholism, the bitter fights between his parents, his father's leaving the family for a period, and his preoccupation with her dying. He felt his father hated him, and he hated his father. There was a pronounced tone of bitter, utter contempt as he spoke of his parents. In sharp contrast to his opening communications, I began to feel an intensely bleak, lonely desolate state, so bleak that it was unsettling. He went on to say that he had struggled with depression most of his life, was on Prozac, and a veteran of many therapist couches. Capt. B thought the Prozac was helping. There had been times when he felt immobilized, and that he could not get through the day. He added that he was living in a borrowed apartment with no sun and uncomfortable furniture. His partner had kicked him out when the affair had come to light. He was either flying, or at one of the men's houses, or at the lonely apartment.

The end of the hour was approaching. I said to him, "You know, I don't think I have ever heard anyone describe himself in a way that was so sexually exciting and so sad *at the same time*." He began to tear up and said, "Doc, the sadness is beginning to win out, and I am getting scared." Wondering if he had become more depressed in the wake of a ruptured treatment, or if his distress was related to his divided affections, I asked how long he had been out of treatment. To my surprise he replied, " Oh, I am still with Dr. L, I am going to see him after you, then I have to go to couples counseling with Dr. E."

He reiterated that it had been fine, but he felt it was time for a change. He had not discussed this with Dr. L and planned on going in and terminating that afternoon. I asked if he would like me to talk with Dr. L. He looked fearful and a bit angry and said, " No, I like it here, this is where I want to be. I don't want him to know why I am leaving, I just could not bear to talk about it."

As I reviewed the hour, several things struck me. The sharp contrast between his sexually charged presentation and the intensely bleak presentation was so great that I felt I had been talking to two different people. I was wondering why he could not say what was on his mind to a therapist that he had been with for four years. But he did connect the transference implication with his inability to talk. I sensed a man who was coming apart at the seams. I wondered if his therapist was aware of it, but more so, if Capt. B was even letting the therapist see it. Clearly there was a huge resistance that had not been dealt with. Was it the resistance to shameful sexual material as the patient had intimated or was it to an erotized transference that was necessary in order to get to the depths of his depression? Dr. L struck me as quite reasonable with gay people, so what was the problem? Was the treatment an example of what I described in an earlier essay, that a lack of hostility, and being accepting is not the same as being able to respond to mirroring needs around sexuality? Or was there some other disappointment? I found myself counting. Three therapists, four including the partner's therapist, three apartments, two partners.

The early sessions had a definite pattern. Capt. B would begin with his sexual exploits, then shift to his family history, then his long-standing profound loneliness and struggle against debilitating depression. I viewed the sexually charged accounts of his exploits as a defense against the deeper transference necessary to deal with his loneliness, isolation, and despair. I also heard desperate pleas for admiration, and for someone to notice the distress in his at times provocative and highly seductive presentation. Each hour I would respond to the pleas, then shift with him as the depressive material emerged more directly. When recounting his childhood, Capt. B would often appear horrified. The termination with the first therapist had a perfunctory flavor to it, and was accomplished by the third session.

Capt. B filled me in on the personalities of his two men. They were quite distinct. Partner A was a driven, compulsive highly successful entrepreneur; partner C was a quiet, regular guy, not nearly as successful, but more emotionally available.

He loved them both and did not want to choose. But he felt horribly guilty, a liar and a cheat, if not a sociopath. He was going through the motions of couples counseling, just to appease partner A. Capt. B reported that the couples counseling consisted basically of him sitting there while partner A read off a list of complaints while he quietly endured this. He was not at all sure if he wanted to stay with him, and could not bear to stop seeing partner C. He was terrified of being alone, "After all, who would want a 40-year-old faggot?"

I asked how the affair came to be. Capt. B described his partner as a workaholic and just not aware of other people. Capt. B remodeled and sold houses as a hobby, so he had taken the lead in restoring their house, and put in countless hours, but felt his partner did not seem to notice. He began to feel like the carpenter and gardener, not a partner. "One day we were walking along and I asked if he knew my middle name. Without even looking guilty he said 'No.' So I asked him if he knew what cereal I ate in the morning. He did not know that either." I asked Capt. B if he said anything in reply. "No, not a thing, but I kind of died inside, then I started playing on the Internet and meeting guys and found C. It went on for a few months, he was over at the house, I told A that he was a friend, and then A finally figured it out, and there was a huge scene and he kicked me out. I moved into a friend's place who was out of town for a few months. I hate it. It's cramped, there is no sun, it feels like a prison, but after all I was the one that had done bad."

Capt. B related that he spent many hours comparing and contrasting the two, what he liked, what worried him, but to no avail, he could not decide, nor could he bear to break off relations with either one. I offered that getting wrapped up in deciding which one was the right one might be a bit of a red herring. What we needed to figure out was how it came to be that he was disappointed, then hung himself out to dry between two men.

Capt. B replied that his plan was to continue with me, he had just bought another building, and would take one of the apartments as his own. He felt he could tolerate living by himself. He added that he was beginning to feel that his problems could be solved but that he had to get himself together first. He was also going to tell the two men of his plan to live alone for a while and sort things out. I offered that I thought we could work well together, but that he really needed to think about coming in more often than once a week. I felt I needed to be honest and offered that it might get rough, before things got better. He was initially hesitant but agreed to a twice-a-week schedule, and eventually three times per week.

Capt. B became overtly seductive in response to my being on crutches following a stress fracture. Upon seeing me hobble out to greet him, he replied, "You get that tucking your foot behind your ear?" I was initially quite angered by the intrusion. I made sense of his response later in the session when he offered that he felt he got involved with lonely isolated men, because they would not leave him. I chose to not directly interpret the resistance manifested by the erotized transference in that accepting it, and responding to the pleas within it, I was gaining considerable access to his depletion, anxiety, inability to speak, loneliness, isolation, and depression. Also his exhaustion with the current situation was increasingly punctuating his accounts of his sexual exploits.

Many times he would appear haggard and tired. He appeared genuinely surprised that I noticed. A different form of resistance appeared as we moved to twice a week. The first week he canceled. Partner C was angry about partner A, and Capt. B ran to him to fix things up. The second week the reverse happened. When I pointed out what he was doing, Capt. B related how panicked he became when one of them was angry. I pointed out that he seemed to be desperately trying to not disappoint either one of them. He related that on one hand he lived in terror of their anger and would "fold up inside." He associated to the many rages and beatings by his father and that when his father died he boxed up and put away his Air Force ring. "I would never wear it. I ate the ring too many times" (as he gestured being backhanded). I took note that he kept the ring, but boxed it away. On the other hand he would often daydream in an erotic way about the many things he could do for his partners to please them. I began to interpret that *he* was desperately needing something from the two men. He was convinced that neither one knew what he was up to despite each one knowing of his involvement with the other. I pointed out that I doubted it, that they were choosing not to see what was going on. Capt. B also reported that he had begun to speak up in the couple's treatment and to convey his disappointments with the relationship.

Another pattern was that toward the end of a session filled with accounts of his chaotic present and past, he would become quite reflective and say something acutely honest and painful: his inability to live in houses once he had fixed them up because they were too nice, his fear that if he did not keep up his frantic pace, "it" would catch up with him and he would swallow a 9mm and end it. His nickname for himself was "Pepe the burro" who takes care of everything for everyone and does it quietly. Perhaps the real issue with the two men was that by being torn between the two, he was always in pain.

The erotized defensive transference quickly waned as we moved to more frequent meetings. His mood stabilized, and he became less frantic about the prospects of disappointing his partners. Capt. B brought in an article on distorted body images in adolescent boys that appeared in a magazine. He began to talk about his bodybuilding. He was 6 feet tall and weighed 245 pounds, but he still felt like that skinny kid lived on inside. That was why he used the Internet to meet people. When he went out in the gay community, if he saw anyone he thought was bigger than himself, he collapsed inside and would go home in shame. He had a personal trainer, and worked diligently. He often would bring a protein-power shake and drink it during his sessions. I asked if he got any pleasure out of his workouts. He had to think awhile and appeared sad. He replied rarely—sometimes he felt a bit of an endorphin rush, but even when all pumped up, he saw a problem, or something that needed improvement. He then said, "You know, I can't believe I am able to tell you the things I do, they just feel so icky, like shame, but I don't feel threatened here." I respectfully accepted this, but also wondered why. Was he indeed able to approach his shameful feelings with less of a threat? Or was he buttering me up? It felt like a mixture of both. In the early sessions, the transferences floated between a buddy he could intrigue with his sexual exploits and complain to about his needy men; slightly devalued man number three; and someone who just might be able to offer him something. Capt. B also seemed to be reassuring me that he really did not need or deserve that much.

Capt. B's hair started to irritate me. At times it looked like he put a bowl on his head and cut around it. At others, I thought it was a wig. It was so out of place with his general presentation. My attention was being drawn to it, but why? It made sense one session when he began to relate that his mother had wanted a girl, and that in her drunken states she had told him as much. He recounted several devastating and confusing incidents. He came home from school one day and his bedroom was painted pink. He was horrified, confused, and deflated, but said nothing, nor did his parents. He related his humiliation that he had a playhouse in the back, while his father and brother had a tool shed they worked in. One day he came home and the playhouse was pink also. Again, nothing was said, but he was devastated and confused. He also described his fear that maybe he was a woman and the efforts he went to convince himself that he was not: His bodybuilding, his terrible anxiety when his partners did something feminine, at which time he would stop bathing, so he could smell his body odor and fantasize that he was Grizzly Adams living in a cabin in the mountains. In acute despair he declared himself a sham. His truck, his bodybuilding, his efforts to act like a redneck, all were just a sham. I replied that perhaps he did attempt to make himself feel better by these activities, but the men he told me about that he admired as a child were farmers and laborers. Capt. B then recalled a favorite uncle who still had a huge farm in his home state, a big, gentle kindhearted man that was the kind of man he wanted to be. I offered that perhaps he was worried that he could never be that kind of man, that something intolerable inside him led him to disparage himself. The venom returned. "I can't. I am a fag."

The next session, he came in and took off his hat, His hair flew up in the air, and for a split second I saw a woman's "bubble" hairstyle. And yes his mother had strawberry blond hair as did he, which was often matted and in disarray during her binges. I came to view his hair as a reflection of his troubling identification or perhaps more appropriately an interjection of some aspect of his mother's personality that he periodically railed in terror against. I also began to notice his acute reactivity to tension, and that when it came to certain negative ways he experienced himself, it was not that he felt that way but *was that way*. When he presented these aspects of himself, he insisted that I see them as the *way things are*, not the way he felt. After I had "accepted" it as the way things are, then he could loosen up a bit, and reflect on it more as a feeling state that could be explored and understood. The bill began to draw transference feelings. At first, he eagerly paid it, then he began to lose it, and then to appear quite distressed by it. It took several tries to get him to talk about it, but he was eventually able to say that paying me felt like taking care of his mother, and that he wanted a father.

Upon return from a brief vacation with one of his partners to a house he kept out west, I noticed some uneasiness about partner A being in the house. Capt. B returned to the death of his first partner and the withdrawal of his family. He had moved to a rural area and "re-created" their home. He purchased a house with a similar layout, and furnished it with their possessions essentially re-creating the home they shared. In tears he said, "I really thought he was coming back." Capt. B went on to say that he has several hundred pictures of his partner and continues to carry many with him every day in his briefcase. He also filled me in on how he went into a profound withdrawal after the house was finished and became almost phobic of the gay community and sexuality. It was at the point of reemerging into the world, that he discovered bodybuilding. The emergence of material about the deceased partner was noteworthy. Periodically it would surface, and it would feel like the man was in the room with us. The next session, the material would be inaccessible. I decided to wait, let the relationship deepen, and listen for anniversary reactions. I also began to view the death of the partner as repeating some earlier loss.

A bit of a crisis occurred the next session. We had changed some appointments around due to a sudden change in his work schedule. I thought we had an appointment, but he did not appear, which was unusual for him. The next session I wondered if I had gotten confused, but I thought we had an appointment. Capt. B blurted out: "I was circling at 30,000 feet! I couldn't call." I noticed he was trembling and tears were in his eyes. "Hold on," I said gently, "I was just inquiring." He replied, "I thought you were mad at me." We worked through this a bit, and Capt. B emphasized how much he worried about people being mad at him.

The next session he brought in a dream. "I dreamed I was chopping my father into small pieces with a machete." He was worried the dream meant that he was sick and crazy. He could not associate much to it, only that he had dreams before of attacking his father but this one was different; it felt more complete, the pieces smaller. He was very concerned that it meant something bad. I pointed out his worry that I was mad at him, and that we had talked it through. Perhaps the dream was a signal that he could approach his feelings more directly and with less fear. The next session he reported feeling very settled and relieved after our discussing the dream, that he felt more relaxed and less afraid.

He then bought a puppy with partner C. He was thrilled with the dog. He lavished it with attention, and he was elated like a new parent. He was amazed at how smart the dog was, and how quickly he caught on. Capt. B looked forward to the puppy crying in the night, so he could go and comfort it. As he recounted his pride at the dog's progression and how quickly he learned, I would offer that perhaps the dog had a good master. These attempts to acknowledge him were quickly pushed away or ignored. When I pointed this out, he replied that he longed to hear that from someone, but that it made him uncomfortable hearing it directly. He then launched into a current problem with partner C, how he paid for vacations, gave him sex as often as he wanted, paid off his car loan, but then he got angry over a minor issue. Capt. B was horrified whenever C had one of his "fits" and often felt unfairly attacked and deeply hurt. I offered, "No wonder you get confused. You want to be admired as a stud, but treated like a puppy." He thought for a minute and said, "Well, why don't they get it?" I offered that perhaps he wanted them to see the stud, but not the puppy, that he himself was uncomfortable if not disparaging of just how much he wanted and needed.

Capt. B returned from a visit to his brother's family in a highly distressed state. He had returned to his home to watch his nephew play in a high school football game. The brother now lived in the house Capt. B had grown up in, and it was in even worse repair. Capt. B was highly involved with the family, greatly enjoyed being an uncle, and showered his nieces and nephews with gifts and trips. However, he longed to feel close to his brother, but felt his brother avoided him. He wondered if the "gay thing" had anything to do with how they treated him. He recalled how his nieces and nephews related that their mother periodically made disparaging "fag" remarks or wondered "who was the woman" when he brought partner A along on trips. "It's like you're always left wondering if that is it, if they don't like me because I am gay."

At the game, Capt. B remembered with great intensity the pain he felt at football games as an adolescent. His father was the announcer for the games. The cousin with whom he once looked to for sexual contact, but then who abandoned him for girls was a star player. He recalled, "Night after night, I would sit there while my father called out my cousin's name. He thought he was fabulous, but he hated me, but he was the one who fucked me. But why did I do that to myself. Why did I sit there night after night in agony?" I offered that it indeed sounded painful, but also perhaps he was looking for something he desperately needed. Capt. B replied, "I wanted both, I wanted my cousin to still be fucking me, and I wanted my dad to be calling out my name." I began to more fully appreciate my earlier interpretation, "How is it that you get disappointed, then hang yourself out to dry between two men?" There he was, torn between the man he bitterly despised but wanted so much from, and the man who had once given, then withdrawn, leaving him bereft.

Several sessions later, Capt. B reported the following dream. "I was napping on a couch that overlooked the coach house. I felt it was time to replace plants in the flower boxes and thought of what I would put in them, but then I thought, no, it's still winter. Then I thought, 'He is dead. You're the father now.' It made me uncomfortable and I woke up." His associations were to the considerable effort put into restoring his coach house and his father's criticism of his attempts to clean up the yard. If he bought a bush or plant with his allowance "just to try and make it look decent," his father would deride him. He recalled a summer when he worked for his father, took his entire earnings, bought a fountain, and triumphantly placed it in the backyard. When his father was critical, he would say to himself, "And there is not a damn thing you can do about it." He then added that he had put in a fountain in the garden of every home he had lived in since. I asked him about "You're the father now." He related his anxiety at the statement, that he wondered if he really could be a father. He then recalled that, even though he hated his parents and thought they were totally worthless, he would often call them to discuss trivial things, or things they did not have any real knowledge of, such as investments, restoring his houses, and the like. I asked him what he was looking for. He recalled how anxious he used to get, but wondered why if he thought they were total fuck-ups why would he look to them? I offered that perhaps he needed reassurance.

Capt. B replied, "It was like I needed them to say it was okay, but they were the last ones I would believe." I offered that he was being a good father to his dog, and had been of considerable help to his nieces and nephews, but wondered if he felt being a father was something that he was not up to himself. He replied that he worried about it all the time, if he really could be a good man who was not plagued by so many doubts. I offered that despite his disappointment at his father, he still needed reassurance that he himself could handle being an adult. Capt. B offered that he was beginning to realize just how much he himself needed and wanted. He found himself railing against it, but was beginning to feel he could tolerate the idea. I offered that perhaps the dream was also about a hope that we could help him feel stronger. I took note of his tendency on one hand to become bitterly disappointed, but on the other hand to desperately cling to relationships. In the following weeks, he began to relate to me his "sensibilities" that he felt his father could not tolerate. His gardening, the efforts he put into rehabbing his houses—into remaking rundown houses really nice—and his plans to make elaborate Christmas wreaths.

The next week, Capt. B began to relate how similar he felt to friends who were raised by survivors of the Holocaust. They talked about how different they felt as a result of growing up with parents that were so traumatized. With an expression of profound horror, he went on to say that *he was different*, that he felt like he went through a holocaust and that he was just beginning to realize that it was a holocaust. With a look of absolute horror, he said "When you're in it, you know it is wrong and crazy, but you're also in it. I am different." He went on to say that he had been trying to explain what he went through to partner C. It made him anxious but he was determined that he hear it. Partner A was just clueless, so there was no use. I offered that he was wanting people to know and to understand him, not just wow them with his efforts and sexual prowess and keeping them happy. He was beginning to feel that it was possible for him to be admired and have his men know about his hurts and tender feelings at the same time.

He kept referring to the Holocaust and how bad he felt. I asked him just what he was experiencing. He related that several times a day recurrent images of his mother passed through his mind. Then he would feel horrible, get a sick feeling in his stomach, and think, "Oh, its still there, she will never go away, I will never get over it" The images were of the time he feared his mother dead when he found her passed out, raging fights between his parents, the time she drove off drunk and he worried for hours that she would be killed in a wreck. At the end of the session, Capt. B thanked me for the way I was so interested in what he experienced. He had tried to talk about how awful it was with other therapists, but felt that others were afraid of it, and just did not want to deal with just how messy and awful it really, really was. Capt. B also began to offer that he was tired of sex, it was not exciting anymore, that all he wanted was to be held.

The process of the sessions had changed dramatically by this point. Capt. B began bringing in accounts of an encounter in which one of his men or a coworker had become tense, and he felt himself "fold up inside." He would fight the urge to retreat to appeasing and would struggle to present his views and feelings. While this had the flavor of "see how hard I am trying," he was also letting me see, experience, and work more directly with him as he felt himself crumbling. Capt. B began to observe his reactivity, and reflected, "You know, I really have to be careful, I tend to hear everything as someone wanting something."

I am going to end with a dream that occurred in month ten of the treatment: "I was walking along with a father, my father. It felt incredible, as we walked I felt closer and closer. I was sitting in his lap. I got an erection, and it felt so incredibly sexual, I have never felt so aroused and wanting it so bad. Then it changed, we were outside a huge two-story manor house. My brother was on the roof with a TV antenna and wires. My dad was shouting directions. There was a chimney with metal rungs going up it. He climbed up the rungs and started working with my brother. It faded out as we were all inside watching TV." He then presented a subsequent dream, in which he returned to his brother's home. All of his cousins were there and were glad to see him.

His associations were rich and deep with affect, and we worked with the dream for several days. He had returned to the welcoming dream, and feeling close to his father many times, taking in the warm powerful feelings over and over again. The second dream seemed pure wish/need/longing fulfillment; perhaps that was expressed in the first. The first dream associations were his fear of heights, that he was not fond of roofs, but his brother was up on the roof with ease, and his father just climbed right up the big chimney. The intense pleasure he felt sitting in his father's lap, and how wonderful it felt to feel close to a father. As for the manor house, he had dreamed and wished his father was a gentleman living in a big manor house, but he was anything but a gentleman, he was a fat, blowhard, redneck, bully, a failure. He returned to the intense pleasure he felt, that he was realizing how much he was looking for a father himself. I wondered aloud if the dream was about having, then losing his father. He replied sharply that he never had a father to begin with. His father hated him, always did, end of story. He returned to the reverie of feeling close to a big man and how wonderful it felt, that was what he wanted. Suddenly his affect shifted to horror as he spoke of his distrust for women: they were mean and did mean things and he was afraid of them. I was taken by the sudden shift. He offered, "I have never told anyone this, but I played with dolls as a kid." I wondered where dolls would come from in a house full of boys. He replied, "She gave them to me, but then she would make fun of me for playing with them. Women are mean, they can hurt you, but men are not."

He just as quickly shifted back to sitting on his father's lap and how wonderful it felt. Then to the time he watched his father spend time with his brother while ignoring him. His affect shifted to intense sadness as he related just how long he has been searching for a father, and pointed out that he had once brought in a picture of what he thought an ideal father would look like (in sharp contrast to his manifest sexual fantasies, the man in the picture reminded me of Bill Moyers—a quiet, thoughtful, gentle man). His expression shifted to the horrified look that would come over him when he related family arguments and his mother's drunken episodes. Capt. B related the neglect he felt, from both parents, wondering why they abandoned him to fend for himself, why they hated him.

In tears, he said, "I wanted to be on the roof, I wanted to play ball, but you know, if I had a kid that was having trouble, I would just say hey, you need to practice a bit that's all, and I would show him how." I offered that it was clear how much he wanted from his father, but the hurt he was feeling so intensely made me wonder if he did not feel hurt that his father did not love him the way he wanted to be loved. But he seemed to love his brother. He replied, "It's the inconsistency, sometimes he would be okay and then he would be mean." Capt. B recalled several times when his father did do things with him, but then would revert to ignoring him. It took awhile to help Capt. B regain his composure as the hour was ending, he was quite shaken, and really did not want to leave.

As I reviewed the dream and associations, I found myself wondering if this was about having but then losing, feeling rebuffed by his father for his sexual longings, or sexual longings causing the father to feel dangerous. Or if it were a case of never having, or sometimes having, and sexualization serving to bridge a gap he felt as a result of crushing disappointment. The dream seemed to convey a segment of development, a time when intense longings and needs became combined with sexuality or perhaps sexualization. Clearly he was hungry for a man to idealize. The more I thought, the more I felt that it was sexualization replacing ruptured idealization. I was also struck by the intensity of the affect he was able to relate to me as we worked on the dream—utter bliss, intense sexuality, bitter disappointment, the horror of feeling hated and the hope of one day feeling loved. But I was struck by the seeming intrusion out of nowhere of maternal material, seemingly unrelated to the dream at all. It did seem to account for why he felt his father hated him, but I also recalled his telling me of scenes of her flashing through his head during the day. Was the intense longing for a man to idealize also an effort to deal with this intrusion? I also realized that in contrast to his usual manner of being sprawled out on the couch, at times displaying his crotch, during the dream description he had pulled his leg up as if inviting me into him. I also recalled that the session before he had thanked me for wanting to deal directly with his trauma of his past, and its effect on him. I also realized that I had gotten so caught up in the intensity and richness of the associations that I had not addressed the transference aspects of the dream.

The next hour he came in and very casually talked about the weather, then remarked that it was quite a session we had the other day. I agreed and added that a lot of powerful feelings were expressed. He then plunged into more associations. Capt. B began recalling his deceased partner. That he was the perfect father, and went on to fill me in with the details of their meeting and life together. He was puzzled because he was not a big man, but was steady and solid as a rock emotionally, could always calm him down and never retaliated when Capt. B was angry. He then went into more detail of the dream, that when sitting on his father's lap he wanted his penis inside him so bad, he really, really wanted it. Again he was puzzled, he and his partner never had anal intercourse, in fact he was quite phobic about the idea. I offered that perhaps it was about wanting to feel the power, comfort, love, and bliss of having a good father inside of him. Capt. B. then turned to his bodybuilding and about how much he wanted to be held, to be enveloped the way he was in the dream. He offered, "In a way, this bodybuilding thing of mine, it's like wanting to build those strong loving arms around me, it doesn't make sense because it's all me." I offered that it made a lot of sense, but perhaps he was trying to build something inside of himself. "I have been the father to them, but I really want a father for me." Capt. B related that he loved it when fathers asked to bring their sons into the cockpit of the plane. He offered that part of the reason he was so into entertaining was so people, especially fathers and sons, would ask to see. He would then pay close attention to how the fathers dealt with their sons and the excitement of being in the cockpit, and he would "rate" them on what kind of father they would be.

He then returned to his current men. He felt partner C loved him because he had taught him so much, the way his deceased partner had taught him, and the way he wished his father would have taught him to play ball. He felt partner A loved him because he would hold him, and fuck him the way he wanted his father to fuck him in the dream. He added, "It's weird, but it's like I have been giving them what I wanted. I think I felt that if I fucked them long enough, they would turn into the father I wanted."

As the hour wore down, I wanted to return to the transference. I offered that the dream also said something about our work together. Capt. B appeared befuddled. I pointed out that it did occur after he had thanked me because he felt I was not afraid of his painful, traumatic feelings and that perhaps some feelings of being taken care of had been rekindled. Capt. B looked at me incredulously and replied, "Naw, I have been aware of this all the time. I just decided I did not give a shit about what you think." My suspicions were confirmed. The transferences were sharply divided. I was the idealized father that he wanted to be close to and borne up by, and on the other hand, I was devalued, unimportant, of minimal consequence and he could handle things quite ably on his own. But I also realize that at this point, the transference is primarily a mirror transference,and despite his considerable longings to experience an idealizing transference, there is much repair to done. The next session, he apologized for saying that he did not give a shit what I thought. He had trouble discussing his feelings directly, but his associations were to his reactions to his pârtners and that sometimes he heard them asking for things when they were actually trying to give him something. We came to understand that he felt that I was wanting to take credit for his dream.

Following this dream it became clear that prior to meeting partner A, Capt. B was quite sexually inhibited and that the use of intense sexualization to engage others was not an overt aspect of his adult functioning. It appears to have emerged in response to his partner's depression and withdrawal. Their sex life became very intense and at times exotic, but Capt. B found the combination of intense sexuality and withdrawal acutely disorganizing and distressing and in his disappointment engaged partner C. The sessions have settled into bringing in and reexperiencing with me interactions with his partners during which he feels himself crumbling, fights his anxiety, and struggles to present his views and feelings. Again, it has a "see how hard I am trying" feel to it. As we have worked more deeply with this, it has become clear that part of what he experiences is his fear that he will have to tell someone that he has no more to give. On one level, it feels like teaching him to play ball, on a deeper level, tending to a toddler that upon becoming overwhelmed with the world's demands, turns to his mother for reassurance.

Conclusion

The title of this presentation is a reference to one of Freud's most benign theories on the development of homosexuality: if the boy has an excess of tender feelings toward the father, he takes him as his love object. This theory is rarely referred to. Indeed Lewes's (1988) monumental study of the evolution of analytic theories of male homosexuality does not consider it one of Freud's four theories. Unlike his others, this theory, while subtly implying a lack of progression, does not rely on regression. My substitution of longings points to the theory of the self and the assumption that parents are more than the target of drives and wishes. They are, rather, selfobject needs that, when met, result in a different kind of structure building. As many theories discuss, the taking of a love object is fraught with potential pitfalls, anxieties, and attempts to manage. Though an idea in need of further elaboration, it may well be that the combination of father as sexual object, combined with ongoing self needs for idealization, response to mirroring needs, and twinship create a potentially more complex situation for the homosexual male child.

On a clinical level, these ideas must be considered within the context of the individual patient and the myriad of parental personalities. If we think of sexualization as one attempt to manage disappointments, then we must remember that these defenses concern disappointments and efforts to manage distressing affects. The more primary selfobject needs are often quite different, and, though sexualization often presents itself in dramatic and noisy manifest manners, the nature of the primary transferences is often quite hidden and emerges via dreams and the qualities of the transference versus its contents.

Reference

Lewes, K. (1983), *The Psychoanalytic Theory of Male Homosexuality.* New York: Simon & Schuster.

Transference Availability: Discussion of R. Dennis Shelby's Clinical Case

RALPH ROUGHTON

The psychoanalytic situation is not an assembly line production. Psychoanalysts are not interchangeable parts. In focusing on the initial engagement in an analytic process, Dennis Shelby's presentation beautifully and evocatively illustrates this point of view. I believe that many otherwise highly competent analysts would not have been able to engage this man so quickly and so effectively. In reaching for an explanation, it is tempting to call on some mystical alchemy of intuitive knowing and communicating. But perhaps we can do better than that.

Shelby's therapeutic work, sampled here near the beginning of his analytic career, stands in stark contrast to the prevalent attitude at the beginning of my analytic career a generation earlier. Before I was exposed to Heinz Kohut's work, Leo Stone's landmark monograph, *The Psychoanalytic Situation* (1961), came as a welcome revelation. It affirmed my own discomfort with what I perceived as the role of the classical analyst. Stone proclaimed that the analyst's arbitrary authoritarianism and devotion to the principle of deprivation were often carried too far. Rather, he said, the analyst should "provide a palpably human context for the transmission of understanding" (p. 108). He also challenged an older colleague's assertion that his patient would have developed the same vivid transference to him if he had been a brass monkey. Stone declared that this was just not true.

Now, 40 years later, having benefited from advances in self psychology, from the transference-countertransference emphasis of the contemporary British school, and from the relational and intersubjective perspectives, I believe that I have almost caught up with the starting point of our young colleagues today. As a supervisor of analytic candidates, I am struck by the progress that has been made in what we teach and what can be didactically learned. I also believe that there are aspects of analytic engagement that cannot be taught. Over and above talent and skill and knowledge, there is the ineffable match of two personalities.

Patient–analyst match has been studied in recent years by Kantrowitz (1986, 1995), who regards the match as one determinative factor in the course and outcome of some analyses. On the other hand, Vaughan and Roose (2000) have questioned the usefulness of the concept: "By suggesting that match exists as a reality outside the domain of transference and countertransference, analysts may overlook the importance of psychoanalytic technique in creating a sense of match" (p. 885). Their critique, however, is aimed primarily at the use of patient–analyst match as an explanation for stalemates in treatment. They do also suggest that some largely intuitive and unconscious factor may be crucially involved in the patient–analyst dyad's decision to work together. It is in this latter sense that I want to focus my discussion on the initial engagement that occurred between Shelby and Capt. B.

Few of us today would argue that, given a skilled and well-analyzed clinician, one blank screen is the same as another for the projections of conflicts and transferences. In our day of postmodern thinking, where relational and intersubjective perspectives augment attention to the needs of the self in the therapeutic setting, we no longer pretend that one size fits all.

In the large center of average expectable needs of the patient and average expectable capacities and talents of the analyst, most dyadic matches seem to work. At the edges of the expectable, however, the dyadic fit becomes more important, sometimes the crucial difference in whether analysis can occur. In referring to the "edges of the expectable," however, I do not mean to imply anything about the degree of pathology in this patient, but rather his life experiences, his essential defenses, his compensatory structures, and—most importantly—his prior experiences with trust.

I believe that this case illustrates the situation where the particular patient–analyst match is vital to the engagement, and I believe that Shelby is uniquely qualified to be this patient's analyst. But is it because of who he is or what he is able to do? Perhaps that is a false dichotomy.

In choosing as my title, "Transference Availability," I refer to the analyst's capacity and availability to function as the particular transference object that the patient requires in order to engage in and benefit from an analytic process. The scope of this transference availability depends on many factors, which I will not attempt to discuss here. Suffice it to say that, for this particular patient, the previous therapist did not have it and Shelby did.

Let's look at the initial encounter. The man Shelby came to refer to as Capt. B had been in therapy with a straight male therapist but was requesting referral to a gay therapist, feeling that he could not talk with the first therapist about sex. Capt. B was currently involved with two men, one a partner of four years who had lapsed into depression, the other a sort of insurance policy against his terror of being left alone. Similarly, he did not end treatment with the first therapist until after he had bonded with Shelby. An earlier partner, who provided the first feeling he had ever had of being loved, died of AIDS. History revealed a bleak and lonely childhood, dominated by his need to rescue and attend to his alcoholic mother and left to that task by a critical and uncaring father.

Against this backdrop of loss and deprivation, Capt. B had developed a defensive facade of swagger and sexualization to blunt and manage his "considerable depletion, depression, and disavowed longings." As later clinical material bore out, Capt. B was in search of a nurturing and idealizable father, which he felt he had, but lost, in the first lover who died.

In the initial session, Capt. B, who says he could not talk with his straight therapist about sex, immediately launched into a lengthy, graphic description of his sexual activities, then paused and said, "Damn, it feels good to finally be able to say these things." That is the first point: he gave himself license to talk about sex, knowing that he was speaking to a therapist who was also a gay man. That may have been a necessary condition for engagement, but it was not sufficient. Not just any gay therapist would have been able to engage and work effectively with this man.

Point two: This sexually charged presentation masked a profound isolation, fear, and self-depreciation. Shelby allowed himself to be in tune to the extent that he experienced in himself evoked feelings of a lonely, desolate state.

It was out of the stark juxtaposition of these two presentations that Shelby formulated his hypothesis that this eroticized transference was necessary in order to get to the depths of his depression. And in that first session—without the benefit of reflective time or immersion in further material, which is why I attribute it to "transference availability" rather than knowledge and skill—Shelby said to Capt. B: "You know, I don't think I have ever heard anyone describe himself in a way that was so sexually exciting and so sad at the same time."

I can imagine some colleagues cringing—telling a patient that he is sexually exciting? Or that his presentation was beyond the expected bounds? Actually, I think it was a brilliant stroke. What Shelby said in that pithy yet movingly empathic intervention was this: I can hear your sexy talk and not be shocked or seduced, and I can also hear beyond the sexiness and feel the sadness and loneliness you are so afraid of revealing. And I am ready to be affectively engaged and to work with you on all of this.

Capt. B's response confirmed that a bond had been established. Moved to tears, he said, "Doc . . . the sadness is beginning to win out, and I am getting scared." And he indicated that his decision was made: "I like it here, this is where I want to be."

What Shelby demonstrated was his *unblinking* acceptance of Capt. B's transference needs. I emphasize the "unblinking" quality as going beyond a willing and uncritical acceptance of the patient's transference needs. As Shelby wrote, wondering why the previous therapist had not been able to get beyond Capt. B's resistance, "being accepting is not the same as being able to respond to mirroring needs around sexuality."

The course of treatment has proved this patient–analyst match to have been solid and workable, despite the intense and sudden onset, which might in other dyads result from intense anticipatory projections that bear no relation to the reality of the match. Shelby wisely avoided getting too caught up with interpreting the erotized transference and instead simply let it be there and responded to the pleas within it, in order to gain access to the underlying depletion, anxiety, and depression. And, as the patient's needs were met by the increasing frequency of sessions and by Shelby's transference availability, the defensive sexualized transference waned. The analysis moved on into an intense process, with a full range of affect, evocative dreams, and mirroring and idealizing transference work.

A longer discussion would dwell on the rich material from these first ten months of analysis, but instead I return to the initial question about the match and engagement. Was it who Shelby was or what he did? Or rather, in what balance were the two blended? I would venture the guess that in the initial session, the engagement was already almost established by what Capt. B experienced of what he observed and felt with Shelby prior to the interpretation at the end. But the just-so-right interpretation confirmed the rightness of his choice.

However poorly he may have understood his needs, at some level Capt. B was in search of a loving, nurturing father whom he could idealize. He described his deceased partner as "the perfect father." It was the first time in his life that he had felt loved, and he described the partner's voice as "like warm chocolate syrup flowing over me." The partner was "steady and solid as a rock emotionally, could always calm him down and never retaliated when Capt. B was angry." I am confident that this is the way he experienced Shelby in that first session. In addition, his readiness to hear the sexy talk, his seeing through that defensive facade to the pain and depression, and his ability to put it together and offer hope all combined to form the necessary transference availability that this man so desperately sought.

With his interpretation and his subsequent analytic work, what Shelby *did* came to the fore; but initially I suspect it was more of a snapshot of who he was that was the determining factor. Ultimately I believe there *is* a degree of mystical—that is, difficult to document—alchemy of connection, of intuitive knowing, of mirroring, of role responsiveness (Sandler, 1976), and of transference actualization (Roughton, 1993).

There may also be a negative side to such intuitive matches. The immediate, intense sense of "fit" may be based on projected expectations, rather than on real qualities of the analyst, or it may stem from complementary needs in the dyadic pair that lead to collusive impasses (Roughton, 1994). But those only require careful assessment of the roots of intuition, not its discrediting or elimination as a mode of knowing.

I have not said anything about the question of whether a gay analyst is preferable for gay patients. For Capt. B, it certainly was a conscious factor in the consultation request and in his being able to risk talking about sex. Beyond that, I do not think it was a very important factor. It is far more important that Shelby is a sensitive, skilled, empathic clinician than that he is gay. I think what he has accomplished in the first eight months of treatment with this man would be the same, regardless of his sexual orientation.

To what extent his transference availability—especially his initial unblinking acceptance of the transference—might be influenced by his own life experiences, which include being gay, is another question that is beyond the bounds of this discussion.

Shelby has provided us with a fascinating introduction to his clinical work with a patient who presented with what might have been difficulties in engagement, given that he had been in extended therapy without ever being able to talk about his sexual life or, presumably, without being able to open up emotionally. Shelby made it look easy, and, in doing so, he raises questions about what makes for a good patient–analyst match, what constitutes intuition, and how the subtleties of communication facilitate or inhibit an engagement in the analytic process. Let us hope that he will publish this case as a completed analysis some time in the future. There will be much to learn from this analytic dyad's work together.

References

Kantrowitz, J. (1986), The role of the patient–analyst match in the outcome of psychoanalysis. *The Annual of Psychoanalysis*, 14:273–297. New York: International Universities Press.

——— (1995), The beneficial aspects of the patient–analyst match. *Internat. J. Psychoanal.*, 76:299–313.

Roughton, R. (1993), Useful aspects of acting out: Repetition, enactment, and actualization. *J. Amer. Psychoanal. Assn.*, 41:443–472.

——— (1994), Repetition and interaction in the analytic process: Enactment, acting out, and collusion. *The Annual of Psychoanalysis*, 22:271–286. Hillsdale, NJ: The Analytic Press.

Sandler, J. (1976), Countertransference and role-responsiveness. *Internat. Rev. Psycho-Anal.*, 3:43–47.

Stone, L. (1961), *The Psychoanalytic Situation: An Examination of Its Development and Essential Nature*. New York: International Universities Press.

Vaughan, S. C. & Roose, S. P. (2000), Patient–therapist match: Revelation or resistance? *J. Amer. Psychoanal. Assn.*, 48:885–900.

Discussion of R. Dennis Shelby's Clinical Case

ELISABETH YOUNG-BRUEHL

I have read R. Dennis Shelby's rich and interesting case report as both a historian of psychoanalysis and a psychoanalyst, a dual role that I especially enjoy when a case report sparks in me an association to a locus classicus in our literature. This is what happened when I read Shelby's paper, and the text that came to mind was Riviere's (1936) "A Contribution to the Analysis of the Negative Therapeutic Reaction."

This text rose into my consciousness for several reasons. First, Shelby's patient, Capt. B, is a man who has not been able, in many therapies, to get well, or even to make progress—he is a serial patient—and he makes it clear to Shelby that he does not think he can get well. Second, he is in mourning for his first lover, lost to AIDS, and presents his world, and his inner world, as a scene of devastation, a holocaust, the kind of scene Riviere invoked in her paper. Third, I suspected that Capt. B held himself responsible for a crime, the deterioration into alcoholism and madness of his mother, so that he could not get well himself until he had paid for this crime and redeemed the damaged mother as she existed in his internal world, an inner world where all the objects were, to one degree or another, damaged, deathly, blighted in the plague. She and the others have to be cured before he can be cured, the imperative Riviere studied. But it is just that redemption that feels impossible, for allowing depressive anxieties to become activated in treatment feels to this patient—as Riviere put it—like bringing about the death and disaster he fears. He fears his own suicide or madness will ensue.

Riviere's paper was, of course, one of the key ones in our literature for delineating the internal world of objects and for developing Melanie Klein's notion of the depressive position. In a famous passage, Riviere (1936) wrote:

> The content of the depressive position (as Melanie Klein has shown) is the situation in which all ones loved ones within are dead and destroyed, all goodness is dispersed, lost, in fragments, wasted and scattered to the winds; nothing is left within but utter desolation. Love brings sorrow, and sorrow brings guilt;

> the intolerable tension mounts, there is no escape, one is utterly alone, there is no one to share or help. Love must die because love is dead. Besides, there would be no one to feed one, and no one whom one could feed, and no food in the world. And more, there would still be magic power in the undying persecutors who can never be exterminated—the ghosts. Death would instantaneously ensue—and one would choose to die by one's own hand before such a position could be realized [p. 144].

Shortly before the end of the paper, Riviere reminded her readers of the perspective she was developing, of the focus she was putting on the inner world of objects (or as we would say now, of object relations):

> I hope that while I have spoken of the patient's unconscious aim of making others well and happy before himself, you will have borne in mind that the others I refer to always are the loved ones in his inner world; and these loved ones are always at the same moment the objects of all of his hatred, vindictiveness, and murderous impulses! His egoistic and self-seeking attitude corresponds accurately enough to one side of things in his unconscious mind—to the hatred, cruelty and callousness there; and it represents his fears for his own ego if the love for his objects becomes too strong. We all fear the dependence of love to some extent [p. 150].

Let me come, now, to Shelby's report. I want to note initially two silences in it. First, Shelby is silent about the conditions of the treatment.[1] Is it an analysis? It started as a once-a-week psychotherapy, then moved to twice a week after Shelby suggested greater frequency—but then what happened? Toward the end of the report, we hear of the patient "sprawled out on the couch," but was it on the couch all along? Similarly, the conditions of the previous treatments are unspecified. Capt. B is said to be a "veteran of many therapist couches." Does this mean his previous treatments (other than the couples therapy) were analyses? Why don't we know? I think it is because the negative therapeutic reaction (never called such) is frightening: Is this a patient who cannot be reached? Who, despite all his "eroticized transference" (if it is such), will not let himself be engaged, helped; who fears the dependence of love far, far too much to be analyzed?

The second silence in Shelby's report, and apparently in Capt. B's presentation of himself, is about Capt. B's childhood. There is no childhood. From the start, he flooded Shelby with his story, both the present tense story of his sexual relations with his two lovers, and his relationship story from the onset of his sexual life, which was with a cousin, at age nine. But childhood material was sparse and very slow in coming; apparently, it was under very heavy repression.

---

[1] Note from the editors: We have asked Dr. Shelby to address Dr. Young-Bruehl's questions about the conditions of treatment in the version of his paper we are publishing.

One revelation was very striking: in association to a dream, Capt. B said: "I have never told anyone this, but I played with dolls as a kid." His mother gave these dolls to him, and then ridiculed him for playing with them. This experience, so important (to my mind) for his gender identity development, is not woven into the case presentation, or, apparently, into the reconstruction of his story by his therapist. We do learn that Capt. B's mother had hoped that he would be a girl, so we can suspect that the dolls were part of her wishes for him, as was her painting of his bedroom pink. We are told of "his fear that maybe he was a woman" and that he hated any feminine behavior in himself or his partners. And there is a suggestion that his hair (blond like his mother's), which was kept—or unkempt—in a womanly way, was "perhaps . . . an interjection of some aspect of his mother's personality." But the whole topic of his gender identity is underdeveloped and unrelated to the common finding that a mother's desire for her son to be a girl typically plays a key role in so-called "gender identity disorder."

It is particularly the patient's childhood with his mother before her decline into alcoholism that is a blank. We learn that the decline began after her father died. And we can infer—although we are not told this explicitly—that the decline began soon after the patient became sexually involved at age nine with his male cousin (or was it cousins in the plural?). This, I hypothesized before, was his crime, which one can imagine made him imagine that he drove his mother away, hurt her, made her reject him further—as she had already rejected him for being a sissy, playing with dolls. The father cruelly told him "This is all your fault!" We do not hear any details about the beginning of the mother's decline in the report, however, for the report focuses, instead, on the patient's relationship with and very strong longing for his father. The mother appears only as the drunk, the parent who had to be endured, hospitalized, rescued, the parent who gave no care at all. There is no sense that she once gave care and then withdrew it.

We really do need to know more about the mother, and more about the way in which Capt. B's sense of disappointment—so palpable when it emerges in relation to his father and toward Shelby in the transference—was related to his mother. One of the further consequences of the absence in the case of the childhood and the mother is that other key dimensions of the patient's family context are missing. The second brother in the sibship, for example, makes no appearance in the beginning of the report; we hear only about the (oldest?) one who followed the paternal pattern of failing into bankruptcy, and who washed out of the flight training that Capt. B successfully completed. Later, we hear only about "his brother," which one is not clear. This sibship was split, with a gap between Capt. B and the two older boys—why? Was there a miscarriage in between? Or a period of sexual alienation? Did the mother want her third child to be a girl to replace a lost girl? We don't know, but this kind of information would be crucial for understanding the parents' attitudes toward their third and youngest child, as well as for understanding why (to use Riviere's formulation) he has to fix them before he can be fixed himself. "His inability to live in houses once he had fixed them up because they were too nice. . . . His nickname for himself, 'Pepe the burro' who takes care of everything for everyone and does it quietly."

I have noted two silences in the case, and now I want to make a second note, which follows from the first. I think that Shelby was so struck by the dramatic way the treatment opened—by the immediate revelation of so much "sexual stuff" that his patient had been unable to tell his previous therapist or any other therapist and by the immediate establishment of what he calls "an eroticized transference," which (he comes to conclude) was defensive—that the patient's childhood experiences did not seem very significant to him. He got caught up in the way Capt. B posed his problem: He has two lovers, and he cannot choose between them or understand why he is unable to move, why he is so afraid that one or both of the lovers will leave him. Shelby decides that what he is dealing with here is a split, so that the real question is: "How is it that you get disappointed and hang yourself out to dry between two men?" And he comes to view the situation as a repetition: the patient had once hung himself out to dry between his cousin (the first sexual experience), who withdrew and left him bereft, and his father, whom he bitterly despised but also wanted so much from.

To me, it does seem that the question of why there are two men is key, but not as it is formulated or pursued in Shelby's report. The patient really goes from man to man to man; that is, his love pattern is like his therapy pattern, he goes from one to the next, never leaving one until the next is in place—and even then having a period of overlap. He repeats the pattern in his avocation: He goes from one rehab project to the next, one garden building project to the next. He has great trouble leaving at all—and, in a sense, he has never left his first lover, who died so horribly of AIDS, losing half his body weight with uncontrollable diarrhea before he collapsed. Capt. B does not leave because he must take care, repair, rescue, build up his own body weight, compensate all the loved ones, who are all—starting with his mother, who also collapsed—damaged or dead people, in the manner Joan Riviere described. In the present tense, he cannot imagine himself moving on to the next lover—even though there is just offstage "a little hustler"—because he feels himself to be so damaged: he is just "a 42-year-old faggot," worthless. He's unable to go out into the gay scene because he is not big enough, not built up enough, so that whenever he meets someone who is bigger he "collapses internally." This phrase and its equivalents recur: he dies inside, he collapses, he folds up, and so forth whenever he meets a bigger man. To me, this sounds like he becomes a woman—not a powerful guy who can penetrate others but a weak woman.

Capt. B's self-disparagement is in the transference, too, of course. He disparages Shelby: "I don't give a shit about what you think." About this, Shelby comments: "I was the idealized father that he wanted to be close to and borne up by, and on the other hand, I was devalued, unimportant, of minimal consequence, and he could handle things quite ably on his own." I'd like to suggest that Shelby feels just like the patient himself—"a worthless, bad piece of shit," to use his terms, and a woman, damaged like the mother.

I wonder about viewing the transference this patient established so immediately and so forcefully as an "eroticized transference." Rather, it looks to me like the opening "I am a queer" was the first step in a negative therapeutic reaction that has continued throughout the treatment, although the treatment has also alleviated it somewhat. The sign of this alleviation was that Capt. B's eroticism in general diminished and a need for affection surfaced. At this time "[h]e related that several times a day recurrent images of his mother passed through his mind. Then he would feel horrible, get a sick feeling in his stomach and think 'Oh, it's still there, she will never go away, I will never get over it.' But at the same time he also was able to express to Shelby his gratitude that he was being heard out on the horror of his past and that he has grown "tired of sex, it was not exciting anymore, that all he wanted was to be held."

This brings me to a third comment. It is, of course, very valuable for gay patients to have gay therapists, for all the obvious reasons. The gay therapist is often able to understand and empathize with the patient's experience, lifestyle, with all the special conditions and conventions and language of the subculture, and so forth. However, it is also important to realize that the gay therapist will be the recipient in the transference of all the patient's self-hatred and the self-destructiveness surrounding that self-hatred, and the therapist will be the legatee of the homophobia the patient experienced as well (in this case, particularly the father's homophobia, but also the mother's and brother's). When the patient encounters Shelby on crutches after an injury, he disparages him, implying with his remark that Shelby has gotten injured while "getting fucked," which may very well mean that Shelby became womanized (and thus Shelby would be quite right in feeling the patient's remark as "an intrusion"). Capt. B is too nice a person to make his projected self-hatred plain, but it is there from the start. It begins when he considers Shelby to be the kind of "faggot" who can receive all his "sex stuff," who can give him enormous momentary relief by being the kind of "little shit"—like himself, he fears—who can have all this "shit" dumped on him. His description of sexual exploits is what Riviere and the Kleinians knew as "manic defense," against his terrible fear of being a worthless, depressed, crazy woman, as well as against his bleak inner world.

Reference

Riviere, J. (1936), A contribution to the analysis of the negative therapeutic reaction. In: *The Inner World of Joan Riviere: Collected Papers 1920–1958,* ed. A. Hughes. London: Karnac Books, 1991, pp. 134–154.

Yearning for Love and Cruising for Sex: Returning to Freud to Understand Some Gay Men

PAUL E. LYNCH

As a psychiatry resident, I was once told, "That's what people do in analysis: when they don't have someone, they talk about finding someone, and when they have someone, they talk about how to get along with him or her."

In my work with gay men in psychotherapy and psychoanalysis, I found that the difficulties of some gay men's finding and getting along with partners were not openly described in the psychoanalytic literature and seemed to be different in significant ways from the difficulties of other patients. I have never encountered a man who, yearning for true love, spent hours cruising a park in hopes of finding a beautiful woman who would have sex with him right then and there, without so much as exchanging names. Perhaps more men would do this if there were women who would oblige. Among the gay men in my practice, this "cruising" phenomenon is not so unusual and often is the source of great frustration, confusion, and shame. Is it to be understood as essentially different from the promiscuity in play in a single's bar, or from any other promiscuity for that matter? Can psychoanalysis help gay men who yearn for love, yet end up in a frustrating cycle of cruising for sex, or men who find love in a relationship which then loses the excitement of sex? In other words, can analysis help gay men whose conflicts interfere with their hope of finding and getting along with partners who can be known, respected, and loved, without losing the pleasure of sex?

Freud (1912) referred to the separation of love and sex, as a "Universal Tendency to Debasement in the Sphere of Love" (p. 179). He wrote about men who could perform sexually with women whom they either didn't know or didn't respect, and about men who were sexually inhibited or impotent with women, particularly their wives, whom they faced in day-to-day social situations and whose respect they needed to maintain. He stated that, other than anxiety, impotence was the primary reason for men to consult a psychoanalyst. His view was that the "madonna–whore" syndrome—impotence with a loved one while maintaining sexual prowess with debased others—is caused by a difficulty in the development of the libido, which he saw as universal.

Freud described a developmental task requiring the unification of affectionate and sensual currents into a libido that could love its sexual objects. Although Freud wrote about heterosexual patients, I hope to show that his ideas are exquisitely well suited to explain some of the difficulties in love and sex for which many homosexual men seek treatment.

For decades after Freud, the extension of his ideas to the psychic experiences of gay men was virtually lost to psychoanalysts. Lewes (1988) has chronicled the decades of effort within psychoanalysis to define homosexuality as a disease. Only in recent years have analysts commonly conceived of nonpathological homosexuality, and begun to consider psychic conflicts in gay men independent of the etiology of sexual orientation (Roughton, 2001). Traditionally, analysts began with a belief that the etiology of homosexual orientation is pathological, and then understood all difficulties that gay men experienced as secondary to this pathology. In this way, analysts not only missed an opportunity to consider the effects of the environment on development, but I believe they recapitulated the disapproving environment that forged psychic conflicts in the first place. I return to this point, and use a recent work by Bollas (1992) as an example of the tendency to envelop an understanding of behavioral phenomena in gay men into a theory of a pathological etiology of sexual orientation itself, thereby tending toward a pathological view of the behavior. First, I begin with a demonstrative vignette—one example of a homosexual madonna–whore syndrome.

A "Double Life" or Two Half Lives?

I answered my ringing phone, and an elderly man was already asking, "What does psychoanalysis do for you anyway?" As I fumbled a bit for an answer, he pushed on to tell me a few things. "First of all, I am, and always have been, homosexual." His wife, who had seen my name in a gay newspaper, was insisting that he make an appointment to talk to me because he had made a friend in an adult movie theater. "I think I might be falling in love, if that's what it is."

My new patient had more than 70 years of life experience to discuss with me. In our early sessions, he focused on his history of sexual activities and relationships. In his college years and early adult life, sexual activity was almost entirely limited to trips to New York City, where he would engage in anonymous sex with men in bathhouses. Men were always the object of his desire in dreams, fantasies, and conscious attractions, yet he vigilantly avoided being in the presence of any man in his social sphere whom he suspected could be homosexual. He was terribly judgmental toward such people, and feared that others might associate him with them.

As he approached forty in the 1960s, he sought the help of a psychologist due to his concern that bachelorhood was becoming a social liability at his advancing age. Within a year of starting psychoanalytically oriented psychotherapy, he had met and married a woman. Prior to marriage, he told her of his therapy for homosexual inclinations, and she was not dissuaded. He remained in therapy for three years, but the topic of homosexuality never came up again, as he and the therapist considered him "cured." The therapy focused on how to get along with his contentious wife. Sexual relations with his wife were perfunctory and lacking altogether in passion or intimacy. When the therapy ended, this gentleman returned to anonymous homosexual contacts on a regular basis. Not able to leave his wife and small children for trips to New York, he discovered parks, public rest areas, and other public places where men would meet for quick, anonymous sexual contact. The next decades proceeded with success in his career, the growth of his family, and very regular anonymous sexual activity. He found these encounters with unfamiliar men to be exciting and pleasurable on the one hand, and believed them to be absolutely forbidden and wrong on the other. He rarely conversed with his sexual contacts and dreaded seeing any of them out and about town.

One day in the early 1990s, a man in an adult theater slipped him a hotel phone number. My patient surprised himself by calling the number. They met a few times under assumed names "just to have sex," and gradually they revealed bits of their true identities. Before long they had a steady, albeit untraditional, relationship. Sex with this man was exceptionally pleasurable, and he looked forward to their meetings. He thought more and more about his new friend, took an interest in his friend's hobbies, and hesitantly acknowledged that he had feelings for him. As he put it, for the first time in his life, now in his seventies, he was enjoying sex with someone he cared about. "Could I be falling in love?" he asked, "and what can talking to you do for me?"

Can One Desire Where One Loves?

I use the term "homosexual" to indicate a stable same-sex orientation, and "gay" to include a self-defined identity associated with homosexuality. When I speak of a homosexual or a heterosexual man, I refer to a man whose sexual fantasies, dreams, and attractions have been steadily focused on other males from childhood. I do not speak about the full range of bisexuality, or about men in whom there is significant uncertainty about their sexual orientation. I am not speaking about women because I have more experience treating gay men than lesbians, and it seems to me that the behavioral phenomena I am addressing are more common in men than in women, regardless of their sexual orientation.

Many gay patients come into treatment today without doubt about their basic sexual orientation, and wanting help with the difficulties they experience in life.

This is clearly more common as social and legal oppression of homosexuality has waned in the past three decades. As indicated earlier, I think that some types of psychic conflict may be more common in gay patients, or at least have intrapsychic constellations that are characteristic of a homosexual's social context. For example, heterosexuals may seek help due to frustrations in establishing and maintaining a satisfying intimate relationship, or due to unwanted sexual behaviors, but these types of problems certainly form in a different social context for the homosexual, given our society's different set of standards for homosexual behavior.

Freud's 1912 ideas about difficulties with integration of the affectionate and the sensual are useful across social contexts and aid our understanding of the influence of the environment on psychic development. His ideas regarding "frustration in reality"—the environment's limitations on the youth's sexual expression—direct our attention to an aspect of psychosexual development evident in adolescence. This reminds us that the neurotic conflicts of adulthood are not fixed by the time of adolescence, and that they continue to accrue form and meaning as they are reworked over and over in new contexts. Freud's theories on our subject involve the environment and (what we understand as) early object relationships in the development of psychic conflicts. His particular idea, which I apply to the psychosexual development of gay men, is that when the environment withholds approval of an individual's sensual desires, the mind finds a way to maintain a separation between love and sex.

Of course Freud (1912) understood the development of the libido in terms of drives, and in his essay on debasement, he discusses the effect of the social context during adolescent development on the evolving expression of the drives. The affectionate current of the libido, which was present early in childhood, was "formed on the basis of the interest of the self-preservative instinct and is directed to the members of the family and those who look after the child" (p. 180). At puberty, Freud states, affectionate fixations are joined by the sensual current, "which no longer mistakes its aims" (p. 181). The barrier against incest must then force the libido away from forbidden incestuous objects, toward socially sanctioned objects outside the family, objects "with which a real sexual life may be carried on" (p. 181). Freud adds that in the course of time the new sexual objects will attract to themselves the affection that was tied to the earlier ones, "affection and sensuality are then united" (p. 181).

Freud went on to describe what could get in the way of the unification of the affectionate and sensual currents:

> Two factors will decide whether this advance in the developmental path of the libido is to fail. First, there is the amount of *frustration in reality* which opposes the new object-choice and reduces its value for the person concerned. There is after all no point in embarking upon an object-choice if no choice is to be allowed at all or if there is no prospect of being able to choose anything suitable. Secondly, there is the amount of *attraction* which the infantile objects

> that have to be relinquished are able to exercise, and which is in proportion to the erotic cathexis attaching to them in childhood [pp. 181–182].

Where there is sufficient "frustration in reality" or opposition to the choice of sexual objects, Freud describes that the sensual current is forced to avoid the affectionate current (reserved for familiar objects). In order for the sensual to find some partial outlet into reality, it is forced to seek new objects that do not recall the forbidden objects.

As Freud puts it:

> The whole sphere of love in such people remains divided in the two directions personified in art as sacred and profane (or animal) love. Where they love they do not desire and where they desire they cannot love. They seek objects which they do not need to love, in order to keep their sensuality away from the objects they love [p. 183].

Impotence and inhibition appear when an object inconspicuously recalls the prohibited object. Thus, becoming too familiar runs the risk of inhibiting sensual interest. According to Freud, the main protective measure for men against such an inhibition is the *debasement* of the sexual object. Familiar objects of affection (representatives of incestuous objects) are *overvalued*, and therefore do not arouse the forbidden sensual current. Sexual potency is enjoyed with the "whore" objects, whereas pure love is reserved for the "Madonna" objects.

Isay (1989) described a type of distant interaction between fathers and homosexually inclined boys, based on the fathers' reaction to their perception of difference in their children. Even without such perception of difference, which I agree is likely to be present, heterosexual parents and our heterosexually oriented culture generally flood children with the message that normal boys fall in love with girls. Having regularly received this message as a basic fact of life, the adolescent boy has a daunting task if he is to reconcile yearnings for boys and men with his wish to be loved and respected by his family and community.

It is easy to see, even in the age of gay television characters on shows such as *Will & Grace,* that most families do not envision the possibility of same-sex relationships for their offspring. They do not romanticize same-sex "oedipal" yearnings in the way that they do heterosexual ones (e.g., "Daddy's little girl"). Pointing out this difference, Goldsmith (2001) notes that the oedipal drama of the homosexual boy does not enjoy the clearly marked arenas in which it can move from the realm of inner conflict to safe enactment. Not only does the father not participate in a romanticized same-sex relationship, but may unwittingly act competitively. In addition, "and perhaps [the] central point [of Goldsmith's paper], is that the homosexual boy has competitive and aggressive feelings toward a mother who may unwittingly but quite reasonably be anticipating a 'childhood romance' with her son" (p. 1275). It may be in these dissonant oedipal experiences, as elaborated by Isay and Goldsmith, that gay men first learn that they are different and that these differences are shameful.

As an example of what Freud (1912) refers to as "extra frustration in reality," (p. 181) the social environment of the homosexual adolescent likewise fails to recognize, or opposes, all objects to which his youthful homosexual libido is attracted. Considering the social context, not only current satisfaction is prohibited, but also dreams of future satisfaction are forbidden and ridiculed. In order to skirt the practically absolute prohibition, same-sex objects must be maintained at a distance—sometimes existing only in fantasy, and sometimes, as in my 70-year-old patient, existing only in a sphere apart from the individual's social life. For some, the prohibition itself becomes eroticized, adding excitement to the thrill of the cruise.

Referring to the animal nature of all genital sexuality, "and thus love, too," Freud (1912) states:

> The instincts of love are hard to educate; education of them achieves now too much, now too little. What civilization aims at making out of them seems unattainable except at the price of a sensible loss of pleasure . . . we may perhaps be forced to become reconciled to the idea that it is quite impossible to adjust the claims of the sexual instinct to the demands of civilization [pp. 189–190].

I began this discussion with the story of a man who has experienced a profound "loss of pleasure" resulting from the psychic compromise that appeases his lifelong sensual longings and his forbidding environment. For him, it is more than a matter of sociological interest that he was born in 1920s America, into a family environment that did not fathom healthy and happy homosexual relationships, and therefore could not sanction the possibility of such as this for their boy. Homosexual attractions are among his earliest memories, and the psychic compromises he made to satisfy both his sensual longings and the demands of his environment are deeply embedded. In an adult theater, the sensual components of this man's libido are given free range, unencumbered by his fuller identity and social persona. Conversely, in the high standing of his position in society, he allows no taint of base sexuality. Barriers exist against awareness of desire for people he loves and cannot afford to lose the respect of, and against knowing too well the objects of his desire. Shame presents itself when either world encroaches upon the other.

The compromise formations that individuals develop to cope with the shame of unsanctioned longings result in an array of behavioral phenomena, surely as varied in homosexuals as in heterosexuals. From the hopeless romantic who cannot act on any sexual wishes, to the compulsive cruiser who cannot spend a peaceful moment without sexual excitement and activity, shame appears to play a great role in the private explanations that propel these truncated experiences.

The social context is relevant, as Freud recognized, to the development of the particular psychic dynamics that will eventually negotiate between the demands of sensual pleasure and the limits set by the environment.

I offer a composite clinical example involving the psychic separation of affection and sensuality. I hope to illustrate the clinically relevant role of shame as a barrier between affection and sensuality, and that awareness of such shame can lead to deeper understanding of the unique aspects of each individual's dynamic constellation. The oedipal dynamics are important here, and it may be fairly said that what I am addressing are some aspects of an oedipal situation in a homosexual man. Sensitivity to the particularly shaming atmosphere in which the homosexual man's "oedipal" dynamics develop may allow for a more comfortable and honest exploration of those dynamics. Of course, one expects that such an exploration may lead to a fuller range of functioning in love and sex. As I discuss later, I propose that my use of Freud's ideas to understand the patient's disconnected attempts to enjoy both affection and sensuality is more neutral to the patient's conflict than are psychoanalytic approaches which link all conflicts of homosexual love and sex to a pathological etiology of homosexuality.

Excitement and Shame in a Toilet Stall

Brian was born in 1964, five years before the Stonewall Riots that mark the beginning of the gay liberation movement in America. Like the patient discussed earlier, he was aware of homosexual attractions as far back as he can recall, and he grew up believing that he was "wrong," "sinful," and "sick" to have such feelings. However, by the time he sought treatment with me at 30 years of age, he was a self-identified gay man. He lived in the heart of the city's gay community, where he volunteered his time to an AIDS service organization and participated in gay political activities. He had good relations with his moderately religious, Protestant family. After his parents adjusted to Brian's disclosure of his homosexuality, they got involved with the social and political organization Parents, Families and Friends of Lesbians and Gays (PFLAG), and his father later became president of a chapter in their small town. Brian knew that his good looks and winning personality had afforded him many advantages, and among his many acquaintances he counted several good friends. He entered treatment with concern that he could not maintain a long-term relationship, having ended several relationships with men he considered to have been "good relationship material."

The pattern that Brian saw disturbed him. The relationships had developed at a mutually comfortable pace, such that he enjoyed the growing interdependence, the identification as a couple, and the deepening intimacy, but subsequently experienced an inexplicable decrease in sexual desire for his partner. His libido was not decreased overall, and it troubled him that he felt greater sexual interest in men he had never met than he felt for his partner. He felt frustrated in his wish to maintain a relationship with one man who would be his best friend, loving partner, and sexual playmate. He considered at least two of his former boyfriends to be close to his image of "Mr. Right," and therefore felt that there had to be something wrong with him for being unable to maintain sexual interest as they grew closer in other ways.

This patient had requested referral to a gay psychiatrist, and began treatment with me emphasizing his sense of frustration for not succeeding in a relationship. He and his boyfriends had the looks, the talents, the intelligence, and the kindness, caring, and other virtues that he felt should have easily allowed them to live happily ever after. In sessions, he was relatively quiet about his sexual feelings and fantasies, often defensive, and whenever he would get a bit unsettled he would return to the themes of his pride in being gay and his frustration that he could not keep up his part in what were otherwise good relationships. Analysis of punitive, unconscious self-criticism as described by Kris (1990) allowed Brian to see that he was in fact harder on himself than he realized, and that some of his pride and frustration belied a deep sense of shame.

In time, Brian began to discuss with great embarrassment his sexual feelings for strangers, and an incident occurred that plagued him as particularly inexplicable. He was driving to visit his parents with Tom, a man with whom he'd been living for one year. In the toilet stall of a highway rest area, he noticed that an older man in the next stall was spying on him through a peep hole in the divider. He was filled with nervous excitement as he looked back to see the other man's erect penis. Brian lifted his T-shirt to show more of his well-muscled body, and although nervous, he masturbated to a fast orgasm. He returned quickly to the car, frightened and ashamed, confused about what he had done. He could not understand why the sight of a physically unappealing man in that unappealing place had aroused him so intensely and so quickly. He was irritable with Tom and with his parents throughout the visit.

Brian had heard about men having sex in public bathrooms, but it had not been, and did not become, a regular occurrence for him. For a long time, he attributed his discomfort during the visit with his parents to his shock and mortification over this incident. He remained confused about what he had felt, and feared that others would learn how sick and disgusting he was. He was sure that I would be repulsed by him, and think of him as a "disgusting pig" or a "sexual animal." In time, as Brian became less defensive with me, he became more aware of pervasive feelings of shame. Little by little he realized that shame was associated with many and various routine incidents and daily activities, and that it persistently colored the way he felt in relation to me. Some aspects of routine incidents reminded him of the incident in the rest room, and as he elaborated the shame and humiliation he felt, he remembered more and more details of that strange day.

Most surprising to Brian was the realization that on that visit home he had been struggling with shameful feelings prior to the stop in the rest area. He had believed that it was a "wonderful opportunity" to bring Tom home for the holiday, and was confident that they'd be welcomed by his parents who had by this time declared their acceptance of his homosexuality. The townspeople knew that he was gay through his father's public promotion of a PFLAG event. Yet, as he recalled some of his daydreams from the car ride prior to the rest stop, he saw that he had in fact been anxious about the visit. He had fantasized about how he would introduce Tom around town. "This is my spouse" or "this is my significant other" didn't sound very warm or human. "Boyfriend" didn't show that they are more than that, and a "partner" could be in business with him. To say "my husband" as he often did with friends in the city, would confuse their elderly neighbor who would automatically link the term "husband" with "wife." "Lover" would make him blush. Although he hadn't made much of it on that day, he later recalled his anxiety that people would look at him and Tom together and think sexual thoughts, perhaps wonder graphically about their bodies and what they did with them in sex. He felt humiliated just imagining what they'd think, how they'd be disgusted, or how they would laugh at such thoughts. He had wondered what name could do justice in describing his relationship with Tom, without calling attention to sex.

Also, one of his father's comments had lingered on his mind during the drive. He'd said that he and Mother had assigned Brian and Tom to stay in a particular guest room, one that had a double bed. Initially this had pleased him as a sign that his parents were making another conscious effort to accept him and his homosexuality. But as they drove, he thought of the house, the bed, and Tom in the bed with him. Tom would snuggle up close, expecting affection in return. Brian had felt that he should appreciate his parents' openness, and enjoy and reciprocate Tom's affection. Once again, he felt this was a wonderful opportunity and that he could not have felt anything negative due to such a situation. He could not account for his irritability, where he had expected joy.

Brian was proud of his parents' attempt to welcome him and his partner, and it was some time before he allowed for the repulsion he'd felt on thinking about Tom snuggling up to him in that bed in his parents' house. He remembered that as accepting as his parents were of his homosexuality by community standards, he had not always expected that they would be. He recalled times from his school days when he had feverishly masturbated and fantasized about handsome older boys, followed by fear that they would ridicule and hate him if they knew what he was doing. He had believed that he was not normal, and that his parents would be horrified if they knew his thoughts about men and other boys. He had felt fortunate to be popular with girls because he knew that it made his attraction to boys less obvious. His parents had expected him to date girls, and he knew that it had pleased them when he did. This had brought some relief. He hadn't escaped, however, the feeling that what he really desired was shameful and forbidden.

The more Brian became intimate with his partners, the more his sexual relations with them deteriorated. In his everyday life, he tried to be open about his sexual orientation, but in treatment we discovered that he experienced a great deal of punitive unconscious self-criticism related to it. In this regard I would include what many have referred to as "internalized homophobia"—an unconscious (and, in some, also conscious) hatred of himself for being homosexual. Brian's shame inhibited sensual pleasure when his objects recalled too closely the desired objects forbidden in his youth (Tom in the bed in his parents' house, recalling his adolescent fantasies and feelings of humiliation), and he experienced a greater degree of sexual excitement when sensuality was temporarily unleashed from such familiarity and punitive unconscious self-criticism (the stranger seeking sexual thrills in the public toilet).

With the "strange man" in the toilet, Brian experienced an intense release of feelings that he usually kept deeply repressed—sexual excitement from looking at the older man's erect penis, and added exhilaration from showing off and masturbating for his appreciative audience. In those brief moments, he acted out his adolescent fantasies of looking at his father and the boys at school, and of being seen, admired, and desired by them, too. In a mix of projection and identification with the old voyeur in the next stall, he became an active phallic sensualist, as well as a passive desired object. In addition, he elaborated on his experience of himself as a passive phallic sensualist (showing his erect phallus and masturbatory activity "on request") and an active desired object (using his erect penis and masculine physique to actively elicit the desire of the other). Active, passive, looking, being seen, wanting, being wanted, being wanted while being overtly sexual—all pushed forth in a rush of sexual tension and sexual release in the protective debasement of the toilet stall walls. Of course, this all gave way to guilt, shame, and humiliation (punitive unconscious self-criticism), as he returned to the interpersonal world of Tom and his parents.

Cruising for a Sexual Self, or Annihilation?

My experience, confirmed by Lewes's (1988) scholarly review, is that once we move beyond attempts to define homosexual orientation as pathological, the psychoanalytic literature offers sparse commentary on the complaints and conflicts that are particular to, or more common among, our gay patients. However, one recent contribution directly takes up the topic of compulsive anonymous sex, or cruising. Bollas (1992) considers the dynamic underpinnings of homosexual men's anonymous sexual encounters in his chapter "Cruising in the Homosexual Arena" (pp. 144–164). This contribution stands out as a creative exploration of a type of experience of particular concern to gay patients, yet

I believe it still falls into the old trap of conflating a conflict in a homosexual with a pathological etiology of homosexual orientation.

Bollas's theory of the homosexual cruiser's experience is similar to the one that I derive from Freud in that there is "an erasure of self." Bollas (1992) describes a total erasure of self, directly retraceable to an experience in which the mother uses the boy as an object in her internal world. In his terms, the mother annihilates the boy's self by using him as her "it." Although he warns against "any effort to constitute an encompassing theory of homosexuality" (p. 152), he persists in focusing on mother's annihilatory role in the life of homosexuals, and particularly in the homosexual cruiser's "it-to-it" erotics. For Bollas, the erasure of self in the cruising arena is a reliving of mother's annihilation of the child's self.

Bollas (1992) tells us about a patient, Bruce, who has suffered traumatic experiences wherein his mother "gained a leisured obsessive pleasure in dressing him in feminine clothing, [and] took him for long exhibitionistic walks to display her son" (p. 152). Certainly such traumatic experiences caused problems in Bruce's experience of himself as a true self, but it does not necessarily follow, as implied, that his mother's objectification made him homosexual. Why didn't Bruce choose women as the replacements for his mother in her annihilatory role, and, conversely, how did so many other gay men become homosexual without engulfing, annihilating mothers?

In my experience of treating many gay men, I have not found extensive maternal annihilation to be among their common experience. I also cannot agree with Bollas's (1992) claim that homosexual patients have an "overwhelmingly consistent preoccupation with the mother." Even as he acknowledges that not all mothers of homosexuals are domineering, he continues to speak of the type of parents who have been traditionally thought to cause homosexuality. "Yet other homosexuals' mothers seem quite different, objects of preoccupation because they seem to offer reliable refuge from an otherwise anxiety-provoking world, often supplying love and affection unavailable from a distant or remote father" (p. 151). So Bollas warns us against an encompassing theory, yet stays close to long held myths. If mother is not always overwhelmingly domineering, she remains consistently an object of preoccupation, and father remains distant.

The focus of Bollas's chapter (1992) is promiscuous cruisers, with particular emphasis on characters of early gay literary fiction—characters who, like the authors who created them, grew up without benefit of the gay liberation movement. He explores a world of desperately lonely souls. The patient and the characters that Bollas presents surely did have little hope in their early lives of integrating their own desires with those of their environment. Rather than experiences of sexuality that are compartmentalized or detached from familiar identifications, Bollas sees the anonymous encounters more often as annihilation of self, and deadness. With Freud's (1912) idea of debasement and my clinical experience in mind, I would see it not usually as a total erasure of self, but more often as a partial erasure—an erasure of one's social self, in order to give lively expression to one's prohibited sexual self.

The anguish and pain resulting from sexual activity in the cruising arena need not necessarily be a total annihilation. It is true that intense cruising can warrant a diagnosis of obsessive compulsive disorder, and self-esteem suffers when whole hours and days are lost and regretted. Yet for some men cruising can bring to awareness the disconnection and lack of recognition they have experienced in the rest of their lives. It can even be a restorative process: a playing out of desired object connections that have not been achieved in reality, or a joining in the arena with others who have had similar experiences. In this way, cruising and anonymous sex can be enlivening for some sexually repressed gay men. On this point, Bollas and I seem to agree.

Where we differ is on the relative frequency and importance of the pathologically engulfing mother in the genesis of self-erasure in sexuality. Bollas's theory of the psychic dynamics that drive anonymous sex follows from traditional theories about the etiology of homosexuality, and I suggest that his otherwise rich contribution is thereby skewed. If the origin of homosexuality is pathological, then naturally the homosexual behavior that follows is sick, too.

Yet, in line with my reading of Freud's emphasis on the role of environmental influence on the psyche, or in Freud's words, the amount of "frustration in reality," Bollas quotes Michel Foucault (1982):

> Homosexuals were not allowed to elaborate a system of courtship because the cultural expression necessary for such an elaboration was denied them—the wink on the street, the split-second decision to get it on, the speed with which homosexual relations are consummated: all these are products of an interdiction [p. 160].

As I stated, I don't see the experience of extreme maternal engulfment commonly or consistently in gay patients. Their experience of interdiction, on the other hand, is essentially ubiquitous. Mothers obviously do play an early and important role, but fathers, siblings, teachers, and peers participate also.

Bollas (1992) describes very nicely the participation of "the heterosexual" in the objectification of "the homosexual" (an experience for which annihilatory maternal objectification is not a prerequisite). So why put the entire burden of early objectification on the mother, and only see the role of heterosexual culture in adulthood? Lacking evidence that mothers of gay men are likely to be more engulfing than any other mothers, I would recognize that mothers, too, are vulnerable to the heterosexual saturation of the world in which they live. For the average mother, the ability to fully appreciate her homosexual son's inner experience has been limited by her own immersion in a heterosexist world. Without engulfing her son to the point of annihilation, the average mother in our society would likely miss those aspects of her son's experience for which she has limited awareness. In particular, she would have a greater propensity for blind spots for repressed areas of sexuality—sexuality that her upbringing has rendered undesirable and often even unthinkable.

All the gay men I have treated had a sense early in life that they had longings for men or other boys that should not be revealed, and of which they were deeply ashamed. As discussed earlier, the roots of these feelings of shame may be in the failure to engage the parents in the boy's particular oedipal drama, or in the failure to be recognized and appreciated for his true oedipal desires. Whether parents recognize and actively oppose the boy's same-sex oedipal strivings, or they simply fail to appreciate them and unwittingly shame him, they may still recognize and value other aspects of an independent other in their child, such that his self need not be entirely obliterated.

I suggest that Bollas (1992) unwittingly participated in a bit of psychoanalytic objectification of "the homosexual patient." Like the well-intended mother, Bollas does a commendable job of understanding the independent experience of his patient. Yet in my reading of his chapter, like the mother who has culturally overdetermined blind spots, he is a bit hamstrung by the limitations of his traditional theory, which precedes and colors his exploration of cruising behavior. The patient is used to some extent as an object in a world of psychoanalytic tradition and theory.

Necessary Etiological Understanding or Insidious Shaming?

It seems to me that the biased and cumbersome encompassing of the etiology of homosexuality unnecessarily burdens psychoanalytic exploration of the experiences of gay men and women. This self-imposed burden has stilted psychoanalytic understanding, causing even contemporary theorists such as Bollas to view conflicts in homosexual patients through the prism of their theories of the etiology of sexual orientation. If psychoanalytic inquiries can be freed to explore dynamic conflicts in homosexuals without burden of incorporating the etiology of sexual orientation, then I maintain we will be in a better position to hear our gay patients' experiences with something closer to that ever-elusive psychoanalytic neutrality. Perhaps what makes it difficult is the unfamiliar ground the analyst is on when asked to maintain a homosexual outcome as possibly normal. As Roughton (1997) points out in a discussion on neutrality, "The unfamiliar stance of simply accepting the patient's homosexuality as normal for him may make it appear to skeptics that the analyst is encouraging the homosexuality" (p. 298).

Attempts to explain the cause of homosexual orientation are generally based on an assumption of pathology, and this assumption can be insidiously conveyed in the treatment by the most well-meaning analyst who does not have the capacity to envision a satisfactory homosexual object choice that is not pathological. In this case, the analytic experience is not neutral at all, but stilted in the same way that the early social environment was—with the implicit message that there is something wrong with the patient's object choices. In this re-creation of the disapproving or unempathic early environment, the analyst unwittingly exacerbates the shame that the patient feels over unsanctioned or unappreciated sensuality.

To approach a homosexual patient's experiences with neutrality, I maintain that the analyst must not only be neutral to the individual conflicts, but also first must be capable of accepting without prejudice the sex and gender of the patient's sexual objects. Like mothers and fathers, all well-meaning analysts grew up saturated in a heterosexist environment, and most trained in a psychoanalytic environment that theorized the heterosexist cultural norms to be scientific truths. Some of the leaders in that quest, such as Socarides (1995), remain dedicated beyond reason in their attempts to define homosexuality as a disease. It is the analyst's job, therefore, to turn his analytic tool on the cultural and theoretical messages with which he has been inundated, in order to expose the limiting influences of his own prejudices. Only then will the analyst be in a position to explore individual conflicts without marked antihomosexual bias.

It is my hope that exposure and appreciation of prevalent antihomosexual bias, including attachments to unfounded traditional theories, will make psychoanalysis a safer, more "neutral" forum for the exploration of conflicts in gay men and women. In the examples used in this essay, the analyst would then be prepared to explore with the gay patient the full range of loving and sexual experiences, allowing for greater possibility of their coexistence and integration.

Summary

Freud's ideas about how the environment's opposition to a youth's sexual objects results in a barrier between sex and love are useful for understanding some of the difficulties in sex and love for gay men, who almost always grow up in an environment that opposes their sexual objects. There is a wide range of experiences and behaviors in which sensuality and affection remain divorced from one another in varying degrees, and analysis of shame and self-criticism often links current experience with earlier shame and humiliation associated with sexual attractions in a forbidding or unempathic environment.

Psychoanalytic theories that require a pathological etiology of homosexuality, and analysts who are unable to envision a nonpathological homosexual object, re-create the unempathic early environment, thereby exacerbating the shame that separates affection and sexuality. When there is true neutrality to sexual orientation, then shame may be analyzed and the barrier between sensuality and affection may be lessened, allowing for a greater degree of integration of love and sex.

References

Bollas, C. (1992), *Being a Character: Psychoanalysis and Self-Experience.* New York: Hill & Wang.

Foucault, M. (1982), Sexual choice, sexual act: An interview with Michel Foucault. *Salmagundi,* 58/59:10–24.

Freud, S. (1912), On the universal tendency to debasement in the sphere of love (Contributions to the psychology of love: II). *Standard Edition,* 11:177–190. London: Hogarth Press, 1957.

Goldsmith, S. (2001), Oedipus or Orestes? Homosexual men, their mothers, and other women revisited. *J. Amer. Psychoanal. Assn.,* 49:1269–1287.

Isay, R. (1989), *Being Homosexual: Gay Men and Their Development.* New York: Farrar, Straus & Giroux.

Kris, A. O. (1990), Helping patients by analyzing self-criticism. *J. Amer. Psychoanal. Assn.,* 38:605–636.

Lewes, K. (1988), *The Psychoanalytic Theory of Male Homosexuality.* New York: Simon & Schuster.

Roughton, R. (1997), Review of *Becoming Gay: A Journey to Self-Acceptance* by R. A. Isay. *J. Amer. Psychoanal. Assn.,* 45:293–298.

——— (2001), Rethinking homosexuality: What it teaches us about psychoanalysis. Plenary address, American Psychoanalytic Association meeting, New Orleans, Louisiana, May.

Socarides, C. (1995), *Homosexuality: A Freedom Too Far.* Phoenix, AZ: Adam Margave Books.

About Cruising and Being Cruised

R. DENNIS SHELBY

Efforts to explain the phenomenon of cruising have periodically appeared in the psychoanalytic literature. To date, authors have offered rather oblique yet fantastic accounts of what they consider cruising to be, rather than defining the phenomenon, as is if we all knew exactly what it is. Narrow, dramatic, if not pornographic descriptions result: men seeking out sexual encounters with other men in public areas such as the street, restrooms, or parks. As a consequence, analytic authors have approached cruising as an activity unique to men seeking sex with other men. It has been approached in libidinal dynamic terms and is often seen as a repetition compulsion and a retreat from Oedipus, accompanied by elaborate dramatic dynamic formulations as evidence. The phenomenon has been viewed as an acting out of some sort of unconscious dynamics and/or a replay of a traumatic event from childhood (Calef and Weinshell, 1984; Willick, 1988; Bollas, 1992). With the exception of Goldberg (1995), who offers a more complex interplay that includes selfobject dynamics, self-structure, and disavowed affects, self psychology has yet to adequately contribute to this much misunderstood area of human behavior. What I focus on in this paper is the *clinical utility* of cruising when the patient brings this activity into the treatment relationship.

The title of this paper may have a familiar ring because it was indeed inspired by Anna Freud's (1967) paper, "About Losing and Being Lost." In her paper, she examined the range of losing objects, from identification with the lost object, to losing people, to being temporarily lost, and, finally, to being chronically lost and wandering. The central themes are the libidinal bond that keeps our objects in our possession, the dynamic unconscious factors that result in losing, and the observation that losing tends to be the exception rather than the rule. Central to this paper, she posited that children who get lost are neglected children, and that it is at a point of distraction or disruption in maternal vigilance that the child finds himself or herself lost and alone. From a clinical standpoint, she asserted that when a patient reports losing a physical object during an analysis, it offers us access to deeper layers of the unconscious via the psychic object to which it is associated.

Let us explore the phenomenon of cruising with the idea that the self can become destabilized, the person on some deeper level feels lost, and manifestly feels an acute need to connect with another person. In this view, cruising is a form of searching and hoping/needing to be found. In working with the idea of neglect, we can posit that a lack of responsiveness to selfobject needs is a form of neglect. Indeed, we often encounter patients whose development was marked by parental pathology that prevented wide sectors of the self from being acknowledged and responded to, or parents who, for whatever reasons, were not idealizable, available for idealizing functions, or able to respond to mirroring needs. In the course of treatment with men who cruise, either impulsively or compulsively, we often encounter wide-ranging deficits born of a lack of vigilance and responsiveness if not outright assault.

I want to emphasize that I am talking about seeking out sexual partners in a frantic, impulsive, or compulsive manner, not what Cohler (1998, personal communication) has referred to as "partner seeking" which reflects a smooth functioning self, striving for enlivening connections in a process that is accompanied by a reasonable degree of anxiety and anticipation. Nor am I equating all sexual activity with distress. Rather, this paper explores the motivations, dynamics, and self needs of partner seeking that has a desperate, "emergency measure" feel to it or what a patient referred to as a "sex tantrum."

Cruising is a wide-ranging phenomenon—from looking at pornography, or passersby, or performers that stimulate a private sexual reverie, to longing for an admiring response from someone, to an intense desire for a sexual encounter. Clearly there is a difference between entertaining a private reverie and an acute need for sexual contact. Kohut (1971) posited that the central difference between a self that was content with a private sexual fantasy and a self that needed to act it out was structural in nature. The need to enact a sexual fantasy indicated the presence of a vertical split. Goldberg (1995) states that the crucial distinction between intrapsychic dynamics and selfobject dynamics is that the latter includes the concept of self-structure. Pertaining to sexuality, Tolpin (1982) discusses the danger of misunderstanding the self's motivations: "Manifestations of the self falling apart, or defensive measures used to prevent it falling apart, are seen as fixations or regressions to archaic wishes and their objects" (p. 174).

In order to analytically understand the phenomenon of cruising at the deepest levels of individual patients' minds, we must deemphasize sex, and emphasize a self that is either temporarily or chronically unstable and acutely vulnerable. We need to emphasize what *the self is searching for* rather than the sexual object and the orgasm that tend to signal the temporary end of the search. In this context, libidinal dynamic thinking does not adequately account for some forms of cruising. We must include the idea of selfobject needs and self-structure for a more complete analytic understanding.

Case 1

Mr. A presented for treatment describing himself as "a recovering alcoholic, bisexual and HIV positive." He presented a history of drinking to acute intoxication that increased dramatically during and after his first marriage to an ambivalent and chaotic woman. After his marriage dissolved, he discovered adult bookstores and began visiting them frequently while intoxicated, and eventually he contracted HIV. When he entered treatment, Mr. A was very involved with a woman he met at an HIV support group. He was dedicated to his daughter by his first marriage, visiting her at least once a month, which required a six-hour drive to a remote rural area. He related that he had had my number for three years, having obtained it from the outpatient alcohol program that he used to achieve sobriety. The precipitant for entering treatment was somewhat vague, but appeared to be that the woman he was dating realized that he was still cruising bookstores, which resulted in an upheaval in the relationship.

Mr. A tended to be politely compliant and eager to explore the complexities of his current situation: the ongoing injury and uncertainty of being HIV positive, his desire for sex with men, his desire for a relationship with a woman, and his devotion to his daughter and fear of not seeing her grow to adulthood. At the same time, he appeared "cut off" from his feeling states. A sturdy, robustly masculine man sat across from me. He was very compliant and eager to please. He seemed quite calm and reflective, yet reported a chaotic history. He was now on the corporate fast track, very involved with women, yet periodically drawn to men.

As I gradually got to know Mr. A, a distinct pattern emerged with his cruising. He tended to visit the bookstores on Sunday evenings after a less than fulfilling weekend with the woman he was involved with (she sounded very depressed and inhibited), and always on the way back from visiting his daughter and parents. As soon as he left the small rural town for the six-hour drive back he would begin fantasizing about the many bookstores along his route home, often visiting each one until he found the kind of man he was looking for: an older, hopefully kind and gentle man, with whom Mr. A would engage in passive anal intercourse.

This raised the question of what was so upsetting at his parents' home that he used the bookstores and cruising to hold himself together on the long drive back to Chicago. In exploring this issue with Mr. A, it became clear that he was aware to some degree that his self state changed dramatically after leaving his daughter and his parents' home. One weekend he met a friend upon his return to the city who told him that he looked and acted "spooky," that there was something different and unsettling about him that she had never encountered before. This enabled Mr. A to reflect on this change in himself. He began to relate the depth of his rage and disgust with his father. His father was retired and spent his days and evenings in a drunken stupor, focusing on the television while ignoring his family, periodically flying into paranoid ranting about the government or whatever sent him into a rage at the moment.

As the treatment relationship deepened, an enactment of a sort began to happen between us. At the end of every session, Mr. A would turn his head and look back as he walked down the hall. I was not sure what this meant, but I made sure I was there and visible for him as he left. Associations I had to this were of a latency age boy at a Little League game, checking in with a parent before he stepped up to bat, or a toddler checking back before venturing further away from a reassuring presence. Eventually this was understood more fully when he offered, "You know, I was never able to look at my father. I still can barely manage to look at him to this day."

Several months later his mother was diagnosed with cancer. Shortly after the diagnosis, his parents came to visit him. Mr. A was rehabbing a house and was very anxious about them seeing his home in a half-finished state. The following session he quietly, without much affect, reported that the visit went well and that his mother was quite admiring and excited about his ideas for the project. Mr. A casually mentioned that he had also taken his parents to visit his office. He then reported the following dream. "I was looking out my office window and a tornado was coming. People were screaming, debris was flying. I was paralyzed. It crashed through the window and shattered my office." His associations were to his mother's diagnosis and his fear of losing her, his father's pathetic state, and the prospects of being left with such a man, who surely would shrivel and die without his wife to look after him. As we worked with the dream, I asked how his mother had responded to his office. Mr. A beamed and reported that she was thrilled, kept saying how proud she was, and had spent a great deal of time looking out his window, impressed that her son had an office overlooking a pond with fountains and swans.

I also understood this dream as an indication of deeper engagement with his considerable anxieties and offered to meet more frequently. After some deliberation, Mr. A said that he feared falling apart if his mother died, and agreed to more frequent meetings. Mr. A was then able to relate the complexity of his relationship with his mother. He described how she and his grandfather had sustained him in the face of his father's rages, neglect of his children, and repeated humiliation. However, he was also angry at her for not protecting her children. In tears he remembered an instance when he and his sibs complained to her about their father's behavior. Mother responded by saying if she had to choose between her children and her husband, she would choose her husband. Once Mr. A was able to acknowledge his anger at his mother, the transference deepened, and Mr. A was more able to work with the depth of his feeling states.

Very gradually the cruising diminished, except during times of acute distress. He began dating another woman who was much more responsive and available. It became clear that Mr. A was deeply involved with her, and marriage was planned. During a series of family reunions in which they introduced each other to their prospective families, he came in quite shaken. At each reunion (both families had extensive alcohol histories, and at each reunion most of the adults were intoxicated), he noticed at least one lost child, a child with seemingly no vigilant adult, who was wondering around aimlessly. Mr. A found himself looking out for these children, playing with them and helping them participate in activities they were too timid to engage in. By the end of the weekend, the children were "orbiting" around him. In tears he related, "That was me. Those lost kids were me."

In a broader sense one can view cruising as a rather ordinary human behavior, a common human activity. If we define cruising as looking for and hoping to find some form of sexual stimulation either in fantasy or actual sexual contact, we identify a more wide-ranging phenomenon. In this light, cruising is an activity participated in by both heterosexual (a young male patient refers to it as "scamming girls") and homosexual men. Kaplan (1997) offers several case examples of cruising by heterosexual women. I could find no specific reference, but lesbian colleagues confirm that forms of cruising are to be observed among the lesbian community. With the advent of the Internet, people of all genders and orientations report spending time searching for pornography to gaze at, engage in highly sexual conversations with people they will never meet, or search out actual sexual partners. Cruising takes many forms, occurs in many contexts, can have many meanings or motivations, and can involve a wide variety of self states and selfobject needs or longings. A cultural aspect is most likely at work as well. What heterosexual people would consider flirting, homosexual or bisexual men might consider cruising. Indeed there is a difference between cruising our fantasies, cruising other people for an admiring response, and cruising other people in hopes of engaging them in a sexual encounter. The selfobject longings may be similar, but the structure of the self that is searching for something it needs is the crucial distinction.

Desperately seeking out a sexual encounter occupies but one end of a wide spectrum of human behavior. The caricature of construction workers admiring female passersby during their lunch break occupies another. Careful observation will show us that passersby have often watched these very men as they labored. Whether being admired for their various skills, the heavy equipment they operate with seeming ease, or the way they fill out their blue jeans, they, too, have been watched, and often admired. Freud (1905) did point out that the eye is an integral part of the erotogenic zones, with an admiring gaze often the starting point for a rise in sexual tension.

From an analytic perspective, one does not have to leap far to embrace the possibility that those who look and admire breasts, or legs or long blond hair, or wonder if a man is wearing boxers or briefs may also be longing for something that is out of their immediate or conscious awareness. Or that the person who needs more than a reverie, and must have a sexual encounter, is in need of something quite different than the momentary distraction of a pleasant daydream. In one the self may be bored or lonely, in the other the self may be destabilized and lost. The need that is out of awareness, most often through disavowal, is desperately wanting/needing to be wanted. Instead of viewing sexual fantasy as revealing solely libidinal dynamic workings, let us also view sexual fantasy as carrying selfobject longings and needs. In viewing cruising in this wider perspective, we are able to extrapolate a range of self-states, self-structures, and psychodynamics, and avoid identifying the male homosexual as the ultimate cruiser. After all, prostitutes must be sought after, and the streetwalker is there to be found.

From the standpoint of clinical process, we can call cruising an enactment, a regression, or an indication of fragmentation, or we can call it an opportunity to engage the patient at a deeper level. When people cruise for a sexual encounter, they are hoping to be cruised and engaged in return, hence when the cruiser finds someone to engage with, he is simultaneously being found. As clinicians we must strive to help these patients find us in the transference.

The case of Mr. A raises questions about the role of sexual fantasy in the functioning and maintenance of the self. As is discussed later in this essay, there appears to be considerable confusion in the literature around homosexual fantasy. Clearly there is considerable difference between homosexual fantasy used to hold the self together in times of distress and homosexual fantasy that orients men toward potential love objects. Shelby (1998) states, "In work with gay men we need to view sexualization within the context of the orientation" (p. 181). Sexualization, the defensive use of sexuality (Coen, 1981) and orientation, the capacity to fall in love with a person of a particular gender (Money, 1988) are by definition two different phenomena. The viewpoint of this essay is that one can observe homosexual sexualization in men who are homosexual, bisexual and heterosexual. The clinical focus then becomes the function of the sexualization in the maintenance of the self. When it comes to homosexuality, psychoanalysis has tended to confuse these two central concepts.

Indeed there are gay men who spend considerable time cruising, apparently looking for sexual encounters. Apparently, because if one listens closely to our patients or actually observes people in their cruising activities, it becomes obvious that searching often occupies far more time than actual sexual contact. Could it be that in some cases *searching* is the central activity (with a corresponding self state) and that achieving orgasm is something one does before going home? In this view, unmanageable affects are deflected into the search for a sexual partner. For some people, searching and hoping to find and be found by a sexual partner becomes a dominant mode of handling distressing affects.

If cruising were as indiscriminate as some analysts have made it out to be, then everyone could quickly dispatch their sexual tension and return to the ordinary tasks of life. The sexual behavior seizes and focuses our attention in much the same manner as it does for the cruiser. Focusing on and attempting to explain the sexual behavior threatens to take us away from the needs of a self that is lost , and needing to be found, a *self that is wanting/needing to feel wanted.*

In the writings that are reviewed later in this essay, cruising has been approached as a rather egregious, depersonalizing activity. From a clinical perspective, it is a highly useful activity in that, when properly handled, it can help us access unmodulated affects and disavowed aspects of the self. Kohut (1996) did point out that when a patient is able to tell us about his perversions, it indicates a deepening of the analytic relationship. Cruising is also an opportunity for engagement: the patient is letting us into the more private, heavily defended, and vulnerable areas of him or herself.

Rather then seeing a patient's cruising being brought into the transference as a welcome sign, the clinician tends to become anxious, to view the cruising as acutely dangerous, and to feel an often exacerbated responsibility to stop it. Fear of the patient contracting HIV or spreading HIV, or being physically assaulted, are often offered as manifest reasons for the clinician's concern. The patient feels betrayed, angry, and hurt, and the treatment is threatened. The paradox is that this is the point at which the alliance can and needs to deepen, not be shaken.

The opposite of acute concern can be problematic as well. Therapists who take a stance that gay men are just more sexually active, or who indulge their own need for stimulation by delighting in the patients' account of their sexual exploits, are problematic as well. This stance also threatens to ignore the patient's distress. If we think in terms of *clinical utility*, the patient's report of cruising activity potentially gives us access to disavowed affects and meanings, deficits in tension regulation, and efforts to cope with unreliable grandiosity. As with many behaviors, the clinician must accept and strive to appreciate the manifest activity until the latent aspects can be accessed. Defenses reflect the complexity of the patient's self. And one of the central efforts of analytic work is to bring as much of the personality into the process as possible.

Case 2

Mr. B presented as a bright, gifted professional, who was able to orchestrate highly complex business dealings, and was considered a rising star in his area of expertise. He rather nonchalantly presented a childhood history of chaos, disruptions, and loss. Mother developed manic depressive illness; there were many hospitalizations, a divorce, time spent in foster care, and mother's suicide when Mr. B was 16. As the oldest of three, Mr. B felt a great responsibility to be strong and steady for his younger siblings during his parents' divorce and the ensuing chaos. Father became the custodial parent after the children were removed from mother's home by a state agency. Mr. B's father was a rather grandiose and vulnerable man who, although he claimed high ideals and presented himself as a long-suffering victim, tended to be highly critical of his children and intolerant of sadness and insecurity, as well as overly concerned about appearances. Over the course of his childhood, there were many accusations of affairs by his mother, and after the divorce Mr. B witnessed both parents engaging in sexual relations with strangers.

Mr. B presented considerable difficulties in modulating affect states, and suffered from chronically unstable self-esteem. During the first year of treatment, he began to request double sessions. Offering to meet twice a week instead of doubling on demand was initially met with considerable resistance, but he eventually agreed to a more regulated schedule. Initially, if I mentioned the word "mother" he became quite resistant and accused me of making a big deal out of nothing, pointing out that was long ago, over and done with. The message was quite clear: "Back off!"

Late in the first year of treatment, his partner of several years, who was HIV positive, began to act in a highly erratic, sexually impulsive manner that was truly out of character, if not outrageous. Mr. B was concerned and realized things were not quite right. He also presented considerable disavowal, a kind of "Yes, it is worrisome and enraging but what can I do?" The nature of the partner's actions suggested organic neural involvement. While these early signs that something was amiss with his partner were occurring, Mr. B mentioned that he had gone out, become intoxicated, and ended up having sex in his car with a man, whom he allowed to insert his penis in him without a condom. Again he was, and was not, alarmed by this, but when I offered that perhaps he was more distressed by his partner's actions than he allowed himself to feel, he dug in his heels and so much as said "Back off!" Eventually the partner went into status seizures and was hospitalized, and considerable neurological involvement secondary to HIV was diagnosed.

While the partner was in the hospital, it became clear that he could be stabilized, but the location and size of the lesions in his brain indicated that he would never return to normal intellectual and emotional functioning. Mr. B began to report more and more cruising. He began to appear curious if I offered that perhaps he was distressed, but that was about it. One day he came in looking quite shaken. He reported that, while at work, he felt the need to cruise and had engaged a man in the rest room of a department store. In the middle of things, he became overwhelmed with sadness, and had to fight back tears. He realized what he wanted was to be held and comforted. He then began to relate the horror of his mother's periodic descent into manic psychosis, and her outrageous, often sexualized behavior. He was very tuned into her comings and goings, and knew how to calm her down and how to deal with her to prevent further escalation, but on the other hand, he was also enraged and embarrassed by her behavior. He also felt responsible for her suicide. One day he sensed something was not right, and went to visit her, but, as he sat in his car outside her apartment building, he felt enraged, exhausted, and unable to deal with her that particular day. That was the day she suicided. As his partner became more and more disabled by brain infection, Mr. B continued to relate the complexity of his sadness, rage, and, in sum, the unmourned loss of his mother.

Mr. B became so involved in exploring and relating the complexity of the relationship and loss of a mother who was able to mirror and nurture his considerable talent, but then descended into psychosis and overstimulated him, that I was concerned that he was neglecting his partner. He may have sensed my concern. Several times he brought his partner to sessions in his wheelchair on their way to the park for an outing. I was truly impressed by his ability to respond to and deal with a man who was so severely neurologically impaired.

If we listen closely to our patients, we will see that cruising may involve many different self states. For some men, cruising will have an impulsive quality in which a disappointment or potentially overstimulating affect can clearly be identified. The patient goes out, cruises, meets (or just as often does not meet) a sexual partner, and all is over and done with. The person returns to his daily activities, perhaps with a smile and renewed ability to focus, perhaps with a sense of shame and wondering what happened. For other men, something that may be harder to isolate from clinical data will set off a compulsive cycle of cruising and fantasizing about cruising lasting several weeks. Some men may exhibit a mix of impulsive and frantic or compulsive cruising over their life span. And many gay men rarely, if ever, seek out sexual partners in this manner.

From a social standpoint, cruising has a long and interesting history in the gay community. It was not that long ago that bars frequented by homosexual men were sparse, located in large cities, subject to considerable police harassment, with patrons being jailed and names published in local newspapers. Cruising in certain public and semipublic areas became a way of seeking partners with less risk of public exposure. As Chauncey (1994) illustrates, however, there have always been other venues for homosexual men to meet than public cruising, and many men availed themselves of partner seeking in arenas more private and secure from public scrutiny.

From a life span developmental standpoint, pressure created by new challenges to the self may leave the person feeling highly vulnerable, unprepared, and unable to form needed selfobject relationships. Cruising may be a central activity during a period in a person's life, then disappear. From an intrapsychic view, a variety of self states and selfobject longings can be surmised. In many cases, far from a repetition of a discreet traumatogenic event, what is being experienced is a destabilizing separation from the self's constituent selfobjects, or the lack of an internalized function to comfort and orient the self as it meets new challenges. In this view the self is lost and needing to be found. Cruising for sexual encounters becomes a useful emergency measure for modulating affect states, serving a function that the self is unable to perform on its own.

From a clinical perspective, we must ask ourselves, just what is this patient attempting to communicate to me, as he tells me about his cruising experiences? What is the self in need of and longing for? What is the patient needing to find in me? Perhaps, most important, what needs to happen in order for us to be able to talk about and respond to these needs, rather than the patient seeking to assuage them outside of the clinical hour in a way that minimizes the possibility of their being met? Although Kohut's (1996) statement about the deepening of the analytic relationship addresses one aspect of cruising in the transference, the patient who tends to fill up the hour with accounts of cruising may be resisting the deepening of the transference.

Psychoanalytic Literature on Homosexual Cruising

A review of the analytic literature on cruising indicates several tendencies: (1) to conceptualize cruising as an exclusively homosexual act; (2) to see it as a repetition compulsion; (3) to see it as a flight from Oedipus and to attribute the standard dynamics supposedly inherent to homosexuality as motivational forces; and (4) to clinically describe men who are highly conflicted and unsure about their sexual orientation and imply that this is the nature of the homosexual psyche in general and gay men's cruising activities in particular.

Calef and Weinshel (1984) view cruising and homosexual fantasy in oedipal terms: an act of restitution, an effort to resurrect the father, to contradict the ambivalent wishes to rob and murder him, to make sure that he is alive and well and not the victim of the cruiser's competitiveness and destructiveness, to idealize him and render him into an object of love; thus to avoid anxiety and to preclude the father's wrath and retaliation (p. 52). The authors view cruising as a regressive act. An anxiety producing situation triggers a libidinal regression to homosexual cruising. Although the authors acknowledge a relationship to transference manifestations in their patients, it is treated as an avoidance, a resistance to reexperiencing the oedipal conflict in the treatment relationship as well as intrapsychically.

In a highly similar vein, Willick (1988) takes up cruising, and offers the following considerations: dealing with conflicts inherent in homosexuality, attempting to deny the vulnerability inherent in intimate relationships, creating a new and fantasied reality in which the cruiser is never rejected and finds a new love each time. Cruising provides the opportunity for the individual to deny the possibility of strife, rejection, and hostility that might lead to the destruction of relationships. The author places great emphasis on anonymity and multiplicity of partners as being absolutely necessary in order to deny the yearnings for love and acceptance that are forever plagued by doubt. Cruising is also seen as a desperate attempt to deal with the turmoil of oedipal conflict by creating a new scenario. "He [the patient] wants to deal with neither the murderous rage derived from his oedipal rivalry nor with the destructive hostility toward his mother that is the consequence of his disappointment in her love" (p. 448). Willick's patient sought out men who were "masculine, with manly physiques . . . his partner, an imagined strong male, would choose him and affirm for him his masculinity" (p. 448). The idea that homosexual men are damaged men, forever searching out a more perfect man to counter their damaged self-image, is a recurring theme in the analytic literature. This idea paints us into a corner in which there is no possibility of a homosexual orientation, only homosexual sexualization. From the viewpoint of self psychology, the hyperidealized, sexually exciting masculine man is the sexualization of a more basic need, not a primary motivation.

Bollas (1992) takes several steps in a promising direction, but then retreats to repetition compulsion. Bollas makes an important point in that he sees cruising as a rather depersonalizing act that is participated in and sustained at least in part, by the heterosexual community. He suggests that the depersonalization gay men often experience by heterosexuals is somehow repeated in homosexual cruising. Bollas viewed his patients' cruising as a repetition of maternal tendencies to use the child in a narcissistic manner. Employing the concept of dissociation, Bollas paints a dynamic and dramatic picture in which the cruiser seeks an "erotic victim into which this loss of control can be passed" (p. 154). He sees cruisers as sexually executing each other, finding the object of desire then dispatching him with the moment of orgasm. Although purporting to go beyond previous theorizing, Bollas, too, relies on the thought that the cruiser is seeking out a perfect image to counter his damaged image. As clinicians we observe patients searching for a range of fantasied partners that men look for in their times of cruising whether it be socially or on an emergency basis. Although Bollas concedes that there are similarities between heterosexual singles bars and homosexual bars, he clearly views homosexual arenas as far more depersonalizing than heterosexual arenas. Could it be that psychoanalysis itself, no matter how well intentioned, has participated subtly, and at times dramatically, in the depersonalization of gay men?

If we focus on libidinal dynamics, as Willick and Bollas do, we end up focusing on sexual acts, not the search and the need to search. For example, Socarides (1978) views cruising as an attempt for a true object relationship, which always fails. Bollas (1992) goes to great lengths to describe the depersonalization that accompanies sexual acts in cruising arenas, and Willick (1988) asserts, "Any discussion of cruising however, must take into account the specific characteristics of the anonymity and multiplicity of partners." If we carefully read these authors, we see a common tendency in their writings. Although the authors purport to be moving us along in our understanding, they are offering dramatic descriptions and dynamic explanations, taking us around in circles, and subtly encouraging us to analyze the object of the search, rather than the self of the patient who is searching. None of the authors offered how, or if, they were able to bring the complexity of the dynamic explanations they offer into the transference, and how or if the transference was resolved. These viewpoints also emphasize dynamic formulations at the expense of clinical process.

Lynch (this volume) offers a more even-handed view of cruising, utilizing the concept of debasement. Although there are instances where the need to cruise appears to be pressure related to the tendency to debase the love object, there are many instances where this is not the case. Indeed, there are patients for whom the concept of debasement is a useful dynamic explanation, however, the economic issues of the anxiety and often frantic behavior that result still need to be addressed. Perhaps cruising is too complex and variable to be understood with concepts that are related to the more structuralized neuroses.

Freud (1905) pointed out, "Here again we cannot escape the fact that people whose behavior is in other respects normal can, under the domination of the most unruly of all the instincts, put themselves in the category of sick persons in the single sphere of sexual life" (p. 27). It is this dramatic change in psychic functioning that is the center of this discussion. To what factors do we attribute the dramatic and often abrupt shifts in the psyche that in many instances accompany cruising? Do we incorporate the concept of libidinal regression to a fixation point, or do we look to the structure of the self? Why are some people content with indulging a fantasy when bored or narcissistically injured, whereas others need to engage in sexual behavior? This is where self-psychology parts ways with drive theory. Fragmentation or threatened fragmentation and presence of a vertical split in the self is posited rather than a regression to primitive drives and wishes.

Kohut (1971) sent us in a very different direction when he proposed that perverse behavior was an attempt to forestall further fragmentation rather than an indication that a regression had occurred. He thus recognized that manifest sexual acts often obscure the area on which treatment needed to focus: the needs of the self. Tolpin (1997) points out that "[t]he selfobject is not an 'object' at all in the traditional psychoanalytic sense—it is not a target of drive wishes, but a vitally important human environment consisting of needed 'others' whose [parental] functions maintain and restore the self and its potential for growth and fulfillment" (p. 175).

Goldberg (1975) elaborated the idea of perverse sexual behavior as being an attempt to manage distressing affects. In Goldberg's view, to be considered a perversion, sexual behavior must have three components: individual dynamics, a vertical split in the self that leads to disavowal, and sexualization. The emphasis is on the use of sexual behavior to manage affects, the overall structure of the self, its strengths and weaknesses, and the use of sexual acts to manage self-deficits. The presence of a vertical split, which leads to the person being of "two minds," with widely varying unintegrated affects, which lead to widely differing self states, offers far more explanatory power than libidinal dynamic regression. Goldberg also makes a crucial distinction regarding depersonalization. There is a difference between depersonalizing the sexual object, and separating one's self from one's feelings. In many cases, lust replaces crushed tender longings, and it is often the tender longings, not rage, that the cruiser most deeply disavows.

A point that needs to be emphasized is that a germ of selfobject longing is often present in even the most dramatic sexual fantasies. If we get too wrapped up in our countertransference or conceptualizations, we may not see that there is indeed a "forward edge" of selfobject longing (Tolpin, this volume), and miss the opportunity to observe what happens in the course of attempts to have it fulfilled.

For example, one patient began his evening of bar cruising with the fantasy of finding a bigger, darker, stronger, slightly intimidating man who would tenderly dominate him but who would also be his friend, protector, and mentor. As the evening wore on, he would become increasingly anxious, and would use cocaine and alcohol to calm and fortify himself as he searched, hoping to find and be found. Often, if he did observe someone who resembled his longed-for partner, he would become acutely anxious, and use more alcohol and cocaine. Consequently, he became so compromised that he could meet no one. He would then return home alone, intoxicated, disappointed, discouraged, and high on cocaine. In the course of masturbation and the attendant fantasies, his longed-for partner became menacing and sadistic, which would lead him to pierce his nipples and genitals. The search for a kind, gentle man can be understood as the forward edge of selfobject need, whereas the sadistic, wounding man can be viewed as the trailing edge (the wounding man was not a man at all, but rather reflected the patient's attempts to manage his desperation in relation to his depressed and suicidal mother). In this case, treatment focused on the patient's massive disappointments and the considerable anxiety that prevented him from establishing the kind of relationship he so desperately needed.

Purely libidinal dynamic thinking can also blind us to the complexity of the self's structure and needs. Although men may be searching for a male sexual partner, the deficits in the self that unleash the need to desperately search may in some cases be maternal in nature. Time and time again, I have observed cruising diminish when a reasonably stable idealizing transference has evolved (as Goldberg observed in his 1975 paper). Data secondary to the maternal mirroring transference are often vital to understanding disavowed affects. Often the most crucial integration occurs when a transference similar to that discussed by Ornstein (1983), the desire to be mirrored by the idealized same sex parent, has been established. In cases of a significant vertical split, the ability to engage both sides of the split is crucial. Focusing on analyzing the object of the search may lead us astray. Certainly these are important clinical data, but more often the point is the self structure and deficits that have unleashed the need to desperately search. Once the more basic selfobject transferences are stabilized and the deficits modulated by the transference, the treatment may indeed proceed to an analysis of libidinal dynamics. As the following case illustrates, one often observes a mixture of deficits associated with maternal as well as paternal selfobjects.

Case 3

Mr. C sought out psychotherapy because of diffuse anxiety and difficulty in concentrating and writing. A student at a prestigious university, he felt woefully unprepared to compete in such an esteemed setting. He grew up in poverty and was a member of an ethnic minority group. Father eked out a living at a job that required him to travel and be away a great deal. Mother was intermittently psychotic and rageful toward Mr. C, as well as overstimulating the patient with her concerns and accusations over father's infidelities. When father was home, his supposed affairs were the topic of vicious arguments. However, Mr. C was quite bright and the nuns in the school he attended nurtured his intellect. Through a series of scholarships, he gradually worked his way up to more prestigious universities and ultimately the highly competitive and coveted department in which he was studying. Although his intellect saved him, a traumatic telescoping memory of his mother in a rage, ripping up his beloved schoolbooks, and his fear of returning the ruined volumes to school was recalled. Fortunately the nuns were a forgiving lot. Perhaps they sensed his circumstances at home, and there was no additional humiliation meted out.

Mr. C looked around his department and found students from wealthy and socially prominent families, who had access to more in-depth educational experience than he. In reality he did have to work to catch up and familiarize himself with the philosophical concepts that were beginning to influence his field of study. However, his worldview as a minority person enabled him to conceptualize ideas that were becoming highly relevant to his field. Although his dissertation area was underexplored and the faculty were excited by his ideas, he felt extremely inadequate. Mr. C felt he was a profound disappointment to his advisor. He was only waiting for the day when the advisor would give up, castigate him, and deny him further funding. There was an element of sexualization to the complex fantasies about his advisor, which left him feeling further ashamed. He could not fathom the idea of having a Ph.D. after his name. It just did not fit into his concept of who he really was. In addition to all this, Mr. C was struggling to integrate a more positive gay identity. He tended to feel that his homosexuality was a sign of further defect. He felt horribly isolated and surrounded by straight people; to counter this alienation he made many forays to the gay neighborhood in the city, many miles from campus. Although he did rely a great deal on his charm and was popular, he felt this, too, was a sham. Even though he felt quite competent in finding sexual partners, he sensed this was a substitute for something more sorely needed.

Mr. C was having considerable difficulty studying and completing his written tasks. He would go to the library and find himself cruising instead of doing his research. He was further ashamed of the men he sought, that is, white men, not of his ethnic group. As treatment progressed, the extent of his distress, his feeling lost in a demanding strange new world, and his difficulty using the relationship with his advisor in inspiring and stabilizing ways became evident. The cruising was becoming more time-consuming, and he fell further and further behind in his work and helpless to right himself and focus on his tasks. Initially, he would beg for mirroring responses from me time and time again, and then, just as quickly, reject them.

Another dimension of transference longings was expressed in the following: "I wonder who you are outside of the office. Are you a butch daddy type that hangs out at the bars head-to-toe in black leather? Or do you live in an *Architectural Digest* apartment and hold salons visited by the gay *literati* of Chicago? Or do you live in the suburbs with a partner, have dogs, and have friends over for barbecues who drink beer and wear flip-flops while you grill burgers?" Clearly, Mr. C was also searching for a gay man to idealize who would provide him some comfort and who could help him remediate his sense of defectiveness in terms of his being gay, his sense of masculine confidence, and his generally shaky grandiosity.

When he next began to talk about his various anxieties with his mentor, about his cruising, and whether his new boyfriend would eventually discover how defective he really was—I offered that perhaps he felt he was better able to please a man sexually than to please a man intellectually. Mr. C then burst into tears and wept. Out flowed just how tortured by doubt, how lost he felt, how unprepared; that he should be learning and producing, but instead felt himself crumbling. I suggested that the crux of his distress was his difficulty in developing an alliance with the male advisor that would help him feel oriented, and believing in himself and his abilities. He felt all he had to offer men was sex, but his advisor, ultimately, wanted a dissertation.

Following this, the transference stabilized into a mirroring one with secondary idealizing characteristics. What evolved next was a truly creative solution. Mr. C began to take his laptop to coffeehouses in the gay neighborhood of the city where he would work peacefully and productively for hours at a time. He was not cruising but felt comfortable, focused, and contained. The frantic cruising waned and disappeared. He subsequently achieved a very useful relationship with his advisor and was able to develop his unique and valuable ideas.

Summary

This paper has offered a different view of the complex phenomenon of cruising. A more complete discussion would include an elaboration of the interplay of social, intrapsychic, and clinical dimensions of this human phenomenon. Further elaboration of working with cruising in the transferences is called for. Although the case discussions have focused on men, women do it, gay and straight and in between do it. We all may do it in some form during the course of our lives, whether it be looking and longing, hoping for an admiring response, or perhaps a more involved sexual situation. From a clinical perspective, we may surmise that something else is needed as well.

Enough time has been spent in the analytic literature attempting to analyze specific unconscious dynamics that purportedly account for all cruising behavior. I have taken a different tack and attempted to emphasize its clinical utility, and clinical process. If we view sexualizations or perversions as representing split-off, disavowed, or unmodulated affects, and an attempt to connect with another person to prevent further fragmentation, then the empathic handling of cruising when it comes into the treatment relationship and transferences offers us access to those aspects of self. This may be of even greater importance in psychotherapy than in psychoanalysis where we do not have the luxury of both the extent of clinical data and the depth of transference immersion.

Although the sexual behavior may grab our attention and focus, it may lead us astray from the needs of the self. In many cases, cruising signals a self that has become lost through separation from its constituent selfobjects and is in need of a stabilizing encounter. The clinician must strive to understand the specific need that is being searched for, as well as the self structure that is prone to cruising, the event and the meaning of the event that resulted in the need to desperately search. In the cases of the men presented in this paper we see a range of paternal and maternal deficits. Although they may have been searching for a male sexual partner, considerable maternally based deficits were evident as well, and may have been the basis for the structural aspects that resulted in the need to desperately search.

In many cases of chronic and impulsive cruising, the restoration is only temporary, and what is needed can be found only through the restorative selfobject transferences. Cruising may at times be a resistance to the deepening of the transference, but it may be a sign of the deepening of the transference as well. If we understand sexualization as being born of massive disappointments in selfobjects, then analyzing the sexualization is not analyzing the "object." It is understanding the affects related to, and efforts to deal with, disappointment in primary selfobjects. Sexualizations are often highly visible, dramatic, and "out there for all to see," often in hopes that another person will see and approach, and want what is being offered. Tender feelings and longings that may have been crushed in the course of development are hidden and may take a great deal of work before they emerge in the transference. Appreciation and acceptance of the defense will pave the way for the emergence of the forward edge of a selfobject transference. Anxiety, befuddlement, or rejection of the defense may obscure, prevent, or delay the more basic and healing aspects of the transference from emerging into the analytic relationship.

Empathic handling of the behavior can solidify the therapeutic alliance and extend the selfobject transferences into highly vulnerable and disavowed aspects of the self, aspects that are in desperate need of being found and responded to so that development can be rekindled, so that the person feels more whole, integrated, and less alienated from his history, and ultimately his self.

This paper has emphasized an "opening phase" approach to cruising and the alliance necessary to bring the selfobject needs into the treatment relationship. The next phase involves working with these transferences once they are engaged. Once the transferences are engaged, the treatment may move far away from issues of sexuality and into the deeper, more basic needs of the self. A reappearance of cruising may then became an indicator of a rupture in the transference which, once understood, offers even deeper understanding of the patient and the needs of the self.

References

Bollas, C. (1992), Cruising in the homosexual arena. In: *Being a Character*. New York: Hill & Wang.

Calef, V. & Weinshel, E. (1984), Anxiety and the restitutional function of homosexual cruising. *Internat. J. Psychoanal.*, 45:45–53.

Chauncey, G. (1994), *Gay New York: Gender, Urban Culture and the Making of the Gay Male World.* New York: Basic Books.

Coen, S. J. (1981), Sexualization as a predominate mode of defense. *J. Amer. Psychoanal. Assn.*, 4:893–920.

Freud, A. (1967), About losing and being lost. *The Psychoanalytic Study of the Child*, 9:9–19. New York: International Universities Press.

Freud, S. (1905), Three essays on the theory of sexuality. *Standard Edition*, 7:130–243. London: Hogarth Press, 1953.

Goldberg, A. (1975), A fresh look at perverse behavior. *Internat. J. Psychoanal.*, 56:335.

——— (1995), *The Problem of Perversion: The View from Self Psychology*. New Haven, CT: Yale University Press.

Kaplan, L. J. (1997), *Female Perversions*. Northvale: Aronson.

Kohut, H. (1971), *The Analysis of the Self.* New York: International Universities Press.

——— (1996), *The Chicago Institute Lectures,* ed. P. Tolpin & M. Tolpin. Hillsdale, NJ: The Analytic Press.

Money, J. (1988), *Gay, Straight, and In-Between*. New York: Oxford University Press.

Ornstein, A. (1983), An idealizing transference of the oedipal phase. In: *Reflections on Self Psychology,* ed. J. D. Lichtenberg & S. Kaplan. Hillsdale, NJ: The Analytic Press, pp. 135–148.

Socarides, C. (1978), *Homosexuality.* New York: Aronson.

Shelby, R. D. (1998), The self and orientation: The case of Mr. G. In: *Conversations in Self Psychology: Progress in Self Psychology, Vol. 13.* Hillsdale, NJ: The Analytic Press, pp. 181–202.

Tolpin, M. (1982), Self-objects and oedipal objects: A crucial developmental distinction. *The Psychoanalytic Study of the Child,* 33:167–183. New Haven, CT: Yale University Press.

——— (1997), Sexuality and the self. *The Annual of Psychoanalysis,* 25:173–188. Hillsdale, NJ: The Analytic Press.

Willick, M. (1988), Dynamics of homosexual cruising. In: *Fantasy, Myth and Reality: Essays in Honor of Jacob A. Arlow, M.D.,* ed. H. P. Blum. Madison, CT: International Universities Press.

V

FEMALE HOMOSEXUALITY

Mirror, Mirror: An Enactment That Stalemated a Psychotherapy

KAREN MARTIN

The term enactment is used in psychoanalysis to refer to unconscious symbolic repetitions of early trauma. When enactments occur in a treatment relationship, both therapist and patient unconsciously contribute to and participate in them. The term is also used, at times, to refer to unconscious symbolic repetitions of early trauma that occur outside of the treatment relationship (see Brothers, 1997). Enactments, sexual or nonsexual, that occur between psychotherapists and patients, are also conceptualized as transference-countertransference collusions. However named, these unconscious symbolic repetitions of early trauma suggest that there is an unconscious push to repeat and/or to relive early experience, understood and conceptualized first by Freud (1914) as the "repetition compulsion."

Holly, the young woman whose case I present, is a lesbian. During the first several years of psychotherapy with me, Holly's relational involvements would be characterized, in my view, as sexual enactments rather than healthy homosexual relationships. That Holly engaged in these sexual enactments outside of the treatment for as long as she did was indicative of a parallel, unseen, and therefore unanalyzed enactment, of the nonsexual variety, between her and me in the treatment. The enactments in which Holly engaged with her various lovers and with me during many years of this treatment were unconscious repetitions of her early trauma at the hand of her mother. I think this becomes clear as I give an account of Holly's history and as I describe the psychotherapy.

Holly is the third of four daughters born to parents who remained married until she was ten years of age, then divorced, remarried one year later, remained married for two more years, and then divorced again. Mother was actively alcoholic throughout Holly's childhood and until Holly was 30 years old. Mother was extremely narcissistic and emotionally unavailable to Holly and her sisters. Drunk or sober she was haughty, arrogant, and narcissistically self-absorbed. In drunken states mother engaged in raging and roaring encounters with Holly's father in which she berated him endlessly for his inadequacies as a husband and for his failure as a "breadwinner" for the family.

Father, for his part, was indeed a rather weak, unassertive, passive man who did not fare well as a breadwinner. Father's employment history throughout his life has been problematic, characterized by losing jobs, changing jobs, and engaging as a would-be entrepreneur in one unsuccessful business scheme after another. His own inadequacies aside, Holly's father appeared to remain endlessly available, out of his own masochism, for his wife's debasing, castrating attacks. It was Holly's mother who filed for both divorces. After she left the father, Holly's mother became more successful in the business world than her father had ever been. But for all that Holly's father was not—not altogether idealizable for instance—he was warm, and he was able to be somewhat emotionally responsive to Holly. Father virtually disappeared, once released from the sadomasochistic enactment he had been trapped in with Holly's mother for years. At the time of this writing, he still has no contact with any of his four daughters. He not only makes no effort to see them but also fails to return phone calls when any of his daughters reach out for contact.

For virtually all her life, Holly doted on her mother. Each time her parents divorced, Holly redoubled her efforts to care for and please her mother. Holly would be a better, more gratifying, and more responsive partner to her mother than her father had been. With her brightness and facility with words (her mother is a wordsmith of sorts), by becoming a budding artist (her mother has artistic talent), and by being endlessly attentive to and available to her mother as an audience, Holly could eke out of her mother minimal, albeit conditional, attention and affirmation.

I first met and began working with Holly when she was a senior in high school. I saw her at the behest of her mother. Both Holly and Mother's chief complaints were that Holly was failing to meet her mother's expectations, was abusing alcohol and drugs, and was doing poorly in school. Her poor academic performance was particularly alarming because Mother placed a high value on academic achievement and because, according to both Mother and Holly, Holly was exceptionally bright. Holly's sexual orientation was not at issue at this time. She did not identify as a lesbian in high school. She dated infrequently, but when she did, it was with boys. She presented, however, as unquestionably male-identified.

In my initial sessions with Holly, she was clever and obviously bright and would have been very entertaining had her "false self" persona not been so painfully transparent. That entertaining me and touching me (emotionally) and impressing me were desperately important to her was obvious, but unacknowledged and unexamined by either her or me. I found myself engaging in a kind of playful, affectionate challenge of Holly's bravado, containing as it did a vulnerability that was denied on a preconscious level and only shakily defended against. Given Holly's experience that my appreciation of her would not be diminished by disclosing some of her vulnerabilities, Holly was able, in time, to let me in on them, in particular how important it was for her to be "best" and to "shine" in the eyes of admired, idealized others, mostly female teachers and always her mother. We came to understand that her withdrawal from sports activities and her lack of motivation for her academic studies were defensive attempts to protect herself from the narcissistic vulnerability and injury that would occur whenever she could not be "the best." If she couldn't be the "best" basketball player, she would lose interest in basketball. If she weren't "number one" on the debate team, she would drop out of debate. If she weren't sure, almost before opening a book, that she could be the "number one" student in a particular course, she would have the conscious experience of boredom and disinterest in the subject matter. In time she would find herself depreciating the course and the instructor as well. She was not studying because whatever course she was taking was stupid, trivial, and unimportant to her life.

In response to my growing appreciation of her brightness and quick wit, "growing," I might add, as she was able to let go of some of the "false" bravado, Holly's functioning improved enough to allow her to graduate from high school and get better control of her drinking and marijuana use. We met weekly for about nine months until she went away to school. My emotional reliability and responsiveness and mirroring appreciation of Holly had seemingly had salutary effects.

One year later, toward the end of her freshman year in college, I heard from Holly again. She wrote me indicating that she was having a terrible time in school. She was on probation, was flunking at least one course, and had "incompletes," in others. She was abusing alcohol and drugs. She also told me that she had engaged in her first lesbian relationship. She was in an acute crisis. In what in retrospect was a countertransference error of presumed identification, I called to tell her that there was nothing wrong with her newly discovered sexual orientation, and I "came out to her," based on the assumption that it would reassure her. Her disclosure had struck a chord with me as I remembered all too well, at that moment, the self-esteem crisis that getting in touch with my own homosexuality had created in me. I shudder, in retrospect, at this unprocessed, spontaneous self-disclosure.

Although my admission was alarming to me, as much, if not entirely, because it was so lacking in self-reflection, Holly gave no evidence at the moment or subsequently of having been affected in any significant way. I believe this is because she already knew about my sexual orientation. (Holly was a client seen through a community based clinic that I directed at the time. Many people in the community were aware of my sexual orientation.) For Holly the "good news" was the emergence into consciousness of her sexual orientation as a lesbian; the "bad news" was that she was experiencing considerable anxiety and insecurity in her new, first really serious intimate relationship. No amount of what would normally have been reassuring responsiveness from Micki, her then current love interest, could quell Holly's anxiety. When not with Micki, Holly could do nothing but obsess about where Micki was, what she was doing, and whether she was still "in love" with her. The intensity of Holly's feelings and preoccupation with this woman left her immobilized. She could think of nothing else, and consequently she could do nothing else. It was this obsession, characterized by an anxious insecure attachment, that made it impossible for Holly to do her academic work. It was the need to quell the anxious, painful, insecurity surrounding her relationship to Micki that drove Holly frequently into the anesthesia offered by abuse of alcohol.

Holly could tell me little about the woman who had captured her so completely, but from what she related, it appeared that Micki, for her own part, was responsive to Holly but was far from consumed by her. Micki continued to function and invest in the rest of her full and busy life, which included many activities and many people. The relationship with Micki ended before the end of Holly's sophomore year. Micki ended it. Micki was to have been the only woman that Holly was to be intimate with who, during the wooing and courting stage of the relationship, was actually homosexual.

Holly came back for treatment at the end of the academic year. She had flunked out of school, and was not invested in returning to it.

She found herself drawn intensely over the next several years to women who were "straight." As had been true in her relationship to Micki, what was paramount for Holly was that she was able to experience her partner as needing her, and as being affirmingly responsive to Holly's exquisite attunement. Holly's relationships were anchored in an unconsciously driven need to repeat an initial childhood trauma. As had been the case with her mother, in these enactments Holly split off or disavowed aspects of her own "self" in order to secure the admiring responsiveness of an "other." That Holly in an intimate relationship might need anything in this world other than admiring responsiveness was not at these times conceivable to her.

As with Micki, each of four relationships over the next several years was to become Holly's obsession. While engaged in a pursuit of a particular attachment, and continuing for several months once the attachment had been secured, Holly was vitalized, and her spirits were dramatically lifted.

It was obvious to me that the women Holly pursued were troubled and severely compromised in their capacities to respond reliably and more than minimally to the normal emotional needs of any partner. For her part, Holly was blind to their considerable limitations and to the ultimate toll they would exact from her. When on a quest to win the loving responsiveness of a would-be partner, Holly was in startling disavowal of the deficits of the other and in startling disavowal of myriad emotional needs and wants within herself to which these women were patently unable to respond.

Holly and each of her partners over the next several years moved in together and made a commitment to "forever" within no more than two months of the date of their first meeting. In each of these relationships, within several months of moving in together, Holly would invariably become lethargic, depressed, silently resentful, and increasingly emotionally withdrawn, although not sexually withdrawn, from her partner. Her emotional state of depression and unexpressed resentment worsened as time went by.

Having secured an attachment, previously disavowed needs in Holly erupted. This is what accounted for her predictable depressive episodes and withdrawn, resentful, emotional states. She now could experience the other side of the "split" within her. A year or more into each relationship, depressed and disillusioned, Holly would "happen" upon another woman with whom she felt the possibility of this particular "special" connection. She would begin a surreptitious, unacknowledged-to-even-herself, titillating courting of her next would-be lover, and when sufficiently certain that she could "win" her, sometimes after engaging in only the briefest sexual affair, she would end her current relationship. Each of three relationships ended in this way, each having lasted about two years. (Although by no means universal, the pattern I describe is common among lesbian couples, and, needless to say, or on second thought, perhaps necessary to say, this pattern is also common among heterosexual couples.)

A similar pattern to the one I've described was in evidence in other areas of Holly's life. During the period discussed, Holly returned to school on at least two occasions. Each time she began, she felt enlivened by her instructors' responsiveness to her. They clearly recognized her obvious talent. Each time, by the end of the first semester, her interest waned, and she failed to complete assignments and eventually dropped out. In her employment as well we observed the same pattern. Holly was enlivened initially on the job in response to the appreciative affirmation of her employers, but this state of enlivened pride in her "self" would never last for long. Within a year she would begin to complain about her employer, feel bored, and subsequently quit or be fired after about two years into the job.

Holly was seeing me in once weekly psychotherapy during the six years I have just briefly described. The alliance between us seemed strong. Idealizing and mirroring transferences were present, but unacknowledged and unanalyzed. Much of the six years was spent examining the repetitive pattern that characterized all of her endeavors—her love relationships, her education and her career—initial enlivenment followed by disillusionment and empty depression. We came to see that in each of her relationships she eventually felt what she had felt as a child and continued to feel as an adult in her relationship to her mother.

She continued to dote on her mother during this period. Holly, not surprisingly, still got very little in this relationship. But doting on mother protected Holly from being retraumatized by the complete lack of responsiveness or biting criticalness that would have emerged had she not continued to court her. Holly continued to split off her own legitimate needs to be cherished for who she was rather than for what she did for her mother. Something was better than nothing, and in addition Holly needed to sustain the illusion that she was her mother's "chosen one."

At one point, while doing a postmortem on a recently ended relationship, Holly was able to see all of the deficits in her partner. She was then in touch with the many aspects of herself and her needs and interests that from the beginning, given who her partner was as a person, had precluded a "good fit." But Holly's sightedness was selective. While in pursuit of a new love interest, she could not "see" who the other was. Perhaps it is more apt to say that she could not consciously register who the other was. On an unconscious level, it seems all but certain that what Holly "saw" was that her would-be partner would engage in the particular unconsciously driven enactment in which Holly was endlessly compelled to engage—and therefore her partner, like her mother, had to be a "bad fit."

I became frustrated over time that our growing understanding was seemingly having no impact on Holly's compulsion to repeat this increasingly destructive pattern, especially as it played out in her intimate relationships. It was clear to me that the women Holly selected for were simply new editions of her narcissistic, unavailable mother, and I was amazed that Holly really could not see this at all, except, of course, in retrospect. I pressed her with the ending of each relationship to take time before becoming lost in another so that we could get at what was being avoided in her internal reality by her throwing herself repeatedly into these relationships that seemed doomed to fail. Holly understood the logic of my suggestion but, of course, could not control, at least for long, her compelling need to repeat this early trauma in her life.

Actually once during this period, I'm sure in response to my mounting frustration, and fueled by the unanalyzed transference-driven need for my affirming responsiveness, Holly managed to "survive" without being embroiled in one of these enactments for about two months. She actually tried "dating" as contrasted with throwing herself heart and soul into the other by the second encounter. She became so anxious and insecure and miserable in these engagements with other women who were healthy enough not to get lost in her and healthy enough not to tolerate her getting lost in them that she simply couldn't bear it. She was in the throes of another enactment by the end of this two-month period.

Approaching the sixth year of examining, trying to understand, and trying to interfere with the destructive enactment that informed and shaped Holly's life experience outside the treatment, which I at least could clearly see, I made an egregious, clearly countertransference-driven, error. Holly had once again fallen in love, this time with an unhappily married woman who, by the way, in physical appearance so closely resembled Holly's mother that it was eerie. No sooner had they moved in together than Holly began complaining bitterly, as she had in every other relationship, that she was not understood and appreciated and that her partner was not interesting to her. In response, out of my mounting frustration I'm sure, with firmness and authority, I strongly suggested, verging on insisted, that Holly make her current relationship work. My misinformed reasoning, which I shared, was that if she could not break the pattern at the point of entry to a new relationship, then perhaps she could learn something by interfering with the pattern at the point of exit, when the impulse surfaced to flee into another relationship as it had so often in the past. She stayed in the relationship another five years. This was three times as long as she had ever remained in any other intimate relationship in her life.

Our treatment was interrupted a year into this relationship when Holly took a job in another state. She took her partner with her. She returned three years later and resumed her treatment. She complained minimally about her relationship and indicated that she was in couples treatment with another therapist. This struck me as progress. The work during this part of the treatment focused on her relationships with her mother and oldest sister.

Holly had returned to Illinois because she had predictably become disenchanted with her job and because her oldest sister's business was failing. At mother and sister's urging, Holly invested a sizable amount of her own money in her sister's business. This won Holly the attention and considerable esteem of her mother. That this was an inordinate sacrifice for Holly to make, and an act of poor judgment in a business sense, was never reflected on by mother, sister, or by Holly herself.

Holly's having inserted herself into her family in such a consuming, self-sacrificing way after all these years was to prove to be a painful but invaluable catalyst for a significant piece of work in the psychotherapy with me and consequently a significant level of psychological growth and development for Holly. After being initially enlivened by the prospect of saving the day, Holly predictably became disillusioned, felt burdened, complained bitterly about how unrewarding the challenge actually was, and became increasingly critical of her sister. Holly's pattern of becoming enlivened and then disillusioned and filled with empty depression, which we had looked at for years in her intimate relationships, was now fully engaged in her work life. And her work life had now become one and the same with her life with her family.

As we examined and explored her motivations for the decision to throw herself into this thankless position, Holly began to become painfully, not just intellectually, aware of how she had sacrificed herself to her mother at every turn. Until now Holly had disavowed her own needs and was not consciously aware of them in relation to her mother. Even as she saw and felt this reality, she was unable to extricate herself from it. Withholding her own reality secured a certain kind of responsiveness from mother and protected Holly from being retraumatized by her mother's cold, unempathic withdrawal and scorn. For many months Holly lived out the relationship she had established to her mother so many years earlier, only now with consciousness and with no pleasure at all.

It was at this time, and in this context, several months into the latest resumption of the therapy with me, that what had been split off in a transference-countertransference enactment in our work entered into the room, into our room, into our relationship. With considerable apprehension, Holly announced that she needed to talk to me about her relationship to her intimate partner. Holly disclosed that her partner was alcoholic and emotionally and physically abusive to her. This had been going on for the last four years of the relationship and had become steadily worse with each year. Holly was in the position she'd been in with her mother all of her life, at least from the age when her parents divorced. It was common that Holly found herself taking care of her partner in drunken states. It was never the case, as it had never been the case with her mother, that her partner showed any remorse or had any appreciation for Holly's experience in these episodes. When I asked why she hadn't told me about all of this sooner, and about why she was so fearful about doing so and about why she hadn't left the relationship, Holly broke down in a way that she had never done at any other time in our many years of work together. She explained with considerable hurt and rage that I had directed her to stay in the relationship and make it work! She went on to ask rather rhetorically if I had in fact any idea of how important I was to her. Did I not realize that she could not risk my disapproval or disappointment?

It seemed in a way that the treatment had just begun. A blindness that had beset me years before and that I had steadfastly, unconsciously clung to left me in a flash. It was like a "bolt of lightning." I was shaken immensely at the reality of what had been disavowed between us all these years, and shaken to have to know inside of myself that I had been an active participant in this tragic enactment. Certainly there were other factors that contributed to Holly's staying in this abusive relationship, one being that she had been living out of state for three years and had very few other relational supports. I have also wondered whether in finding this last partner to her enactment Holly had found someone who was closer to being like her mother than any of her previous partners. Recall how I said that it was eerie how much this woman actually looked like Holly's mother. But all that having been said, it is also true that my frustration-driven countertransference directive to Holly to make her relationship with her partner work had no small impact on her.

That my participation in the enactment had contributed to my patient's remaining in an abusive relationship for five years was almost more than I could bear to know. Holly had been terrified to tell me this. She was certain that her reality would be denied as it had been endlessly throughout her life at the hand of her mother, her various lovers, and her "self." She expected me to blame her. She expected me to deny my part in our jointly constructed tragedy. She expected me to turn critical and haughty and arrogant and cold. She expected me, in a word, to turn into her mother. She imagined she would lose me.

It goes without saying that neither of us was aware of the enactment we had been engaged in. Throughout the entirety of this very long treatment until this point there had never even been a hint of a negative transference. *That this did not strike me as rather odd, and that I never therefore questioned within myself that there might be something defensive operating in our "blissful" connection, was evidence of the enactment in which we were both participating.* My affirming responsiveness was still contingent, in Holly's view, both preconsciously and unconsciously, on an only partial presentation of herself. As she had done with her mother, Holly split off and disavowed needs and feelings about me that would in her view threaten my affirming connection to her. What Holly had to put aside nearly completely, for all the years of this treatment, was her own rage and despair at having to be the mirror to the mother from whom she so desperately needed mirroring. It was these needs and these affect states that Holly had to disavow, which now resurfaced. Holly's own alcohol and drug abuse numbed the dim awareness of her rage and the acute, nascent sense of her own emptiness.

In the enactment what I experienced as an idealizing transference that was a manifestation of an archaic need (Kohut, 1971) was actually an instance of defensive idealization. Holly did need to idealize me in the transference, but an actual idealizing transference that was not defensively driven did not get mobilized until the unwitting enactment in which we both participated surfaced into consciousness and was worked through. Had the split off sector of Holly's "self" been able to be brought into our relationship earlier, she would not have had to engage endlessly in the traumatizing enactments outside of the treatment.

Given Holly's history and traumatizing relationship to her mother, that I remained unaware, for as long as I did, of the defensive aspects of her idealization of me and that I was not alarmed that no negative transference ever entered the work, was indicative of my own countertransference-driven participation in this enactment. I mention now that when writing the preceding sentence I originally made a "slip." Instead of saying "given Holly's history and traumatizing relationship to her mother," I originally wrote, "given Holly's history and traumatizing relationship to *my* mother." I disclose this because I think it gets to the heart of the matter. In fact my relationship to my mother was very similar to Holly's relationship to hers. During the greater part of this treatment, I was not engaged in my own psychoanalysis. A split existed in me that mirrored the split in Holly. I could not help Holly bridge a split in her "self" that had not yet been bridged in mine. In all likelihood it was because I was well into my own psychoanalysis by the time Holly and I became aware of our enactment that we then were able to do what we needed to do.

During the next year in treatment, there was in evidence more change and growth in all sectors of Holly's life, internally and externally, than we had seen during the entirety of the treatment to that point. In her intimate relationships, delighting a sought after "other" was no longer enough. Holly experienced herself as having other appropriate relational needs. Over the next year, Holly brought more of herself, in particular the "other side of the split," the sector of herself that admitted to having her own needs and desires, into the once weekly treatment. She was depressed with me. She was angry with me. She was consciously and admittedly aware of being hurt on one occasion or another "at my hand." After considerable work on the egregious enactment that I had participated in with her, she was strengthened enough out of my appreciation of her fuller reality that she was able to extricate herself from her lifelong sadomasochistic relationship to her mother. She pulled out of her dysfunctional sister's failing business. She has confronted her mother time and again with the reality of what Holly's relationship to her had really been all about. She has left her alcoholic and abusive partner of five years without having to defensively flee into another illusory love relationship. She has lived alone now for over a year. She has entered into a "dating," not live-in, relationship with a woman who seems far healthier than her previous partners. Holly maintains interests in her life that do not include her new relationship. She has begun pursuing her artistic talent which is indeed considerable. She has stable work.

I chose to write about this case for many reasons. I believe it is an excellent example of a client whose relationships were for many years actually a manifestation of sexual enactments. It also demonstrates rather well I think how an unanalyzed enactment within the therapist–patient dyad was at the root of my being unable to help this patient extricate herself from this destructive pattern. And, finally, I chose this case because in my clinical practice over the last 20 years I have treated many women who identify as lesbians and who are hopelessly caught in a repeating cycle of serial relationships that last two to three years. I believe many of these women are trapped, as Holly was, in an unconsciously driven compulsion to relive early trauma embedded in their childhood relationships to their mothers. This is not to say that every lesbian is a lesbian because of an unanalyzed enactment relating to her mother.

As homosexuals we have been maligned, marginalized, and pathologized for so long in the culture that we are reluctant to examine the psychological meanings of and functions served by our sexual orientations. Homosexuality in my view is not a manifestation of a conscious choice, nor is it a manifestation of a biological predisposition—neither is heterosexuality. But, sexualities are carriers of health and pathology—there are many homosexualities. I, granted, have been privileged to see only some. Similarly there is not one heterosexuality, but myriad heterosexualities. There are people for whom the particular dynamics of their heterosexual orientations are pathological. Similarly, there are people for whom the particular dynamics of their homosexual orientations are pathological. All relationships, regardless of orientation, can be healthy or unhealthy. I consider my own homosexuality to be a developmental alternative, in contrast to a developmental derailment, to a heterosexual orientation that predictably would not have emerged for me given the psychologies and pathologies of my parents and the dynamic interplay of these within my family.

It seems to me that the psyche is intrinsically motivated in development to construct itself in such a way as to best meet its needs given what it has to work with in both the internal and external environment. Each of our idiosyncratic psychological configurations represents the "best" psychic package that can be put together given variables too numerable to ever be ferreted out. Sometimes the "best package" that can be put together supports healthy interpersonal relationships, and sometimes the package is not good enough and is rightly deemed pathological, regardless of orientation.

References

Brothers, D. (1997), The leather princess: Sadomasochism as the rescripting of trauma scenarios. In: *Conversations in Self Psychology: Progress in Self Psychology, Vol.* 13. Hillsdale, NJ: The Analytic Press, pp. 245–267.

Freud, S. (1914), Remembering, repeating and working-through (Further recommendations on the technique of psycho-analysis: II). *Standard Edition,* 12:145–156. London: Hogarth Press, 1958.

Kohut, H. (1971), The analysis of the self: A systematic approach to the psychoanalytic treatment of narcissistic personality disorders. In: *The Psychoanalytic Study of the Child,* 26:37–56. New York: International Universities Press.

Discussion of Karen Martin's Clinical Case

SALEE JENKINS

Martin's description of her work with Holly has a biphasic before-and-after-the-enactment quality that I think often characterizes our retrospective analysis of a lengthy treatment process. Although these behavioral events, with their dramatic intensity and reorganizing impact on both the patient and therapist are important nodal points in organizing a compelling narrative, it is upon the earlier bit by bit construction of an environment in which they can unfold that I wish to focus. Within that context I briefly discuss the multiple transference meanings inherent in both the chronic and discreet enactments that occur between Holly and her therapist.

Martin beautifully describes the disregulated deadened state in which her patient entered treatment and which plagued them from time to time throughout their work together. Holly's efforts to vitalize herself through drugs, alcohol, and, later, addictive liaisons to transiently idealized but flawed women were only temporarily enlivening. The repetitive cycle of obsessional fantasy and relentless pursuit of her love objects, followed by crushing disappointment and withdrawal, Martin suggests, had its roots in Holly's adaptation to her explosive alcoholic mother. In an attempt to garner her mother's highly contingent attention and approval, Holly had become a one-way mirror—reflecting flattering air-brushed images of her mother, but sequestering her own needs and affects behind a vertical barrier of disavowal. Her father, a "not not idealizable figure," warmhearted and friendly, after years of "endless availability" for his wife's excoriating attacks, abandoned the family when Holly was 13.

Holly's lengthy (11-year) psychotherapy was dominated by her need to feel supported, affirmed, and special in the eyes of her therapist. From her earliest hours, her approach was to "entertain . . . touch . . . and impress" Martin, whose "playful, affectionate" response evolved into a stabilizing appreciation of this young woman's "brightness and quick wit."

During these years, Martin states, there was no awareness or interpretation on either her own or Holly's part of the negative transference, that is, the distrust underlying the accommodations Holly automatically made in order to ensure her therapist's responsiveness.

Martin goes on to suggest that she missed something in the transference due to unacknowledged countertransference. She implies that this "mutually negotiated . . . resistance" (Boesky, 1990) to awareness of a central transference/countertransference dynamic took the form of a chronic enactment and contributed to the interminable quality of her work with Holly. Her later insight into the ways in which her disavowal paralleled that of the patient and her interpretation of this process achieved impressive new integrations.

Martin's candor in describing the evolution of her identification with Holly and the occasional missteps this engendered was refreshing. Her discovery of the "split" in herself undoubtedly changed the relationship, charging it with greater emotional immediacy and freeing her to provide the interpretations so notably absent in the previous years.

I would, however, like to offer an additional construction of the meaning of this lengthy period of interpretive hiatus, that is, that it was an implicit response to the patient's (paranoid) need to control the relationship, and in this sense it represented, not an avoidance, but a necessary precondition for the later mobilization of deeper needs and feelings.

Patients like Holly epitomize the humbling complexities of those whose early traumas and losses have left them refractory to change. Their symptoms form a fragile web, barely containing a self riven by structural weakness. Their deficits or malformations may take the form of a depleted self in need of enlivenment though sexualization, a schizoid self whose fear of affects leads to obsessive isolation, a delinquent self whose petty acts of theft provide reassurance of unassailable power. Psychotherapy often reaches a plateau and takes on an interminable cast as the therapist, filling in or bolstering up a weakened self, is cemented into place by the patient's uncompromising need. The underlying vision of the therapist as an untrustworthy object who must at all costs be controlled reveals the early bad selfobject tie upon which later relationships have been constructed (Bacal and Newman, 1990). This unconscious bond to the pathological object pushes the patient into a Faustian bargain: in order to maintain the self organization and preserve the illusion of having a good parent, the patient must deny both internal and external reality.

Early trailing edge (Tolpin, 2000)[1] interpretation of the defensive features of such repeated relationships (Stern, 1994), as they take form in various therapeutic exchanges, can be experienced by a patient so divided within him-or herself

[1] Tolpin (2000) illustrates the importance of working with the "total" transference, emphasizing that our traditionally exclusive focus on childhood pathology and its derivatives has "obscured the subtle hints of bonafide transferences which derive their force and momentum from still visable

as reproaches or rejections—which then serve to entrench old accommodative patterns, variously conceptualized as the false self (Winnicott, 1960) or the defense transference (Schlessinger and Robbins, 1983). Mitchell (1988), in his description of the "delicate balance" between the defensive and reparative features of narcissistic transference illusions, cautioned against too early interpretation of these archaic configurations, stating: "To challenge . . . idealization vigorously and to interpret it prematurely only as a defense against rage or separation would . . . preclude a deep transferential engagement " (p. 233).

Martin decries her lack of interpretive activity and ascribes it to a split-off identification with the patient's need to idealize her and eschew negative perceptions and affects. However, her genuine admiration of Holly and her acceptance and active participation in the broadening twinship transference also point toward an implicit appreciation that the patient's search for a new beginning is mediated through ties with the old object.

Martin's work with Holly conforms to a paradigm frequently encountered with patients who have suffered severe trauma or loss (in Holly's case, her father) during their childhood years. These patients often attempt to recreate with the therapist those aspects of the pre-loss or pre-trauma relationship that provided comfort and a sense of security. Embedded within this repetition is a denial of the reality of the pain and loss. As the new object seamlessly replaces the lost object in the patient's eyes, the experience of grief or frustrated rage is avoided for the time being.

Early studies (Fleming and Altschul, 1963; Fleming, 1972) of young adults who, as children, had lost parents, viewed this clinging to the illusion of union with the lost object as derailing the developmental process. As long as the unconscious tie to the preloss figure was guarded and preserved, genuinely new relationships, including a transferential attachment to the therapist, were avoided. Technical strategies emphasized vigorous confrontation of the patient's denial in an effort to bring home the reality of the loss and to initiate a mourning process. By contrast, later approaches (Shane and Shane, 1991) focused on the provision of those regulatory functions previously supplied by the missing parent as the route through which the painful affect states could be faced and integrated. A lengthy and often silent acceptance of the patient's need for an illusory bond with the absent parent, embodied in the therapist, preceded its explanation.

In Holly's work with Martin, her desperate attachment to a negative maternal object occupies center stage. Her tie to the "not not idealizable" absent father

tendrils of healthy childhood motivations, strivings, expectations and hopes of getting what is needed, now, from the analyst" (p. 3). These latter transferences she positions at the "forward edge" of development, contrasting them with "trailing edge" transferences, representing reeditions of the formative childhood pathology. Interpretation of forward edge strivings revives "remaining healthy needs and expectations of responsiveness" while trailing edge interpretations, in their delineation of the patient's defensive response to early environmental failures, often unwittingly repeat them.

waited in the wings and was evoked in her sustained involvement with Martin, reminiscent of her father's steadfast albeit passive presence during her early years. Although the cycle of idealization and disillusionment inherent in her "serial relationships" repeated the failures of the maternal object, Holly's persistent pursuit of a warm and responsive mirroring selfobject could have represented an effort to recapture what she had lost with her father. The sequelae to Holly's traumatic early years, that is, her limited accessibility and openness, might have inadvertently influenced Martin's approach to the patient, her intuitively noninterpretive stance preserving an illusory relationship while seeding the possibility of a new one. A heretofore silent but healthy sector of the self, residing within the connection to the father, might have been discovered in Martin's nonintrusive, reliable presence.

In this sense, the layering of defense and adaptation in Holly's personality encompassed both the pseudoidealizations Martin discusses, which aimed at securing affirmation at the cost of denying core needs and affect states, and possibly a more camouflaged effort to reestablish the regulating and containing features of the relationship with her warm and more sustaining father. Even though Martin's lack of interpretation was an enactment, in addition to avoiding the negative transference, it could have also been based on an acceptance of the narrowly defined potentially healthy paternal transference.

At the conclusion of her presentation, Martin tells us of a specific enactment that she regards as the denouement of her work with Holly. Following a series of painful insights into the dynamics of the relationship with her mother, Holly hesitantly confides that she has kept secret her masochistic involvement with an abusive partner rather than risk her therapist's disapproval. Martin, who had unwittingly encouraged this relationship, attributes her blindness to the defensive (accommodative) aspects of Holly's idealization to a "split in . . . [herself] . . . that mirrored the split in Holly." This painful insight (Martin says, "That my participation in the enactment contributed to my patient's remaining in an abusive relationship for five years was almost more than I could bear to know") ultimately serves as the platform for the construction of integrating interpretations that permit therapist and patient greater access to "what Holly had to put aside nearly completely, for all the years of this treatment, . . . her own rage and despair at having to be the mirror to the mother [therapist] from whom she so desperately needed mirroring."

As I read these passages, I was once again struck by the honesty and thoughtfulness of Martin's description of her work with Holly. However, the detail with which she generously tells their story lends itself to alternative constructions. Just as the patient's clinging to old object ties can be motivated by a broad spectrum of needs and affect states, so might Martin's reorganizing insight be understood within a variety of clinical perspectives.

Katz (1998), in writing of enactment, emphasizes its communicative aspects. Actions often become the central modality for conveying meaning and even words may not be used symbolically but instead become assimilated features of the enactment. Martin intuitively grasps that effective communication with this patient occurs nonverbally. In fact, she describes a "now moment" (Stern et al., 1998), a spontaneous dramatic departure from habitual modes of relating in which both her own and the patient's awareness of unconsciously motivated agendas lights up and spurs new levels of intimacy, as well as greater momentum in the treatment. Martin's newfound capacity to illuminate and begin integrative work around the split transference/countertransference, she believes, moves the two of them out of their becalmed state. However, it is also possible that Holly, in blaming her therapist for all the pain she had suffered, revealed a core transference fantasy/wish, expressing a readiness to engage Martin as a potentially new object, capable of surviving disillusionment and abandonment. The therapist's immediate affective response, assuming responsibility for her patient's pain, actualized that wish and introduced the possibility of a disconfirming experience. Far from being "egregious," Martin's earlier confrontational "advice" might have signaled, for the patient, an emotional availability that laid the groundwork for the later reorganizing encounter.

Gehrie (1996), in his broadened definition of empathy, emphasizes that the "patient will 'hear' the analyst's emotionality with . . . (a) preverbal 'ear' in a way that no higher level symbolically encoded communication alone could accomplish" (p. 168). The reverse, for the therapist, may be true as well. The jarring intensity of Martin's shocked response ("I was shaken immensely", to Holly's explosive revelation finally opened her eyes ("like a bolt of lightning") to a core experience of herself and of her accommodative tie to her own mother which had not been represented verbally but had been enacted with her patient. As Martin's need to side-step Holly's distrust (through advice and reassurance) diminished, Holly was able to differentiate viscerally as well as cognitively a therapist who could tolerate her negative affects from a mother who could not. Newman (1999), discussing Winnicott's notion of usability, underscores the importance of "reliving" in making interpretations that closely connect to the patient's world and thereby provide for the patient a new object experience that facilitates the integration of feelings. Again, the bidirectionality of influence was especially significant in this case presentation. It was Holly's "interpretation" (paraphrasing, "Don't you know how important you are to me?") that brought the full impact of her avoidance to life for Martin, catalyzing a process of "more change and growth in all sectors of Holly's life, internally and externally, than we had seen during the entirety of the treatment to that point."

This case illustrates, once again, the hard-won knowledge achieved in the last few decades, that is, the recognition of how early object ties—especially negative ones—become embedded in the very core of the self and influence its development, layer by layer.

Although we have long cherished the overall paradigm that recognizes character as defense and resistance, and transference as requiring carefully titrated and timed interpretation, we often discover, via countertransference enactments, just how delicate another psychic organization can be. Years of preparatory work in which the therapeutic relationship is strengthened in barely discriminable ways precede and subtly influence the intense transactions described in this case. We can be alert to our patients' needs to evolve in their capacities to form healthier selfobject bonds and to engage unintegrated and often unknown affect states. However, the whole endeavor proceeds at a pace ultimately determined by the complex interplay between the patient's growing security and the therapist's expanding awareness of the possibilities of engagement—within the immediacy of the present relationship.

Summary

I have focused on the background features, that is, the patient's need, sometimes for a lengthy period, to relate to the therapist through the scrim of his or her characterological defenses. The urge to control the "other" in the relationship can stem from a variety of motivations. In the case of this patient, it was postulated that the combination of early trauma and parent loss resulted in both disavowal of the toxicity of the environment and denial of the loss. The patient's need to reestablish the preloss relationship, experienced as a safe haven, contributed to the interminable nature of the work. The enactments that punctuated the treatment derived meaning from the insight they produced and the intensity of the affective engagement they generated, both facilitating the integration of split-off aspects of the self.

References

Bacal, H. & Newman, K. (1990), *Theories of Object Relations: Bridges to Self Psychology.* New York: Columbia University Press.

Boesky, D. (1990), The psychoanalytic process and its components. *Psychoanal. Quart.*, 59:550–584.

Fleming, J. (1972), Early object deprivation and transference phenomena: The working alliance. *Psychoanal. Quart.*, 41:23–49.

——— & Altschul, S. (1963), Activation of mourning and growth by psychoanalysis. *Internat. J. Psychoanal.*, 44:419–431.

Gehrie, M. (1996), Empathy in broader perspective: A technical approach to the consequences of the negative selfobject in early character formation. In: *Basic Ideas Reconsidered: Progress in Self Psychology, Vol. 12,* ed. A. Goldberg. Hillsdale, NJ: The Analytic Press, pp. 159–179.

Katz, G. (1998), Where the action is: The enacted dimension of analytic process. *J. Amer. Psychoanal. Assn.*, 46:1129–1167

Mitchell, S. (1988), A delicate balance: The clinical play of illusion. In: *Relational Concepts in Psychoanalysis.* Cambridge, MA: Harvard University Press, pp. 204–234.

Newman, K. (1999), The usable analyst: The role of the affective engagement of the analyst in reaching usability. In: *The Annual of Psychoanalysis,* 26/27:175–194. Hillsdale, NJ: The Analytic Press.

Shane, E. & Shane, M. (1991), Object loss and selfobject loss: A consideration of self psychology's contribution to understanding mourning and the failure to mourn. In: *The Annual of Psychoanalysis.,* 18:115–131. Hillsdale, NJ: The Analytic Press.

Schlessinger, N. & Robbins, F. (1983), *A Developmental View of the Psychoanalytic Process.* New York: International Universities Press, pp. 193–216.

Stern, D., Sander, L., Nahum, J., Harrison, A., Lyons-Ruth, K., Morgan, A., Bruschweiller-Stern, E. & Tronick, E. (1998), Non-interpretive mechanisms in psychoanalytic therapy: The "something more" than interpretation. *Internat. J. Psychoanal.,* 79: 903–921.

Stern, S. (1994), Needed relationships and repeated relationships: An integrated relational perspective. *Psychoanal. Dial.,* 4:317–345.

Tolpin, M. (2000), Forward and trailing edge transferences: An enlarged framework. Unpublished.

Winnicott, D. W. (1960). Ego distortion in terms of true and false self. In: *The Maturational Processes and the Facilitating Environment.* New York: International Universities Press, 1965, pp. 140–152.

Countertransference Dominance: Discussion of Karen Martin's Clinical Case

BEVERLY P. KEEFER

It is important to write openly about our experiences as therapists and analysts so that we can learn from one another. The author's interest in enactments seemed to be a guiding force for her to look critically at her work with Holly, a late adolescent. Her paper is the author's retrospective account of her struggle with countertransference in her work with a lesbian-identified adolescent. The author emphasized the lesbian identification of the patient as the predominant stimulus to her countertransference as a lesbian-identified therapist.

In the third to last paragraph of her paper the author clarifies its purpose. Martin says,

> I chose to write about this case for many reasons. I believe it is an excellent example of a client whose relationships were . . . a manifestation of sexual enactments. It also demonstrates . . . how an unanalyzed enactment within the therapist–patient dyad was at the root of my being unable to help this patient extricate herself from this destructive pattern. And, finally . . . in my clinical practice over the last 20 years I have treated many women who identify as lesbians and who are hopelessly caught in a repeating cycle of serial relationships that last two to three years. I believe many of these women are trapped, as Holly was, in an unconsciously driven compulsion to relive early trauma embedded in their childhood relationships to their mothers. This is not to say that every lesbian is a lesbian because of an unanalyzed enactment relating to her mother.

I organize my discussion to address these three points.

Sexual Enactments

The author opens her paper with a discussion of the term enactment, referring to it as "unconscious, symbolic repetitions of earlier trauma." She continues, saying that these unconscious enactments comprise a repetition compulsion. She then hypothesizes that her patient, Holly, (presumably) age 17 or 18 when she began a once a week psychotherapy, enacts with female partners her unanalyzed and unconscious "repetitions of her early trauma at the hand of her mother." This use of repetition compulsion is not sufficient to understand the sexual dynamic of this multifaceted, complex young woman. I question whether the author's use of the term enactment is reductionistic and offered in place of a dynamic case formulation.

The many enactments suggest a replication of Martin's description of Holly's parents' marital relationship. Holly is described at different times as obsessed with the other and unable to leave. This is the transference. Could this be a defensive, masochistic identification with the absent father who surrendered to his wife? The description of this case suggests that Holly sacrificed herself to her partners and to the therapist to keep the attachment. This is sadomasochism; the therapist felt tortured and Holly suffered. The patient seems to be blamed, or in the author's eyes, responsible in part for the enactment. I suggest this is a case of countertransference dominance (Maroda, 1998) and a reductionistic formulation (e.g., trauma at the hand of the mother) by the therapist.

Notably absent is any discussion of the late adolescent developmental context of this patient and its role in her enactments. Forming a firm sense of identity including sexual identity, is the developmental achievement of late adolescence, with failure to do so resulting in identity diffusion (Erikson, 1950; Blos, 1977). Profound regressions and progressions are known hallmarks of this period (Erikson, 1974; Blos, 1977). In infancy there is a "hatching" to individuate from the mother (Mahler, Pine, and Bergman, 1963). In adolescence the hatching occurs again with a shedding of family dependencies, a loosening of infantile object ties, and ultimately the consolidation of one's identity. In both periods, there is a heightened vulnerability of the personality or character organization.

Contemporary feminist writers (Chodorow, 1978; Butler, 1990; Brown and Gilligan, 1992) have argued that the process of identity formation for female adolescents is harder and differs from that of male adolescents (see Ollech and McCarthy, 1997, for a review). Heterosexual girls experience greater increases in anxiety, conflict, shame, and self-doubt. As their sexuality comes to the fore, heterosexual adolescent girls often learn they are identified chiefly by their physical selves, reproductive capacity, and appearance. These girls often subject those who are unfeminine to derision, scapegoating, and ostracism.

Psychic restructuring can only be accomplished with regressions in service of ego development. It is unavoidable, obligatory, and phase-specific. Many patients who are action prone demonstrate through sexual relationships their age-appropriate regressions and desperate attempts to avoid annihilation anxiety, separation anxiety, depression, and mourning through exciting, sexual engagements (Coen, 1992). Sexual conquests can also be viewed as a defensive attempt to preserve an illusion of infantile omnipotence and the wish for regressive merger.

An additional developmental perspective may be helpful to understand this young woman's repetitive sexual enactments. She is action prone. Her use of drugs and alcohol and her sexual acting out are better understood as painful expressions of her adolescent struggle with identity formation, particularly the regression from, and progression toward, attempted consolidation of her sexual identity. Her behavior at any and all points is multidetermined (Waelder, 1936).

One question often asked at the beginning of psychotherapy is, "Why now?" Why in her senior year did this "extremely narcissistic" and "unavailable" mother bring this girl for help? We are told she abuses drugs and alcohol, but this has been going on for some time. Could it be that the mother is experiencing anxiety, and brings her daughter for therapy as a college separation is in the air, because she finds separation unbearable, a narcissistic injury she would like to deny?

Once she is a patient, I wonder what Holly's expectations of therapy are for herself. Missing, in the entire paper, are any quotes of what the patient actually said. We hear no dialogue between the therapist and the patient. We never hear Holly's voice, and we have no visual image of her. As readers, we do not get a sense of the patient's mind, her constructions, memories, or fantasies.

The Therapist–Patient Dyad

What absorbed Martin's interest in this paper is that both she and the patient are described as lesbian. It becomes clear that their sexual identities play a powerful role in the author's countertransferential enactment in the therapy. Papers such as this one are important teaching vehicles. The case was difficult for the therapist, and this fact is apparent and acknowledged.

In writing about her patient, Martin is contradictory.One contradiction has to do with the description of the mother. The author describes the mother as having no redeeming features but says, on the other hand, that the woman "is a wordsmith of sorts," The author seems to reduce and simplify the patient's report of her parents and may need to consider a more complex multifaceted picture of them.

Holly is described as male-identified. What does this mean to the therapist, and what does it mean to the patient? Does this mean she dresses in a masculine way? Does she enjoy traditionally male activities such as riding motorbikes, or has she masculine features? It may be important as to whether this masculinity separated or isolated Holly from her female peers.

The author gives evidence of Holly's withdrawal from sports to protect herself from narcissistic injury. She does not tell us if she recognizes Holly's sense of worthlessness that could identify her with the father. Was her dating of boys defensive against emerging libidinal attractions to girls or women? Was it a weak attempt to conform to peer pressure, to avoid ostracism? Or, could her attraction to women be defensive, a masochistic identification with a father who submitted to his wife's rages and who abandoned Holly.

The father is described by the author as impotent and absent from the family. She gives him no contributing power to the patient's early childhood. There is no discussion or formulation of the possible effect of his absence (e.g., there are suggestions that girls of divorced parents turn away from boys, and identify with the [maternal] aggressor, so as not to feel conflict, shame, and humiliation for the libidinal longings for the lost parent). Possibly Holly's early relationship and identifications with, and the loss of, the father contribute to her choice of partners.

The countertransference of the therapist seems to reach a zenith with the patient's letter to her from college. The patient is described as having a lesbian identity when she writes from college and reports that she is flunking out, continues to use drugs and alcohol, and "had engaged in her first lesbian relationship." She was in an acute crisis. What acute crisis? Flunking out of school should not seem surprising. The way the paper reads, it refers to the relationship with the woman. Perhaps this is what unconsciously stimulated the author to call her patient and reveal her sexual identity, under the guise of reassurance for Holly. Goldberger (1993) writes about bright spots, those occasions where because we have something in common with our patient, we imagine we know their experience.

I wonder if this "enactment" was provoked by "a crisis" in the therapist as her writing tells us. Maroda (1998) suggests either party may initiate an enactment. Gabbard (1995) noted that mutual projective identification refers only to the stimulation of repressed intense affect. Enactment requires an additional action. It is not merely an affectively driven set of behaviors; it is necessarily a repetition of past events that have been buried in the unconscious due to unmanageable or unwanted emotion. The therapist is shocked because she did not know this (crisis) part of herself.

Maroda (1998) points out there has been no serious discussion in the literature of the impact of the therapist's past, rather than the patient's, being reenacted to the point of dominating the treatment, and even its outcome. A therapist under a strong countertransference is under the influence of the same repetition compulsion as the patient. The therapist is in a position to be certain her reality prevails. The patient's reality can be subjugated to the therapist's, resulting in countertransference dominance throughout the course of treatment (Maroda, 1998). This is damaging for the patient and the therapist. Holly may blame herself for therapeutic failure, and this therapist tells us about her guilt, conflict, and defensiveness—about a therapy that does not go well. Although the author does not reference Maroda, it is a valuable paper in that it validates Martin's experience.

The therapist seemed unaware of the internal difficulties that led to her over-involvement and the ensuing difficulties until six years into the therapy. If Holly was about 18 when she started, she would be about 24 when she confronted her therapist about her suggestion she stay with her partner. It is likely she had developmentally arrived at a place of greater identity consolidation.

Martin's Concluding Clinical Observations

The author's concluding statements about lesbians "hopelessly caught in a repeating cycle of serial relationships" are tangential to the paper. Psychoanalytic psychotherapy is informed by knowing a particular, individual patient. Since Freud, we have been deeply influenced in our practice by the developmental history of the patient and the particular point at which a person commences treatment. Serial relationships lasting two to three years may be age appropriate in late adolescence and have very different meanings in midlife.

Because of their unique experiences of cultural and familial restrictions and personal shame, lesbian adolescents cannot formulate a sexual identity with the supports given to heterosexual, female adolescents. It is suggested that the formulation of one's same-sex sexual identity takes longer and is more complicated than for heterosexual girls. This is in addition to the character structure previously developed. It would have been helpful for me if Martin had commented on the age group she is referring to in her practice. Perhaps it is normative for lesbian women to experience two to three year serial relationships during their late adolescence or early adult years. Is this the age of the population on which Martin is basing her generalizations? Another possibility is that in the process of coming out, one experiences an adolescence of sorts at any age, and short-term relationships are a practicing phase in which sexual identity becomes consolidated and the capacity for long-term commitment is developed.

Conclusion

Martin's paper serves as a reminder of the importance of experiencing and then examining our own countertransference, especially when a case does not show progression over a lengthy period of time. Instead of looking to the term enactment for explanatory power in understanding Holly, I think the author would have been better served by understanding the complex developmental tasks of adolescence for girls and the additional difficulty of forming a lesbian identity. The lesbian therapist acknowledged her unanalyzed countertransferential effects on the patient's therapy. I hope she continues to do more reflecting, reading, and writing in this important area.

References

Blos, P. (1977), When and how does adolescence end: Structural criteria for adolescent closure. In: *Adolescent Psychiatry, Vol. 5,* ed. S. C. Feinstein and P. Giovacchini. New York: Aronson, pp. 5–17.

Brown, L. & Gilligan, C. (1992), *Meeting at the Crossroads: Women's Psychology and Girls' Development.* Cambridge, MA: Harvard University Press.

Butler, J. (1990), *Gender Trouble: Feminism and the Subversion of Identity.* New York: Routledge.

Chodorow, N. (1978), *The Reproduction of Mothering.* Berkeley: University of California Press.

Coen, S. (1992), *The Misuse of Persons: Analyzing Pathological Dependency.* Hillsdale, NJ: The Analytic Press.

Erikson, E. H. (1950), *Childhood and Society.* New York: Norton.

——— (1974), *Dimensions of a New Identity.* New York: The Jefferson Lectures.

Gabbard, G. (1995), Countertransference: The emerging common ground. *Internat. J. Psychoanal.*, 76:475–485.

Goldberger, M. (1993), "Bright spot," a variant of "blind spot." *Psychoanal. Quart.*, 62:270–273.

Mahler, M. S., Pine, F. & Bergman, A. (1963), *The Psychological Birth of the Human Infant.* New York: Basic Books.

Maroda, K. J.(1998), Enactment: When the patient's and analyst's pasts converge. *Psychoanal. Psychol.*, 15:517–535.

Ollech, D. & McCarthy, J. B. (1997), Impediments to identity formation in female adolescents. *Psychoanal. Psychol.*, 14:65–80.

Waelder, R. (1936), The principle of multiple function. *Psychoanal. Quart.*, 5:45–62.

Reply to the Discussions

KAREN MARTIN

I am grateful to Salee Jenkins and Beverly Keefer for their thoughtful responses to my clinical case.

Jenkins has broadened and deepened my understanding of my work with Holly. She looked at my case through the lens I was using and discovered things there I had not seen. She has provided me with important additional ways of thinking about and understanding my patient, myself, and our treatment. Jenkins elucidates complexities in my case that I missed, and she generously suggests that my unconscious awareness of these may well have informed my work. Jenkins's major focus in her discussion is on "the bit by bit construction of an environment" in which what I identified as a crucial turning point in Holly's and my work could develop. The turning point to which I refer was the bursting into consciousness of an unconscious vertical split in myself that mirrored that in Holly and that had "trapped" us for years in an enactment. In so doing, Jenkins has contributed a great deal to my own appreciation of the "unfolding" quality of my work with this patient. Although she acknowledges that specific enactments by the therapist constitute "important nodal points" in a psychotherapy, she argues throughout her discussion for a more sensitive and deeper understanding of the "multiple transference meanings inherent" in the interactions that precede and facilitate such major enactments.

Jenkins suggests that a period of time, even an extended period, during which the therapist finds herself not interpreting the resistances may in fact be less collusive with a patient's avoidance than responsive to the patient's need for paranoid-like control of the treatment relationship. Although I welcome this idea and even feel that I can in retrospect value its merit in helping me to understand the early period of the treatment with Holly, I also find myself a bit apprehensive about latching onto it, fearful that such a notion offers an "easy way out" of potentially valid therapist guilt for not having been more diligent in attending to the transferences and countertransferences for the therapist's own unconscious or conscious reasons.

In Jenkins's words, "Patients like Holly epitomize the humbling complexities of those whose early traumas and losses have left them refractory to change." She observes it is common in work with such patients for the psychotherapy to "reach a plateau and take on an interminable cast" in which little appears to be happening. But Jenkins suggests that during this seemingly interminable period of "no change" the therapeutic relationship is over time shoring up the patient's weakened self, and the patient is silently transforming her unconscious belief that the therapist is untrustworthy and needs to be controlled. As I reflect on that point in the treatment with Holly when I "insisted" that Holly remain in a relationship that she had an impulse to flee, I have to wonder whether my own impatience was a result of not recognizing her need for this extended period of "filling in or bolstering up of a weakened self." I attempted to break through what I took to be my patient's defenses, without due consideration of the idea that Holly was herself dictating the speed of the process, based on her own selfobject needs. In essence, I underestimated the strength and profundity of the pathology—the "unconscious bond to the pathological object" that made Holly enter into a "Faustian bargain: in order to maintain the self organization and preserve the illusion of having a good parent, the patient must deny both internal and external reality." (I wish I'd been able to make my main point as clearly and eloquently as Jenkins has stated it here.)

Yet, consistent with the entire tone and intent of Jenkins's discussion of my case, she suggests that even my "confrontation" of Holly—while probably motivated consciously by my frustration and underappreciation of her need for the extended period of "filling in and bolstering up" of her weakened self—may indeed have had a salutary effect by having signaled for Holly "an emotional availability that laid the groundwork for the later reorganizing encounter."

Jenkins states that patients like Holly, who have experienced early loss and trauma, "often attempt to recreate with the therapist . . . aspects of the preloss or pre-trauma relationship." In doing so, she goes on, "the experience of grief or frustrated rage is unnecessary." I take it Jenkins meant that Holly recreated with me the early childhood experience of warmth and responsiveness flowing toward the "real her" emblematic of her relationship to her father. In Jenkins's words, "A heretofore silent but healthy sector of the self, residing with the connection to the father, might have been discovered in Martin's nonintrusive, reliable presence." In a sense, then, Holly reunited her parents in fantasy as she played out with me in the transference the crucial aspects of her relationships with both of them. Conceptualizing the predominant transference as containing simultaneously defensive and reparative dimensions is facilitative of my deeper understanding of my case.

In her discussion, Jenkins reminds us that more recent theoretical formulations suggest that "a lengthy and often silent acceptance of the patient's need for an illusory bond with the absent parent, embodied in the therapist, must precede vigorous confrontation of the patient's denial." The interminable quality of this 11-year treatment, exaggerated as it was by the span of 20 years in which we worked, made it difficult for me to "keep the faith." My having insisted that Holly suppress an impulse to leave yet another relationship is perhaps indicative of my "crisis in confidence" surrounding more recent contributions to theory which emphasize provision and abiding commitment to following our patients' leads rather than leading our patients. Having reminded me of the essential rightness of more recent contributions to our work, Jenkins is able to point out that it is actually Holly who first opens the door to our disentangling ourselves from the enactment, when she functions as interpreter to me, her therapist, by asking rhetorically, "Don't you know how important you are to me?" Does this then signal a readiness on my patient's part to proceed in the work? Has she sensed something in my responses to indicate to her that I am finally up to handling that which she has put aside all of these years? But then, as I previously referenced, Jenkins suggests that perhaps my vigorous confrontation a few years earlier, even though not compatible with more recent theoretical contributions, may actually have signaled an "emotional availability that laid the groundwork for the later reorganizing encounter." This would suggest, and it appears that Jenkins may concur, that enactments may indeed be an essential component in a psychotherapy. If, in Jenkins's mind, not an essential component in psychotherapy in general then at least in the case of Holly, she indicates that "the enactments that punctuated the treatment derived meaning from the insight they produced and the intensity of the affective engagement they generated, both facilitating the integration of split-off aspects of the self."

Jenkins quotes from Newman (1999) in his discussion of "usability" that when a therapist is with a patient "reliving—as an insider—makes it possible to offer interpretations that truly grasp the world in which the patient lives—thereby providing a new object experience, facilitating the integration of feelings, and strengthening the matrix of the self." In her discussion, Jenkins seems to have somehow relived this case with me "as an insider." This clearly made it possible for her to offer observations, understanding, and interpretations "that truly grasp the world in which" this therapist lived. In doing so, Jenkins has "strengthened the matrix" of my professional self. I am greatly appreciative.

Jenkins's response signals, by her omission of any discussion of it, the relative insignificance of the question of sexual orientation in this treatment. This resonates with my own analysis that shared sexual orientation and sexually identitifying as lesbian are of minor importance in understanding the obstacles and outcomes in this case.

It is my impression that Keefer does not share this view. In the very first paragraph of her discussion, she indicates that I "emphasized the lesbian identification of the patient as the predominant stimulus to my countertransference as a lesbian-identified therapist." This is not my understanding of what I said. Clearly my spontaneous, unreflected upon self-disclosure to my patient of my sexual orientation is an example of countertransference related to both of us being homosexual. However, my paper is not about countertransference per se but about enactments. My self-disclosure obviously was not an enactment, by definition, and it did not make a meaningful contribution to the difficulty we encountered in the psychotherapy. It was simply a single instance of countertransference that actually occurred when Holly was not even actively engaged in psychotherapy with me. The predominant stimulus for the enactment that the paper was written to demonstrate was that an unanalyzed split in me, of which I was unaware, mirrored a split in Holly. Holly's costly psychological adaptation to an emotionally unavailable and unresponsive mother was to split off and disavow myriad psychological needs and to replace those needs with a solitary compensatory need to win the mirroring responsiveness and affirmation of her mother by becoming exquisitely attuned to her mother's needs. Holly's destructive compulsion to relive in "real time" this traumatic relationship to her mother characterizes her contribution to the enactment that she and I became trapped in. That a similar unanalyzed split lay dormant in me, and that I therefore did not see through Holly's defensive and adaptive accommodation, is what informed my part in the transference-countertransference collusion that constituted the enactment in the psychotherapy.

That we were both homosexual was only tangentially related to my countertransference difficulties in the case and was virtually not related at all to the enactment we became trapped in.

Keefer continues her discussion of my case by indicating that "the use of repetition compulsion is not sufficient to understand the sexual dynamic of this multifaceted, complex young woman." She wonders whether the "use of the term enactment supplanted dynamic case formulation." She states that "notably absent is any discussion of the developmental context of this patient and its role in her enactments." She continues her theme with a brief rendering of adolescent developmental theory and indicates that perhaps "an additional developmental perspective may be helpful to understand this young woman's repetitive sexual enactments." In Keefer's view my patient is "action prone." She believes that my patient's use of drugs and alcohol as well as her sexual acting out are "better understood as painful expressions of her adolescent struggle with identity formation, particularly the regression from, and progression toward, attempted consolidation of her sexual identity." Keefer notes that my patient's behavior at any and all points is multidetermined. That my patient's behavior and symptoms at all points are multidetermined goes without saying, and that in the beginning of treatment she was adolescent and therefore struggling with many developmental issues characteristic of that stage of life goes without saying. That I did think of her in relation to her developmental issues during the initial years of her treatment I believe also goes without saying. That she struggled with the same unremitting set of symptoms for many, many years, while in treatment and during one- to two-year hiatuses from the treatment until she was in her early thirties made it clear to me that her behavior and symptoms were about something other than "normal" developmental period instability and fluidity. And, finally, "that the use of repetition compulsion is not sufficient to understand the sexual dynamic of this multifaceted, complex young woman" also goes without saying. "Mirror, Mirror" was about one pivotal element in this complex case with this admittedly complex young woman; it was not intended to be a complete case study and indeed is not a complete case study. That I am only writing about a major enactment that Holly and I were unwittingly "trapped" in and that proved to be a major obstacle to her becoming free of a similar repetitive enactment that she was engaged in outside of the treatment does not mean that this is the only dimension of the treatment or the only psychological dimension of Holly. It is simply the one dimension of the case about which I chose to write.

Keefer continues in her discussion by noting that I contradict myself in my characterization of Holly's parents, and that these inconsistencies in my rendering contribute negatively to my dynamic understanding of the case. For example, I characterize Holly's mother as alcoholic, extremely narcissistic, and emotionally unavailable to Holly. Keefer translates this into my alleged belief that Holly's mother has "no redeeming features" and points out that I describe the mother as a "wordsmith" and "artist." According to Keefer, mother's being a wordsmith of sorts, an artist, and most importantly, taking the initiative to seek treatment for her daughter, constitute evidence that it is not true that mother has no redeeming features. Again, Keefer seems to have misunderstood. I did not characterize Holly's mother as having no redeeming features. I characterized the mother as being alcoholic, narcissistic, and unresponsive and unavailable emotionally to Holly, and I saw no evidence to the contrary in the many years of our work together. Keefer suggests that perhaps the mother was experiencing difficulty with the anticipation of separation from Holly as she prepared to leave for college. Of course anything is possible, but I am curious that Keefer could imagine that I would not have come to that understanding myself during the many years I have worked with Holly if there had been any evidence in support of it. Holly was failing to function as a good selfobject to her mother by behaving badly and not being successful. This was the stimulus for mother's initiating treatment. If anyone was having anxiety in anticipation of separation it was Holly, who was indeed not well prepared to take this next developmental step because of not having had "good enough" maternal responsiveness in her life.

In a similar vein, Keefer observes that I describe the father as "impotent and absent from the family" and says that I give him "no contributing power to the patient's early childhood." In fact I indicate that though impotent, masochistic, absent, and "not altogether idealizable . . . he was warm and he was able to be somewhat emotionally responsive to Holly." I think my statement suggests that the father did have contributing power to my patient's childhood, in both negative and positive ways. In fact, it was probably her father's emotional responsiveness and attunement that Holly tried to use to compensate for the glaring psychological deficits in her mother. This is one way then, in my view, to think about Holly's having become so strongly "male-identified."

Keefer indicates on the first page of her discussion that it is not until the third to the last paragraph of the paper that I clarify my "purposes" for writing it. Herein lies a clue, I believe, to Keefer's slant on the paper. I make clear on page one that I will demonstrate how an unwitting enactment in the treatment functioned for many years as an obstacle to the successful outcome of the work. On the final page, I add that intimate relationships, heterosexual and homosexual alike, "are carriers of health and pathology." I then observe that in my practice I have seen many lesbians whose serial relationships, marked by a pattern of idealization followed by traumatic disillusionment, are trapped in relationships that are manifestations of the compulsions to relive originally traumatizing attachments rooted in childhood relationships to unavailable and unidealizable mothers. Nearly all Keefer's remarks seem at least tangentially related to this point. By this I mean that most of her comments are directed to other ways in which I might have understood the psychological issues manifested in my patient's "sexual enactments" (serial relationships) outside of the treatment. In addition, Keefer devotes virtually none of her discussion to the singular purpose that I identified on page one for writing the paper in the first place. That purpose being, once again, to demonstrate how an unseen and therefore unanalyzed enactment in the psychotherapy with Holly functioned as an obstacle to reaching successful termination of the work.

Keefer suggests that my "concluding statements about lesbians being 'hopelessly caught in a repeating cycle of serial relationships' are tangential." She goes on to indicate that "psychoanalytic psychotherapy is informed by theory, and by knowing a particular, individual patient." She reminds me that "since the time of Freud, we have been deeply influenced in our practice by the developmental history of the patient and the particular point at which a person commences treatment." And further, she states "serial relationships lasting two to three years may be age appropriate in late adolescence and have different meanings in midlife." I trust a more careful reading of the case will highlight that Holly's pattern in relationships, as well as work and school, lasted well into her thirties. I trust that I have responded to Keefer's other hypotheses about my patient's psychological dynamics, conflicts, and deficits sufficiently to have demonstrated how and why I arrived at my conclusions. It would appear that Keefer assumed that because I did not produce an extensive case history, explain how I came to the diagnostic understandings that I did, and speak to the patient's motivations for treatment, that I had really not done the careful dynamic formulation that functioned as the background to my paper. Finally, to observe that many people, heterosexual and homosexual alike, engage in relationships that are pathological rather than healthy and that "sexualities are carriers of health and pathology" does not strike me as an overgeneralization. Had Keefer accused me of stating the obvious I could have easily concurred.

Female Adolescence:
Difficult for Heterosexual Girls, Hazardous for Lesbians

BEVERLY P. KEEFER
KELLY REENE

I'd rather you be a prostitute than be a lesbian. You could be a murderer. You could be a prostitute, and that would be fine. We'd still love you.
—Sharon Thompson. *Going All The Way: Teenage Girls' Tales of Sex, Romance, and Pregnancy*

Developmental theories that describe the process of adolescence for girls assume heterosexuality (Blos, 1962; Erikson, 1968; Ollech and McCarthy, 1997). What about this process for a subset of adolescent girls, those who begin to identify attractions for other girls and eventually identify as lesbian? The focal developmental task of adolescence is a "second individuation," a reworking of the earlier oedipal drama, with new resolutions attempted and integrated. Individuation is facilitated through gaining satisfactory and ever more complicated notions about love, affection, and sexuality. Central to facilitating this process are peer and social experiences and family values as they impact on the ego in its progressions and regressions (Erikson, 1963, 1968). For lesbian-identified adolescents experiencing same-sex attractions, the "trying on" of sexual roles, peer and familial affirmation of one's emerging sexual feelings, and the typical behaviors associated with promoting one's evolving sexual identity (e.g., dating, locker room talk) are probably much different from those of their heterosexual counterparts. This paper discusses normative, female, heterosexual adolescence, and the social and cultural demands that reciprocally influence intrapsychic demands and processes. These are then compared with and contrasted to the unique demands of culture and society when one is a lesbian adolescent. Given certain cultural impediments to heterosexual female identity formation, the task of identity consolidation for the lesbian identified adolescent is almost certain to be different and more difficult.

What does this mean for those who treat lesbian-identified patients? For young, lesbian-identified women, is the process of identity consolidation simply delayed and elongated? Or do the difficulties cause symptoms of identity diffusion at worst, as evidenced with symptoms such as aggression, impulsivity, and sexual acting out, or severe sexual inhibition, constriction, and depression? Or, is it possible that lesbian-identified girls, unlike their heterosexual counterparts, do not generally subordinate important aspects of themselves in adolescence, and overvalue the opinions of others, leading to a stronger, more consolidated self?

Adolescence: Heterosexual Female Identity

Adolescence is known as the second individuation (Blos, 1967). The developmental thrust through this period is to restructure the psyche as the body and mind develop new adult capacities and ultimately consolidate an enduring sense of identity. Sexuality surges during midadolescence and takes its final form during late adolescence (Blos, 1962). If unable to master the developmental tasks of adolescence, identity confusion may result. Successful resolution of adolescence results in a firm sense of identity, i.e., an internally consistent sense of self, including a sense of pride in one's sexual identity.

Horney (1945) and other contemporary writers (Chodorow, 1989; Butler, 1990) maintain that in general the process of identity formation for female adolescents differs from that of males. In middle and late adolescence, having several positive experiences with loving and sexual feelings seems to further facilitate identity consolidation. It is generally believed that adolescent infatuations help resolve homosexual, heterosexual, and bisexual trends, or having it all, to having a primary identification (Blos, 1967). Our cultural climate with normative and generally mandatory heterosexuality implies a different and probably marginalized experience as detailed below for lesbian-identified female adolescents.

Ollech and McCarthy (1997) hypothesize that cultural, social, and psychological factors attenuate the development of ego strengths throughout girlhood. In their review of impediments to identity formulation, they suggest that girls experience greater anxiety, conflict, shame and self-doubt faced with choice, and lack of differentiation from the family and culture at large. This results in a heightened dissonance about differentiation and renders girls' identity formation process more difficult and attained identity more tenuous.

Heterosexual adolescent girls often learn that they are defined chiefly by their reproductive capacity and by their appearance, or by how others see them. They lose the strong sense of self that they seem to have gained and voiced during the latency years (Gilligan, Lyons, and Hammer, 1990; Brown and Gilligan, 1992). Thus, adolescence becomes a time of increased interest in "feminine behavior" in order to win approval and affirmation from authorities, male and female peers and the wider culture. Hill and Lynch (1983) explained that the emphasis on being feminine that adolescent girls encounter is due to a "gender intensification" that occurs at this time of life. This process involves a decrease in self-esteem, an increase in greater self-consciousness, and a heightened receptivity to the needs and opinions of others.

It is not coincidental that adolescent girls subordinate important aspects of themselves in order to appear likable and maintain relationships in a society that in general devalues and sexualizes women. Their preferences, opinions and needs generally remain secondary to the desires, views, and requirements of others. If this is true for heterosexual female adolescents, does this apply to lesbian-identified adolescents?

The Ego Ideal

Blos (1962) emphasized the need for adolescent revision and expansion of the superego to encompass emerging aspirations for sex, intimacy, and work or career achievement. Adolescent developmental processes result in the formation of the new psychic structure, the ego ideal. It contains the individual's highest future expectations for herself. Infantile idealization of the parents and their expectations for their child, already internalized, are diminished and reformulated. This process of deidealization begins in early adolescence when loving, idealized feelings are transferred from the parents to a new best friend or friends who acquire an intense emotional significance; it offers affirmations and identifications often in contrast to those of the parents. The peer group emerges as a central presence of seminal importance (Dunphy, 1969). General banter among girls includes such questions as, Should you kiss on the first date? Do you think he's cute? How far do you go? Should you maintain your virginity? What if you get pregnant? In this way, the peer group is a significant molder of adolescent values and probably constitutes a profound influence on modifying the superego and establishing the ego ideal. These relationships help support movement from the dependent child to a differentiated, autonomous adult. New standards emerge, reflecting the adolescent's sexual and mental maturity, ambitions and goals, and the reflection of influential friends, lovers, and mentors.

Because of the preoedipal and oedipal ties with the mother, there is a preoccupation and orientation toward relationships and exemplary femininity. The female ego ideal exemplifies nurturance, selfless caretaking, a pleasing appearance, and a disavowal of aggression (Ollech and McCarthy, 1997). It has as its precursor "the idea of an unaggressive, clean, neat and physically attractive little girl who is determined to renounce sexual activities" (Jacobsen, 1964). The crystallization of the ego ideal in adolescence and the resurgence of childhood bonds, plus the potential shaping effect of social pressures, initiate and support curtailment of identity formation in female adolescence (Gilligan et al., 1990; Brown and Gilligan, 1992).

Through her clinical work, Kaschak (1992) recognized that although women's gender-based identity is constructed from birth, the developmental phase of adolescence is "the crucial stage for full emergence and crystallization of gendered and embodied meaning" (p. 90). Jack (1991) noted the dilemma of the female adolescent in choosing whether to fabricate a self in order to obtain "male favor, safety and security" (p. 85).

Adolescence: Lesbian Identity

There are numerous psychoanalytic writings on identity formation in adolescence. Generally, heterosexual models are implicit, thus equating all female development with heterosexual female development. Gonsiorek and Rudolph (1991) describe "coming out," the process of identifying with and becoming a member of one's minority group, as an additional developmental effort unique to lesbian and gay adolescents. Valuing one's budding sexuality both as being attractive and in terms of another's attractiveness are of primary importance. If this is true, what happens with lesbian attraction? If a girl admits a same-sex attraction to her peers, loss of affection, peer exclusion, and isolation are probable consequences for her "deviance." It makes sense that for any adolescent who does not engage in the normative, heterosexual activities, there is a high price to be paid.

Martin and Hetrick (1988) noted, in a study of 2000 lesbian and gay teens, that not being part of the dominant social group results in a profound sense of isolation. They note the isolation in three areas. Cognitively, there was lack of accurate information about lesbian sex and positive models of lesbians. Socially, there was a negative view of the self, including identification with the aggressor, with profound self-loathing. Emotionally, one could "pass" or "not pass" (e.g., acting in a counterphobic manner such as dating lots of boys, or at worst getting pregnant connoted being more accepted, and therefore "passing"). The other possibility was not to pass.

In religious groups, there is generally an equal pressure to pass or be disenfranchised. Similarly, coming out or hiding confronts a lesbian-identified adolescent with her parents. Generally, parents are interested in having heterosexual children. Coming out can mean a lack of support, rejection, verbal abuse, or even violence. Simple openness can be viewed as flaunting (i.e., a hostile act, resulting in violence or sexual or physical abuse). It is thought that lesbian-identified adolescents learn to compartmentalize which further intensifies social isolation. Hiding to pass further isolates, coupled with the fear of discovery. The social isolation is thought to increase sexualized same-sex relationships. Being part of other minority groups (e.g., African American, Jewish) does not risk family expulsion. Thus, college or post–high school years may offer the first opportunity for a same-sex relationship without the fear of parental knowledge or expulsion.

If a girl is shamed about her sexual object choice and sexual expansion, the likelihood of developing an integrated superego ideal could be inversely proportional. Lies, secrets, and shame could negatively affect one's self image and aspirations. Burch (1993) however, noted that bisexual expressiveness is a sign of health, compared with exclusive primary hetero- or homosexuality. To maintain bisexual or lesbian expressiveness in the face of gender conformist pressure may structure a greater capacity for independence, resilience, or creativity and tolerance for internal, conflictual pressures. A lesbian identification may deemphasize heterosexual ideals of deferential femininity. Conversely, some heterosexual women claim that homosexual relationships have enhanced their femininity and maternality (Kirkpatrick and Morgan, 1980).

Cultural Factors

Important cultural impediments to females' identity formation have been identified. The devaluation of women and girls, and the acceptance of male prerogatives in many places are still normative. Benjamin (1998) noted there's an idealization of the father and a devaluation of the mother that constitute a profound split that has infused our culture at large and shaped our very notion of individuality.

Horney (1945) and Westcott (1986) noted there is a cultural expectation in the patriarchy that daughters should affirm their fathers and help their mothers. Mothers turn to other women and children and provide reciprocal nurturing; often fathers do not. A daughter learns from both parents that she is valuable to the extent that she meets the needs of others. This may produce subjugation and a dependent character structure in some women that is compulsively other-oriented, or masochistic. For these women a conflicted altruistic orientation may defend against self-loathing. If identified with the aggressor, a mother can utilize the daughter as a vicarious proxy for thwarted self-satisfaction. Feminist theorists who emphasize the cultural context of adolescence suggest female altruism and the need to nurture develop from the subordination of the girl and parental demands for nurturance. These implicit cultural norms impact female development.

Discussion

There is an implicit presumption of heterosexuality of adolescents in almost all writings on identity. Forming a firm sense of identity for girls is fraught with difficulty in adolescence. With the onset of gender intensification, there is a turn to looking to others for validation about appearance and desirability, and a concomitant disavowal of her emotional and achievement needs. Preoedipal and oedipal identifications with the mother are transformed to prepare the girl to selflessly nurture and be flawlessly attuned to the needs of others. She becomes familiar with her social position as secondary to that of the male. Feminist psychoanalytic theorists, (Horney, 1945; Chodorow, 1989; Butler, 1990) argue forcefully that the second individuation becomes tainted with being sexualized, objectified, and devalued. In addition, a contradiction exists in that women are expected to have a career and be independent while conforming to a cultural standard of femininity.

Adolescents who identify as lesbian may negate or fail to be equally subordinated by these influences. Butler (1990) suggests that the culture punishes those who do not "do gender" correctly. The very ostracism, marginalization, and isolation that are so punishing in adolescence may increase the capacity of the lesbian identified girl to think outside the box. It is a cliché, but what doesn't kill you often makes you stronger, or disidentified from the dominant norms.

It would seem that for lesbian-identified adolescents the harsh realities of conditional love, social isolation, and marginalization are experienced far ahead of these experiences for heterosexual girls. For example, it may not be until the death or divorce of a husband that a heterosexual woman experiences these. Perhaps lesbian-identified girls are less influenced by gender intensification (Hill and Lynch, 1983) and depend more on achievements and excellence to foster a stable ego. Or, the converse, there is a plunge into identity diffusion and corresponding inability to negotiate intimate relationships.

In text chapters on adolescence, Colarusso (1992) used in at a least one psychoanalytic institute, says that he will "not discuss the developmental line leading to an adult homosexual orientation because there is little agreement" and in his opinion, "insufficient knowledge about the developmental processes which result in an adult homosexual orientation." And "despite the position statement by the American Psychiatric Association that homosexuality is not a pathological entity, considerable controversy remains about the normality or pathology of adult homosexuality" (p. 98). I wonder if this mirrors the lack of analytic attention to the adolescent lesbian experience?

In treatment, whether analytically informed psychotherapy, or psychoanalysis, the practitioner may need to conceptualize the adolescence of lesbians as significantly different, and possibly elongated, from that of her heterosexual cohort. It may be elongated because of prohibitions to experiencing support of her budding sexuality at the appropriate time. A "second individuation" may be normative at a later time in life and does not match that described in "textbook" accounts of adolescence. A careful and detailed attention needs to be paid to exactly the experience of this female person as an adolescent and the meaning of her behaviors within a normative, heterosexist context.

"Coming out" as an additional developmental process and lesbian adolescence as a normal developmental pathway need psychoanalytic attention and research. A search of the Psychoanalytic Electronic Publishing database (PEP CD-ROM 1920–1977) used to search the major psychoanalytic journals located no articles under the key words, lesbian adolescent. Does this reflect a belief of the larger psychoanalytic culture that there are no lesbian-identified adolescents? Or that this topic is not of significant importance to be discussed in mainstream psychoanalytic journals? Historically our society has emphasized a gender hierarchy, with men at the apex, and women valued when compulsorily heterosexual, particularly for reproduction (Butler, 1990). In this old paradigm, the lack of inclusion of mention of lesbian adolescents is not surprising. It is probably the case that analytic writing in major journals mirrors what is considered valuable and is a microcosm of the larger culture. It is my hope that this paper will help stir the thinking of those interested in adolescence to include gay and lesbian youth as a normative practice in their theoretical and research formulations.

References

Benjamin, J. (1998), *The Bonds of Love: Psychoanalysis, Feminism, and the Problem of Domination*. New York: Pantheon.

Blos, P. (1962), *On Adolescence: A Psychoanalytic Interpretation*. New York: Free Press.

——— (1967), The second individuation process of adolescence. In: *The Psychoanalytic Study of the Child*, 22:162–186. New York: International Universities Press.

Brown, L. & Gilligan, C. (1992), *Meeting at the Crossroads: Women's Psychology and Girls' Development*. Cambridge, MA: Harvard University Press.

Burch, B. (1993), Heterosexuality, bisexuality and lesbianism: Rethinking views of women's object choice. *Psychoanal. Rev.*, 80:83–99.

Butler, J. (1990), *Gender Trouble: Feminism and the Subversive Identity*. New York: Routledge.

Chodorow, N. (1989), *Feminism and Psychoanalytic Theory*. New Haven, CT: Yale University Press.

Colarusso, C. (1992), *Child and Adult Development: A Psychoanalytic Introduction for Clinicians*. New York: Plenum.

Dunphy, D. (1969), *Cliques, Crowds, and Gangs*. Chesire, UK: Chesire Publishing.

Erikson, E. (1950), *Childhood and Society*, rev. ed. New York: Norton, 1963.

——— (1968), *Identity, Youth, and Crisis*. New York: Norton.

Gilligan, C., Lyons, N. & Hammer, T. (1990), *Making Connections: The Relation Worlds of Adolescent Girls at Emma Willard School*. Cambridge, MA: Harvard University Press.

Gonsiorek, J. C. & Rudolph, J. R. (1991), Homosexual identity: Coming out and other development events. In: *Homosexuality: Implications for Public Policy*, ed. J. C. Gonsiorek & J. D. Weinrich. Newbury Park, CA: Sage, pp. 161–177.

Hill, J. & Lynch, M. E. (1983), The intensification of gender related role expectations during early adolescence. In: *Girls at Puberty: Biological and Psychological Perspectives*, ed. J. Brooks-Gunn & A. C. Peterson. New York: Plenum, pp. 210–228.

Horney, K. (1945), *Our Inner Conflicts: A Constructive Theory of Neurosis.* New York: Norton.

Jack, D. C. (1991), *Silencing the Self: Women and Depression.* Cambridge, MA: Harvard University Press.

Jacobsen, E. (1964), *The Self and the Object World.* Madison, CT: International Universities Press.

Kaschak, E. (1987), *Engendered Lives: A New Psychology of Women's Experience.* New York: Basic Books.

Kirkpatrick, M. & Morgan, C. (1980), Psychodynamic psychotherapy of female homosexuality. In: *Homosexual Behavior: A Modern Reappraisal,* ed. J. Marmor. New York: Basic Books, pp. 357–375.

Martin, A. & Hetrick, E. (1988), The stigmatization of the gay and lesbian adolescent. *J. Homosexuality,* 15:163–183.

Ollech, D. & McCarthy, J. (1997), Impediments to identity formation in female adolescents. *Psychoanal. Psychol.,* 14:65–79.

Psychoanalytic Electronic Publishing database (PEP CD-ROM 1920–1977). London: Institute of Psychoanalysis, Byron House.

Thompson, S. (1995), *Going All the Way: Teenage Girls' Tales of Sex, Romance, and Pregnancy.* New York: Hill & Wang.

Westcott, M. (1986), *The Feminist Legacy of Karen Horney.* New Haven, CT: Yale University Press.

VI

PSYCHOANALYSIS AND HOMOSEXUALITY IN CONTEMPORARY SOCIETY

Making a Gay Identity: Coming Out, Social Context, and Psychodynamics

ROBERT GALATZER-LEVY
BERTRAM J. COHLER

People feel vital when they can maintain a sense of personal coherence over life's course. The experience of oneself as self continuous over time and situations results from an integration of desire, a presently coherent life story, satisfying relationships with others, and shared expectations within family and community. Being able to tell a coherent life story and to share this story with others greatly contributes to the sense of personal integrity and coherence (Winnicott, 1960). We feel less coherent and whole to the extent we feel forced to dissemble, particularly in important relationships such as those with parents and other family members.

Lichtenstein (1961) points to the cardinal role of sexual desire as a fundamental aspect of this sense of personal integrity in the stories we tell about ourselves. Contested sexual identities, such as being gay or lesbian, pose particular problems for the management of a sense of coherence. Our culture distinguishes between an inner, private self and an "outer," public self. Discrepancies between these two aspects of onself contribute to shame and lowered self-regard which may be felt as diminished morale or even depletion. Feeling different in an important way and not living up to presumed family and community expectations often leads to problems in managing personal coherence and a resulting need to disavow this difference. Acceptance of alternative forms of desire, first for oneself, and then from family, friends, and the community, can provide a renewed sense of personal integrity. "Coming out," the process of accepting same-gender desire as an aspect of one's identity, telling others, and seeking others' affirmation for this contested sexual identity, often fosters personal coherence.

Many factors enter into awareness of sexual identity (Cohler and Galatzer-Levy, 2000). It is clear that our society, with its strong emphasis on heteronormativity, stigmatizes alternative sexual identities, such as that of men who seek other men and women who seek other women as the focus of sociosexual desire. A large psychoanalytic literature maintained that homoerotic interests reflect either conflict or deficit in personality development. However, recent study guided both by relational and self-perspectives in psychoanalysis, and also systematic studies of gay and lesbian people not seeking psychotherapy, has refuted the assumptions of these earlier accounts based on an essentialist psychology and biology (E. Stein, 1999). However, as Herek (1996) and Meyer (1995) showed, the experience of antigay prejudice and the resulting stigmatization by family and community regarding an important aspect of one's own identity may compromise sense of personal coherence.

The Politics and Psychodynamics of "Coming Out" Gay

The role of psychoanalytic inquiry about homosexuality should be less the exploration of the origins of same-gender desire than the examination of the meanings of sexual orientation for lived experience.[1] As in other areas of clinical psychoanalytic investigation, the study of early origins is undertaken only as part of an effort to understand current meanings and narratives about the self. All aspects of sexuality have meaning in a particular time and place (Chodorow, 1992; Herdt, 1997). Understanding and expression of sexual desire change between societies and over time; generalization from one society or time to another is difficult.

In American society the significance of sexual orientation for both men and women has changed dramatically across the past half-century. In contemporary urban America, sexual orientation is usually assumed to be fixed over time. The historian George Chauncey (1994) showed that the meaning of men choosing to have sex with other men has changed dramatically across the past century. Early in the morning of June 28, 1969, the patrons of the Stonewall Inn, a bar in New

[1] We have little understanding of the factors leading to the expectable heteronormative or "straight" sexual identity, let alone the variety of alternative sexual identities or lifeways (Chodorow, 1992; Hostetler and Herdt, 1998). Philosopher of science Edward Stein (1999) describes our society as believing in natural essences. This belief follows from the paradigm of rational explanation first invoked by 17th century philosophers seeking answers for human dilemmas in the wake of the Reformation which questioned the Church's power to provide such answers (Toulmin, 1990). Answers to the question why men and women experience same rather than opposite gender desire have taken the course of other explanations of conduct, searching for essential differences in "natural kinds" or biological explanations. Nearly all discussion about the question of the origins of homosexuality have focused on male homosexuality. There has been much less concern with the origins of homosexuality among women. Perhaps this reflects the greater anxiety in contemporary society about same gender sexual expression among men than among women (Nungesser, 1983). The foundation for same gender sexual orientation among men has been claimed by some to have its basis in genetic transmission or variation in hormonal development during gestation. Edward Stein (1999) has carefully dissected these and other biological explanations, concluding that there is little evidence at present to support any of them.

York's Greenwich Village, resented a police raid on the bar and took to the streets (Duberman, 1993). The purpose of the raid was ostensibly to catch men and women dancing with same-gendered partners, which was then illegal under city liquor laws. Over the next several days, there was continued community pressure which finally forced the police to renounce harassment in the gay community. The Stonewall Riot sparked the emergence of a gay rights movement which was modeled in large part on the politics of the civil rights movement of the preceding decade and fundamentally changed the place of gay men and women in American society.

Over the next three decades, there was a dramatic change in discourse about sexuality and sexual identity. Currently this discourse has reached a point of viewing same-gender socioerotic identity as "virtually normal" (Sullivan, 1995; Clendinen and Nagourney, 1999) . Although the Stonewall Riot was itself the outcome of several decades of political activity extending back to the postwar period (D'Emilio, 1983; Loughery, 1998), the intense political fervor that followed this popular uprising, reflected in the Pride Parade, an annual commemoration of the emergence of the gay rights movement (Herrell, 1992), and the enhanced visibility of a gay identity over the ensuing decade posed unique opportunities and challenges for men and women with same-gender desire to reconcile this desire with the heteronormative expectations of family and community while creating a new positive and proactive gay identity.

Coming to self-identify as a homosexual (more recently termed gay or queer) man or woman, followed by disclosure of this identity to friends and family, is often termed "coming out" (of the closet). Chauncey (1994) notes that the meaning of this term has changed several times in the past century. It appeared first in the 1930s satirizing debutante balls (Loughery, 1998, p. 70). Immediately before the Second World War, there were enormous drag balls in many cities mocking and emulating the debutante events (Chauncey, 1994). However, in the postwar period the term was refined to mean coming out into the (gay) life or the gay world, and out of hiding (used in conjunction with "closet"), including first discovery of same-gender sexual desires and, more recently, disclosure of same-gender sexual desire to family and community. The term "gay" may itself be traced to the 1920s as an effort to turn a spoiled identity (Goffman, 1963) into a less charged adjective, referring to a positive sense of satisfaction.

Although the history of this recent gay rights political and social movement has been well documented (Kaiser, 1997; D'Emilio 1998; Clendinen and Nagourney, 1999), there has been much less systematic discussion of the meaning of this experience for several generations of men and women struggling to reconcile personal desire and public presentation of self. Several generations of self life-writing in the form of memoir and autobiography (Cohler, in preparation) reflects both the changing shared understanding of same-gender sexual desire and also the effort to come to terms with the experience of this desire for oneself. The very possibility of "going gay" (Plummer, 1981), including both the temptations and the fears associated with accepting a gay identity, may be a source of personal struggle for many men and women dealing with conflicting same-gender desire. Since the late 1970s, gay newspapers and magazines listing community activities have been widely available. Further, particularly within more affluent, liberal suburban communities, boys and girls aware of same-gender desire are increasingly able to acknowledge this desire safely and to receive support from gay-affirmative groups at school, protection from harassment, and support from an accepting family. An example of this sort of development can be seen in a college student:

Case 1

A university student from a religious right family had elected to stay in Chicago for the summer and work rather than returning to the small Midwestern community which had been his lifelong home. He reported feeling desire for other guys since junior high school but was tormented by shame imagining his family discovering his wishes. He knew of gay men in his college house and wanted to get to know them. But he feared where this might lead. He read in one of the gay newspapers available at several points around campus of the annual gay pride parade, which attracted crowds of about 200,000.

Feeling ashamed even to be going to the parade, when he saw the large number of people, he began to suspect that his shame about his desire must have to do with himself. He sought psychotherapy, hoping to deal with issues that made it hard for him to be a part of the gay community and to act on his desire. Seeing the parade both strengthened his desire to go gay *and* fears about realization of this desire. After a long personal struggle, coming to terms with his concerns about disappointing his family and uncertain of their response following his disclosure that he was gay, he was able to join the gay-straight student alliance in his college where he met another student from a similar conservative Midwestern small town background who had overcome much of his own sense of stigma. The two became best friends and ultimately lovers in a mutually satisfying and supportive relationship; however, to date neither has told his family of his gay identity.

The increased visibility of the gay community means that it is possible to find others with similar desires without the furtive searches of earlier times, but on the other hand it also increases the pressure for coming to terms with one's gay identity. Even more recently, the Internet has opened new possibilities for self-exploration across the junior high school and high school years. Carefully monitored sites designed for young people make it possible to read stories of the struggles of others, and to talk with other teens also trying to come to terms with their own gay identity.

Our own clinical work, supported by the literature on emergence of gay identity across the course of life and over time (Sadownick, 1996; A. Stein, 1997; Parks, 1999; Cohler and Galatzer-Levy, 2000), suggests that in contemporary urban society the process of self-discovery leading to the experience of a gay identity, though occurring most frequently during child and adolescence, may also occur in middle and later life. Men who grew up in the postwar years, when intense stigma was attached to same-gender desire were particularly likely to suppress such desire. They married only to discover later in life that it was difficult to continue to suppress this desire. The increased visibility of gay life in contemporary society supported the longing of these men to realize their same-gender desire. These men often divorced and found their way into the gay world (Gochros, 1989). Although men most often tell stories of "always having been gay," and finally realizing this desire, women are more likely to move back and forth between same and other gender relationships. Other men and women often first become aware of same-gender desire only in middle or later adulthood. Consider the following variations on the discovery of same-gender desire across the adult years.

Case 2

A man in his early forties, married while still in college to his childhood sweetheart, had been aware of his same-gender desire since junior high school. Growing up in a strict religious family he had suppressed this desire, married and had several children. One day, while commuting to work, he had exchanged looks with another man and immediately fell in love. Each had been married, and each had known he was gay since childhood. Summoning up his courage, he approached the other man and they soon became lovers. At first they were furtive, finding time to be together in the late afternoon and on business trips. Gradually they decided that they could not be apart, and each sought divorce in order to be together.

Case 3

A successful lawyer in his forties, who was married to another successful attorney whose work often required short trips, was working late in his office one evening while his wife was out of town. Another member of the firm known to be gay invited him to a favorite gay bar for a drink. Accepting the invitation on a whim, the lawyer caught the eye of another man at the bar. The two became immediately acquainted and have now lived together for nearly two decades. The lawyer maintains that he had no awareness of his homoerotic desire until that evening. He and his wife divorced amicably and he feels life has been good to her, his lover, and himself.

Case 4

A university student in the sciences was totally unaware of any same-gender desire. One night at a party, he met another student and felt an immediate attraction to him. This attraction turned out to be reciprocal, and the two are now living together as lovers. This student does not consider himself gay. As is true of many members of his generation, he eschews all labels as forcing him into a category. Rather, he see himself as passionately in love.

Case 5

A woman with three teenage children met a coworker who had just joined her firm. Although her marriage was satisfactory, she discovered in her growing relationship with her newly found friend, a recently divorced mother of teenage children, a degree of comfort and intimacy which she had not known in her marriage. She had not previously been aware of same-gender desire. She found both spiritual and sexual intimacy with her new friend, which led her ultimately to get a divorce, and they moved in together. The two women and their former husbands have an amiable if strained relationship, while their children all live with them in a large, cheerfully unkempt Victorian era house.

Viewed from a life-course perspective, there are multiple sexual lifeways (Herdt, 1997; Hostetler and Herdt, 1998), and persons may opt for one sexual lifeway at one point in life and yet choose another at some later point. Some men and women opt for a gay identity across the young adult years, then decide to marry. Increasing options for raising a family, regardless of sexual identity, have diminished the link between parenthood and heterosexual marriage. Still, we should ask why these men and women decide to permit themselves to get in touch with their own same-gender desire at some particular time. Each of these men and women had been in psychotherapy for problems unrelated to same-gender sexual desire. Among middle-aged men and women, chronological age and generational changes in freedom to express same-gender desire played some part. Particularly the man long aware of his same-gender desire felt that the landmark birthday of 40 meant that if he was ever to realize a longed-for gay relationship, he had better not put off this possibility. His relationship with his wife and children was satisfactory, and although things at work were a bit unpredictable because of an economic downturn, he believed that his firm would weather the economic storm. There was little to suggest that this decision to come out as gay was a breakdown product or evidence of a disorder related to enactment of neurotic conflicts at midlife.

The other three instances also have meaning not necessarily related to psychopathology. The university student belongs to a generation of students who refuse to classify their sexuality. Sometimes using terms like "queer" or "trans" (meaning not heteronormative) or spectrum (meaning somewhere other than "0" or completely heterosexual on the seven-point Kinsey-Klein scale of sexual orientation), these men and women eschew all labels and categories, including even "bisexual," to portray their sexual identity. Although a vocal minority of university men and women self-define as gay or lesbian, other students are comfortable sometimes being in romantic relationships with others of the same-gender, sometimes with others of the opposite gender.

The man who met his life partner at a gay bar portrayed his marriage as not very fulfilling. His career-oriented wife did not want children, was emotionally distant, and had a distaste for intimacy. From the first, this man was attracted to his lover's magnetic personality and personal warmth. Their relationship continues to be fulfilling for each partner. This man reports little regret but some surprise at how his life has turned out. The experience of the women with children from a heterosexual marriage entering into a long-standing lesbian relationship is consistent with what is known about same-gender sexuality among women. Women are more likely than men to move back and forth between same-gender and heterosexual ties. More than a third of women in lesbian relationships have been married and have had children. Although both gay men and women are beginning to adopt or to have children through alternate means, combined families of women, each with their own children, are also an expected element of the lesbian lifeway (Burch, 1993; Bradford, Ryan, and Rothblum, 1994; Patterson, 1995; Laird, 1998).

Sexual Identity and the Adolescent and Adult Life Course

Wishes and their expression are shaped out of the interplay of personal circumstances and sociohistorical contexts. For example, following Toulmin's (1990) discussion of the foundations of modes of understanding, Drescher (1998) noted that the traditional psychoanalytic understanding of homosexuality resulted from a distinctive theoretical perspective characteristic of psychoanalysis in New York following the Second World War. Influenced by Rado's (1945, 1949) concept of adaptational psychodynamics, many analysts who received analytic training in the postwar era were taught that same-gender sexual desire (then called homosexuality) was a form of psychopathology. The appeal of the underlying theory reflected the particular historical moment of their training. For analysts of this postwar generation seeking a rational explanation for the nonrationality evident in the war in which many of them had fought, drive theory and a focus on adaptation seemed to provide an answer to the problem of irrationality.

Rado (1949), Socarides (1968), and others portrayed same-gender desire as inevitably reflecting fixation and regression, and Bieber and his colleagues (Bieber et al., 1962) asserted that homosexual men overwhelmingly came from families characterized by an overly intrusive mother and a distant and absent father. Recently, some of those within psychoanalysis continuing to insist on this older view of same-gender desire as necessarily evidence of psychopathology have allied with the religious right, which attempts to covert gay men and women to heterosexuality in the belief that same-gender desire is sinful. The dismal impact of this mistaken belief was that gay men and women who sought help for psychological disturbance not necessarily even related to their sexual orientation were confronted with the overwhelming and fruitless task of attempting to change their sexual orientation.

Case 6

When fifteen-year-old Jay came out to his father, he confirmed his father's "worst fears." Jay's father was an anxious man whose own psychotherapy seemed to have left him with a long list of ideas about the ways he had failed his son. He saw his son's homosexuality as the outcome of his paternal failings and sought advice about how to manage "the crisis." Jay was indeed distressed, but not by his sexual interests, which he found pleasurable and for which he found considerable support among friends. He was, however, deeply pained by his father's constant disapproval of him, which included not only his sexual orientation but also his academic interests and personality style. Consistent with what father reported, Jay said that his father often let Jay know how he wished that Jay were different in many ways but, other than communicating his dissatisfaction, did little to assist the boy in developing in ways that the father consciously hoped he would.

Jay's father focused on the boy's treatment. Through the Internet he found a therapist whose attractive website was funded by a Christian organization. This therapist held that homosexuality was pathological and resulted from the psychological absence of the father. The cure for this condition was to provide the youngster with a surrogate father who would be closely involved with the boy and advocate for conventional masculine interests. The father found this idea appealing on a number of grounds. The website's appearance and its authoritative clear sounding claims carried more prestige than the less impressively presented and less certain statements of the several therapists he had interviewed.

The story of the genesis of homosexuality in paternal absence initially proposed by Bieber and his associates (1962), and widely known among parents of gay offspring, was consistent with his own guilt-laden thoughts about his role in his son's sexual orientation. At the same time, the proposed therapeutic intervention again spared him from being involved with his son. He decided to undertake this rehabilitation program at great expense. Jay resigned himself to the proposed treatment, saying that he realized that he had been mistaken to think that his father would ever accept anything about him that did not fit his father's fantasies. He planned to appear compliant with the treatment as long as necessary to get himself discharged and to remain secretive about his sexual interests in any context that might involve his family. As to treatment for his quite significant depression, he said, "My friends were right! Get near a shrink and they'll mess you up. When I get rid of this jerk, I'll never talk to another one of your kind!"

The historical moment always affects psychoanalytic thought. The ten-year period between 1965 and 1975 was a tumultuous time in American society (Foucault, 1976; Tipton, 1982). During this time, relational and self-perspectives emerged as relatively coherent frameworks for understanding development and intervention. These viewpoints were driven partly by attempts to work with patients for whom older techniques seemed not to work, but also derived from the shifting nature of thinking about people within the society generally. With the disappearance of the orthodoxy characteristic of much of psychoanalysis in the postwar period, many analysts recognize that their work could be understood as a form of narration designed to create a life story fostering an enhanced sense of coherence and integrity over that which the analysand brings to analysis (Schafer, 1980, 1992), and recognition of the clinical psychoanalytic process as a relationship between two people (Gill, 1994; Hoffman, 1998).

Consistent with sociologist Glen Elder's (1995, 1996, 1997) discussion of generational cohorts and social change, history and social change influence both clinical psychoanalytic theory and the lives of analysts and analysands. For example, in the 1980s an increased commitment to solidarity among gay people, reflected in part by the belief that it was morally right to be open and public about sexual orientation, supported a strong feeling of liberation among many younger gay men. Yet many middle-aged and older gay men were threatened by the expectation among younger gay men and women that the workplace and community should accept and nurture their alternative sexual identity. They believed that this demand jeopardized hard-won community tolerance given in exchange for hiding gay sexual identity. The same shift to being open about sexual identity transformed the experience of gay adolescents. For a teen becoming aware of erotic interests in the same sex while having access to the Internet or television, the question that haunted gay adolescents of a few decades before, "Is there anyone like me?" was not only given an affirmative answer but a concrete, and often positive, face.

Our understanding of important psychoanalytic concepts such as identity also changed. Initially elaborated by Erikson (1958, 1959) as a personality attribute particularly salient during adolescence, the concept of identity referred to both a sense of continuity of personal experience and to a sense of coherence with the ideals of family and community (Lichtenstein, 1961). Although Erikson eschewed efforts to reduce this concept to a measurable attribute of personality, he used the term identity to refer to a sense of self-realization integrating personal goals and ambitions and those of family and society. Recent discussions regarding the formation of identity (Sarup, 1996; Holland et al., 1998; Mishler, 1999) suggested that reports of lived experience are always recounted in the context of a particular time and place which establishes priorities for talking or writing all aspects of lived experience. Mishler (1999) calls this historical and social context "figured worlds of interpretation" (p. 52), meaning that reports of lived experience are always recounted in the context of a particular time and place which establishes priorities for talking or writing about lived experience.

Figured worlds of interpretation provide the foundation for our understanding of ourselves and others. Meanings of lived experience are always mediated by figured worlds. Identity is, in Mishler's term, a "situated retelling" (p. 50) which may be better understood through close attention to the ways in which we talk about our lives, including within the psychoanalytic situation. Retelling the life story takes place both at a particular time and at a particular place, with a particular listener assumed (Sarup, 1996). These situated retellings involve some selection of lived experience recounted as a part of a presently comprehensible story told to another with some intent. Life events may be arranged in varying ways, guided by culture and life circumstances, in an effort to make sense of remembered and anticipated aspects of personal circumstances. This view is fundamental to psychoanalytic listening in which we focus on the analysand's selection of particular aspects of lived experience during particular analytic hours with the understanding that this selection is guided by the analysand's experience of the analyst and their relationship. Understanding identity as the confluence of shared understandings of self and others in particular cultures, generation or cohort growing up, and at particular historical moments in particular life circumstances transforms the expectation that identity will be static to an expectation that identity will reflect dynamic process. It admits the possibility of continuing change in identity across the life course. This view of identity as sense of personal integrity as revealed as a story of lived experience is profoundly salient to the study of sexual orientation.

Generation, Social Change and the Meaning of Going Gay

Comparative study of the life stories of people across generations highlights how social context shaped people's understanding of their own life stories. Boxer and Cohler (1989) and Cohler and Galatzer-Levy (2000) note the importance of studying sexual identity in the context of shared understandings of sexual orientation among persons of particular ages across cohorts. Parks (1999) and A. Stein (1997) have studied narratives of lesbian young adults dealing with their same-gender orientation across several generations. Sadownick (1997) has contrasted understandings of gay sexuality among men across generations from the post-war years to the present based on narrative accounts. However, with the exception of Sadownick, who reported on archival material, these reports contrast conceptions of sexual identity among persons born at different times but interviewed in the present. Thus, separating the impact of age from historical experience is difficult in these studies. It is important to understand how cohort membership leads to differences in the use made of social change in telling the life story (Crites, 1971).

Generational differences over the postwar period have been important in how women and men have organized their life stories and understood the meaning of their alternative sexual identity (Sadownick, 1997). Parks (1999) and A. Stein (1997) have reported on the life stories presently told by women from these two generations. These written life stories inevitably are created in the light of subsequent personal and social change. Sadownick (1997) reports archival material, including life story accounts, from men of about the same age across two generations. Summarizing the life stories of 11 women in the generation entering middle age at the time of the 1969 Stonewall riots, Parks (1999) reports that these women felt very much alone during their youth and young adulthood. They experienced a sense of pervasive stigma that lowered their self-esteem. They described themselves as delayed in the realization of their lesbian identity, and their life stories are organized around the theme of silence about their desire. The 11 women who were young adults at the time of Stonewall organized their life stories around both an increased sense of personal freedom and sociality. They report being younger than the middle-aged generation when they started to define themselves as lesbian and had their first same-gender socioerotic experiences; they believed that the earlier timing of same-gender identity facilitated the transition into physical intimacy.

A. Stein's (1997) report contrasts the young adult generation at the time of Stonewall, presently middle-aged, with another, younger generation of women who were young adults in the 1990s. The life stories of the presently young adult generation are less explicitly organized around themes of political activism than those of the presently middle-aged generation. They had grown up in a decade marked by increased privatization of experience (Putnam, 2000). These younger women appear more willing to accept contradictions and inconsistencies in their story of sexual identity. Some organized their life stories around ambiguous sexual identities. This young adult generation moves with greater ease between same-gender and opposite gender partnership. Their story is of a more fluid sexual identity than that of their middle-aged counterparts whose young adulthood was marked by social activism and a commitment to feminism and lesbian politics. It also includes making a transition to parenthood in greater numbers and at earlier ages than the presently middle-aged generation who were young adults at the time of Stonewall. Oswald (2000) reported that lesbians in this generation view coming out in the context of relationships with friends and family. They work to build networks of social support for their newfound sexual identity.

Coming Out Gay from Adolescence to Later Life

The emergence of conscious same-gender socioerotic may occur at any point in life (Cohler and Galatzer-Levy, 2000). It will be understood in terms of values learned from early childhood and preexisting attitudes regarding one's own self. Responses may range from denial that the wish has much significance to convictions that same-gender desire is the core of one's being. Sometimes recognition of this desire is welcomed, explaining the absence of heterosexual interests; sometimes it is treated with easy acceptance from the first; sometimes the person is profoundly revolted by same-gender desire to the point where suicide seems like the only way out. Especially among men or women who have substantially internalized homophobic attitudes, recognizing homoerotic desire for oneself may lead to great anxiety.

Not infrequently the issue of coming out to oneself, while apparently focused on homosexuality, has more to do with the discovery of strong erotic wishes of any kind. Two examples illustrate what we have in mind.

Case 7

John, a neurotically inhibited young adolescent boy, claimed not to have "figured out" how to masturbate. Occasional nocturnal emissions were accompanied by dreams of touching or seeing other boys' genitals, and John was aware of sexually exciting fantasies of fondling other boys. This represented a shift in the content of his fantasies from earlier, prepubescent longing to be physically close to older boys and occasional fantasies, which puzzled him, about structures he could see on the underside of trucks. (Later, in analysis, he recognized that these unconsciously represented a scrotum.)

Case 8

John, who grew up in a sophisticated upper middle class family, had heard about homosexuality and repeatedly reread sections of books on child development he found in his parents' library concerning it. He was greatly reassured to learn that homosexual experimentation was common among pubescent boys and convinced himself that he was going through a "phase" out of which he would soon mature. At the same time, John's overall attitude remained that of a latency age child. He wanted more than anything to be "good" and to win parental approbation. He equated expressions of erotic interest and mild aggressiveness in his peers with "juvenile delinquency" (a term that was much in use by the press at the time he was growing up). He would be different from the other "bad" kids but consciously feared that as he grew older he would inevitably become as "bad" as teenagers did.

In analysis it became clear that the anxiety John manifested about homosexuality was, in fact, distress about thinking of himself as in any way sexual. Under his incapacity to "figure out" how to masturbate lay a wish that sex could be treated as an intellectual puzzle and because it was so puzzling something in which he could not engage. Beyond this lay a fear that were he to allow himself to follow his impulses he would be overwhelmed by them. The issue for John, who happened to be homosexually oriented, was not coming out as gay but coming out as sexual in any way.

A similar issue was raised by an older patient.

Case 9

At 45, Harold's conscious sexual interests had always been "healthy and reasonable." Although as an adolescent and young man his emotional attachments were deeper with male friends than with the women he dated, his erotic fantasies were exclusively about women. Sexual relations were generally "pleasurable." However, sexual interest was never allowed to interfere with his "life," that is his professional and social worlds. He married a woman he liked and got on with well. They had three boys. He summarized his situations as "quite comfortable."

While on a business trip, following a tense day of work, Harold noted an ad for an escort in a local newspaper. Though he says that he would now quickly recognize that advertisement as offering sexual services, at the time his conscious understanding was that there was no erotic element to the service. When an attractive young man was announced at his hotel and he met him in the lobby, Harold became aware of some sexual excitement which grew extremely intense as they took the elevator up to his room. Hardly was the door closed when the escort began taking off his clothes and urged Harold to do the same. Ultimately, the escort performed oral sex on him and Harold experienced an orgasm that was far more intense than any he could remember.

This experience initiated a group of activities and fantasies that were both profoundly exciting and frightening to Harold who felt dominated by his sexual urges. Whereas he had been previously able to keep his sexual interests neatly circumscribed in a fashion that did not disturb his "life," Harold now found the longings for homosexual encounters and his actual sexual activity intruded into and disturbed his daily existence. Although it troubled him that his marriage might be disrupted were his wife to learn of his homosexual activity (and he took considerable precautions that she not find out about it), this was not Harold's major source of discomfort. Rather he was simultaneously anxious and greatly pleased by the very intensity associated with this sexual encounter, which was different from anything he had experienced in his life up to that time.

Coming out in Adolescence

Much of the literature concerning acknowledgment and disclosure of same-gender sexual orientation has focused on the era of adolescence and youth. In part this is a consequence of the larger focus on the issue of identity and its management as young people first struggle with issues of futurity and the expectation of a connection between the remembered past, experienced present, and anticipated future (Erikson, 1959; Greene, 1986, 1990). Sexual identity is one aspect of this larger issue of identity management. It is during adolescence that young people first come to terms with sexual desire in the context of family, school, and community. Living at home, generally with brothers and sisters, sexual identity is particularly visible. Parents, anxious that their children grow up right, may seek to reassure themselves that their offspring is able to cope with the expectations of the social world, including dating and finding friends and dates whom they regard as appropriate within social position, religion, and other social categories.

Disclosure of alternative sexual lifeways generally poses issues for families, but particularly so for parents and adolescents. Children and parents ordinarily serve each other as essential others, supporting and promoting the development of and support the others' sense of self, across the entire life course (Galatzer-Levy and Cohler, 1993). The process is mutual, in that the interactions of parent and child fit together each individual's essential other needs into a mutually satisfying interaction. The parent who effectively calms an upset infant has obviously functioned as an essential other for that infant providing organization and soothing to the point where the infant can function and feel more coherently. The same interaction, viewed in terms of the parent's essential other needs, has provided that parent with a sense of effectiveness and being of value that supports the parental self and its development. Although more subtle, the mutual essential other functioning of parent and child continues across the life course.

Parents often measure their own worth in terms of the well-being of their offspring. Inevitable disappointments with the child, such as learning that the adolescent or young adult identifies with an alternative sexual lifeway, may threaten parental self-esteem and upset important hopes for the child founded in the parents' ambitions. For parents, learning of same-gender sexual desire threatens traditional expectations regarding marriage, becoming grandparents, and continuation of the family line. Tension within the family often appears when parents attempt to fulfill their own ambitions through their children. These problems may manifest themselves in the relationship of parent and child or may result in difficulties for the child resulting from internalized versions of this scenario. Analytic authors have often emphasized the pathology that can be generated through the narcissistic use of children (Miller, 1981). The problems that can arise from such a situation have been the topic of innumerable novels and endless personal discussions. However, when interest in the child's well being remains an overriding theme, parental idealization of the child and the compensatory function of the child with regard to parental grandiosity serves as an important and desirable function in ordinary parent-child interdependence, which fosters the child's sense of self-worth and promotes achievement in school and in the community.

Initial social science studies of adolescent coming out emphasized age and stage "models" for explaining human behavior. They portrayed this process of disclosure in terms either of disclosure of alternative sexual identity and its exploration as "rite of passage" or stage of the life cycle loss (Van Genep, 1909; Herdt, 1992), following the model developed by Kubler-Ross (1969) for the study of response to death of a family member, or a stage model of arriving at a new identity (Cass, 1984; Troiden, 1988). These experience distant models were invoked in order to provide some sense of the adjustment required of family and friends to the disclosure that a family member had gone gay, together with a means for accounting for the process by which young people arrived at a gay identity.

Detailed narrative study failed to support these models (Beeler and DiProva, 1999; Savin-Williams, 2001). In part these models appeared irrelevant because of dramatic social changes across the past decade regarding opportunities for young people to talk about their sexual identity and to learn about what it means to go gay from the Internet and gay–straight alliances in high school. In part, the visibility of gay culture has made it possible for parents and other family members to see that sexual identity need have little relevance to continuing close family ties and even to having grandchildren. Finally, as the means for study in the social sciences has shifted from more formal, experience distant and realist perspectives to one emphasizing story and factors entering into the construction of social experience, study of sexual identity has moved away from formal models to the means we use to talk about sexuality and intimate relations (Ben-Ari, 1995a).

Some gay men report having always known they were gay. In one of the few detailed, systematic studies to date, Savin-Williams (1998d) reports on the lives of a group of self-identified gay and lesbian university students volunteering to take part in an interview and survey study. Although by no means a random sample of gay men or lesbians, Savin-Williams reports that more than four-fifths of his group reported awareness of same-gender desire prior to adolescence. Corbett (1998) has described for himself this sense of awareness of being different from other boys in terms of his attraction to male classmates. The boys destined to realize a gay identity sought the caring and company of men, expressed nonstereotyped gender interests, and reported being sufficiently nonmasculine that they were often subject to bullying. Lesbians reported less conflict with peers because being a "tomboy" was more readily accepted. About the same time, about two-fifths of the boys in Savin-Williams's (1998d) study did not have a name or a label for their same-gender desire. This awareness was first realized across the years of junior high school and high school, although the specific identity as gay and participation in sex with other men came somewhat later. (In the decade intervening between Savin-Williams's first interviews and the present, this process of self-awareness and the labeling of personal socioerotic desire seems to have become ever earlier with many boys in particular identifying as gay already while in junior high school and even well before puberty.) Finally, Savin-Williams (1998d) reports that nearly all the participants in his study were able to arrive at a positive gay identity by the college years, often fostered by acceptance among peers and parents to this self-disclosure.

The response of others upon hearing this information is an important determinant of the outcome of self-disclosure of a gay sexual identity or "coming out." Findings regarding the probability of disclosing sexual orientation to parents varies considerably across studies (Savin-Williams, 1998a). Although more than 80 percent of activist gay teens have disclosed their gay or lesbian sexual identity to their parents, less than a fifth of gay or lesbian college students surveyed had made a similar disclosure. However, many of these young people believe that their parents are aware of their gender atypical interests and have tacitly recognized their offspring's nonnormative sexual orientation. There has been much less systematic study of young adult disclosure to family and friends. Presumably with time an ever-increasing proportion of young adults make such a disclosure. Disclosure becomes particularly important when a young adult seeks to bring a lover or partner home for the holidays or other important family gatherings. Further, the offspring's lifestyle and romantic interests becomes increasingly visible in the postcollege years as parents visit with their young adult offspring. Efforts to hide the reality of same-gender sexual orientation become increasingly awkward. Parents may become increasingly concerned with offspring plans to marry and have children; persistent parental inquiries and concern regarding offspring romantic interests often force the disclosure of same-gender sexual identity.

Among young adults disclosing their sexual orientation, most tell a friend first and then a family member, most often their mother. Some studies (Devine, 1984; Cramer and Roach, 1988) suggest that gay or lesbian young adults are more likely to disclose their nonnormative sexual orientation to brothers and sisters before disclosing to parents, assuming that as members of the same generation they will be most likely to understand and support a nonnormative sexual identity and lifestyle. However, when brothers and sisters are told, it is most often after coming-out to friends (Savin-Williams, 1998c, 2001). What is clear is that once learning of gay or lesbian sexual identity, more than three-fourths of brothers and sisters are supportive of this decision (Savin-Williams, 1998c).

Savin-Williams (2001) reported that for most youth, the pattern is for disclosure first to friends (for young men, often another friend believed or known to be gay or gay-friendly, or for a young woman friend), then brothers and sisters, then mother, and finally father. Ben-Ari (1995a) suggested that it is the very act of disclosing or coming out that creates an identity as gay. Reporting on a detailed study of the discourse of an adolescent son coming-out to his mother and her response, Ben-Ari (1995a) showed that such disclosure helps each generation to make sense of such previously confusing experiences as the son's reluctance to ask girls out on a date. Findings from Ben-Ari's (1995b) report, together with those of Savin-Williams (2001) focusing on parental response to this disclosure, suggest that parents often have harbored suspicions or had accumulated evidence regarding their offspring's sexuality which they had not been able to talk about with their offspring.

Parental adjustment to adolescent offspring disclosure of same-gender socioerotic desire has been described both by parents themselves (Borhek, 1979; Dew, 1994; Baker, 1998) and in accounts co-authored by parents and their gay offspring (Fricke and Fricke, 1991; Shyer and Shyer, 1996; Wythe et al., 2000). Study of parental response to adolescent offspring disclosure has been reported by Ben-Ari (1995b), Herdt and Koff (2000), and Savin-Williams (2001). In accounts by parents themselves, there is a striking degree of ambivalence upon hearing of this aspect of their son or daughter's life (Cohler, in preparation). Parents report worrying about the difficulties their offspring's sexual identity will pose at school and in the workplace. Parents also worry about AIDS and other sexually transmitted diseases, although this is less often a particular focus of concern.

To date, there have been only three systematic studies of parental response to offspring disclosure regarding gay or lesbian sexual identity: the Chicago study initially described by Boxer, Cook, and Herdt (1991) and by Herdt and Koff (2000), the San Francisco Bay area study reported by Ben-Ari (1995b), and the study of parents of youth attending college in Ithaca, New York, portrayed by Savin-Williams (2001). These studies rely on convenience samples of parents of gay and lesbian offspring either nominated by offspring or obtained through the assistance of Parents and Friends of Lesbians and Gays (PFLAG). There has been little systematic study of families in which there is a gay or lesbian adolescent or young adult offspring, studied together with the parents of these offspring.

Learning from their offspring of their gay or lesbian sexual identity, parents interviewed in the study reported by Boxer et al. (1991) were concerned primarily about discrimination and presumed increased risk for AIDS. Their principal concern appeared to be for their offspring, not themselves. Parents also reported that offspring disclosure led to a period of enhanced self-reflection and reordering of priorities and expectations. These middle-aged and older parents struggled with such implications as the possibility of having fewer grandchildren.

Parents of daughters disclosing lesbian sexual orientation had greater difficulty reordering their expectations and priorities than did parents of sons. Presumably, daughters are seen as the key to realizing grandchildren; for fathers, this means the possibility of carrying on family traditions whereas for mothers, as daughters first marry and then become parents there is enhanced role complementarity (Low, 1978; Cohler, 1987–1988). Boxer et al. (1991) report that parents had the greatest difficulty accepting the nonnormative sexuality among offspring who were somewhat older at the point of explicit acknowledgment of being gay or lesbian. Among offspring of younger age at disclosure, there may be some hope that this is a transient experience of youth; among those offspring older at the point of disclosure, it is more difficult to maintain such hope.

Parents and offspring had each implicitly acknowledged the reality of the offspring's sexual identity before officially coming out. Many of the offspring in the study reported by Boxer et al. (1991) were in their midtwenties at the time that they and their parents explicitly acknowledged their gay or lesbian sexual identity, but it was clear that each generation had implicitly acknowledged this reality earlier. Such tacit acknowledgment may evidence a demilitarized zone (Hagestad, 1981). But this avoidance of explicit acknowledgment of the offspring's gay or lesbian sexual identity may have interfered in greater closeness between the generations in ways less common in families in which offspring expressed normative sexual orientation.

Herdt and Koff (2000) report on six dimensions of family life central to this group of parents of gay and lesbian offspring: (1) extent to which parents felt shame or guilt connected with offspring disclosure and parental decisions regarding informing friends and relatives; (2) extent to which disclosure either fostered or interfered with closeness between parents and offspring; (3) extent to which parents could be empathic with the offspring's disclosure and efforts to make a comfortable gay or lesbian sexual identity; (4) extent of parental contact with the gay and lesbian community, including use of groups such as PFLAG; (5) extent to which parents were able to be inclusive of the offspring's lover or partner and his or her own family; and (6) extent to which parents were able to see a future for their gay or lesbian offspring. Although some parents were able to be supportive regarding these issues, a very few parents were outright rejecting, and most parents remained ambivalent, wanting what was best for their offspring.

Although the Chicago area parents interviewed by Boxer and his colleagues (Boxer et al., 1991) were often isolated from contact with the gay community, the Bay area families interviewed by Ben-Ari were living in the midst of a community which over the preceding two decades had become a center of gay life. Most parents in this study reported a better relationship with their offspring following disclosure. Just as in the Chicago study of Boxer et al. (1991), parents were most concerned about the impact upon offspring of possible social stigma and discrimination, followed by concern with the possibility that offspring would be at increased risk for AIDS which, by the nineties, had become a pandemic in the Bay area. However, Ben-Ari (1995b) maintains that concern about AIDS was less significant than concern regarding social discrimination. Once again, parents of lesbians expressed greater difficulty than parents of gay sons accepting their offspring's disclosure. The greatest guilt about presumed contribution to offspring nonnormative sexual identity, however, was expressed by mothers of gay sons and fathers of lesbian daughters.

Fear of rejection appeared to be an important determinant of parental response to issues of disclosure of offspring sexual identity in this study. Offspring anticipating the possibility of parental rejection found reality in this fear in the sense that their parents also reported it more difficult to accept their offspring's disclosure. Parents more isolated from the liberal attitudes and lifestyle of the Bay area were also less able to accept offspring disclosure. Finally, it should be noted that parental response is often tied to how offspring disclose their sexual orientation. When offspring disclose their gay sexual identity as leading to increased happiness and life satisfaction, parents respond with greater affirmation than when offspring present their nonnormative sexual identity as a "problem." Mothers found it easier than fathers to accept offspring nonnormative sexual identity. Significantly, within this Bay Area group of parents, more than three-fourths of the parents had found a parent support group in dealing with their offspring's disclosure. Mothers are most likely to spur this effort to join and use support groups in dealing with their own feelings following offspring disclosure (Henderson, 1998).

Discussing parental response to offspring disclosure of nonnormative sexual identity, Savin-Williams and Dubè (1998) report on findings from Savin-Williams's continuing study of gay youth and their parents that initial parental response was primarily one of shock or denial, followed by anger at those in society who fostered the possibility that their offspring could go gay, bargaining with offspring to postpone making a decision regarding their sexual identity, and sometimes maintaining that offspring disclosure was a "phase." Less often, parents were able to be fully accepting of the offspring's decision regarding an alternative sexual lifeway. Consistent with Ben-Ari's (1995b) report, in which parents of younger offspring were more likely than parents of older disclosing offspring to view this disclosure as a phase, findings from Savin-Williams's study (1998b, 1998c, 2001) suggested that fathers were at least as likely as mothers to respond in a positive manner. In fact, largely stemming from the belief in our culture regarding the importance of maternal care for offspring personality development, mothers initially felt guilty and tended to reject their offspring. Fathers, however, appeared to be emotionally distant from other family members more generally, and found it difficult to be close to their offspring either before or after disclosure of alternative sexual identity. It appears that there is a complex interplay between gender of parent, offspring age at disclosure, and the nature of parental response which requires attention in further study.

Clearly, mothers and fathers of older and younger gay and lesbian adolescents and young adults react in quite different ways to this disclosure. Findings reviewed by Savin-Williams (1998b, 1998c, 2001) suggest that parents initially react with feelings of guilt when hearing of their offspring's gay or sexual identity. However, over periods of time, both systematic study and parental narratives suggest an accommodation by the parents following offspring disclosure of an alternative sexual orientation. For example, parents or parents-in-law are generally responsible for the forward socialization of offspring and spouse into the role of married offspring. When a gay man or woman finds a partner, the offspring more often helps his or her parents modify their understanding of the role of spouse or "in-law" through backward socialization now understood in terms of relations both with the partner and the partner's family (Serovich et al., 1993).

Coming Out Gay Over the Adult Years

It is often assumed that issues of coming-out gay or lesbian are restricted to the adolescent epoch. However, more recent evidence, much of which is founded on reports from men and women seeking psychotherapy, suggests that the issue of going gay and realization of this alternative sexual identity is important across the course of life. Circumstances for going gay across the adult years differ between men and women and across generations—particularly among men, while the "dominant or master narrative" (Plummer, 1995) is of having felt desire toward other men since earliest childhood (Corbett, 1998). Many men, however, report their first awareness of such desire across the adult years. Social change occurring across the past two decades in the expression of sexual desire has contributed to awareness of same-gender desire among men who might not have encountered the possibility for exploration of this desire in earlier times. Other middle-aged and older men had been aware of this same-gender desire from childhood or adolescence but had suppressed it in an effort to comply with the expectations of family and community. For these men, too, increased visibility of a gay community has offered support in realizing this long suppressed desire.

The mistaken assumption that sexual orientation is necessarily stable across the life course (Cohler and Galatzer-Levy, 2000) adds further to the burden of addressing same-gender orientation during adult life. Retrospectively, adults are likely to "recognize" indications of homoerotic interests earlier in life and feel additionally guilty in the belief that they might have spared the family distress by recognizing and avowing those interests before enmeshing others in the complexity of the current situation. The accomplishments of the marriage are likely to be seen as inauthentic. Expectable rage and disappointment from the spouse, although not universally forthcoming, interact with the individual's guilt and shame, raising issues about whether the person who has come out is not only disrupting the family, but also has a long history of fundamental dishonesty.

Fears are common that children's normal idealization of the parent will be interrupted and social embarrassment will result for the child as a result of a father's coming out. Our clinical experience is consonant with research findings (Buxton, 1994) that adult men who are coming out tend to anticipate far more negative responses from their children than they actually receive. Two powerful fantasies seem to converge to lead to this anticipation. One fantasy arises from internalized antigay prejudice, believing that gay men and women cannot be admirable. The second is the idea that the parent must be a greatly admirable figure in order to perform his necessary psychological role in the child's development. For example, when a son becomes a father himself, he is likely to experience a new appreciation and admiration for his own father's skill and care as a parent. When the father's sexual identity differs from that expected in our society, the father may fear that he can no longer be idealized by his son.

Case 10

Alex, a man in his mid-twenties was markedly sexually inhibited. His limited sexual contact with both women and men was characterized by great anxiety and concern about his analyst's opinion. Although his erotic fantasies were exclusively about women, he once allowed himself to be seduced by a male acquaintance. He responded to his analyst's inquiry about whether he had enjoyed the experience by believing that the analyst recognized that he was latently homosexual and that his analyst was giving him permission to become involved in a gay lifeway. However, just as in his experiences with women, Alex's sexual experiences with men involved no pleasure, a feeling of confusion about why he was engaged in the experience, and a sense that he was acting compliantly with his analyst's wishes. Alex's own wishes remained obscure to him, except for the wish to know his own desires. This state of mind had many determinants of which very early interferences with Alex's sense of personal initiative turned out to be perhaps the most important. However, in the sexual arena an additional contributing factor concerned Alex's perception of his father's sexuality. Following his parent's divorce, when Alex was a young boy, Alex's father had lived in a manner that was marginal in many ways. In particular, he appeared to have no sexual partners, something that made Alex feel ashamed and contributed to his fantasy that he was limited in this regard, just like his father.

Far into the analysis, Alex pressed his father for an explanation. At first, the father said that he had just never gotten around to finding another partner following the breakup of the marriage. Later, with much embarrassment and anxiety about what Alex would think of him, he came out to Alex, explaining that he feared Alex's contempt, that he would be a poor role model for Alex, especially since his sexual life consisted in numerous furtive relationships with men he picked up in bars—at least at this point in his development

Alex responded very differently from what his father had anticipated. He felt greatly relieved that his father had erotic interests and satisfaction. The partner's gender was of minor importance to Alex, who was actually pleased with his father's homosexual orientation because it meant that father was acting on his own desires, rather than simply following social convention in his erotic life.

The realization that father had at least a somewhat satisfying sexual life contributed to Alex's greater ease with his own erotic interests.

The situation of men who first discover their same-gender desire during the adulthood years and those in which men have long been aware of same-gender desire but have either suppressed this desire or enacted it in furtive ways represent two quite different pathways to adoption of a gay sexual identity across the second half of life. Evidence from the study of women in a heterosexual marriage at one point of life and in a lesbian relationship at another suggests that women are less likely to maintain a dominant narrative of their sexual identity and are much more likely than men to move back and forth between heterosexual and lesbian relationships across the course of adult life (Blumstein and Schwartz, 1983; Bradford et al., 1994; Lewin, 1993; Laird, 1998; Cohler and Galatzer-Levy, 2000). When women move from a heterosexual to a same-gendered relationship and have been married with children, children most often join them in this blended family. The very process of divorce is less painful and complex than when men in heterosexual marriages with children suddenly announce that they are gay and plan to live with a lover. Divorce in these circumstances is likely to be more painful, and children most often remain with the wife and mother. Courts are still less comfortable awarding custody to gay fathers than to lesbian mothers. Lynch and Murray (2000) report that both men and women, parents of young children and coming out gay, are particularly sensitive about disclosing their newfound sexual orientation to their children and that the children are able to accept their parents' alternative sexual identity.

At least to some extent, coming out gay in adulthood is viewed as inappropriate and off-time for expected life changes. Adolescence and youth is viewed as a time of finding one's own identity, and work on sexual identity is presumed a part of that process. Adults, however, are less often presumed to struggle over such core identity issues as sexual desire. Although there has been little discussion of adolescent realization of same-gender identity in the contemporary mental health literature (although some mental health professionals, just as some parents, view this as experimentation or as just a "phase" in a process that will eventually lead to a heterosexual identity), adults coming out gay, particularly men, are more likely presumed to be struggling with some significant psychological issue. Isay (1989) discusses same-gender sexual fantasies among married men and presumes much of this fantasy to reflect psychological issues which, if addressed, will relieve these men of their same-gender desire. He does acknowledge that it is possible for gay men to have complied with social expectations by being married and having a family, but is hesitant to acknowledge that these heterosexual men might—as a result of further personal growth or changing family circumstances—decide to go gay.

In his most recent discussion of this issue, Isay (1996) acknowledges that some older men subjected to particular opprobrium attached to homosexuality in their youth might have hidden this desire for a lifetime and then come out gay in later life. Other gay men remain married and have furtive affairs which, if discovered, may force these middle-aged and older men to come out as gay. Isay (1996) notes the complexity involved in the decision on the part of men living a straight lifeway to go gay. In the case of one such older man consulting him regarding the decision to come out, Isay advised that this man not disclose his same-gender desire, work on his relationship with his wife, enjoy his children and grandchildren, and satisfy his same-gender sexual desire through contact with sex workers.

Goldberg (1995) is equally suspicious of the motives of men coming out gay across the adult years. He views this decision as the consequence of a midlife crisis and fragmentation leading to feelings of depression. Too often, Goldberg suggests, coming out gay in midlife represents the sexualization of a disorder of the self, using sexuality as a means for feeling alive in an existence marked by feelings of depletion and inner deadness. Goldberg believes that analysis will show that homosexual fantasies represent a perversion (that is, the use of sexual interaction for nonerotic ends) used in an effort to ward off feelings of fear of pending personal breakdown, which, if analyzed, may lead to a heterosexual adjustment. Although he admits that some men feeling same-gender desire from earliest childhood may be truly gay, he is less certain that this is the case among men coming out gay in adulthood. Our own clinical experience suggests that although coming out gay in adulthood may for some men reflect a breakdown product of the self, for other men this decision may reflect personal growth and provide an enhanced source of personal and sexual fulfillment.

Although some men with strong homoerotic interests that are not put into action remain single well into adulthood, either denying or suppressing same-gender desire as a result of antigay prejudice learned in early childhood and felt as a sense of shame, most men in earlier generations felt social pressure to marry and have a family. At some point across the adult years, these men either become aware of the intensity of their longstanding same-gender desire or of such desire for the first time, and they seek partners of the same-gender. This issue of the decision among married men to come out gay has been addressed in a study of more than a hundred middle-class, middle-American wives, most with two children, whose husbands had come out gay during their marriage (Gochros, 1989; Buxton, 1994). Most wives inadvertently learned of their husband's sexual interest in men, often after finding letters from a lover, discovering gay pornography, or having been told by others. On the basis of her clinical work and systematic study, Gochros (1989) reports that there is no single predictable response to learning of her husband's sexual orientation. Often, husband and wife agree to marital separation, which may lead to divorce; however, in some instances the couple remains together and view each other as a "best friend and confidante."

Case 11

A man seen in psychoanalysis had experienced same-gender desire since childhood. Although he had a positive relationship with his wife and satisfying sexual intimacy, he felt a nagging desire for intimacy with men. Discovering that a coworker, somewhat younger, was gay, he sought out and became friends with his coworker. This soon led to a sexual intimacy that he found immensely satisfying and meaningful in the manner that he had always imagined. His wife discovered a birthday card to her husband from his companion expressing his own love and the pleasure of being together. With several children, and caring for each other, the couple agreed not to separate. Rather, this man arranged to spend three nights a week with his lover. Because his work is at some distance from his home and he had often been away on business, the children didn't find this odd. To date, this arrangement has worked satisfactorily for all. Although husband and wife no longer have a sexual relationship, they remain each other's best friend.

Less is known about the impact of a wife's decision for a lesbian relationship than that of a husband's decision to go gay. Unfortunately, much of the literature on both gay men and women coming out or being out in the adult years is based on work carried out in the 1970s in the aftermath of the emergence of the gay rights movement. The social changes of the past three decades suggest that circumstances for both gay men and lesbians are markedly different from those three decades ago. Traditionally, when married men go gay, marital separation and divorce follows from that decision, with custody awarded to the wife because courts still mistakenly believe that it is not good for children to be raised in a household consisting of two men as parents. It is considered less onerous for children to be raised in a household with two women parents. Somewhat less acrimony is present in divorce when the wife comes out lesbian than when the husband comes out gay (Bozett, 1993). While obviously it is a difficult time for the wife of a man going gay, Buxton (1994) and Gochros (1989) report that very few women ultimately judged this turn in life in negative terms. After some period of crisis, most women divorcing husbands coming out as gay report being as happy or more happy than during their marriage.

Understanding coming out among women over the adult years is more problematic than it is for men. First, women's role in society has been defined either in terms of the absence of male characteristics (Chodorow, 1978), or in heavily stereotyped terms. Second, It was long presumed that women have less sexual desire than men, so that there has been little study of the course of life among women beginning same-gender sexual intimacy across the adult years. There is a belief that women are less specific than men in their sexual desires and have an easier time managing bisexuality, which makes it possible to move back and forth between same and opposite gender sexual intimacy. As Jensen (1999) reports, many women have dated both men and other women and see few contradictions in this pattern of dating. In contrast, most men going gay seek only same-gender sexual partners. Jensen (1999) also notes that women identify less readily than men with their own sexuality. Relationship and sexuality appear to be more tightly integrated than among men. Particularly in more traditional communities, women are brought up from girlhood to view their role in society in a traditional manner, to be a wife and mother rather than a person with her own desires. Movement toward a lesbian sexual identity may be as much a consequence of a marriage felt as empty and not fulfilling as adoption of a positive identity based on long-standing sexual desire.

In a study parallel in many respects to that of Gochros (1989), Jensen (1999) reports on findings from a study of 25 middle-class women in a Midwestern community who had come out lesbian in adulthood. These women had married without thinking of any alternative lifeway because that was the expectable course of adult lives for their postwar generation (Coleman, 1989). These women had typically been married for more than a decade before realizing same-gender desire. Often, first lesbian relationships followed some women's social event such as a concert. Kirkpatrick, Smith, and Roy (1981) report that lesbian women ending marriages had a less stormy divorce than divorcing heterosexual women, and were less likely to have accepted abuse by their husband before the divorce. The heterosexual women were more bitter and angry about men than lesbian women ending their marriage. There has been little systematic study of the husbands of women going gay, but the husbands seem to react with surprise and rage and then to move on to another marriage. Jensen (1999) reports that more than half of the women she studied were not aware of same-gender desire at the time of their marriage. Other women found it easy to deny such desire when marrying even though they had been aware of this desire for some time. Finally, Laird (1998) reports that regardless of the circumstances leading to adoption of a lesbian identity, lesbians remain firmly attached both to their own parental families and to the care of their own children. Gay men coming out in adulthood have a somewhat more difficult time maintaining ties with both their own family and continuing relationships with their own children.

The issue of commitment among same-gender couples is one that has relevance both for mental health and social policy. Sullivan (1995) has observed that legal recognition of such same-gender relationships may foster monogamy and stability in the gay community. Vermont now legally recognizes civil unions between two men and two women and has set a precedent for other states to follow. Regardless of the label attached to these enduring commitments the reality of enduring commitments among same-gender couples is increasingly visible. Such relationships inevitably involve same-gendered couples with family and community in a more complex manner than simply living together. It involves the two women or two men coming out to their own families together, implicitly demanding that each partner's family recognize the relationship. Each of the partners acquires in-laws just as in heterosexual unions (Serovich et al., 1993). It sometimes happens that one prospective partner is out to his family, and the other is not. LaSalla (2000) reports that when gay couples disclose their civil union to both sets of parents, even though there is some initial parental and in-law disapproval, each family comes to accept their offspring's partner and actively works to include the partner in holidays and other family events. Over time, strong intergenerational ties are created that benefit each generation and foster the gay couple's own relationship.

Conclusion

The process of disclosing one's sexual identity, first to oneself and then to others, must be understood in terms of the course of life as a whole and in terms of expectations of family and community at particular times and in particular places. It is said that one never stops coming out. In each business or personal situation, gay and lesbian people are always confronted anew with the question of whether to "tell" and whether telling in that situation is warranted. Clearly, factors relating to a lifetime of growing up in a heteronormative world lead many lesbians and gay men to harbor enduring feelings of shame and stigma. Even those gay men and lesbians growing up in ordinary devoted households and managing in other respects feel some sense of shame about same-gender desire and adoption of a gay identity.

In some more liberal, educated, and affluent communities, the assumption of deviance associated with same-gender orientation appears to be diminishing. Many high school and college students at this time in history do not regard persons with same-gender desires as significantly unusual. The extent to which homoerotic desire will be accepted as just another sexual lifeway without prejudice may reshape the meaning of going gay in contemporary society. Much of the discourse concerning same-gender orientation and coming out arises from the assumption that going gay is a statement about a core aspect of one's being. If something is part of one's essence, then to change it is to negate an aspect of the self, to deny it is to be inauthentic, and to attempt to transform it seems, at best, challenging. The assumption that an aspect of one's identity needs changing is contrary to common psychological experience in the sense that one's actions grow out of one's essence, and that there is a self at the core of the personality whose qualities determine actions, including psychological actions, and which weighs legitimate, though often highly conflicted, claim to determining actions.

There is little evidence to support the assumption that going gay across the years of adulthood has particular significance for mental health. Men and women may be in a heterosexual relationship at one point in their life and in a same-gendered relationship at another. In itself, this decision to come out gay or lesbian has little significance for present or future personal adjustment. It is clear that disclosure of same-gender sexual identity is always one that is potentially a source of uncertainty in terms of the response of others. Whether a high school student comes out to friends first, then sisters and brothers, then mother, and finally father, it is never clear in advance how family members will react to this news. In the same way, men and women deciding to tell friends and coworkers face a similar paradox.

Savin-Williams (2001) and Herdt and Koff (2000) both provide guides for young people deciding whether to come out to their family. Ben-Ari (1995b) reports that young people who come out in a positive manner to their family enjoy a more positive response than young people who present coming out as a problem. Parents want their offspring to be happy, and if the gay son or daughter tells of being in a wonderful relationship, parents are more likely to respond positively regardless of initial uncertainty. Savin-Williams (2001) and Herdt and Koff (2000) both note the importance for family members coming to parents and others of working through one's own sense of shame and ambivalence and recognize in an empathic manner parents' own struggle to understand this disclosure. It is here that psychoanalysis is able to be of real help to gay youth and adults; dealing with feelings of shame and making peace with the experience of not having a gender atypical childhood affirmed by parents who, themselves, may have been confused about what this means for later development. Working through the experience of disappointments across the childhood years, struggle for acceptance among peers in high school and, perhaps, college as well, and more recently at work, all are important in arriving at the positive gay identity so essential for a continued sense of personal vitality across the years of adulthood.

References

Baker, J. M. (1998), *Family Secrets: Gay Sons—A Mother's Story*. New York: Harrington Park Press.

Ben-Ari, A. J. (1995a), It's the telling that makes the difference. In: *The Narrative Study of Lives, Vol. 3. Interpreting Experience*, ed. R. Josselson & A. Lieblich. Thousand Oaks, CA: Sage Publications, pp. 153–172.

——— (1995b), The discovery that an offspring is gay: Parents', gay mens' and lesbians' perspectives. *J. Homosexuality*, 30:89–112.

Beeler, J. & DiProva, V. (1998), Adjustment of families following disclosure of homosexuality by a family member: Themes discovered in narrative accounts. *J. Marital & Family Therapy*, 25:443–459.

Bieber, I., Dain, H., Dince, P., Drellich, M., Grand, H., Gundlach, R., Kremer, M., Rifkin, A. Wilbur, C. & Bieber, T. (1962), *Homosexuality: A Psychodynamic Study of Male Homosexuals*. New York: Basic Books.

Blumstein, P. & Schwartz, P. (1983), *American Couples: Work, Money, Sex*. New York: Morrow.

Borhek, M. (1979), *My Son Eric: A Mother Struggles to Accept Her Gay Son and Discovers Herself.* Cleveland, OH: Pilgrim Press.

Boxer, A. & Cohler, B. (1989), The life course of gay and lesbian youths: An immodest proposal for the study of lives. In: *Gay and Lesbian Youth,* ed. G. Herdt. New York: Harrington Park Press, pp. 315–355.

——— Cook, J. & Herdt, G. (1991), Double jeopardy: Identity transitions and parent–child relations among gay and lesbian youth. In: Parent–Child Relations Throughout Life, ed. K. Pillemer & K. McCartney. Hillsdale, NJ: Erlbaum & Associates, pp. 559–592.

Bozett, F. (1993), Gay father: A review of the literature. In: *Psychological Perspectives on Lesbian and Gay Male Experiences,* ed. L. Garnets & D. C. Kimmel. New York: Columbia University Press, pp. 437–458.

Bradford, J., Ryan, C. & Rothblum, E. (1994), National lesbian health care survey: Implications for mental health care. *J. Clinical & Consulting Psychology,* 62: 228–242.

Burch, B. (1993), *On Intimate Terms: The Psychology of Difference in Lesbian Relationships.* Urbana: University of Illinois Press.

Buxton, A. (1994), *The Other Side of the Closet: The Coming-out Crisis for Straight Spouses and Families.* New York: John Wiley.

Cass, V. C. (1984), Homosexual identity formation: Testing a theoretical model. *J. Sex Research,* 20:143–167.

Chauncey, G. (1994), *Gay New York: Gender, Urban Culture, and the Making of the Gay Male World, 1890–1940.* New York: Basic Books.

Chodorow, N. (1978), *The Reproduction of Mothering.* Berkeley: University of California Press.

——— (1992), Heterosexuality as a compromise formation: Reflections on the psychoanalytic theory of sexual development. *Psychoanal. Contemp. Thought,* 15: 267–304.

Clendinen, D. & Nagourney, A. (1999), *Out for Good: The Struggle to Build a Gay Rights Movement in America.* New York: Simon & Schuster.

Cohler, B. (1987–1988), The adult daughter–mother relationship: Perspective from life-course family study and psychoanalysis. *J. Geriatric Psychiat.*, 21:51–72.

——— (in prep), *Writing Lives, Reading Lives: Generation and the Experience of Same Gender Desire among Men.*

——— & Galatzer-Levy, R. (2000), *The Course of Gay and Lesbian Lives: Social and Psychoanalytic Perspectives.* Chicago: University of Chicago Press.

Coleman, E. (1989), The married lesbian. In: *Homosexuality and Family Relations,* ed. F. W. Bozett & M. Sussman. New York: Haworth Press.

Corbett, K. (1998), Gross-gendered identifications and homosexual boyhood: Toward a more complex theory of gender. *Amer. J. Orthopsychiat.*, 68:352–360.

Cramer, D. W. & Roach, A. J. (1988), Coming out to mom and dad: A study of gay males and their relationships with their parents. *J. Homosexuality*, 15:79–91.

Crites, S. (1971), The narrative quality of experience. In: *Memory, Identity, Community: The Idea of Narrative in the Human Sciences*, ed. L. P. Hinchman and S. K. Hinchman. Albany: State University of New York Press, 1997, pp. 26–50.

D'Emilio, J. (1983), *Sexual Politics, Sexual Communities: The Making of a Homosexual Minority in the United States, 1940–1970,* 2nd ed. Chicago: University of Chicago Press, 1998.

Devine, J. L. (1984), A systemic inspection of affectional preference orientation and the family of origin, *J. Social Work & Human Sexuality*, 2:9–17.

Dew, R. F. (1994), *The Family Heart: A Memoir of When Our Son Came Out*. New York: Ballentine Books.

Drescher, J. (1998), *Psychoanalytic Therapy and the Gay Man.* Hillsdale, NJ: The Analytic Press.

Duberman, M. (1993), *Stonewall.* New York: St. Martin's Press.

Elder, G. H. Jr. (1995), The life-course paradigm: Social change and individual development. In: *Examining Lives in Context: Perspectives on the Ecology of Human Development,* ed. P. Moen, G. H. Elder Jr. & K. Lüscher. Washington, DC: American Psychological Association, pp. 101–139.

——— (1996), Human lives in changing societies: Life course and developmental insights. In: *Developmental Science: Multiple Perspectives,* ed. R. Cairns, G. H. Elder Jr. & E. Costello. New York: Cambridge University Press, pp. 31–62.

——— (1997), The life-course and human development. In: *Handbook of Child Psychology, Vol. 1, Theory,* ed. R. M. Lerner. New York: Wiley, pp. 939–991.

Erikson, E. H. (1958), *Young Man Luther: A Study in Psychoanalysis and History.* New York: Norton.

——— (1959), *Identity and the Life Cycle.* New York: Norton.

Foucault, M. (1976), *The History of Sexuality, Vol. 1, An Introduction,* trans. R. Hurley. New York: Random House, 1990.

Fricke, A. & Fricke, W. (1991), *Sudden Strangers: The Story of a Gay Son and His Father*. New York: St. Martin's Press.

Galatzer-Levy, R. & Cohler, B. (1993), *The Essential Other*. New York: Basic Books.

Gill, M. (1994), *Psychoanalysis in Transition: A Personal View.* Hillsdale, NJ: The Analytic Press.

Gochros, J. S. (1989), *When Husbands Come Out of the Closet*. New York: Harrington Press.

Goffman, E. (1963), *Stigma: Notes on the Management of Spoiled Identity*. New York: Simon & Schuster.

Goldberg, A. (1995), *The Problem of Perversion: The View from Self Psychology.* New Haven, CT: Yale University Press.

Greene, A. L. (1986), Future time perspective in adolescence: The present of things future revisited. *J. Youth & Adolescence,* 15:99–113.

——— (1990), Great expectations: Constructions of the life-course during adolescence. *J. Youth & Adolescence,* 19:289–306.

Hagestad, G. (1981), Problems and promises in the social psychology of intergenerational relations. In: *Aging: Stability and Change in the Family*. ed. R. W. Fogel, E. Hatfield, S. B. Kiesler & E. Shanas. New York: Academic Press, pp. 11–46.

Henderson, M. G. (1998), Disclosure of sexual orientation: Comments from a parental perspective. *Amer. J. Orthopsychiat.*, 68:372–375.

Herdt, G. (1992), "Coming out" as a rite of passage: A Chicago study. In: *Gay Culture in America: Essays from the Field*, ed. G. Herdt. Boston, MA: Beacon Press, pp. 29–67.

——— (1997), *Same Sex, Different Cultures: Gays and Lesbians Across Cultures.* Boulder, CO: Westview Press.

——— & Koff, B. (2000), *Something to Tell You: The Road Families Travel When a Child Is Gay.* New York: Columbia University Press.

Herek, G. M. (1996), Heterosexism and homophobia. In: *Textbook of Homosexuality and Mental Health,* ed. R. Cabaj & T. S. Stein. Washington, DC: American Psychiatric Press, pp. 101–113.

Herrell, R. K. (1992), The symbolic strategies of Chicago's gay and lesbian community: Pride Day Parade. In: *Gay Culture in America: Essays from the Field,* ed. G. Herdt. Boston, MA: Beacon Press, pp. 225–252.

Hoffman, I. (1998), *Ritual and Spontaneity in the Psychoanalytic Process.* Hillsdale, NJ: The Analytic Press.

Holland, D., Lachicotte, W. Jr., Skinner, D. & Cain, C. (1998), *Identity and Agency in Cultural Worlds.* Cambridge, MA: Harvard University Press.

Hostetler, A. & Herdt, G. (1998), Culture, sexual lifeways, and developmental subjectivities: Rethinking sexual taxonomies. *Social Research,* 65:249–290.

Isay, R. (1989), *Being Homosexual: Gay Men and Their Development.* New York: Farrar, Straus & Giroux.

——— (1996), *Becoming Gay: The Journey to Self-Acceptance.* New York: Pantheon.

Jensen, K. L. (1999), *Lesbian Epiphanies: Women Coming Out in Later Life.* New York: Harrington Park Press/Haworth.

Kaiser, C. (1997), *The Gay Metropolis, 1940–1996.* Boston, MA: Houghton Mifflin.

Kirkpatrick, M., Smith, C. & Roy, R. (1981), Lesbian mothers and their children. *Amer. J. Orthopsychiat.,* 51:545–551.

Kubler-Ross, E. (1969), *On Death and Dying.* New York: Macmillan.

Laird, J. (1998), Invisible ties: Lesbians and their families of origin. In: *Lesbian, Gay, and Bisexual Identities in Families: Psychological Perspectives,* ed. C. J. Patterson & A. R. D'Augelli. New York: Oxford University Press, pp. 197–230.

LaSalla, M. C. (2000), Gay male couples: The importance of coming out and being out to parents. *J. Homosexuality,* 39:47–71.

Lewin, E. (1993), *Lesbian Mothers: Accounts of Gender in American Culture.* Ithaca, NY: Cornell University Press.

Lichtenstein, H. (1961), Identity and sexuality—A study of their interrelationship in man. *J. Amer. Psychoanal. Assn.,* 9:260–279.

Loughery, J. (1998), *The Other Side of Silence: Men's Lives and Gay Identities: A Twentieth-Century History.* New York: Henry Holt.

Low, N. (1978), The relationship of adult daughters to their mothers. Paper presented at the Annual Meetings of the Massachusetts Psychological Association.

Lynch, J. M. & Murray, K. (2000), For the love of the children: The coming out process for gay and lesbian parents and stepparents. *J. Homosexuality,* 39:1–24.

Meyer, I. (1995), Minority stress and mental health in gay men. *J. Health & Social Behavior,* 36:38–56.

Miller, A. (1981), *The Drama of the Gifted Child,* trans. R. Ward. New York: Basic Books.

Mishler, E. (1999), *Storylines: Craftartists' Narratives of Identity.* Cambridge, MA: Harvard University Press.

Nungesser, L. (1983), *Homosexual Acts, Actors, and Identities*. New York: Praeger.
Oswald, R. F. (2000), Family and friendship relationships after young women come out as bisexual or lesbian. *J. Homosexuality*, 38:65–83.
Parks, C. (1999), Lesbian identity development: An examination of differences across generations. *Amer. J. Orthopsychiat.*, 69:347–361.
Patterson, C. (1995), Lesbian mothers, gay fathers, and their children. In: *Lesbian, Gay, and Bisexual Identities over the Life Span*, ed. A. R. D'Augelli & C. Patterson. New York: Oxford University Press, pp. 262–292.
Plummer, K. (1981), Going gay: Identities life cycle and lifestyles in male gay world. In: *The Theory and Practice of Homosexuality*, ed. J. Hart & D. Richardson. New York: Routledge & Kegan Paul, 3–110.
——— (1995), *Telling Sexual Stories: Power, Change, and Social Worlds*. New York: Routledge.
Putnam, R. D. (2000), *Bowling Alone: The Collapse and Revival of American Community*. New York: Simon & Schuster.
Rado, S. (1945–1955), *Adaptational Psychodynamics*, ed. J. Jameson & H. Klein. Northvale, NJ: Aronson, 1995.
——— (1949), An adaptational view of sexual behavior. In: *Psychosexual Development in Health and Disease*, ed. P. H. Hoch & J. Zubin. New York: Grune & Stratton, pp. 159–189.
Sadownick, D. (1997), *Sex Between Men: An Intimate History of the Sex Lives of Gay Men Postwar to the Present*. San Francisco, CA: Harper.
Sarup, M. (1996), *Identity, Culture, and the Postmodern World*, ed. T. Raja. Athens: University of Georgia Press.
Savin-Williams. R. C. (1998a), Lesbian, gay, and bisexual youths' relationships with their parents. In: *Lesbian, Gay and Bisexual Identities in Families: Psychological Perspectives*. ed. C. J. Patterson & A. R. D'Augelli. New York: Oxford University Press, pp. 75–88.
——— (1998b), Parental reactions to the child's disclosure of a gay, lesbian/bisexual identity. *Newsletter, Society for Psychological Study of Lesbian, Gay, and Bisexual Issues, American Psychological Association*, 14:16–19.
——— (1998c), The disclosure to families of same-sex attractions by lesbian, gay, and bisexual youths. *J. Res. on Adolescence*, 8:49–68.
——— (1998d), *. . . And Then I Became Gay: Young Men's Stories*. New York: Routledge.
——— (2001), *Mom, Dad, I'm Gay*. Washington, DC: American Psychological Association.
——— & Dubè, E. M. (1998), Parental reactions to their child's disclosure of a gay/lesbian identity. *Family Relations*, 47:7–13.
Schafer, R. (1992), *Retelling a Life: Narration and Dialogue in Psychoanalysis*. New York: Basic Books.
Serovich, J. M., Skeen, P., Walters, L. H. & Robinson, B. E. (1993), In-law relationships when a child is homosexual. *J. Homosexuality*, 26:57–76.
Shyer, M. F. & Shyer, C. (1996), *Not Like Other Boys: Growing Up Gay: A Mother and Son Look Back*. Los Angeles, CA: Alyson Books.
Socarides, C. (1968), *The Overt Homosexual*. New York: Grune & Stratton.

Stein, A. (1997), *Sex and Sensibility: Stories of a Lesbian Generation*. Berkeley: University of California Press.

Stein, E. (1999), *The Mismeasure of Desire: The Science, Theory, and Ethics of Sexual Orientation*. New York: Oxford University Press.

Sullivan, A. (1995), *Virtually Normal: An Argument about Homosexuality*. New York: Knopf.

Tipton, S. (1982), *Getting Saved from the Sixties: Moral Meaning in Conversion and Social Change*. Berkeley: University of California Press.

Toulmin, S. (1990), *Cosmopolis: The Hidden Agenda of Modernity*. New York: The Free Press.

Troiden, R. (1988), *Gay and Lesbian Identity: A Sociological Analysis*. New York: General-Hall.

Van Gennep, A. (1909), *Rites of Passage*. Chicago: University of Chicago Press, 1960.

Wythe, D., Merling, A., Merling, R. & Merling, S. (2000), *The Wedding: A Family's Coming Out Story*. New York: Avon Books.

Winnicott, D. W. (1960), Ego distortion in terms of the true and false self. In: *The Maturational Processes and the Facilitating Environment*, ed. D. W. Winnicott. New York: International Universities Press, pp. 140–152.

Queering Psychoanalysis

GARY GROSSMAN

In a footnote in his book *Reverie and Interpretation*, Thomas Ogden (1997) reports a personal communication from James Grotstein, who was analyzed by Bion: "Grotstein responded to one of Bion's interpretations by saying, 'I understand.' Bion paused and then calmly said, 'Please try not to understand. If you must, superstand, circumstand, parastand, but please try not to understand" (p. 208). As analysts, we are constantly oscillating between positions of understanding our patients and being confused. To the extent that we become comfortable in our understanding, we risk also becoming closed to new ideas, new ways of seeing and understanding. Although I believe maintaining an open mind without sacrificing understanding is a challenge we all face in every aspect of the analytic encounter, and one that has received increased attention throughout all spheres of psychoanalytic discourse, the realm of sexuality has presented our profession with some of its greatest challenges. Queer theory, a multidisciplinary approach to cultural studies that first emerged within the academy in the early 1990s, has also articulated this paradox in regard to gender and sexual identity. For example, in the process of deconstructing labels such as "homosexual" and "heterosexual," William Turner (2000), a literary critic who has traced the history of queer theory, draws attention to the fact that "cultural categories simultaneously constrain and enable subjectivity" (p. 110). It is in the overlapping arenas of gender, sexuality, identity, and the tendency to categorize that "queer theory" has much to offer psychoanalysis.

Psychoanalysis encompasses theories of human development, mental functioning, and psychotherapy. The development of a "sense of self" and individual "identity" is part of all psychoanalytic theories. Although there are some basic components common to all schools of psychoanalysis, each has its own unique perspective on development and treatment. Within a contemporary ego psychological/conflict model of psychoanalysis, any self-reported identity will have developed in the service of expressive, adaptive, and defensive functions.

Gender theorists such as Judith Butler (1990), Virginia Goldner (1991), Adrienne Harris (1991), and Jessica Benjamin (1996) have challenged psychoanalytic notions of a fixed core gender identity (Stoller, 1964). Butler especially has explored the role that culture has played in the construction of gender and challenges the rigid dichotomization of male and female. Concurrently, queer theorists (Sedgwick, 1990; de Lauretis, 1994; Grosz, 1995) have also questioned common assumptions about the essence or nature of sexual orientation. Queer theory rejects notions of essential and fixed identities. Drawing on the writings of Michel Foucault (1978), queer theorists such as Annamarie Jagose (1995) have asserted that "the recent critique of identity politics . . . has not arisen simply because the reification of any single identity is felt to be exclusionary. It has occurred because, within poststructuralism, the very notion of identity as a coherent and abiding sense of self is perceived as a cultural fantasy rather than a demonstrable fact" (p. 82).

The postmodern critique of gender and sexual identity has captured the attention of psychoanalysts and has catalyzed efforts to revise our theories of sexual object choice and gender development (Elise, 1998; Hansell, 1998). Identity, like other aspects of the personality, develops as a compromise formation serving multiple aims. Existing models of "gay identity development" have been based on a theory of sequential and universal stages (Cass, 1979; Minton and McDonald, 1984; Troiden, 1989). In contrast, contemporary psychoanalysis recognizes the influence of both intrapsychic and interpersonal dynamics in all developmental processes, resulting in a multidimensional identity unique in each individual.

How, then, does the theoretical deconstruction of gender and sexuality, in the mind of the psychoanalyst, materialize in the analytic endeavor? How do we reconcile the decentering of sexual identity and our belief in the value of challenging concepts of the "core" or "true nature" of an individual, with the very real patient in our consulting room who says, "I'm gay. Always have been; always will be"? And what of the analyst's sexual orientation and identity? What impact does it have and how is it used in the minds of analyst and patient?

Although there is a growing body of literature linking queer theory with psychoanalysis (de Lauretis, 1994; Dean, 2000; Dean and Lane, 2001), the majority has focused on the contributions that psychoanalysis provides queer theory. Contributions illustrating the applicability of queer theory to psychoanalytic practice are still in their infancy.

Queer Theory

A postmodern, social constructionist approach to understanding identity, queer theory challenges the notion of identity as essential and fixed, particularly in regard to gender and sexuality. Queer theorists also question the binary perspective toward gender (male or female)[1] and the bipolar perspective towards sexuality (heterosexual and homosexual at opposite poles with gradation between them), arguing that such dichotomous models are social constructions and fail to adequately describe the actual diversity of people.

The term queer has its roots in lesbian/gay culture and politics. A term used to describe something that was strange, odd, or peculiar (OED, 1989), queer was adopted as a derogatory word for homosexual in the early 20 twentieth century. It wasn't until the late 1980s that queer was reappropriated by gay men and lesbians as a self-identifying term of empowerment. With the formation of the political action group Queer Nation in 1990, the use of queer as a self-affirming and inclusive word to refer to someone of nontraditional sexuality became more popular.

As an academic discipline, queer theory has its roots in gay/lesbian studies, feminist theory, critical thinking, and philosophy. In the process of documenting gay/lesbian history, a debate between essentialists and social constructionists emerged around the origins of sexual identity. How were we to understand and describe individuals across time periods and cultures who participated in same-sex relations? The essentialist/social constructionist controversy and the prolific contributions from each side provided much of the intellectual fuel for the emergence and growth of queer theory within the academy (Stein, 1992).

According to the essentialists (e.g., Boswell, 1980, 1992), homosexuality is something basic, a natural component of a person, which transcends and is independent of culture. Although different cultures may use different words to describe same-sex relationships, and these relationships will vary in their meanings and functions in a particular society, the erotic attraction is understood as something intrinsic to the individual.

From the social constructionist perspective, the sexual orientation of a person cannot be considered separately from the culture in which that person lives. Although there may be biological forces at play in a person's sexuality, the meaning and form they will take and the manner in which such experiences are signified will be determined by the culture.

Although the voices for each side of the debate come from many disciplines and can present compelling arguments for their positions, the debate has yet to be resolved (Stein, 1992). There are also those who confused the debate between essentialism and social constructionism to be another version of the

[1] Although this binary perspective toward biological sex is most prevalent, Fausto-Sterling (2000), a biologist and a feminist, has introduced a bipolar model that identifies gradations: "[H]uman males and females all begin life with the same structures; complete maleness and complete femaleness represent the extreme ends of a spectrum of possible body types. . . . Knowledge of biological variation, however, allows us to conceptualize the less frequent middle space as natural, although statistically unusual" (p. 76).

nature versus nurture controversy or voluntarism versus determinism (though usually the arguments are raised specifically in discussions about the origin of homosexuality). Although "nature" might fairly represent the essentialist model that explains sexual orientation as innate, "nurture" fails to capture the complexity of social construction. The social constructionists are not arguing that sexual orientation develops as a result of upbringing or an individual's interactions with environment. Theirs is not an explanation of the origins of a person's sexuality, but, rather, a means of understanding sexual identity in the context of culture.

An essentialist position which argues that sexual orientation is innate and independent of culture would also consider sexual orientation, and, therefore, sexual identity, to be fixed and stable. For the social constructionist, sexual orientation and a person's sexual identity is constituted via the interplay of an individual with society. "Sexual orientation" as an identifier is considered problematic in that orientation implies an innate characteristic. The concept of sexual orientation is instead a construction and therefore fluid. For the essentialist, sexual orientation is an aspect of oneself that is discovered by the individual in the course of sexual maturity. This fluidity of sexual orientation has a bit of a dilemma for some social constructionists who may be more comfortable with the term "sexual preference," as Turner (2000) points out: "constructionism implies a measure of choice that no one wishes to claim" (p. 113). It is here that psychoanalytic theory aids the social constructionist position by introducing the role of unconscious choice throughout all stages of development. Erotic preferences and object choices develop unconsciously early in life and are differentiated from conscious choices an individual might make as a child or an adult. Queer theory embraces these aspects of social constructionism in its efforts to describe the functions and meanings of sexuality and gender in contemporary society.

Annamarie Jagose, an Australian professor of English, has written one of the most accessible books describing the history of queer theory within the academy. The term queer, according to Jagose (1995),

> . . . has come to be used differently, sometimes as an umbrella term for a coalition of culturally marginal sexual self-identifications and at other times to describe a nascent theoretical model which has developed out of more traditional lesbian and gay studies. What is clear . . . is that queer is very much a category in the process of formation. It is not simply that queer has yet to solidify and take on a more consistent profile, but rather that its definitional indeterminacy, its elasticity, is one of its constituent characteristics [p. 1].

Jagose describes further a term whose very basis resists definition:

> [Q]ueer describes those gestures or analytical models which dramatize incoherencies in the allegedly stable relations between chromosomal sex, gender and sexual desire. Resisting that model of stability—which claims

> heterosexuality as its origin, when it is more properly its effect—queer focuses on mismatches between sex, gender and desire . . . queer locates and exploits the incoherencies in those three terms which stabilize heterosexuality. Demonstrating the impossibility of any "natural" sexuality, it calls into question even such apparent unproblematic terms as "man" and "woman" [p. 3].

Queer theory begins by challenging the prevailing beliefs about gender and sexual identity. The impetus for this endeavor is both academic and political. It is academic in its aim to shake up existing theories and beliefs, to foster the expansion of ideas and understandings, and to promote new ways of seeing, describing, and explaining human experience. It is political in its aim to highlight social injustices, and especially the disproportionate distribution of power in our society.

Queer theory's mission is to elucidate the manner by which creative productions (i.e., art, literature, film, music, performance and science, all reflections of our culture) serve to perpetuate the disproportionate access to power. The categories as defined by culture are ubiquitously used to both describe and determine experience. Fausto-Sterling (2000) has demonstrated that even in biology, culturally determined conceptions about gender and sex silently influence and distort allegedly scientific interpretations of objective data.

In his exhaustive exposition of the genealogy of queer theory, Turner (2000) highlights the challenges of critiquing the status quo:

> Because categories continue to function in the face of criticism, however—partly because many persons are invested in their continuation—pointing out the inadequacy of categories is not sufficient. Queer theorists also see the need to examine the functional modes of identity categories and figure out ways to undermine them [p. 137].

Queer theory strives to undermine the functional modes of identity categories because such categories limit access to power and serve to marginalize and disempower persons assigned to certain categories, that is, "queers." Turner (2000) is succinct in his explanation:

> [Q]ueer theorists would like to reveal how assumptions about gender and sexuality informed the positive unconscious[2] of our culture not simply with respect to scientific inquiry but also with respect to virtually every aspect of the culture. . . . Assumptions about gender and sexual identity inform our perceptions and understandings of the world at the most basic level, and they inform our conceptions of who is and is not a person [p. 123].

---

[2] A term used by Foucault to refer to the "historical unconscious" of the culture in contrast to the psychological unconscious of the individual.

Psychoanalytic Theory Meets Queer Theory

The tenets of queer theory rely on the presumption that there are social forces that are so ingrained in our culture that they exert influence on our perceptions, experiences, definitions, and beliefs without conscious awareness. It is, therefore, no grand leap to see the compatibility between queer and psychoanalytic theory. Both theories rely on a notion of unconscious determinants to meaning and experience. Both also focus attention on the role that language and symbols play in shaping and defining our experience.

> For queer theorists, language plays a crucial role in producing persons . . . our understanding of the world comes to us through language, with the result that, whatever else may exist in the world independently of language, our knowledge of those things is always already bound up with the terms that we use to describe them [Turner, 2000, p. 137].

As psychoanalysts we recognize, for example, that regardless of the biological determinants of an individual's symptoms, it is the meaning that is attributed to them that we consider important in treatment. Similarly, though we recognize the relevance of what actually happens as a child interacts with the environment (and how responsive that environment is to the child's needs), we focus on the meanings that the individual has attributed to his/her experience. It is within the realm of language and symbol that psychoanalysts strive to intervene.

Classical psychoanalysis has frequently been criticized for its limited focus on the individual to the point of ignoring social influences on development. The interpersonal, object relations, and more recently, the intersubjective schools of psychoanalysis have successfully brought our attention to the interplay between the social and intrapsychic in human development. At the same time that queer theory was proliferating with the academy, analysts working within the intersubjectivist model drew attention to the role that authority played in psychoanalysis (see Hoffman, 1992, 1996; Friedman, 1996; Renik, 1998). The conception of the neutral objective analyst was challenged, as was the sharp division between naïve, sick patient and knowing, healthy analyst. Foucault (1965, 1973), who was vehemently critical of the authoritarian role that institutionalized medicine and psychiatry wielded as the ones who "knew," would likely be pleased by this contemporary revision in psychoanalysis.

Who holds knowledge, what is the knowledge, and what are the functions that knowledge is playing are all questions that analysts are asking more and more in their work with patients. It is in this spirit that I believe Bion's comments to Grotstein on understanding can be considered. Although the process of psychoanalysis involves the pursuit of understanding, the actual experience of achieving understanding both enlightens and conceals. The challenge to analysts is to work within this paradox, to strive to obtain understanding in themselves, and foster it in their patients, but at the same time remain open to new ways of seeing and explaining. This is especially relevant when it comes to our approach to a patient's "identity" and specifically gendered and sexual identities, as well as the ways in which patients "know" us.

Although the psychoanalytic literature has begun to explore the effects of gender on the analytic relationship, the role of the analyst's sexual orientation has received only minimal attention. Self-identified gay and lesbian clinicians, practicing primarily within nonpsychoanalytic models of psychotherapy, have been around for approximately 25 years in this country. Professional writings and presentations describing these experiences date back to 1977 with the publication of *We Speak for Ourselves: Experience in Homosexual Counseling* (Babuscio, 1977). It is only since 1991, when Richard Isay's essay "The Homosexual Analyst" was published in *The Psychoanalytic Study of the Child* that gay psychoanalysts have begun to have a voice.

In this essay Isay (1991) expresses his belief that gay analysts should disclose their sexual orientation to their gay patients. He argues that withholding this information is likely to confirm the patient's belief that it is shameful to be gay. There continues to be debate among gay and lesbian therapists about the merits of self-disclosure of sexual orientation (Gabriel and Monaco, 1995; Kassoff et al., 1995; Cabaj, 1996). In the remaining section, I show how, as an analyst, queer theory has influenced my approach to a patient's expressed interest in my sexuality and identity. Using the cases of Ms. A and Mr. B, I illustrate how theory and clinical practice intersect, particularly with regard to a patient's questions about the therapist's identity. Queer theory, in its challenge of common conceptions of identity, complements the premise underlying an "analytic attitude" (Schafer, 1983), which values discovery and meanings over analyst disclosure in response to a patient's questions and curiosity. Through these vignettes I hope to demonstrate the value of responding to patients' questions without revealing the particular stated information sought, as well as the relevance of queer theory to psychoanalysis.

Clinical Illustrations

Ms. A, a 30-year-old self-identified bisexual woman in analysis, assumes early in treatment that I am gay. I respond by inviting her to talk about her assumption, without confirming the accuracy of her belief. Her assumption, she reveals, is based primarily (consciously) on my appearance and my "nurturing" attitude toward her. Psychoanalytic theory suggests exploring Ms. A's assumption as a fantasy, with conscious and unconscious determinants, in an effort to discover the multiple meanings of her belief. I hear her fantasy as a mental construction expressing a combination of wishes, anxieties, and defenses. At this point I am uncertain about the meanings of her belief that I am gay. At the most realistic level, I consider that Ms. A has picked up on some culturally supported cues and has accurately perceived my gay identity. Yet I continue to reflect. Is Ms. A afraid that I am gay and hoping that I am not? Is she thinking I'm gay and, therefore, fears that I won't really be interested in her because she's a woman? Perhaps she hopes that I'm gay and can thereby defend against an anxiety-provoking erotic fantasy.

In a session several months later, Ms. A expressed embarrassment about revealing to me her wish to meet someone and have a romantic relationship. She again referred to her idea that I was gay. Ms. A then revealed her belief that if I were gay, I wouldn't find her attractive or sexually desirable. I responded with a brief, open-ended inquiry, "How come?" which notably dislodged Ms. A from her self-restricting assumption, "Hmmm . . . I don't know. I guess it wouldn't necessarily mean that." In a session several months later, Ms. A talked about a friend whose therapist was frequently self-revealing. "I was thinking about C who saw her therapist with her husband. . . . I wouldn't want that much information about you . . . I guess it could be helpful to have to imagine that stuff . . . but then I thought, so, whatever information you have you're still gonna have a fantasy about a person . . . not necessarily sexual." After a long pause, she continued, "Maybe I want to think you're gay because it makes me feel safer and then if I found out you weren't, I might feel less safe—maybe part of me wants you to be gay and part of me doesn't want you to be. I'm not sure which I prefer."

Three months later Ms. A reported the following dream: "I went for my appointment with you . . . it was in your house . . . you had this huge house and you had this weird cat with hardly any hair on it and a long pointy head. It kept trying to bite me. But you were talking to me all about yourself and I remember thinking 'this is strange cause I usually talk about myself.' Then I thought this was nice, it felt like we were friends. Then I went to the bathroom and saw this picture of a woman. It was your girlfriend or wife. But then I thought, I thought he was gay and was thinking, what if he's being all chatty because he's interested in me."

She then said, "I don't know what to think about it. When I was getting dressed I thought I'd be embarrassed to tell you about it . . . the part about you being interested in me." I said, "Something about the idea of me being interested in you makes you anxious." "In the dream you were interested romantically but, well, yeah, that makes me feel anxious. Not that you are, but I have to wonder why I think about things like that—I wonder if I want you to be interested."

Mr. B, a 32-year-old gay-identified man, specifically sought a referral to a gay analyst. Mr. B had two previous treatments with male analysts who were both married and had children. At the beginning of the analysis, I knew that Mr. B wanted a gay analyst, but the reasons for this were unclear. He had known a fair amount about the personal lives of his previous analysts, whose offices were in their homes. He also described them as self-disclosing and sessions often began with "chitchat" about current political or cultural events. Although he knew that I was gay, he knew little about my personal interests or professional activities, and complained that I revealed very little about myself. He occasionally expressed interest in me but was also uncomfortable with and critical of his curiosity. Mr. B wanted to know about my training and what "school" of psychoanalysis I identified with, but he would not ask me directly. These ambiguities about me made him very anxious, and he expressed the wish to find a category where I would fit.

In listening to Mr. B's questions about me, I chose not to disclose the specific information he sought and, instead, invited him into a joint exploration of his fantasies about me, including his wishes and fears. This proved difficult for Mr. B, who quickly replied, "I don't think I want to go there." It gradually became clearer that Mr. B relied on categorizing in order to restrict his thinking, to close down his mind. By limiting his thoughts, he was unable to recognize his own desires and therefore could defend against experiencing disappointment and frustration. This enabled him to maintain unconscious fantasies of omnipotence and allowed him to ward off feelings of helplessness, dependence, or loss.

Discussion

Based on a social constructionist perspective, queer theory, suggests an optimal stance that an analyst can take toward a patient's presenting complaints, treatment goals, and self-disclosures. An appreciation of queer theory helps us to recognize the assumptions we hold, as well as those that our patients have, about gender and sexuality in particular, and identity in general. By shaking things up within ourselves, we are better able to help our patients broaden their own self-conceptions. Queer theory acknowledges the potential for a multiplicity of identities, recognizes the capacity for individual fluidity, and argues for keeping things open.

Psychoanalytic theory explains the persistent effort within each of us to foreclose, categorize, and simplify experience in order to alleviate the anxiety generated by an open mind. The more open one's mind is, the more likely unconscious wishes, fantasies, and fears will emerge. Although we all develop unique defensive strategies to prevent such anxiety-provoking ideas from entering awareness, unconscious fantasy actively influences our experiences, choices, attitudes, beliefs, and behaviors.

As psychoanalysts, we recognize the centrality of the unconscious and the ubiquity of defenses against knowing. We also have a unique insight into the influence and power of the unconscious. Through our experience as analysands, our immersion in analytic training, and our work as analysts, we have witnessed and experienced the impact of unconscious wishes and the determining effect of unconscious beliefs. Although our goal is to foster enlightenment in our patients and to broaden their awareness and expand their capacity to think, adopting the position of the "authority" who knows can serve more to foreclose than to enable thinking. At the same time, in order to be helpful to patients, an analyst must have conviction in one's understanding of a patient. To have conviction and remain open to new ways of seeing requires humility. If we become too enamored with our own ideas, we risk becoming blind to new ones.

Ms. A had the impression that I was gay. Cultural clues combined with her own fantasies, wishes, and anxieties contributed to her belief about my sexual identity. Although she revealed her assumptions and beliefs about me, Ms. A did not ask me directly. It seemed to me that she did not want her assumption confirmed or disconfirmed. Over the course of several months, various meanings and functions of her belief became apparent. Ms. A could use her "belief" that I was gay in order to ward off her own erotic longings, the awareness of which could lead to feelings of desire, rejection, humiliation, and helplessness. Yet it was her very efforts to defend against these feelings that also interfered in her ability to pursue a satisfying romantic relationship. Confirming Ms. A's assumption, I believe, could have prevented further elaboration of her fantasy and obscured its defensive function.

Like Ms. A, Mr. B also relied on certain ideas in order to prevent the emergence of other ideas. Supplying the answers to his questions, alleviating his curiosity, would support his efforts to restrict his thinking and perhaps collude with his unconscious omnipotent fantasies. His wish to have a gay analyst introduces the possibility of experiencing erotic desires for me. Even though this makes Mr. B uncomfortable, his erotic transference, at this point in his analysis, is preferable to him because it effectively defends against his more threatening infantile wishes and terrifying dependency.

This clinical approach to a patient's curiosity about the analyst will likely appear to many as sound psychoanalytic technique, a position with which I would readily agree. So how, then, has queer theory influenced me in these analytic encounters? Maintaining a position within the paradox of knowing and not knowing is one of the challenges of working analytically. The various factors that enable an analyst to find and maintain this position have rarely been specified. Having a thorough personal analysis certainly helps us tolerate uncertainty and ambiguity, as well as the anxieties that emerge in response to feelings of helplessness in the face of not knowing. Identifications with our supervisors and analysts also aid us in these decentering moments. In addition to these experiential and personal variables, we also rely on theory to help us navigate turbulent and unchartered waters.

Psychoanalytic theory helps us to recognize and begin to identify the multiple functions of a patient's experiences in treatment. In its appreciation for the fluidity of gender and sexual identities, queer theory can help us to resist temptations to label and, instead, to retain an open mind. Both theories can help us to live with uncertainty without abandoning what we know.

Practicing psychoanalytically requires that we work within a paradigm of paradox, in which we are repeatedly pulled by the tensions of opposing aims. The psychoanalytic relationship is intimate and personal, yet professional and detached. We are drawn in to participate and experience it firsthand, yet we must be able to pull back in order to observe, reflect, and think. We must find conviction in our beliefs and ideas, and yet remain puzzled and uncertain. We must be knowledgeable as well as confused. It is in this arena that queer theory is also daring to play.

Familiarizing ourselves with the contributions of queer theory invites and challenges us as analysts to recognize the assumptions that we hold about sexuality, identity, and desire as well as the associated anxieties with which we all must grapple. This self-scrutiny, I believe, increases our freedom to investigate and understand the meanings of our patients' experiences.

Queer theory invites us to think in a more complex manner about sexuality, gender, identity, and desire. Like psychoanalysis, it is in a state of motion; it is continually changing, expanding, and being revised by its diverse constituency. Although it offers no solutions or answers, by decentering our attention, the queering of psychoanalysis fosters our ability to tolerate the dialectical tension between fixed and fluid, knowing and confusion, participant and observer. By living within this paradigm of paradox, we can liberate our capacity to listen and to think, thereby helping our patients expand their minds, discover the multiple meanings of their own unique identities, and live fuller, more satisfying lives.

References

Babuscio, J. (1977), *We Speak for Ourselves: Experience in Homosexual Counseling.* Philadelphia: Fortress Press.

Benjamin, J. (1996), In defense of gender ambiguity. *Gender & Psychoanal.,* 1:27–43.

Boswell, J. (1980), *Christianity, Social Tolerance and Homosexuality.* Chicago: University of Chicago Press.

——— (1992), Categories, experience and sexuality. In: *Forms of Desire: Sexual Orientation and the Social Constructionist Controversy,* ed. E. Stein. New York: Routledge, pp. 133–174.

Butler, J. (1990), *Gender Trouble: Feminism and the Subversion of Identity.* New York: Routledge.

Cabaj, R. (1996), Sexual orientation of the therapist. In: *Textbook of Homosexuality and Mental Health,* ed. R. Cabaj & T. Stein. Washington, DC: American Psychiatric Press.

Cass, V. (1979), Homosexual identity formation: A theoretical model. *J. Homosexuality,* 4:219–235.

Dean, T. (2000), *Beyond Sexuality*. Chicago: University of Chicago Press.
——— & Lane, C., eds. (2001), *Homosexuality and Psychoanalysis*. Chicago: University of Chicago Press.
de Lauretis, T. (1994), *The Practice of Love: Lesbian Sexuality and Perverse Desire*. Bloomington: Indiana University Press.
Elise, D. (1998), Gender repertoire: Body, mind, and bisexuality. *Psychoanal. Dial.*, 8:353–371.
Fausto-Sterling, A. (2000), *Sexing the Body: Gender Politics and the Construction of Sexuality*. New York: Basic Books.
Foucault, M. (1965), *Madness and Civilization: A History of Insanity in the Age of Reason*. New York: Random House.
——— (1973), *The Order of Things: An Archaeology of the Human Sciences*. New York: Vintage Books.
——— (1978), *History of Sexuality, Vol. 1: An Introduction*, trans. R. Hurley. New York: Vintage Books, 1990.
Friedman, L. (1996), Overview: Knowledge and authority in the psychoanalytic relationship. *Psychoanal. Quart.*, 65:254–265.
Gabriel, M. & Monaco, G. (1995), Revisiting the question of self-disclosure: The lesbian therapist's dilemma. In: *Lesbians and Psychoanalysis: Revolutions in Theory and Practice*, ed. J. Glassgold & S. Iasenza. New York: Free Press.
Goldner, V. (1991), Toward a critical relational theory of gender. *Psychoanal. Dial.*, 1:249–272.
——— (2000), Reading and writing, talking and listening: Introducing *Studies in Gender and Sexuality*. *Stud. Gender & Sexual.*, 1:1–8.
Grosz, E. (1995), *Space, Time, and Perversion: Essays on the Politics of the Body*. New York: Routledge.
Hansell, J. H. (1998), Gender anxiety, gender melancholia, gender perversion. *Psychoanal. Dial.*, 8:337–351.
Harris, A. (1991), Gender as contradiction. *Psychoanal. Dial.*, 1:197–224.
Hoffman, I. (1992), Some practical implications of the social constructivist view of the psychoanalytic situation. *Psychoanal. Dial.*, 2:287–304.
——— (1996), The intimate and ironic authority of the psychoanalyst's presence. *Psychoanal. Quart.*, 65:102–136.
Isay, R. (1991), The homosexual analyst: Clinical considerations. *The Psychoanalytic Study of the Child*, 46:199–216. New Haven, CT: Yale University Press
Jagose, A. (1995), *Queer Theory: An Introduction*. New York: New York University Press.
Kassoff, B., Boden, R., de Monteflores, C., Hunt, P. & Wahba, R. (1995), Coming out of the frame: Lesbian feminism and psychoanalytic theory. In: *Lesbians and Psychoanalysis: Revolutions in Theory and Practice*, ed. J. Glassgold & S. Iasenza. New York: Free Press.
Minton, H. & McDonald, G. (1984), Homosexual identity formation as a developmental process. *J. Homosexual.*, 9:91–104.
Oxford English Dictionary, 2nd ed. (1989), Oxford, UK: Oxford University Press.
Ogden, T. (1997), *Reverie and Interpretation: Sensing Something Human*. Northvale, NJ: Aronson.

Renik, O. (1998), The analyst's subjectivity and the analyst's objectivity. *Internat. J. Psychoanal.,* 79:487–498.

Schafer, R. (1983), *The Analytic Attitude*. New York: Basic Books.

Sedgwick, E. (1990), *Epistemology of the Closet*. Berkeley: University of California.

Stein, E., ed. (1992), *Forms of Desire: Sexual Orientation and the Social Constructionist Controversy*. New York: Routledge.

Stoller, R. J. (1964), A contribution to the study of gender identity. *Internat. J. Psychoanal.,* 45:2–3.

Troiden, R. (1989), The formation of homosexual identities. *J. Homosexual.,* 16:43–73.

Turner, W. (2000), *A Genealogy of Queer Theory*. Philadelphia: Temple University Press.

Author Index

Subject Index

For Product Safety Concerns and Information please contact our EU
representative GPSR@taylorandfrancis.com
Taylor & Francis Verlag GmbH, Kaufingerstraße 24, 80331 München, Germany

www.ingramcontent.com/pod-product-compliance
Ingram Content Group UK Ltd.
Pitfield, Milton Keynes, MK11 3LW, UK
UKHW022116190926
475702UK00013B/1469
9781138009837